Better Living through TV

Better Living through TV

Contemporary TV
and Moral Identity Formation

Edited by
Steven A. Benko

LEXINGTON BOOKS
Lanham • Boulder • New York • London

Published by Lexington Books
An imprint of The Rowman & Littlefield Publishing Group, Inc.
4501 Forbes Boulevard, Suite 200, Lanham, Maryland 20706
www.rowman.com

6 Tinworth Street, London SE11 5AL, United Kingdom

British Library Cataloguing in Publication Information Available

Library of Congress Cataloging-in-Publication Data

Names: Benko, Steven A., editor.
Title: Better living through TV : contemporary TV and moral identity formation / edited
 by Steven A. Benko.
Other titles: Better living through television
Description: Lanham : Lexington Books, [2022] | Includes bibliographical references and
 index. | Summary: "The essays collected in Better Living through TV: Contemporary
 TV and Moral Identity Formation analyze a variety of contemporary television shows
 to argue for the role that TV plays in moral identity formation. Audiences take from
 television viewing a better sense of what matters to them, ways of relating to others,
 and a moral sense of the world they inhabit" —Provided by publisher.
Identifiers: LCCN 2022004507 (print) | LCCN 2022004508 (ebook) |
 ISBN 9781793636188 (cloth) | ISBN 9781793636201 (paperback) |
 ISBN 9781793636195 (epub)
Subjects: LCSH: Television programs—Social aspects. | Television programs—Moral
 and ethical aspects. | Television viewers.
Classification: LCC PN1992.6 .B47 2022 (print) | LCC PN1992.6 (ebook) |
 DDC 302.23/45—dcundefined
LC record available at https://lccn.loc.gov/2022004507
LC ebook record available at https://lccn.loc.gov/2022004508

Contents

Acknowledgments

Something never comes from nothing, and this work has been made possible by multiple people and offices at Meredith College. Sarah Roth, thank you for your support and encouragement at the beginning of this project and for helping me navigate some rough waters at the end. Your arrival at Meredith has been transformative in so many ways, but most meaningful of all is your enthusiastic and consistent support of my research. Matthew Poslusny and the members of the Faculty Development and Instructional Technology Committee, thank you for supporting this work with generous research funds.

This book was conceived before, then delayed by, the COVID pandemic. Some people were lucky enough to be able to turn to television as a means of escaping from or coping with very different, very challenging, work and life circumstances. For me, it was a chance to remember the important dialogue that occurs between a story and its audience. Why were certain TV shows more or less popular during the pandemic? What role was TV playing in helping people feel better? Was it to connect with something familiar or to escape from the everyday? And given the unprecedented nature of this time, what role is TV playing in shaping who we are going to be when the pandemic ends? It was an opportunity to revisit the ways that stories create a sense of self, and beyond that, a moral sense of self. This question has been the consistent thread that ties all of my work together. Melanie McKay, it was our conversations about Nabokov's *Pale Fire*, specifically the difficulty of telling our own stories and the ethical dimensions of identity formation that are the foundation of so much of what I think. At Syracuse University, David Miller and Gail Hamner helped me take those questions in directions I never would have thought of on my own. But no one deserves more credit for the way that story and the relationship between story, identity, and ethics continues to reverberate in my thought than James Wiggins. I think he would have liked this book and the continued belief that story is a place where important and interesting things happen. All that being said, none of this would be possible without Janet Nelson and significant role she has played in my personal and professional development.

While my name is on the cover, many hands were involved in the production of this text. Vance Ricks, thank you for your early collaboration on this project; your comments and insights helped get this process started. It is clear that this book would not have made it to its final form without the assistance of a dedicated group of people who saw an opportunity to take on extra work. Laura Fine and Zach Linge, thank you for providing some much-needed polish. Ellie Jones, thank you for writing with me, again. Bailey Birtchet, thank you for the brilliant cover design. My small part in both of your academic and professional successes is something I will treasure forever. It is my hope that as you grow to become whatever you will be—scholars, artists, and thinkers—that I can be included in your projects and enhance them in the ways that you have enhanced mine.

Given all that was swirling around the atmosphere when this work was being done, it was not obvious that this text would cross the finish line. There were those who kept listening and kept encouraging me so that its completion became inevitable, and I will always appreciate the support you gave me: Mike Runy, Andrew Ball, Rebecca Duncan, and Shannon Grimes, thank you. Judith Lakamper at Lexington, thank you for your patience.

Finally, my family endured or enjoyed the time I had to spend away from them to complete this book. Now, hopefully, we can gather together again and watch something good, and good for us, together.

Foreword

Martin Shuster

Writing a preface during a pandemic—now, likely unfortunately an endemic—is a peculiar feeling, as if one is doing something that seems beside the point, as if one should be doing something else. Yet there is something entirely natural in writing *this* preface right now, for a book on television, especially on its ethical significance and potential, seems to be exactly what we might need. After all—globally and seemingly without any slowing down—we have turned to television during this pandemic and its lockdowns and tribulations. Whether it has meant re-watching classic series like *The Sopranos* or *Buffy the Vampire Slayer* or becoming involved with more recent ones like *Snowpiercer* or *The Handmaid's Tale*, we have turned to what I had earlier termed "new television."

While the critical and aesthetic significance of such television is now increasingly—although by no means universally—accepted and celebrated, it is interesting that the potential pleasure of such television was never questioned. Since our very first experience with *Twin Peaks*, we have understood the way in which new television may serve to captivate us, offering us a unique new pleasure, one that somehow mixed televisual duration with filmic sensibility (admittedly, perhaps not in the show's second season). But what is the significance of this pleasure?

When I wrote *New Television: The Aesthetics and Politics of a Genre*, my aim was to make a case for the aesthetic—and thereby political—significance of new television. My suggestion was that here was a medium finally coming of age, that we must take note of it, understanding its qualities and its stakes so as to locate its precursors and future possibilities. The possibility and existence of *Better Living Through TV* is to me a deep confirmation of the thesis of *New Television*, for this book conclusively shows that new television—regardless of how offbeat or quirky or even humorous it may be—is *serious* stuff, capable of inspiring the most fine-tuned and sophisticated moral reflection. And the reader of this book should make no mistake, the more than dozen chapters in this book each pursue cutting-edge readings of particular shows in the new television canon, each chapter expertly informed by deep scholarship in ethical and moral theory, and all of them unified by a deep understanding of the moral possibilities of new television.

To be clear, the cumulative suggestion of the chapters that follow is not the naïve or cross idea that watching new television will somehow make you more moral, as some scholars of, say, literature sometimes assert. The mere act of watching new television is no guarantee of anything. What all of the chapters that follow illustrate, however, is that new television is a site for serious moral contemplation: that it can inspire our moral reflection, can train our sensibility, can expand our imaginative capacities, and can give us—in a time where this is increasingly difficult to find or create—common ground. A volume like *Better Living Through TV* thereby becomes an important project for our social democracy: it is a possible means of forging connection, whether with each other or with a potential past, in the form of a potentially shared philosophical inheritance. Even though about ethics, then, *Better Living Through TV* is also thereby a political book (as it is also a book in aesthetics). And, exactly because it responds—in several ways—to the present moment, it is a book from which we stand to benefit, now and into the future.

Introduction

TV, Better Living with Other People?

Steven A. Benko

Television is ubiquitous in America. According to the A.C. Nielsen company, 99 percent of U.S. households have at least one television; 66 percent of households have three or more televisions. The average television set is on for 6 hours and 47 minutes each day.[1] It was predicted that the internet would lead to a decline in television viewing but the opposite is true: online viewing has increased the overall amount of television viewing by 15 percent.[2] In 2009–2010, television viewing peaked at almost 9 hours per day.[3] It is an imperfect metric, but if you assume a home is empty between 9 am and 5 pm, then television viewing is what Americans do first thing in the morning and as soon as they get home (66% of Americans watch television while eating dinner).[4] The chapters collected in this volume are not about whether Americans are addicted to television. The authors who have contributed to this collection argue that television is a place where important identity work and moral reflection can occur. Each of the chapters begins from the premise that television series are worthy of analysis and are part of how people come to understand themselves and how they identify with and relate to others, and it is the argument of the chapters in this book that the moral reflection prompted by television shows is the occasion for moral improvement. There is no claim that this was intentional on the part of the series creators or writers—moral conflict moves a plot, and moral development makes characters more interesting—nor does it invalidate other interpretations of the show. Instead, the author's argue that there is a moral message that the audience can take from watching the show, be it expanding the moral community to include non-human animals, recovering voices of marginalized groups, how to live decently with other people, or how to think through questions of race and representation in popular media. Television has gotten much better: technological changes in the production and consumption of television has, first, increased the quality and quantity of television shows being broadcast in the United States, such that second, there has been a change in the way viewers connect with a show. Better technology, writing, acting, filming, and so on, have allowed television to become more important culturally and in the lives of viewers. One result has been that viewers are investing more in television shows and, as a result, the moral messages of these shows have come to matter more intensely. The chapters in this volume speak to what the audience may take away from the shows under consideration but the larger point is that viewers are finding themselves, or becoming themselves, in conversation with what they see on the screen.

Technological developments in production, including new visual and sound technologies, digital cameras that are cheaper and lighter, and enhanced computer graphics and editing software, have made the images on the screen sound and look better than they ever have. On the audience side, new televisions with better resolution and sound capabilities have enhanced the viewing experience. An argument can be made that the improved sound and video was the catalyst for improved filming, writing, and acting. Raising the aesthetic level on the production side incentivized writers, directors, and more actors to work in television. These new technologies meant that everything along the spectrum from a subtle gesture or sound to the most over-the-top image, spectacle, and cacophony could be seen and heard more clearly than ever before. The new cameras, editing, and graphics software became the tools with which to frame a scene from alternative angles, or to place characters in new locations, or to use green screen technology to place the characters in those locations without having to go there, or to light the scene or the actors in ways that new televisions with more colors and pixels could display. Digital technologies allowed directors to do multiple takes without worrying about running out of tape or increasing supplies or storage costs. And while it is true that for every example of great television, there is a counterexample that confirms every suspicion that TV appeals to the lowest common denominator (for every Soprano or Shellstrop there seems to be a Kardashian or Real Housewife), it does seem that these new technologies have pushed the medium to heights that rival the most expensive film productions.

The technological improvements that enhance the viewing experience are one part of the story of how television has become better. The second improvement to the viewing experience are changes in consumption that allow for a more personalized viewing experience. It is this change, along with the proliferation of outlets streaming television, that is the catalyst for the move away from broad programming that appeals to the largest possible audience to programming that is targeted at smaller, but more specific, audiences. Audience engagement with content became more intense as television viewing became more personal and intimate. Television viewing opened up new ways of seeing and being that suggested and informed new ways of thinking about oneself, what mattered, and relating to others.

PERSONAL VIEWING HABITS

In its origin and for the first several decades of its existence, television viewing was a social experience because it had to be. Televisions were expensive and not many homes had multiple TV sets. Television shows were appointment viewing because audiences were unable to time-shift when they watched a show.[5] Fast forward to today, recorded television shows are no longer stored on cassettes consisting of "0.5-inch magnetic tape wound between two spools" encased in plastic and sold for $20.[6] While the VCR allowed viewers to shift when they watched a program, no other technology has done more to expand audience control over the viewing experience than the digital recorder. TiVo, the first company to develop set-top boxes with the ability to record, but more importantly pause and rewind live television, improved upon time-shifting and collecting episodes of favorite shows on VHS tapes. TiVo's digital copies did not degrade over time (as was the case with VCRs) and were easier to access and search.[7] Where TiVos and DVRs were limited by their storage capacity, cloud-based storage has largely removed this obstacle. TiVo and DVRs created an expectation that television viewing should conform to the individual's schedule and that shows should be available at the push of a button. Most importantly, TiVos and DVRs allowed viewers to store episodes so that viewers could watch several in one sitting or re-watch them over and over again. Different from, and maybe inspired by, how the TiVo and DVR created something like "TV on demand," streaming services like Netflix, Hulu, and HBOMax enhance the opportunities for viewers to personalize the viewing experience.

The increased personalization of television, coupled with the proliferation of content providers, made the viewer want something that was tailored to their preferences and schedule. Brett Martin, author of *Difficult Men*, highlighted in *The Atlantic* how these new technologies gave rise to more content providers and more diverse content:

> Television was becoming more and more diversified. The big networks were ceding some of their monopoly to cable. Cable was proliferating like crazy. Televisions themselves are becoming better all the time; they were something you could view cinematic work on. And the beginning of a stream of technologies that allowed you to watch at any time. So the network telling you when to watch was starting to fall away.[8]

According to a presentation for Sony, Inc. by media consultant William Cooper, there are at least six reasons why people watch television: to unwind, for comfort, to connect to society, the experience, to escape, and to indulge in guilty pleasures. Cooper's list shows how television viewing is both personal and social: viewing not only satisfies individual needs and desires but also connects the viewer to other people, communities, and larger cultural conversations. From the beginning, television has been the leading distribution method for live information: news, sports, awards shows, and so on. That changes, though, as new technologies allow audiences to demand content tailored to their wants and interests.[9] Though Cooper's list privileges what individuals get out of television viewing more than the social benefits of television viewing, he maintains that "traditional television fulfills our basic need for company, social connection, and participation in a shared experience."[10] Recognizing that viewing habits are changing and becoming more personal Cooper's suggestion for retaining and attracting viewers is for content providers to stress quality over quantity and to grow beyond the belief that the television viewer is a passive consumer of what is on the screen: "the biggest challenge for existing channels is to think not of a massive passive audience, but in terms of valued individuals with their own needs and shared interests."[11] The value that viewers derive from the viewing experience is finding that the program connects to what matters to them. Connecting to what matters to viewers as individuals is the catalyst for connections to others and society because the experience of what matters is always social. Mattering is social because it is comparative. Because the value of what matters comes from it mattering to the individual and that it also matters to others, the individual connection to a particular television show is enhanced when one finds a community of people to share that investment with. An individual, seeing other people invest in something that matters to them, will feel that connection more intensely. Even if that connection is serendipitous or the result of careful market research, it is still validating in that it makes the time spent with that show more than a way to pass the time.

Cooper's call for a move away from quantity television (measured in terms of audience size) to quality television (measured in terms of awards, esteem among television critics, and intensity of fan base) can be seen in which shows were produced, how those shows were marketed, and how they were able to find success in a crowded television landscape. These technological changes and the increased personalization of the television experience came to define a new era of television. While much has been written about the different television eras and the quality of the shows that defined them, this text considers television from this most recent Golden Age of television through the current era of Peak TV. It is these eras of television that have been shaped by the technological changes that increased the quality of television production and respond to the increased personalization of television viewership that allows shows to matter more intensely to audiences.

Writing for the *AV Club*, Emily VanDerWerff cites Syracuse University professor Robert Thompson's declaration that there have been many golden ages of television:

> In his book *Television's Second Golden Age* (published, amusingly enough, in 1997, just two years before *The Sopranos* remade the TV landscape), Robert J. Thompson argues for the '50s as the first golden age and the '70s as a potential second golden age before casting his lot for the '80s as the *actual* second golden age of TV, thanks to the proliferation of intelligent, adult dramas that told serialized stories and didn't have things finish up at the end of each new episode. Shows like *Hill Street Blues* and *St. Elsewhere* codified new rules for TV drama, which were then exploded by everything from *Moonlighting* to *Thirtysomething*. And if comedy was your thing, the '80s were no slouch on that score either, from major hits like *Cheers* to minor cult sensations like *Frank's Place*.[12]

This latest Golden Age of television is said to have begun with the premiere of *The Sopranos* on HBO, January 10, 1999.[13] Peak TV is said to have begun in 2015 when FX CEO John Landgraf told the Television Critics Association that the sheer volume of scripted television available on over-the-air networks, cable channels, and ever-increasing streaming channels meant that there was now more TV, and more quality TV, than ever before. While Landgraf had predicted that the bubble would eventually burst, he returned a few years later to say that he had been wrong: the number of scripted shows kept increasing meaning that his notion that there was "too much TV" had been replaced by there being "too much story! There's too much narrative," making it impossible for viewers to consume all that this new era had to offer.[14] Joe Lipsett provides the data to support this claim: "In 2015, 409 scripted series were produced—nearly doubling the number from 2009. In 2016 that number rose to 455, with speculation that the number could potentially hit 500 series in 2017."[15] Peak TV can also be defined as the beginning of the proliferation of cinema-like quality programming on channels other than HBO (FX and AMC, in particular). Content-wise, it can be argued (as many of the chapters in this volume do) that the transition from this latest Golden Age of television to Peak TV emphasizes connection over self-actualization, community over individuality, and an uplifting vision of humanity, rejecting the nihilism of the previous era. It is clear that TV got better in both of these eras.

While one can talk about television's different eras and the shows that defined it, no one era is without counterexamples. While interesting and important television was produced in the 1960s and 1970s (e.g., *All In the*

Family), the goal was still to attract the broadest possible audience: "In the three-network world that existed until the 1980s, it always paid to pursue the broadest audience, and that meant keeping it simple and uncontroversial. The brave stuff stood out for its quality as well as its ratings, as if the two had to be mutually exclusive."[16] Relative to the time period under consideration here, *The Sopranos* premiered in 1999, but so did *Family Guy, The West Wing, Angel, WWE Smackdown, Strangers with Candy*, and the latest incarnation of *Family Feud*. In order to grow the audience, the shows produced for television had to reflect both the audience's diversity and the diversity of the audience's concerns, values, and interests. This may be, then, the discernible difference between this Golden Age of television and the era of Peak TV and what came before it: instead of finding the broadest possible audience for a show, the goal became to find *an* audience for a show. Where Nielsen rankings estimated the number of people watching a show as a percentage of total viewership at that given time, success in this era prioritizes intensity (in the form of critical praise and fan engagement such as memes, shared clips, and online discussion). Lipsett writes:

> This is the new normal in the age of Peak TV: as audience attention is fragmented across hundreds of series, live ratings (captured the same day an episode airs and represented in audience by millions that are broken down into key demographic metrics) no longer accurately capture how or when audiences engage with their favorite series. . . . Viewers, as a result, no longer simply watch programs; they actively consume, engage and generate content about their favorite series—activities that networks have used to supplement or complement traditional live ratings to demonstrate viewer interest in their programming (effectively monetizing social media engagement to advertisers).[17]

FROM THE GOLDEN AGE TO PEAK TV

The television show *Schitt's Creek* is a perfect example of how a niche show that emphasizes unique characters and plot can thrive in this new media environment. The *Vulture* article "The Unlikely Rise of *Schitt's Creek*" charts the growth of the show from the Pop network to Netflix. On a more traditional broadcast network, a show like *Schitt's Creek* would not survive. The American distribution for the show was on the Pop network—formerly TV Guide Network—which, in 2015, had a subscriber base of 80 million homes. While *Schitt's Creek* was immediately popular in Canada, it struggled in America: Season 1 averaged 263,000 viewers because people did not know how to find Pop among the many other cable channels they subscribed to or how to stream it.[18] The ratings for season 2 grew 26 percent to an average of 331,000 viewers. To promote the show, Pop "let audiences watch the show on as many platforms as possible, and as easily as possible. Instead of limited on-demand streaming of the show to the five most recent episodes—as many cable networks still do—Pop lets its subscribers watch every episode of the series, going back to season one."[19] *Schitt's Creek* debuted on Netflix in 2017 and the ratings on Pop increased every single year. The creators of the show, Eugene and Dan Levy, credit Netflix with making the show a success:

> "I definitely think that the combination of airing on Pop early in the new year and then re-airing in Netflix in the fall—it's kept the conversations happening around the watercoolers in a way," he says. Because Netflix's subscriber base includes a number of younger cord-cutting viewers who don't have a cable subscription (and thus no access to Pop), Levy theorizes a portion of the show's fan base considers its fall launch on Netflix as a season premiere. "Whenever the season drops [on Netflix], it feels like we've just relaunched. We see a lot of social-media activity," he says. "To have two different premieres in a way, in a single year, is an opportunity that few shows get. As someone who wants the show to be seen by as many people as possible, that kind of opportunity is wild."[20]

Similarly, shows like *Breaking Bad* and *Mad Men* saw increases in viewership and cultural relevance when they began streaming on VOD services.

The digression into the minutiae of distribution and streaming is relevant to the chapters in this volume because the television shows they examine are, for the most part, examples of a shift away from the broad comedies and dramas that defined earlier television eras to a turn toward more niche, more sophisticated comedies and dramas. Again, *Schitt's Creek* is illustrative of the shift from content meant to engage as broad an audience as possible to content being produced, distributed, and pushed for a smaller, more specific, and intense audience:

> The CBC, like ABC in America, is a somewhat broad-skewing, over-the-air broadcast network. That might have ruled them out as a potential home, given the Levys desire to go somewhere more amenable to a "niche" idea. But right around the time the Levys were pitching *Schitt's Creek,* the Canadian TV powerhouse was undergoing a bit of a metamorphosis in its comedy development philosophy. "In 2014, we made a decision to prioritize half-hour, single-camera comedies with a unique point of view and authentic, character-driven storytelling," says Sally Catto, general manager for programming at CBC. Or, as Eugene Levy puts it, "They were heading in more of a cable direction for their comedies. The timing was right."[21]

Levy's aside about the CBC heading in "more of a cable direction" reflects important shifts, or possibly the pivotal change, in quality television programming. There is, at least, a change in perception of what was possible to produce and distribute on cable channels. Less concerned about viewership and content ratings (cable channels were given more freedom or cared less about warnings regarding content, language, nudity, and depictions of sexual behavior; as a pay TV channel, HBO was the most free to push the boundary for what could be shown on television), cable channels were able to explore niche topics that were likely to appeal to a small, but intense, group of people. These cable channels eschewed ratings and instead pursued demographics. For example, *The Sopranos* finale was viewed by 11.9 million people. Those numbers are good by HBO standards, but compared to other programs, it would place the show in thirtieth place for average TV viewership that year (equal to the number of people who watched *Law and Order: SVU*, which also premiered in 1999).[22] The series finale of *The Wire*, regarded by some as the greatest show ever made, was viewed by 1.1 million people.[23] HBO's willingness to trade viewership for reputational success (as well as Emmy and Golden Globe awards) set the standard for high-quality programming, and other channels wanted to replicate their success. In deciding to produce *Mad Men* after several networks (including HBO) passed on it, Charlie Collier, president of AMC network, realized that networks could produce quality content and sell commercials at the same time:

"(We asked ourselves,) 'How do we become premium television on basic cable?'" Collier says, noting that the network wanted to find programming that complemented its movie offerings. "If we can offer a premium experience but on ad-supported television, that would be something unique in the cable landscape." . . . Its slogan is now "Story matters here." The competition is no longer Turner Classic Movies; it's now, well, everybody else.[24]

Different from the technological and production side of this latest Golden Age of television and Peak TV is the change in content. What shows like *The Sopranos, Breaking Bad, The Wire, Ray Donovan,* and *Mad Men*—all shows that are included in discussions of the era between 1999 and 2006 as the latest Golden Age of television—have in common is male protagonists who are in crisis. Writing for Slate.com, Willa Paskin defines these shows as "serious dramas about antiheroes and larger issues of masculinity" and, more derisively, "men in crisis on esteemed cable channels."[25] The main characters of these hour-long dramas were "complicated male leads whose actions can be described as morally ambiguous at best. And not only have viewers tuned in to watch these men, but they actually root for them—questionable behavior and all."[26] Tony Soprano was a revelation for the type of character that could lead a show. Martin contends that everything from the casting, to the wardrobe, to the behavior challenged the audience: "It went against everything that people thought they knew about television. People would reject a complicated hero in their own houses. There might be a small sliver that would be entranced by it in films, but you couldn't have a hero be a killer and be that complicated."[27] After him, the male leads in shows like *Dexter, Breaking Bad, Lucifer,* and *Deadwood* could look and behave like Tony Soprano and it did not break television norms. Culturally, this era of television coincided with an upheaval in American masculinity: What did it mean to be a man? How were men supposed to understand themselves as men? How ought they relate to women? And how ought women respond to them? The problem was that, perhaps, too many viewers identified with them or rooted for them.

SINCERITY PEAKED

Peak TV is the decentering of these White men and their replacement by characters with a variety of ethnicities, gender identities, and sexualities who are navigating a wider array of careers and family dynamics. It ceases to be about these men being their most authentic selves to being about how they relate to others and whether they can make space for them to live their lives too. An article by James Poniewozik in the *New York Times* explores how the eras of television covered in this volume went from David Brent of *The Office* to *Ted Lasso.* Poniewozick writes that "In TV's ambitious comedies, as well as dramas, the arc of the last 20 years is not from bold risk-taking to spineless inoffensiveness. But it is, in broad terms, a shift from irony to sincerity."[28] That shift saw the decentering of angry, brooding, White men to characters who are more earnest and direct. Poniewozik explains this shift away from irony as a response to fatigue from the tropes and style of these dramas becoming cliches, to a backlash against a president who distanced himself from the consequences of his words by saying he was always joking. The crisis in masculinity that generated hyper-masculine characters like Tony Soprano, Don Draper, and Walter White was something that the audience should think about, not embrace or root for. However, what was supposed to be a window into contemporary masculinity became, for a segment of the audience, a mirror:

> The common thread of antihero drama and cringe comedy is the assumption that audiences could and should be able to distinguish between the mind-set of the protagonist and the outlook of the author. They asked you to accept dissonance within the story and within yourself: You could see Tony as an animal while acknowledging the beast in you that resonated with him, you could see Larry

David as a jackass while recognizing that you found it thrilling. Audiences did not always observe this nuance, which led to what the critic Emily Nussbaum identified as "bad fans": the aggro "Sopranos" and "Breaking Bad" viewers who just wanted to see Tony bust heads and Walter White science his way to the top of the meth trade, and who got irritated if other characters, fans or even the artists behind the shows suggested that they were anything other than awesome.[29]

If irony fatigue occurs when the audience no longer capable of telling the difference between what the show depicts and what the show intends to say, then there is another explanation of how television has gone from irony to sincerity: if television tells stories, and if some of the stories that television tells are about the audience, then watching a show becomes autobiographical. It may have been the case that people saw or found themselves in *The Sopranos, Breaking Bad, Mad Men*, and *The Wire*. But when that was no longer pleasurable or sustainable—or the pleasure was no longer sustainable—it was time to change the channel. Here, the arc of Stephen Colbert's career is instructive: when politics seemed to be lower stakes, it was possible to approach it with a hip, ironic detachment that expressed an awareness of what was going on. His *Colbert Report* persona had the privilege of playing with meaning and leaving it up to others to figure out what he meant. When the political stakes changed, there was less time and space for irony; the Colbert of the *Late Show* had to start saying it straight.

Poniewozik sees the shift away from irony to sincerity as satisfying a cultural and political need for earnestness and straightforwardness. It may be that the need for sincerity is the result of fatigue, but there is also a moral dimension to it. The crisis of masculinity that animated characters like Tony Soprano and Walter White was also a crisis of authenticity: Who were these men, really? Did they know themselves? Could they make themselves known to others? Their crisis is fueled by how the people around them make it difficult for them to be themselves. Consider Walter White's speech to his wife, Skyler, when she expresses concern for his safety:

> Who are you talking to right now? Who is it you think you see? Do you know how much I make a year? I mean, even if I told you, you wouldn't believe it. Do you know what would happen if I suddenly decided to stop going in to work? A business big enough that it could be listed on the NASDAQ goes belly-up, disappears. It ceases to exist without me. No. You clearly don't know who you're talking to, so let me clue you in. I am not in danger, Skyler. I am the danger. A guy opens his door and gets shot, and you think that of me? No. I am the one who knocks.[30]

White's speech is both a confession of how he sees himself and a demand of how he wants to be seen by others. His frustration stems from the gap between how he sees himself and how others see him, but the more intense frustration is the gap between how he sees himself and the roles that society has assigned to him; these roles are emasculating. However, for the emasculated in the audience there is something invigorating about the power White displays when he explains who he thinks he is. For Howard Pickett in *Rethinking Sincerity and Authenticity*, White's speech is an example of the danger that comes from venerating authenticity at the expense of the social: "self congruence resembles, instead, self-interest, and the narcissism that threatens genuine ethical concern for others."[31] Authenticity is a "purer, more thoroughgoing self-congruence, one stripped of any distracting concerns with others, with their observations and opinions" such that "the one who resolves above all to be himself, is also one lacking the capacity for altruism or a genuine concern for others as others."[32] The social nature of television makes this sort of authenticity impossible to sustain: characters are part of ensembles and must learn to negotiate what those other characters need and want. The viewer may watch alone, but as William Cooper pointed out (see above), television fuels and satisfies the viewer's need for company, social connection, and participation in a shared experience. For some, the shift from the solipsism or individuation of authenticity and irony occurs when it can no longer be sustained culturally and politically. Sincerity, in the form of earnestness, warmth, and straightforwardness, is as much about the viewer feeling good about feeling pleasure while watching a show, as it is a map for how to negotiate this current cultural and political moment. Shows such as *Parks and Rec*, *The Good Place*, *Schitt's Creek*, and *Ted Lasso* show another way forward. These are shows where the window the viewer sees through and the mirror they see themselves in reveal that the best expression of one's self is other oriented. On television, characters become who they are in relationships with others. Characters become who they are when they identify and respond to the other characters' needs. Television viewing satisfies a need for more than just distraction and entertainment: viewers become who they are in dialogue with others, including the characters on television shows.[33] To attempt Eleanor Shellstrop's journey of self-improvement or to try to be as nice, hopeful, and encouraging as Ted Lasso is to attempt better living through TV. The shift away from solipsistic authenticity of the most recent Golden Age of television to the social sincerity of Peak TV reveals that there were television shows—not all of them, but a good number—that linked better television to being a better person.

Each of the chapters in this volume picks up this idea of seeing something on the screen that suggests the possibility of moral improvement. TV got better, but could it make the audience better? That was the idea at the start of this project: in the transition from the latest Golden Age to Peak TV, something about TV had changed. The best that TV had to offer was becoming nicer, friendlier, and more hopeful and optimistic about being better. The truth is much more complicated than that, but it did seem like there was a move away from the dark narcissism and misogyny of the male leads of *Mad Men*, *The Sopranos*, or *Breaking Bad* to Eleanor Shellstrop's belief that redemption was possible even if moral perfection was not. TV was going to show that better living was possible.[34]

THE PLAN OF THE BOOK

It is not the case that these shows were read didactically or that the moral message each author found was intentional or the point of the series or episode, though that is the case for some of these shows. Instead, the authors of the chapters in this volume demonstrated that watching television is an interactive process where the audience tries to make sense of what they see on the screen. The viewer is trying to find a place for the show and the characters in their world and that includes making moral sense of their motivations and behaviors. The chapters are arranged chronologically by release date of the television show because doing so reveals how there has been a move from shows that focus on the individual to shows that place a greater emphasis on a more communal ethic. In some of the early chapters, it took considerable work to bring something like a moral meaning to the fore, whereas the later chapters consider shows that make moral growth a central part of the plot.

If there is a thread that connects these chapters, it is the tension between the individual and society, specifically the struggle to be more than who one has been told or conditioned to be. Also, it was unintentional, though maybe predictable, that shows such as *The Sopranos* and *The Wire* offer a more ambiguous moral message, whereas newer shows, such as *The Unicorn* and *The Falcon and the Winter Soldier*, are obvious in the moral message they want to communicate to the audience. None of these chapters is the final word on these shows—some might be the first word—but they will not be the last word because of central place TV occupies in American culture, and the recent technological developments that make it possible to find and embrace smaller, niche shows that did not have an audience the first time, or to revisit popular shows and find new meanings in them.

The first chapter in this volume, "Sleeping with Fishes and Talking with Horses: Animality, Identity, and Vegetarianism in *The Sopranos*," breaks new ground on what is arguably the best television series of all time, *The Sopranos*. In a show that was never shy about mental and physical violence, Steeves asks the question whether viewers can see in *The Sopranos* a call to be better . . . to non-human animals. *The Sopranos* is a complicated show with many themes and sub-themes running through it, but the show continually returns to the question of inherited violence and whether it is possible to break free from that tradition. Steeves uses that question to think through the unthoughtful way we consume animals for food and asks whether there is something about the care Tony Soprano shows animals that might be a larger lesson for the audience about their own relationship with the animals that become their food or the animals that live around their homes. The larger question Steeves is asking is what *The Sopranos* has to say about community: Who is included? Who is excluded? More importantly, how do we decide who is and is not included in the circle of respect and concern? The work that Steeves encourages the viewer to do in order to think more deeply about the moral meaning of *The Sopranos* is indicative of the type of work that needs to be done to find positive moral meanings in many of the shows that feature a strong, male antihero. By asking if we are up to the task that Tony himself might not have been up to (though the last thing we see him order is a plate of onion rings, a vegetarian choice depending on the type of oil that was used to fry them), Steeves sees in *The Sopranos* the possibility of a better, more inclusive, moral community.

Writing about what is arguably the other best television show ever produced, *The Wire*, John Hillman's chapter, "The Bigger the Lie, the More They Believe: Morality and Ethics in *The Wire*," questions how the show upends the audience's moral sensibilities by making the behavior of the police and the criminals interchangeable and indistinguishable. Of the six reasons Cooper gives for why people watch television (to unwind, for comfort, to connect to society, the experience, to escape, and to indulge in guilty pleasures) having one's expectations frustrated and moral sensibilities called into question might make it impossible to watch *The Wire* for comfort, or to unwind. To identify with the characters of *The Wire* or to see oneself in that world is to become discomfited about one's moral commitments. Ironically, this is a good thing. Instead of identifying with the positive and uplifting, *The Wire* forces an identification with the struggle: the struggle to be better, the struggle to do the right thing, and the struggle to be good. The moral reflection this prompts provides clarity on what matters to the individual and what they value. Different from other shows considered in this volume, *The Wire* is less about validating moral beliefs or values than it is fleshing them out amid the social conditions and relationships that constitute them.

While the first two chapters focus on the relationship between the individual and the community, Rasmussen's chapter, "The Two Walters: Walt Whitman's Poetry and the Moral Vision of *Breaking Bad*," is about something larger than the individual. Mining the connections between Walter White and American poet Walt Whitman, Rasmussen sees in White an inversion of Whitman's democratic and individualistic philosophy. *Breaking Bad* is a cautionary tale about what happens when a man uses science for selfish, individualistic, and capitalist gains instead of encouraging interconnectedness and community. White loses himself and those around him as he justifies his behavior with appeals to libertarianism and neoliberal economics. White's ability to rationalize any behavior serves as a warning to the viewer about what happens when science is unmoored from the greater good. Similar to the essays by Steeves and Rasmussen which had to read against how a character has been interpreted (or valorized in pop culture), Hillman contends that Walter White should spur thoughts about the importance of the common good and the necessity of contributing to it.

No author is more explicit about reading against the popular reception of a character than Kolb who explores the amount of work that women have to do in order to find something for themselves—that is, something more than objectification and misogyny—in these shows. In "Check Your Settings: Change to a Democratic Framework for Feminist Subtitles," Kolb focuses on *Breaking Bad* and *Sons of Anarchy* to explain how the cultural and political situatedness of the audience will open, close, and re-open different interpretive possibilities, which political, feminist, or masculinist themes are more obvious. Her argument is that what people were getting from these shows ebbed and flowed with the changing political and cultural landscape. Finding feminist possibilities in these shows in the early 2000s was easier than it was after the 2016 U.S. presidential election foreclosed some of these readings. Kolb argues that these changes make it difficult to arrive at any common understanding or shared meaning about these shows and, like Rasmussen, worries about the consequences for democracy when selfish individualism is valorized and when we cannot speak with one voice against violence and misogyny. The solution, Kolb argues, is to view these shows through a feminist lens, specifically a lens informed by care ethics, so that one has a place to speak from.

If antiheroes and misogyny are what define the dramas that are heralded as the best of this latest Golden Age of television, then within those broad categories are explorations of where individuals, usually men, fit in a society with an evolved understanding of right and wrong. Shelton's "'The Lord of War and Thunder': The Morality of Nemesis and Retributive Justice within *Justified*," is a thorough investigation of the idea of retributive justice and is an example of how the men of this era did not want to be wrong, or alternatively, needed someone or something to tell them that they were right. Shelton finds in Raylan Givens a character who believes all of his actions are justified even as they cause upset and chaos for those around him. By raising the question of justification—and what can and cannot be justified—the audience is engaged in a debate about the moral appropriateness of retributive violence. On the surface, retributive violence should always be justified because the person suffering that violence did something to warrant punishment. Shelton rightly ponders the nature and scope of retributive justice by asking whether it perpetuates cycles of violence. *Justified* uses the Western genre, specifically the idea of the shootout, to destabilize the morality of retributive justice: Does the good person win because they are good or because they are faster? Is the violence of the shootout always justified or is restraint and mercy a more moral act? Unlike other shows of this era, *Justified* wears its morality on its sleeve and is forthright about the moral questions it is interrogating, but like other shows in this era, it offers no easy answers to the questions it raises. The audience is left to do the work to tease out the moral meaning of the show and is often left unsettled, with more questions than answers.

If there is a discernible transition between this latest Golden Era of television and Peak TV, the next several chapters consider television shows that are examples of what that transition would look like. In "Law and Loyalty in *Hellcats*," Matt Hummel considers how a show about cheerleading that aired on the CW can reverse the emphasis on self-actualization found in shows like *The Sopranos*, *Breaking Bad*, or even *Justified*, to being about finding oneself by making a connection with a larger group. The theme of *Hellcats* is loyalty. Where other shows of this era might show how loyalty is a burden that forces the individual to compromise aspects of themselves, on *Hellcats* loyalty to the group is a positive that brings out the characters' best self. The characters on *Hellcats* might be people that an audience member could aspire to be.

Alternatively, no one should aspire to be a character on *Hannibal*. In "Justice is Served: Bryan Fuller's *Hannibal* and the Evolution of Cultural Morality," Douglas L. Howard traces all of the various properties that Hannibal Lecter has appeared in and explains how changing cultural attitudes and values have made it impossible to ignore Lecter's otherness. In many ways, then, the evolution of audience sentiment about Lecter, which ranged from him being everything from a hero, to antihero, to monster, can serve as a model for how many of the male leads of shows like *The Sopranos*, *Breaking Bad*, and *Mad Men* have been reevaluated. Where the television show *Hannibal* indicates that there is still a desire for morally complex and compromised characters, they will not be given the same latitude for their bad behavior.

While Hannibal Lecter could be said to be the devil incarnate, the lead character of *Lucifer* is literally the devil. Where several of the chapters in this volume consider the burden of inherited morality, the social pressure to conform, and the difficulty of escaping legacies of violence, the main character of *Lucifer* takes those questions to their logical conclusion. By framing this question as one of free will, Liotta and Vanzo shift the debate from the ways that society restricts the individual to the individual being responsible for transcending their origins and cultural situation and becoming responsible for themselves. Relative to the other chapters in this volume, the chapter by

Liotta and Vanzo is a response to chapters by Rasmussen and Kolb: fans were tired of shows where the bad behavior of the main characters was explained by appeals to tradition, culture, or toxic upbringings. What better character to depict struggling against, and overcoming, each of these things than Lucifer? If the Devil can become a better person, then so can anyone else.

Kearney's "Tolerance and Tradition in *Letterkenny*" continues the thread of shows that interrogate the burden and weight of what people and communities pass down from generation to generation and how communities can form around the inclusion and exclusion of others based on their attitude toward that heritage. While *Letterkenny* is not as famous as some of the other shows in this volume, its inclusion is indicative of a shift toward smaller shows that found a niche outside of the mainstream but are supported by a loyal and intense fan base. Kearney sees in *Letterkenny* a sustained interrogation of tradition: tradition is what ought to matter to a person; however, uncritical acceptance of tradition can alienate someone from someone or something that also matters. The solution offered by *Letterkenny* is that progress is more important than tradition; tradition should be jettisoned when it slows or impedes progress, specifically, when it fosters intolerance and exclusion. Similar to the chapter by Liotta and Vanzo that argues that individuals are ultimately responsible for themselves, and adopting the democratic impulse explored in the chapters by Hillman and Kolb, progress and tolerance become the values that supersede selfish individualism. The audience watches as the citizens of Letterkenny become better people by negotiating this tension in a way that rewards openness and empathy.

Although shows like *Letterkenny* might make something like moral improvement part of the plot or part of the relationship dynamics between the characters, moral improvement was literally the point of *The Good Place*. All four seasons were a meditation on the possibility of moral improvement, even going so far as to enlist ethics professors as consultants. One can see Eleanor Shellstrop as one of the boys, fitting right in with the Tony Sopranos, Walter Whites, and Don Drapers of the world, but she was also a meditation on what it would take to become less selfish and give other people the moral respect that they are owed. It would be fair to assume that given the care and effort that went into constructing the moral vision of the show that it would have stuck the landing and presented a consistent and coherent moral vision that the audience could live in. Delston argues in "Morality versus Mortality: The Meaning of (After)Life in *The Good Place*" that the show's ending, where each of the characters gets to choose non-existence as a reward for achieving moral perfection, may be in keeping with the idea that moral growth is part of the process of self-actualization, but the ending is at odds with the theme of the show. For Delston, the theme of the show is that the pursuit of virtue is what makes one good and gives meaning to life. While the show depicts immortality in the Good Place as boring and stultifying, there were still people who needed to be helped. Only Tahani, who opts to become an architect (and whose character arc was most closely associated with virtue ethics) makes what for Delston is the correct choice: she continues to work for perfection because she realizes that the pursuit of perfection is what gives life meaning. Viewed in the context of the other chapters in this volume, Delston's analysis adds a new dimension to the move away from solipsistic self-actualization: one is never done becoming a better version of oneself. There is always more work that one can do on oneself if one is to live morally and meaningfully with others.

Living with others and the ability of television to create meaningful communities is the subject of Denis Newiak's analysis of *13 Reasons Why*. Newiak writes in "How Television Produces Invisible Communities in an Age of Loneliness: A Detailed Look at *13 Reasons Why*" that where loneliness is the condition created by late modernity, television helps to overcome that loneliness by forging connections between audience members. *13 Reasons Why* depicts characters struggling in the aftermath of a suicide that ruptures their world and community. As the characters work through their grief, they gain a new sense of hope and community. He argues that television does something similar by bringing viewers together in the shared experience of the show: viewing a show about loneliness gives the audience shared experiences, shared memories, and a collective set of values with which to be in community with others. Because *13 Reasons Why* deals with suicide, Netflix (the company that distributed the show) took steps to create real-world resources for people who might be suffering from depression or suicidal ideation, further blurring the line between television show and reality, but also expanding the community of people connected to the show. Similar to Delston's argument about our ongoing responsibility for other people, Newiak sees the telos of community to be the mutual support of others to combat the pressures of contemporary life.

The chapter by Steven A. Benko and Eleanor Jones, "Can Watching TV Make Me a Unicorn? TV and the Ethics of Decency," on the CBS show *The Unicorn* further develops the theme that the nature of goodness and key to moral improvement is living among and for others. *The Unicorn* is the story of a widowed father of two and his circle of friends as they negotiate late middle age parenting and careers. The show was an attempt by the network to capitalize on the idea of moral improvement as a show's central conceit (after the failure of *Living Biblically* and *God Friended Me*). Benko and Jones develop the idea of mattering maps to argue that the characters' ability to be decent to one another and grow as people depends upon what matters to them and how they direct their concerns and attention to what else should matter to them. Like other shows of this era, and shows considered in this volume, the central question of the show is how to negotiate what is owed to other people and how to attain and maintain relationships and hobbies that give meaning to one's life. Using the criteria for a decent life developed by Todd May in his book *A Decent Life*, Benko and Jones argue that what sets *The Unicorn* apart from other shows was how clearly it articulated a moral vision for contemporary times; it was a moral vision that responded to the solipsism of the previous eras but did not swing as far as other shows that asked the individual to give up too much of themselves for the common good.

An example of a character bound by a code—or creed—that required the sacrifice of individual desires and wants in order to sustain the common good was the Mandalorian. James Rocha's "The Baby Yoda Effect: A Kantian Analysis of Mandalorian Ethics" examines how the idea of the bounty hunter code and the Mandalorian "way" (as they were depicted in the first season of the show) complicates Kantian notions of duty and universal moral laws. While the second season of *The Mandalorian* changed much about what we know about the main characters, the first season contains a compelling depiction of the pressures one faces when trying to live according to an absolutist morality. Where so many of the shows from this latest Golden Age and Peak TV explore the tension between the individual and the communities one is a part of, the first season of *The Mandalorian* explores whether meaning can only be found in complete fidelity to a moral code. If chaos and violence are the consequences of violating that moral code, Rocha wonders what happens when absolutist moral codes come into conflict with one another or with a higher, more compelling moral virtue. For those who wanted to emulate the Mandalorian because the clarity of his moral system made him certain of what he ought to do, Rocha problematizes that clarity and certainty by showing the limits of absolutist moralities.

The final chapter in the volume, "A Black Captain America: Race in *The Falcon and the Winter Soldier*," considers a show that might not be a show but might be the future of television. Each of the shows analyzed in this volume began as open-ended projects with no publically declared end in sight. *The Falcon and the Winter Soldier* is different because of its intentionally limited run (six episodes) but, like the other shows, was produced for television and released on a weekly basis. Given the short run of shows like *The Good Place*, which eschewed multiple open-ended seasons for a tighter, more satisfying ending, *The Falcon and the Winter Soldier* might be the future of television where the time commitment to complete a show is declared in advance. The chapter by Alisa Johnson and Steven A. Benko does not consider whether *The Falcon and the Winter Soldier* is the future of television; instead, they analyze how the show deals with contemporary issues surrounding race and representation. *The Falcon and the Winter Soldier* continues storylines developed in the Marvel Cinematic Universe but addresses race more directly than any other Marvel property. Johnson and Benko question whether it was successful in doing so by examining how the situatedness of the audience determines their experience of the show: Could a White audience identify with and understand how the Black characters talk about race and their experiences? Does the show go far enough in addressing systemic racism or would a Black audience feel let down by an underwhelming presentation of racial struggle and oppression? How much can a show be expected to do or is it no longer possible for shows to avoid these larger cultural questions? While it is clear that being anti-racist is better than any alternative, can a show make its audience anti-racist or get them to question the racialized perspective they bring to television viewing? Like the other chapters in this volume, Johnson and Benko offer no easy answers to these questions but express a hope that more shows will include complex depictions of race as part of the larger story they are trying to tell.

As the statistics at the beginning of this introduction indicate, television is ubiquitous in American culture. The worlds depicted on the screen contain amazing possibilities for enriching and improving the lives of the viewer if the viewer is sensitive to the moral vision of the show. Each of the chapters in this volume argues that television is a catalyst for something like moral reflection and improvement. But they also indicate that the responsibility for that work is with the viewer, though the burden of that work can be lessened when the moral message is more obvious than not. It also seems to be the case that as the technologies for producing and viewing television improved, television programming got better. As these technologies allowed for more personalized viewing experiences that were more intense for how they connected with and shaped what mattered to the viewer, the shows became better at engaging important social issues. And audiences have been better for it.

NOTES

1. Norman Herr, "Television and Health," Television and Health (Internet Resources to Accompany the Sourcebook for Teaching Science, 2007), http://www.csun.edu/science/health/docs/tv&health.html.

2. Nicole F. Roberts, "Psychological Research Explains Why TV Viewing Is Higher than Ever," *Forbes Magazine*, December 4, 2019, https://www.forbes.com/sites/nicolefisher/2019/12/04/psychological-research-explains-why-tv-viewing-is-higher-than-ever/.

3. Alexis C. Madrigal, "When Did TV Watching Peak?," *The Atlantic*, May 30, 2018, https://www.theatlantic.com/technology/archive/2018/05/when-did-tv-watching-peak/561464/.

4. Herr, 2007.

5. VCRs were introduced in the United States in 1977 and gained in popularity through the early 1980s. Priya Ganapati, "June 4, 1977: VHS Comes to America," *Wired* (Conde Nast, June 4, 2010), https://www.wired.com/2010/06/0604vhs-ces/.

6. Ibid.

7. Brian Santo, "The Consumer Electronics Hall of Fame: TiVo," *IEEE Spectrum*, November 7, 2019, https://spectrum.ieee.org/the-consumer-electronics-hall-of-fame -tivo. Brian Santo calls TiVo's DVR "the least successful, most significant consumer electronics device ever" because it allowed viewers to pause, rewind, and fast forward live television. Eventually, all of the innovations offered by TiVos would be adopted by satellite and cable companies, as well as streaming services.

8. Hope Reese, "Why Is The Golden Age of TV So Dark?," *The Atlantic*, July 11, 2013, https://www.theatlantic.com/entertainment/archive/2013/07/why-is-the-golden -age-of-tv-so-dark/277696/.

9. William Cooper, "Why We Watch Television," Why We Watch Television (Informitiv/Sony Professional Solutions Europe, 2015), https://www.live-production .tv/sites/default/files/why_we_watch_television.pdf, slide 21.

10. Ibid., slide 41.

11. Ibid., slide 42.

12. Emily VanDerWerff, "The Golden Age of TV Is Dead; Long Live the Golden Age of TV," *The AV Club*, September 20, 2013, https://www.avclub.com/the-golden -age-of-tv-is-dead-long-live-the-golden-age-1798240704.

13. Jennifer Keishin Armstrong argues that the true origin of this Golden Age of television begins with *Buffy the Vampire Slayer* (1997), not *The Sopranos*. Her point is that all of the this Golden Age of Television are present in *Buffy*. See Jennifer Keishin Armstrong, "We Should Thank Buffy for Today's 'Golden Age' of Television," BBC Culture (BBC, March 7, 2017), https://www.bbc.com/culture/article/20170303 -we-should-thank-buffy-for-todays-golden-age-of-television. Writing for *The New Republic*, Rachel Syme provides reasons why *Buffy* would not be included, let alone foundational, for defining this Golden Age of television: it has a woman at the center of the narrative. Syme criticizes the continued emphasis on both the male leads and the male showrunners who created them. This is an era of television that is defined by shows made by men about being a certain type of man. Syme's point is that this obscures both the women who work on these shows and shows that center women and their experiences. See Rachel Syme, "The Trouble with Our 'Golden Age' of TV," *The New Republic*, November 21, 2017, https://newrepublic.com/article/145961 /trouble-golden-age-tv.

14. Joy Press, "Peak TV Is Still Drowning Us in Content, Says TV Prophet John Landgraf," Vanity Fair (Vanity Fair, August 3, 2018), https://www.vanity- fair.com/hollywood/2018/08/peak-tv-fx-john-landgraf-tca-donald-glover-chris-rock .VanDerWerff writes,

> I suspect there's another thing driving the end of the golden age of TV narrative: Paradoxi- cally, there's too much good TV on right now. One of the nice things about the golden age of TV was that there were always *maybe* 10 shows on at any given time that one had to be reasonably conversant in to feel caught up. . . . The best shows were on cable; the

best shows had shorter orders; the best shows were dark dramas and wacky single-camera comedies. The best shows, in other words, were the many children of *The Sopranos* and *Arrested Development*, the series that sprang up because those shows blazed so many trails that others followed, then branched off and made trails of their own. VanDerWerff, 2013

15. Joe Lipsett, "Defining Success in the Era of Peak TV: A Case Study of *The Nine Lives of Chloe King* on ABC Family and *Shadowhunters* on Free Form," in *ABC Family to Freeform TV: Essays on the Millennial-Focused Network and Its Programs*, ed. Emily Newman and Emily Witsell (Jefferson, NC: McFarland & Company, Inc.), 16.

16. Todd Leopold, "The New, New TV Golden Age," CNN (Cable News Network, May 6, 2013), https://www.cnn.com/2013/05/06/showbiz/golden-age-of-tv/.

17. Lipsett, 18.

18. Eugene Levy admits the first couple of years on Pop were "a bit of a struggle" to get noticed. "Not everybody knew how to get Pop," he says. "So the awareness factor in the States was not, I would say, extremely high. In fact, I wouldn't say it was high at all. In fact, I would say it was kinda low." In Josef Adalian, "The Unlikely Rise of Schitt's Creek," *Vulture* (Vulture, April 7, 2020), https://www.vulture.com /2020/04/schitts-creek-netflix-pop-success-story.html.

19. Ibid.

20. Ibid.

21. Ibid.

22. "'The Sopranos' Ratings: Only 11.9 Million?," The Take, *Vulture*, June 12, 2007, https://www.vulture.com/2007/06/the_sopranos_ratings_only_119.html.

23. David Zurawik, "'Wire' Finale Premiere Seen by 1.1 Million," *The Baltimore Sun*, March 12, 2008, https://www.baltimoresun.com/news/bs-xpm-2008-03-12 -0803120244-story.html.

24. Leopold, 2013.

25. Willa Paskin, "What Does 'Peak Tv' Really Mean?," Slate Magazine (*Slate*, December 23, 2015), https://slate.com/culture/2015/12/what-does-peak-tv-really -mean.html.

26. Reese, 2013.

27. Ibid.

28. James Poniewozik, "How TV Went from David Brent to Ted Lasso," Critics Notebook (*The New York Times*, July 26, 2021), https://www.nytimes.com/2021/07 /26/arts/television/ted-lasso-the-office.html.

29. Ibid.

30. *Breaking Bad*, season 4, episode 6, "Cornered," dir. Michael Slovis, aired on August 21, 2011, originally released on AMC.

31. Howard Pickett, *Rethinking Sincerity and Authenticity the Ethics of Theatricality in Kant, Kierkegaard, and Levinas* (Charlottesville, VA: University of Virginia Press, 2017), 171.

32. Ibid., 174.

33. Some shows do both. The continued popularity of *The Office* can be explained by the way it ironizes and distracts from the absurdity of contemporary American

work culture at the same time that viewers become attached to characters and their story arc. Thank you to Rebecca Duncan for pointing out that many of these either/ ors are really both/ands.

34. The success of *Succession* (HBO) is a fair rebuttal to this thesis.

BIBLIOGRAPHY

Adalian, Josef. "The Unlikely Rise of Schitt's Creek." *Vulture*. Vulture, April 7, 2020. https://www.vulture.com/2020/04/schitts-creek-netflix-pop-success-story .html.

Armstrong, Jennifer Keishin. "We Should Thank Buffy for Today's 'Golden Age' of Television." BBC Culture. BBC, March 7, 2017. https://www.bbc.com/culture/ article/20170303-we-should-thank-buffy-for-todays-golden-age-of-television.

Cooper, William. "Why We Watch Television." Why We Watch Television. Informitiv/Sony Professional Solutions Europe, 2015. https://www.live-production .tv/sites/default/files/why_we_watch_television.pdf.

Ganapati, Priya. "June 4, 1977: VHS Comes to America." *Wired*. Conde Nast, June 4, 2010. https://www.wired.com/2010/06/0604vhs-ces/.

Herr, Norman. "Television and Health." Television and Health (Internet Resources to Accompany the Sourcebook for Teaching Science, 2007. http://www.csun.edu/ science/health/docs/tv&health.html.

Leopold, Todd. "The New, New TV Golden Age." CNN. Cable News Network, May 6, 2013. https://www.cnn.com/2013/05/06/showbiz/golden-age-of-tv/.

Lipsett, Joe. "Defining Success in the Era of Peak TV: A Case Study of *The Nine Lives of Chloe King* on ABC Family and *Shadowhunters* on Free Form." In *ABC Family to Freeform TV: Essays on the Millennial-Focused Network and Its Programs*, edited by Emily L. Newman and Emily Witsell. Jefferson, NC: McFarland & Company, Inc., Publishers, 2018.

Madrigal, Alexis C. "When Did TV Watching Peak?" *The Atlantic*. Atlantic Media Company, May 30, 2018. https://www.theatlantic.com/technology/archive/2018 /05/when-did-tv-watching-peak/561464/.

Paskin, Willa. "What Does 'Peak Tv' Really Mean?" Slate Magazine. *Slate*, December 23, 2015. https://slate.com/culture/2015/12/what-does-peak-tv really mean.html.

Pickett, Howard. *Rethinking Sincerity and Authenticity the Ethics of Theatricality in Kant, Kierkegaard, and Levinas*. Charlottesville, VA: University of Virginia Press, 2017.

Poniewozik, James. "How TV Went from David Brent to Ted Lasso." Critics Notebook. *The New York Times*, July 26, 2021. https://www.nytimes.com/2021/07 /26/arts/television/ted-lasso-the-office.html.

Press, Joy. "Peak TV Is Still Drowning Us in Content, Says TV Prophet John Landgraf." Vanity Fair. Vanity Fair, August 3, 2018. https://www.vanityfair.com/ hollywood/2018/08/peak-tv-fx-john-landgraf-tca-donald-glover-chris-rock.

Reese, Hope. "Why Is the Golden Age of TV so Dark?" The Atlantic. Atlantic Media Company, July 11, 2013. https://www.theatlantic.com/entertainment/archive/2013/07/why-is-the-golden-age-of-tv-so-dark/277696/.

Roberts, Nicole F. "Psychological Research Explains Why TV Viewing Is Higher than Ever." Forbes. *Forbes Magazine*, December 4, 2019. https://www.forbes.com/sites/nicolefisher/2019/12/04/psychological-research-explains-why-tv-viewing-is-higher-than-ever/.

Santo, Brian. "The Consumer Electronics Hall of Fame: Tivo." IEEE Spectrum. IEEE Spectrum, July 29, 2021. https://spectrum.ieee.org/the-consumer-electronics-hall-of-fame-tivo.

Syme, Rachel. "The Trouble with Our 'Golden Age' of TV." *The New Republic*, November 29, 2021. https://newrepublic.com/article/145961/trouble-golden-age-tv.

"'The Sopranos' Ratings: Only 11.9 Million?" The Take. *Vulture*, June 12, 2007. https://www.vulture.com/2007/06/the_sopranos_ratings_only_119.html.

VanDerWerff, Emily. "The Golden Age of TV Is Dead; Long Live the Golden Age of TV." *The A.V. Club*, September 20, 2013. https://www.avclub.com/the-golden-age-of-tv-is-dead-long-live-the-golden-age-1798240704.

Zurawik, David. "'Wire' Finale Premiere Seen by 1.1 Million." *The Baltimore Sun*, March 12, 2008. https://www.baltimoresun.com/news/bs-xpm-2008-03-12-0803120244-story.html.

Chapter 1

Sleeping with Fishes and Talking with Horses

Animality, Identity, and Vegetarianism in The Sopranos

H. Peter Steeves

INTRODUCTION: WOKE UP THIS MORNING

It can be argued that the new Golden Age of Television began in January 1999 when Mob boss Tony Soprano (played by James Gandolfini) sat down in the waiting room of his psychiatrist's office, clearly anxious about his first therapy session, and began to stare, perplexed, at a statue across the room. It all started, that is, with the puzzling nature of art.

From the first scene of HBO's *The Sopranos* it was clear that we were in a new world—perhaps even a new age. *The Sopranos* was art. And we were going to have a lot to enjoy but also a lot about which to learn and to puzzle. Like all major works of art, *The Sopranos* both altered American culture and mirrored that culture, a weekly rolling hermeneutical circle that reflected back to us who we were while at the same time changing our identities by forcing us to think about what it all meant. In nuanced and sophisticated ways, *The Sopranos* complicated who we, in the cable reflection, took ourselves to be. Most obviously, the show forced us—and continues to force us through means of DVD, OnDemand, general cultural legacy, and the 2021 prequel film—to ponder the moral contradictions in capitalism and the American Dream.[1] But because *The Sopranos* is such a rich text, it is about far more than crime and capital. For all of its apparent violence and denigration of life of all kinds, the moral status of the nonhuman animal is also something with which *The Sopranos* was constantly struggling. Animals, it turns out, consistently form meaningful parts of the characters' community and identity. From Big Pussy and the whacking of "rats," to the equation of murder and meat, from Tony Soprano's successive identification with a duck, a horse, and a bear, to the important allusions to the images of horses and fishes in *The Godfather* trilogy, *The Sopranos* offers a surprisingly morally complex argument concerning the relation between animality and human identity, ultimately suggesting that the two are inseparable, that "we" is far more diverse and multifaceted than previously imagined, and even coming startlingly close to proposing moral vegetarianism.

THE PILOT AND "THE BEAST IN ME"

As a way in, let us begin where *The Sopranos* begins, pointing to some of the appearances of animality in the pilot for the show, just describing with little analysis, at first, in order to get a clear sense of how integral animality is to the meaning of the show.

The pilot introduces us to Tony Soprano, a capo in the north New Jersey Mob, who has been having panic attacks.[2] As a result of these incidents, he is seeing Dr. Jennifer Melfi (played by Lorraine Bracco), a psychiatrist who prescribes him Prozac. If anyone in Tony's Mafia world were to find out about the therapy or the medication, it would be seen as a sign of weakness and he is sure he would be murdered. The initial attack seemed to have been caused by Tony witnessing a family of ducks who took up residence in his backyard pool but are now ready to fly away. Adding to his stress, his nephew, Christopher (played by Michael Imperioli), is dying to be a made man and is making decisions in Tony's crew that are questionable at best. When Czech mobsters, the Kolar brothers, try to move in on the crew's waste management business, Christopher's solution is to murder Emil, their representative in town, without permission from Tony. The rest of Tony's crew, which includes Peter Paul "Paulie Walnuts" Gualtieri (played by Tony Sirico), Sal "Big Pussy" Bonpensiero (played by Vincent Pastore), and Silvio Dante (played by Steven Van Zandt), is in opposition to Tony's Uncle Junior (played by Dominic Chianese) and his crew, struggling in a power vacuum given that their Don is undergoing chemo treatment. Junior's crew wants to kill someone at a restaurant owned by Tony's friend, Artie Bucco (played by John Ventimiglia), which Tony knows will ruin the restaurant forever. At home, Tony's wife, Carmela (played by Edie Falco), is fighting with their daughter, Meadow, (played by Jamie-Lynn Sigler) while Tony's son, Anthony Junior (A.J., played by Robert Iler), who is celebrating his thirteenth birthday, seems to be developing into a simple nothing. Even more potentially troubling is Livia (played by Nancy Marchand), Tony's mother, who is clearly incapable of living on her own anymore due to her age but is scheming, manipulative, and hateful, forbidding Tony from relocating her to a retirement community. Meanwhile, Tony reflects on his life in general and feels as if there is no hope for the future—he wasn't able to get in on the "ground floor" of the Mafia, no one involved has any sense of honor anymore, and perhaps his path ends with him losing everything he cares about, including his family.

So, where, in all of this, are the animals? Everywhere.

Tony's panic attacks seem directly related to the duck family—a group of wild animals that at first was a source of great joy. He builds a wooden ramp for them to make it easier to get out of the pool. He reads books about ducks so he can attend to them better. He even talks to them as if they could under-stand his heavily Jersey-accented English. When the duck family is going to be leaving his pool for good, the babies flying off over the house, he realizes that his connection to these creatures is almost at an end. And he loses con-sciousness. It should be noted, though, that at the same time of this first panic attack, Tony is watching the ducks while also preparing to grill meat in his backyard, the disconnect between the animals he loves and the animals he is about to consume apparently not registering. The first time that Tony can admit that he has been depressed since the duck family left his pool, he is so overwhelmed by the emotion that he walks out on Dr. Melfi, unable to face his feelings. A few days later, he is back in therapy, explaining a dream he had the night before. In the dream, Tony unscrews his belly button, his penis falls off, a bird swoops down, grabs it in his beak, and flies off with it. Dr. Melfi asks Tony what sort of bird it was, and he reveals that it was a water bird of some kind. It takes some work, but she leads him to see that there is a connection here with ducks. Tony admits that he was happy to have "those wild creatures come into my pool and have their little babies. . . . I was sad to see them go."[3] Then, going against everything he has explained he hates about contemporary men who are too emotional and can't stoically take their hits, Tony begins crying uncontrollably.

Meanwhile, there is some confusion as to which of the animal-named mobsters is going to be whacked at Artie's restaurant. Not "Big Pussy," who is part of Tony's crew, but Gennaro "Little Pussy" Malanga. This confusion over the identity of the person who is slated to die is echoed throughout the episode with other confusions.[4] Discovering, and being mistaken about, who you are, who I am, who *we* are—this is a key theme in *The Sopranos*. Later in the pilot, the priest who is visiting Carmela mistakes Meadow for a raccoon (as she is trying to sneak into the house through a window). This interrupts a conversation Carmela is having with the priest about how Tony feels about *The Godfather* movie trilogy and *Goodfellas*.

The equation between humans and animals comes out again when Christopher murders Emil at the butcher's shop (a place of death and murder in general). As Christopher shoots Emil, the scene is edited so that images of famous Italians on the wall look down between each shot, observing and judging. After the final bullet enters Emil's lifeless body, Christopher does a double-take as he sees real pig heads looking at him, too, from the vertical meat case behind him. Observing. And judging.

Characters on *The Sopranos* are often referencing other fictional depictions of Mob life. In fact, it turns out that Christopher came up with the idea of killing Emil as a warning to the Kolar brothers based on the first *Godfather* movie, explaining to Big Pussy that it's like "Lewis Brazee sleeps with the fishes." Big Pussy not only corrects him ("It's Luca! Luca Brasi!") but has to explain to him that there are differences between the movie and their current situation.[5]

Finally, the image of the mother—the matriarch—runs throughout the episode. The nurturing duck mother is contrasted with Livia (who will, later in the first season of the show, sanction a hit on her own son). Tony cannot seem to get a coherent view of his mother to sit in his head: she is strong and to be respected one moment, then seen to be a horrible, plotting, love-less woman in the next. Tony looked up to his father but admits to Melfi that Livia destroyed the man over time—a fact he cashes out by suggesting that his mother destroyed his father's *humanity*. Livia wore his father down, says Tony, until "he was a squeaking little gerbil when he died."[6]

As the episode ends, A.J.'s rescheduled birthday party is taking place (Tony's panic attack having ruined the first party). The pool is empty, duckless, which Tony notes. Livia arrives and, instead of greeting her son, immediately complains that the mesquite barbeque materials Tony is using makes the meat "peculiar." Less than a minute later, the closing credits are rolling while Nick Lowe sings: "The beast in me has had to learn to live with pain. . . . And in the twinkling of an eye might have to be restrained. God help the beast in me."[7]

THE BEAST *IS* ME: COMMUNITARIANISM AND LIBERALISM

There is a classic conception of the self that is tied to modernity, the Enlightenment, and the history of liberalism. This is the metaphysical notion of identity that is part of the worldview of Descartes, Hobbes, Locke, Rousseau, Kant, et al., and as such, it is also our inherited notion of the self. At its core, the liberal self is thought to be selfish, isolated, rational, and autonomous. Rationality, a classical quality that has long been thought to separate humans from animals, ends up meaning, for the most part, rational self-interest: what it is to be an individual is to promote one's own well-being and avoid pain and suffering. We are isolated in this quest, it is thought, because our very nature is to be cut off from each other, nearly to the point of solipsism. *Politically*, this leads Hobbes, for instance, to assume that humans start off alone in a "state of nature" at war with each other, and they only enter into a community by means of a "social contract" that they sign when the conditions of the contract are appropriately in line with their own selfish ends, the contract ultimately enforced through fear. *Metaphysically*, this leads Descartes, for instance, to argue that he can be completely sure that he exists but can never be apodictically positive, never know without some level of doubt, that other selves really even exist. After all, goes the thinking, I can't feel your emotions or be inside your head to know if you are truly aware and conscious: you might be an elaborately programmed automaton and I am the only real self that exists. *Ethically*, the assumption of the liberal self as a model for personhood leads to various forms of ethical egoism in which I believe that my own Good is the only important Good in the world. More "enlightened" versions of liberal ethics begin, still, with the assumption that we are rational, isolated, and self-interested, but then find ways to "extend" morality to include other people. The Golden Rule—treat others as I wish to be treated—is still basically a form of pure egoism, but one based on believing that it might be in my best interest to care for others so that they will care for me in return. Utilitarianism reduces ethics to a calculation—a math problem in which each person is stripped of his or her individual subjectivity and treated as a general liberal self in the grand calculus. Deontology reduces ethics as well, this time to a set of abstract, universal laws that once again strip subjects of what makes them individuals, with culture, history, and context completely irrelevant: other people matter as ends-in-themselves due to their generic nature as autonomous, rational, thinking things.

Although all of this is the norm—although this is the story we are forced to live and tell each other today, the story that founds capitalism, our educational system, our healthcare system, our neoliberal "democracy," and most of the other structures and institutions of our culture—none of it is true.

There are many ways in which the problems with liberalism can be made apparent, and there are many alternatives to this narrative and its lived consequences. Communitarianism, for instance, argues that what it is to be a subject—an individual, a person—is to be inherently connected to others. Liberals are fond of saying, "You're born alone, you die alone, and you're essentially alone in between." Communitarians argue that this is a fundamental mis-description of the human experience. When we are born, we are immediately enmeshed in a web of relationships: someone's son or daughter, someone else's brother or sister, a member of this or that ethnicity, culture, religion, linguistic community, and geographical location. The world, full of history, customs, social norms, and narratives, is already up and running, and so we find ourselves "hitting the ground running," defined and constituted by the various connections that are immediately there with everything and everyone else that exists. We do not need a social contract to bring us together. We are not isolated monads constantly wondering if other people are really robots. We are the point of overlap of all of the roles and relationships we have and inhabit. Liberals see the self as something like a pin cushion: we all have the same generic cushion (isolated, selfish, equal, rational, etc.), and then the "accidental" qualities we have, such as our familial connections or where we live, are like the pins—you can pull them out and replace them with other pins, but the self-underlying this change remains essentially unaffected. Communitarians argue that the pin cushion is a fiction. There is no self without its connection to Others. If we must imagine selfhood with such a metaphor, then imagine the pins to represent our roles and relationships, descriptions of the ways in which we are enmeshed in a web of relations. The pins don't get stuck in a cushion but rather overlap in piles: I am at once a son, a brother, a Midwesterner, an English speaker, etc. The self *is* the point of overlap of these pins. That point of overlap is real. It exists here and not there (I am me, not you). But it is not a "thing" and certainly not a thing that we all have in common that defines something like a generic selfhood. The point of overlap of many pins lying on top of each other is constituted by the pins themselves and nothing more. Remove the pins and the point of overlap vanishes.[8] In other words, I *am* the conglomeration of the roles and relationships that constitute me. Take away how I am related to everything else that exists and I vanish. There is no self without the Other, without an entire community of Others.

Choice is important, but it is not the ultimate creator of identity that liberals take it to be, as if we can just choose to be anything at all, as if freedom is the same as making choices. In the episode "Down Neck," for instance, Dr. Melfi is trying to suggest that Tony has free will, with the implication being that he could leave his life of crime and choose a different line of work whenever he wanted to do so. "How come I'm not makin' fuckin' pots in Peru?" Tony responds. "You're born to this shit; you are what you are."[9] Dr. Melfi rightly responds that within our circumstances there exists a range of choices. The point is, though, that Tony was born into a Mob family and groomed to become a gangster. Had he left the life early-on, he would have been the-man-who-was-born-to-be-a-mobster-but-went-a-different-direction. Of course we have decisions to make within our community, even to the point of leaving our community—but then we would only move on to other Others and be constituted by other roles and relationships.

Consider: in the episode "Boca," Tony learns that Meadow's soccer coach has slept with one of the other underage girls on the team. For Tony, as for all of the mobsters around him, the consequence is clear: the coach must be killed. Dr. Melfi tries to get Tony to think about why he feels it is up to *him* to handle this question of "justice." At first, Artie is all in on this vigilantism, too, but after talking to his wife, he finds Tony at the Bada Bing and tries to convince him that the hit on the soccer coach is being done for the wrong reasons. "You think I don't want to rip him apart like a fuckin' chicken?"[10] Artie says to Tony. But he goes on to argue that this will just hurt the coach's wife, his daughter, and others. Essentially, Artie is making the case that the murder will be an act of selfishness and not an act that takes a wider shared Good into consideration. Tony reacts to Artie violently at first, but eventually calls off the hit. The episode ends with Tony coming home drunk—and apparently happy—explaining to Carmela (and Meadow, listening from upstairs), "I didn't hurt nobody."[11] This is an important moment early in the series. Tony—and we, the audience—are learning that there is no such thing as radical freedom or unbounded free will, but even if we are born into liberalism, we can critique it, reject it, and think about the ways in which ourselves and our Goods are communal.

Importantly, these Others who make us who we are need not be human. Consequently, the thoughtful communitarian realizes that community is constituted by all of the entities and all of the stories around us. Nonhuman animal life, too, makes us who we are. We share common Goods with animals and we share commonly constructed identities. In other words, unlike Artie, we can't speak of exhibiting mercy to human Others at the same time we speak of "ripping apart" chickens and still hope to be in the right.

I am what I am in virtue of the dogs and cats and turtles and frogs and mice and squirrels and rabbits and birds and grasshoppers and etc. etc. etc. that have co-constituted my identity since the first rumblings of my own selfhood. Some more than others have played a special role in making me what I am today—this is always the case with human Others as well. In my childhood, it was my dog; when I lived in South America, it was the iguanas; back when *The Sopranos* was first on TV, it was the possum-rabbit-skunk-chipmunk-duck community that frequented my back-porch restaurant. I am these Others, and they are me. I learned to give without asking for anything in return from my boyhood dog; I learned how to live under the sun and how to eat wild mangoes from my iguana friends; I learned how to respect difference and to balance the goals of privacy and a shared life from my restaurant patrons (the possum would always make little contact and walk off slowly—cool and hipper-than-thou—when our eyes met in the middle of the night; the skunk was grateful for a well-set plate and let me say hello, but always with the threat of potential "violence" in the air; the duck couple were cautious at first but eventually ended up coming inside my apartment and spending time with me most nights in the kitchen). Without these relationships, I would not be me; indeed, I would not be human. Every one of us is constituted by radically different Others. On *The Sopranos*, even the big horse Pie-O-My needs to have a little goat friend.[12]

Just as there is no self without the Other, so there is no personal Good without the Good of Others—without the communal Good. When I act on something I consider to be good or bad, I necessarily affect all of the things around me that can be better or worse off. My Good is but a perspective on a shared Good. If we all were to stand around the Leaning Tower of Pisa, we would all have a different perspective, but it is the same public thing that we are all perceiving. It would be an act not only of hubris but of psychosis to think that the Leaning Tower of Pisa is mine and mine alone just because I happen to have a view of it that is mine and mine alone from here. It is a similar hubristic (and psychotic) act to look out into the world and think that I have my own private, individualistic Good just because I have my own perspective on what helps and hinders my flourishing. Goods are communal in much the same way that buildings are. When you pursue what you take to be of worth from your perspective, you affect me and everyone else. It's not, then, that Pie-O-My has a Good and the goat has a Good and Tony has a Good and all they need to do is enter into some sort of contractual arrangement in the marketplace so that each of their private, selfish Goods is being met by the other.[13] Instead, they are all in it together. Their Goods are intertwined (as perspectives on the same Good) in much the way that their identities are intertwined.

It is hard for most of us to realize this and then live accordingly. It is hard to accept that we are constituted by animal Others when all of the institutions and traditions in our society are telling us otherwise. Amazingly, Tony Soprano comes close to understanding these communitarian truths, even if they never completely bubble up into his conscious life so that he can speak them coherently. Throughout the show, Tony struggles to understand his own identity in terms of what he has inherited from his past (being Italian-American, being part of the Mafia, being "a man," etc.). He finds it difficult to live as the lone, isolated, individualistic self and also come to terms with the fact that his identity seems so deeply constituted by the community and traditions in which he finds himself thrown from the start.[14] Startlingly, though, Tony often seems on the verge of seeing how his selfhood—and the common Good—are tied to nonhuman animals.

No one in Tony's community can understand his relationship to animal life. Everyone, in fact, goes out of their way to separate themselves from animals. Forced to consider using a bedpan, for instance, Junior declares: "I'm not a cat. I don't shit in a box."[15] To call someone an animal is, for most of Tony's crew, the ultimate insult. Yet, Big Pussy's name comes from what is no doubt a misogynist bit of slang, but it also happily attributes to him cat status. In Tony's dreams, when he begins to realize Pussy is working with the Feds, Pussy becomes a fish. And in reality, Pussy is a rat. Before he was "lost at sea," Sal was working his way through the menagerie. Making it even clearer that there is a strong sense of liberal separation in this community, only the vile Livia sees little distinction between human and nonhuman: "[Human] [b]abies are like animals," she claims. "They're no different than dogs."[16] Livia may be right, but for all the wrong reasons.

Even on the verge of a breakthrough, Tony finds it hard to accept his own animal identity. When Artie, for instance, claims that Tony is a hawk (and thus a carnivore) capable of seeing a helpless little rodent from afar, Tony complains to Dr. Melfi: "Am I a fucking hawk? An animal?"[17] Tony hears Artie and associates animality with brutality, with being less than human. This is the view of animality that the liberal culture gives us, and it is troubling, but perhaps Tony is also seeing another alternative. It is no doubt important to recall here Tony's claim that Livia had worn down his powerful father so that he was eventually "a squeaking little gerbil," thus suggesting that after Artie's comment, Tony is worried that he is now the hawk rather than the rodent—that is, that he is more like his mother than his father. A frightening thought, indeed. Still, there is something *even deeper* going on here.

The simple reading of the overall *The Sopranos* narrative is that we are supposed to wonder how Tony could be so violent toward humans while being so tender toward animals.[18] In the second-to-last episode of the series, even, Tony has been let go by Dr. Melfi in part because she has read an academic paper entitled "The Criminal Personality" that states, in part, "The criminal's sentimentality reveals itself in compassion for . . . pets."[19] Such a reading of the show and of Tony's feelings, however, is naïve and does not force us to rethink our own assumed constructions of animality. This work of art is far more complex.

In the second season episode "D-Girl," the newly philosophical A. J. is told not to give much credence to Friedrich Nietzsche when the philosopher says that God is dead because Nietzsche went crazy and "wound up talking to his horse."[20] Of course, this is exactly what Tony winds up doing in the fourth season. Pie-O-My becomes Tony's comfort and confidante. But rather than taking him to be sentimental or crazy (as most others on the show would), let us instead be open to the possibility that Tony is on the path toward a more philosophically thoughtful life. This is, in part, what it metaphorically means for Tony to be in therapy. He is struggling to understand his world and himself.

But the struggle is hard. The fourth season, especially, is a test for Tony, his worst tendencies coming to the surface, his deepest fears realized. Others have less of a struggle, perhaps, because they tend to think less.

The fourth season premiered in September 2002 and was the first season of the show made after the events of 9/11. Though the Twin Towers are removed from the opening credits now, the show itself doesn't change on a fundamental level. Instead, it reacts to the new state of affairs in the United States with occasional mentions of the terrorist attacks but all the while treating this moment as "more of the same"—as if 9/11 was just a moment that was always going to happen. In 1999 when the show premiered, it did so with the understanding that things were coming to an end. The events of September 2001 just confirm this, and Tony feels it more than others because he in some sense "gets it." Post-9/11, the Mafia is not only fading in terms of moving further from its supposed "golden age," but it is fading from public and private interest. RICO suits become less of a priority for law enforcement as the FBI shifts to concerns about terrorism rather than organized crime. What Tony does matters less and less: could it be that *nothing* matters—that nothing has *ever* mattered? On top of this, 9/11 is bringing up questions in the culture and in the show concerning community. Who are "they" who did this to "us"? What do these words even mean? Is violence when it is meant intentionally by individuals different from violence when it is created by a system, a culture, and a set of institutions? Are we all eventually going to get something we aren't expecting?

In the tenth episode of the fourth season, "The Strong Silent Type," Christopher takes heroin and kills Cosette, Adriana's little dog, by sitting on him accidentally. Christopher doesn't really feel bad about the death. In the end, this scene, though, is actually far more complicated than Christopher whacking a dog. As he shoots up, he's watching TV. An episode of "Little Rascals" plays in the background and Buckwheat is talking about meeting, and fighting, a bear: "That bear would have just as much chance as this here porkchop . . . Somebody's going to get something they ain't expecting."[21] The equation between the dead animal for food, the dead animal due to being crushed by the drug addict, and the immorality of the life these humans are living is not acknowledged.

As we move to talk about what all of this shared identity means for our eating habits, it is interesting to note that a blindness to patterns of violence appears in "real life" as well as in some of the character's thinking. Michael Imperioli, who played Christopher on the show, insists, for instance, that "no animals were hurt in the making of *The Sopranos*," but he goes on to explain that Cosette was made, in part, of dead pig. "Little-known fact about Cosette the smushed lapdog," explains Imperioli. "They made the tongue out of pro-sciutto."[22] Do we register this disconnect? Do we agree that because the dog wasn't made of dog but was made out of a dead pig, that "no animals were harmed"? The fact that a pig doesn't count as an animal is telling. Like the criminal sociopath, we compartmentalize our compassion—caring for the pet and not for the pig who becomes dinner.

Though Imperioli still seems capable of a kind of blindness after his experience on *The Sopranos*, it is interesting to note that other cast members emerged changed. Steve Schirripa—who played Bobby "Bacala" Baccalieri, first a helper to Uncle Junior and then, in the final seasons, part of Tony's crew—moved into the food business after the show folded and created Uncle Steve's Italian Specialties, an all-vegan line of pasta sauces.[23] More recently, in a December 2020 episode of Schirripa and Imperioli's entertaining podcast, "Talking Sopranos," Schirripa claimed—with Imperioli goading him about it—that he would never go hunting and would feel horrible if he saw a dead deer (though he's not sure if fish are capable of suffering so he's unsure if fishing is bad), and that it was animal cruelty to force a chicken to play Tic-Tac-Toe against humans in Chinatown (though Schirripa admits that the chicken once beat him at the game).[24] Meanwhile, Edie Falco, who played Carmela, announced that she was a vegan when the show ended, telling *Parade* magazine: "I believe this is at the base of everything bad in society—you can bring it back to cruelty to animals. If you don't have respect for life of any kind, it will manifest in more obvious ways."[25] It's not that Falco is arguing that we must be good to animals because this is a sign of comportment toward other more important beings (which is the best we ever get out of Kant) but rather that violence is violence is violence—and animals are one of "us."

Few of us get this in real life. Tony seems to be the only one starting to get it on the show, the only one to have a sense that something is wrong. Little wonder, then, that Tony takes his silent place in the stable with Pie-O-My and the little goat, having no other real community that appears to accept him or provide him with a sense of belonging. Here, Tony thinks he might find some peace. Pie-O-My seems purely what Pie-O-My is: a pure-bred (unlike the "Italian"-"American" Tony); this horse knows what she has to do to succeed: run, run fast, run faster than everyone else; she knows what she must be and do. As Tony said in the first season episode "Pax Soprano" as he and Hesh looked out over a field of grazing horses, "I envy them."[26] Thus, as the camera pulls back at the conclusion of "Pie-O-My," we are presented with a makeshift nativity, though it is unclear who is divine here. There is apparently no Lamb present, only a goat—as if someone has already done the separating, already arrived, chosen, and moved on. It is Pie-O-My who is "pure" (which is always a dangerous and immoral category to celebrate) and who will soon be murdered, sacrificed to the greed of Ralphie (a capo in Tony's crew who is metaphorically given the silver coins he will collect from the horse's murder from the insurance company). Ralphie is the worst mankind has to offer. Yet Pie-O-My's blood does not even cleanse Tony: soon the latter will have Ralphie's blood on his hands as well, plus a failing marriage on his conscience. Tony is not saved when Ralphie has the stable set on fire. If anything, the image of a horse in flames suggests the apocalypse rather than the virgin birth, an end rather than a beginning, a condemnation and a judgment rather than a salvation and a promise. And so perhaps it is Tony who must do the saving, Tony who plays the role of the Infant King surrounded by his manger animals, his baby-face sad with the knowledge of the violence of the world, of our collective inability to recognize true community and true community members, of our failure to see that the kingdom of heaven is spread upon the earth even in North Jersey. Or perhaps all of these roles are interchangeable, and Tony himself is—as he has always been—Pussy, tiger, horse, hawk, bear, gerbil, duck, dog, goat, and Lamb.

PASS (OVER) THE *CAPOCOLLO*:
BADA-BEING WHAT WE EAT

In the mid-1980s, I realized I had been thoughtlessly eating my friends because my culture had been thoughtlessly serving them up to me, and so I made a choice. Vegetarianism is still hard for me: I salivate after all of these years when I smell the neighbor's sausages on the grill; the capocollo Tony inhales before passing out still looks delicious. How hard it is to question what was never questioned before, what one's society sets up precisely as purposely hidden. But not eating meat was and remains just a single step in learning how to live appropriately with these Others who share my Good, my home, and my identity. As with Others of all species, it is an ongoing project, part of what it means to be alive, getting to know each other and how best to live together.[27]

Ducks, as we have seen, are of paramount importance to Tony. The duck family that takes up residence in his pool in the first episode and then flies away precipitates Tony's panic attack, leads him to therapy, and comes to symbolize his fear of losing his own family. Twenty-eight episodes later, Tony and Dr. Melfi come to the conclusion that the panic attacks might be more closely related to experiences of meat—that it might have been the sausages on the grill rather than the ducks in the pool that led to the initial problem—but the two interpretations are not really at odds. In "Fortunate Son," Tony remembers that his first panic attack actually came when he was a child and saw how his father cut a finger off the local butcher who was behind on his loan payments. The butcher then agreed to give the Sopranos free meat—to the delight of Tony's mother. Seeing the joy with which Livia received the meat—the joy that she took, then, in the violence that made it possible—gave Tony his first attack. Meat, ever since, has thus had multiple and somewhat subconscious levels of meaning for Tony.

Seeing the relationships among human flesh, animal flesh, meat, self, Other, and food is a startling thing. The violence that Tony's father enacted on the butcher was meant to be hidden from his son, just in the way that the butcher's everyday violence against animals is meant to be hidden in our lives as well. Exposing both, and seeing how both can be thoughtlessly enjoyed, is traumatic. Ducks, too, are murdered and eaten, and they have families and exhibit love and care. Seeing both truths at the same time is traumatic. Passing out over a duck family being broken up and passing out over the eating of meat can thus be the same thing. As a result, ducks come to symbolize and foreshadow violence throughout *The Sopranos* narrative. Artie serves duck ragout and a formation of ducks flies overhead during a hit. Carmela refers to Livia as a "peculiar duck" and ducks float across the barren Pine Barrens sky before Christopher guns down a deer (thinking it is a human). Ducks are quacking as asbestos is illegally dumped into the water in the season 6 episode "Kennedy and Heidi." Adriana is feeding ducks with an FBI agent talking about how horrible her life is, all just a few days before she is killed by Silvio (under orders from Tony) for having talked to the Feds. And in "Employee of the Month," the episode in which Dr. Melfi is raped, a television report discusses the Newark Esplanade project (from which Tony hopes to make embezzled millions) and the news camera focuses on a nearby group of ducks.[28]

Ducks have families. Ducks can be in our families. And ducks are served up to us to eat. The crisis of thinking these things together is one that is marked by violence—a rupturing of categories and traditions. But when we rightly equate self and Other, we must not back away from the full implications. Again, *The Sopranos* is always flirting with this. In case the butcher's finger and the roast Livia later serves were not enough of a clue—in case we miss the fact that these violent mobsters keep their office hidden in the back of that same butcher shop—we are given, from time to time, even more graphic images of the ways in which meat is murder and flesh is flesh is flesh. As we saw, when Christopher "shows initiative" and commits that first murder, killing Emil in the butcher shop, he turns immediately afterward, startled to see the faces of the decapitated pigs in the case behind him: animals have faces; animals can look upon us and judge. Later, Brendan—Christopher's partner in crime for the first few episodes—gets pushed into a table of meat scraps by Tony, effectively suggesting his own status as meat and his own upcoming death. More to the graphic point, after Tony's sister, Janice, guns down her fiancé, Richie Aprile, the gang gets rid of the body by feeding it through the sausage grinder at the butcher shop. Richie becomes sausage, his flesh passing just as easily through the grinding machine—through the Machine that is our society—as any other animal's. Interestingly, both Richie and Ralphie (arguably the two most violent characters on the show; both killed in a violent, rupturing manner as well) are killed in their kitchens while eating or preparing food. This is no accident. Most of us have murdered corpses in our kitchens as well, though we do not want to see it. When a *fish* sleeps with the fishes, it takes a thoughtful communitarian to see the crime.

"Sleeping with the fishes," recall, comes to us from *The Godfather*. Luca Brasi has been murdered, his body dumped in the water, sleeping with the fishes, never to be found. In *The Godfather II*, the movie concludes with Fredo waiting to take Michael's son out fishing, only to have Michael invent some pretense to take his son away so that Fredo can be killed alone out on the little rowboat, saying his Hail Mary's and trying to catch a fish—the killer of fish becoming the one who is killed.[29] Animality is a theme that runs throughout the trilogy. Horses, too, have an important place in *The Godfather*. A prized racing horse famously ends up decapitated in the first film, his head placed into the bed of a man to whom Vito Corleone is making an offer that cannot be refused. Accordingly, a horse plays an important role in *The Sopranos* as well. If we look closer at the Pie-O-My arc, we find more interesting details. Ralphie buys the racehorse, and Tony falls in love with the creature, muscling in on Ralphie's action. Eventually, Ralphie starts a stable fire and burns Pie-O-My to death—partly for the insurance money, partly out of jealousy and spite as Tony has recently taken up with Ralphie's ex-*comare* (another thing Tony has loved and "taken away" from Ralphie). Here, *The Sopranos*, though, is importantly an inverse of *The Godfather*. Tony winds up in bed with Ralphie's girlfriend, not with his bloody horse. And in the end, it is Ralphie and not Pie-O-My who loses his head (after Tony kills Ralphie and dismembers his body with Christopher's help). The equation of animality and sex is still there, but the violence toward animals is altered. For Don Corleone, the horse is a thing, an object to be bloodied and used to coerce a man to do his bidding. For the new Don, the horse is a member of the community, an Other whose murder must be avenged. There is no attempt to force Ralphie to do Tony's bidding. Only to force his head into a bowling bag.

Tony does not want to accept that he feels this way about animals. Others continually point out to him that this was "just" a horse, and he seems to want to agree with them even if he cannot. He is sensing the true place of nonhuman animals in the community, though it is too much consciously to accept. From his initial panic attacks at the equation of meat and murder, to his sudden outrage when he finds that Christopher killed Adriana's little dog, Tony is becoming a defender of animals.

One of the last things Ralphie utters to Tony before being murdered is the mocking question, "Are you a vegetarian?!" One imagines that being a secret-vegetarian is more dangerous for a Mafioso than surreptitiously going to a psychiatrist. It would undoubtedly be seen as an act of weakness if Tony came out as a vegetarian or vegan.[30] If he is moving toward vegetarianism, though, and taking us with him, it is not because the killing and eating of animals is forbidden by a universal moral law (such as Kant's Categorical Imperative) or because a set of abstract calculations has determined this to be the case (as in Mill's utilitarianism). Instead, Tony is coming to see the communitarian truth of his enmeshment with Others—including these nonhuman Others—and coming to see the ways in which the Good is complicated and communal as well. Because this is a work of art, he is typically seeing these truths in the form of accumulating narrative moments of encounters with animals taking place at meaningful junctures in his journey when such encounters have metaphorical as well as literal significance. One thinks, for instance, of Tony's unstable, depressed, and prone-to-violence third season girlfriend, Gloria Trillo. Early in their affair, something already marked by darkness and danger, they have sex at the zoo in the reptile house after looking at the gorilla exhibit ("The Telltale Moozadell"). When Gloria's violent attacks against Tony finally go too far in "Pine Barrens," it ends with her throwing a roast beef at Tony's head—what was meant to be his dinner turned into a literal weapon as it smacks Tony upside the head. It is not the first moment Tony will be "harmed" by meat, for the roast that Gloria throws at him is a visual echo of the roast that Tony's father brings home to his family which we learn about in a flashback in "Fortunate Son." Livia, remember, is overjoyed, maybe even "turned on," by the fact that her husband has cut off the butcher's finger and now the butcher gives the family free roasts. She dances around the kitchen with Johnny Boy, Tony's father, eventually saying they need to stop in order to eat while the roast is hot. "The lady loves her meat," says Johnny Boy.[31] Moments later, young Tony collapses—his first ever panic attack overwhelming the boy as he realizes the equation sums up violence, meat, his father's work, and his own position in life.

In this sense, at least, Tony is a role model for us all. We should be outraged when animal Others are abused and mistreated. We should count their deaths as mattering morally. We should all pass out on the floor instead of eating meat, at the thought of eating meat, at the very sight of meat, at the threat of meat harming us, too—meat, which is, after all, murder.

We might note that if there is one person on *The Sopranos* who can be singled out as being the worst when it comes to animals, it would be Artie Bucco. Artie keeps offering up veal, chicken, pork, steak, and other dead animal bodies to his friends throughout the series, the greatest murderer of animals on the show. In fact, in the episode "Luxury Lounge," Artie shoots a rabbit in the head when he sees her eating from his vegetable patch and we later watch Artie prepare the rabbit and serve her in his restaurant. It is interesting to note that although we know Artie is the only one of the guys who all grew up together who doesn't end up working for the Mob in some capacity—Artie is regularly portrayed as the only civilian—we learn in the episode "The Test Dream" that back in school, the boys' teacher and sports mentor, Coach Molinaro, warned Tony to stay away from Artie because he was "the worst of the bunch."[32] It is a comment that only makes sense if we understand

Artie to be a trafficker in animal suffering and death, another subtle way that the show makes its case for vegetarianism.

To be fair, though, it is not just moral vegetarianism that seems to be a refrain repeated on *The Sopranos* but moral veganism in general. Let's trace just one sub-theme, one example of this, to see how powerful the images and arguments are. Just as cooking meat is shown to be a violent activity in the show, cooking and eating *eggs* is as well. There are at least a dozen instances in the series in which eggs are shown to be a symbol of violence and death, the equation between the violence involved in egg consumption and the violence done by these characters to each other spelled out clearly. Perhaps most obvious and most striking is that Ralphie offers to cook eggs for Tony right before Tony kills him, the skillet even being part of the struggle that ensues ("Whoever Did This"). A couple of seasons before, Richie Aprile offers to make Tony eggs when Tony finds him living with Janice ("Big Girls Don't Cry"). Tony feels like killing Richie often, but before he gets the chance, Richie is shot by Janice a few episodes later. In "Long Term Parking," Adriana offers to make Christopher eggs after admitting she has been working with the FBI. She is murdered shortly after. And Tony's fifth season mistress, Valentina, is disfigured horribly in a fire that starts because she is cooking eggs for Tony at the stove ("The Test Dream"). In the episode "I Dream of Jeannie Cusamano," Mikey Palmice is killed while Carmela is home making scrambled eggs. Later in the series, in "Watching Too Much Television," Tony's first mistress, Irina, suggests that she make egg salad right before Tony removes his belt and mercilessly beats Congressman Zellman. AJ makes Carmela an inedible poached egg, which is still in the shell, in "College"—the episode in which his father kills the rat, Fabian Petrullio. As Tony and Uncle Junior have a conversation about the possibility of murdering Johnny Sack, they have the TV on which is playing "Who Wants to Be a Millionaire?" ("The Weight") As Johnny Sacks' hit is contemplated, the contestant fails on the game show, giving the wrong answer to the question: eggs. Uncle Junior, in fact, has a near-obsession with eggs, always at moments foreshadowing great violence. Speaking in his attorney's office about surrendering to the Feds ("Boca"), he sees everyone else eating and remarks, "peppers and eggs? That's what I should have had"—and that egg sandwich is the last thing he thinks about before going under for his cancer surgery.[33] But most importantly, perhaps, in "Rat Pack," Junior asks Bobby to make eggs for him and Tony forgets that he has asked already so he asks again, and then refers to Tony B (Tony's cousin) as "Tony Egg." Moments later the phone rings and they learn that Carmine Lupertazzi, who had a stroke in the previous episode, has died. He had the stroke while eating egg salad. Eventually, Tony will kill his cousin, Tony B, with a shotgun. The last thing he does before committing to the murder is step in broken eggs on the ground ("All Due Respect"). As the end draws near for Big Pussy ("Commendatori"), his wife carries in the groceries and drops the eggs on the kitchen floor. She tells him that the tests are back and she doesn't have cancer, but Pussy is uninterested. The eggs scrambled on the floor, he takes off to whack Jimmy Bones. Finally, in the episode "For All Debts Public and Private," the episode in which Tony tells Christopher who murdered his father and then essentially serves the cop up to Christopher on a silver platter so that he can murder him in revenge, Tony lets Christopher commit this murder privately, having a meal with Bobby at a diner while the deed is done. Tony has a plate of fried eggs. And then, seeing what Bobby has ordered, places a second order for a steak.

We could go on. The point of tracing in depth the single theme of eggs and their relation to violence, though, is to suggest that there comes a point at which the correlation is so consistent that we see a causal link, a point at which a critical mass of inductive evidence accrues and we are forced to say that there is, indeed, something in the narrative that is calling on us to equate eggs, meat, and animal suffering in general with something that is deeply violent and immoral. It might be hyperbole to say that Artie is "the worst of them all," but once it has been said we begin to see that when we watch the show we can think that we are better than most of the characters because we are not going around whacking our competition, beating up our neighbors and business associates, and generally living a life where physical violence against other humans is a daily occurrence. But, the show is asking us, can we so easily separate ourselves and forgive ourselves when it comes to our treatment of animals? Are *we*, in our treatment of nonhuman animal life, perhaps "the worst of them all"?

CONCLUSION: DON'T STOP BELIEVING

If season 4 was mostly about Tony's marriage disintegrating and his "beef" with Ralphie escalating, the next season took up the topics of Tony's cousin, Tony Blundetto, being released from prison and Adriana's increasing *agita* over being an FBI informant.[34] Season 5's patron animal saint is the bear. The penultimate season opens, in fact, with a bear appearing at the Soprano's home—an actual bear. He rummages around the pool area in the backyard, terrorizes A.J., has a seat at a glass end table, and eventually saunters off. Tony, at this point, is no longer living at home, and the bear is an obvious surrogate: he shows up, the possibility of violence is in the air, he sits around, and eventually leaves without even interacting with the family that much. Later in the episode, Tony has one of his crew stationed out back with a machine gun, and the gang talks about bears while they are out with their mistresses.

Paulie: "As far as fucking bears are concerned? I say get rid of them all. They had
their turn and now we got ours. That's why dinosaurs don't exist anymore."
Woman: "Wasn't it a meteor?"
Paulie: "They're all meat eaters."
Christopher: "Meteor, meteor."[35]

Of course, the point is not lost on us that meat eaters are all "meteors"—
destroyers of animals and entire worlds. The one is a moral stand-in for the
other: bringers of death that are acting without thought yet are apocalyptically
spreading terror across the Earth.

This is a season in which doppelgängers, especially of Tony, are everywhere. We are introduced to Tony B, for instance, the cousin recently
released from prison, who is called "Tony B" because he and Tony Soprano
would get confused for one another so often when they were younger. Tony
B is the version of Tony S that could have been if life had gone a different
way—and Tony S knows it and feels guilt over it. The bear is a version of
Tony S that mirrors what he has become. In "All Due Respect," the final episode of the season, Tony reluctantly murders Tony B. At the very end of the
episode, we see a rustling in the bushes at the edge of the Soprano property
and the outline of a large body that could mark the return of the bear. But this
time it is Tony Soprano, lumbering like his ursine cousin through the woods,
on the run from the Feds at Johnny Sacks' house.

Tony's trek home from Johnny's place takes him through quite a bit of
Jersey wilderness. The most rural place we ever see on *The Sopranos*, though,
is probably the Pine Barrens—the site of Christopher and Paulie's failed, or
at least *complicated*, dumping of a body (that body belonging to a very resil-
ient Russian). Deer roam the Pine Barrens, and one is even killed in "Pine
Barrens"—a shooting that foreshadows the fate of Adriana in a later season.

Adriana La Cerva might appear to be a minor character in *The Sopranos*
pantheon, but in some respects she is a linchpin holding many connecting
ethical themes together. As Christopher's longtime girlfriend, Adriana is typically a sympathetic character—and somewhat innocent, at least to the degree
to which anyone can be in this world. More so than any other character, she
is constructed as a metaphorical animal. From her nail/claws to her penchant
for wearing animal prints, Adriana (whose last name, La Cerva, literally
means "the doe") is a deer.[36] Sometimes caught in the headlights of the FBI,
sometimes fawning over Christopher, Adriana lives on the margins with little
apparent agency, yet her role is central. In the episode in which Adriana is
murdered ("Long-Term Parking"), we first see her dressed head-to-toe in a
tiger-print jumpsuit. Later she's wearing something like a glittery zebra print
the last time she's picked up by the Feds. Complaining about her stomach
problems at the Crazy Horse, Silvio suggests to her that she might consider

becoming a vegan. Within 24 hours, Silvio will be driving Adriana into the woods, she will crawl off on all fours like an animal, and he will shoot her in the back. Adriana sleeps with the fishes and slumbers with the fallen deer. In the following episode, Carmela tries to comfort Christopher, who tells the lie that Adriana left him: "There are other fish in the sea."[37]

Tony briefly considers having an affair with Adriana but more or less decides to do the right thing at the end. In "Irregular Around the Margins," Tony and Adriana are injured late at night on the way to buy cocaine when they are in a car accident caused by Tony swerving in order not to hit a raccoon in the middle of the road. Not only does this fit with Tony's care for animals, but it foreshadows the next season's episode, "Kennedy and Heidi," in which there is a similar car accident, this time with Christopher driving and Tony in the passenger seat. But Christopher doesn't swerve to miss an animal; he swerves because he is high on drugs and almost hits another car. This accident is much worse than the one with Adriana. Mostly uninjured, Tony sees Christopher fighting for his life and decides to murder him rather than call 911. Interestingly, two episodes before he kills Christopher, Tony purposely publicly embarrasses Christopher about his lack of barbeque skills. It is as if Tony is reminding himself that he is capable of grilling well so that he can soon be capable of killing well, too. And there, in the tall grass, in the bushes, among the trees, Tony pounces like a wild animal on his prey.

The bear who came looking for food at the Soprano's house—in much the same way Tony would often make his way to the kitchen with an unnamed, primal hunger—was a creature who could have hurt A.J. and Carmela. But he didn't. The animal control officers tell Carmela, in fact, that because the bear wasn't violent, they aren't allowed to do violence to him. There is, therefore, the possibility of anyone hurting anyone else, but also the example of how to live together in peace, how this violence needn't happen: a lesson Tony-the-bear needs to learn. Adriana, it's true, had violated the friendship she had with Tony and abandoned any sense of loyalty to the people in her inner circle by secretly talking to the Feds. But it would have been possible, with a moment's pause, to realize that Adriana, the doe, was always forced into the role of prey within this group. She had little chance of being anything else, and little chance of escaping in the end. Friendship and loyalty are important, but they always appear in context, in the lives of real people in real historical situations. They are not overarching values that tell the whole story. Communities are not closed-off and communitarianism is not relativism. When a group of people is not truly appreciating the Other's perspective on the Good, we do not have a true community. When one's identity is being constituted in a way that does not lead to mutual flourishing, something must be done.

Do we have the ability to question the traditions we are handed and overturn the false definitions of community we are served? Are we, like Tony, capable of seeing the truth about the immoral way we treat animals, but apparently unlike Tony, capable of seizing the opportunity to make real change based on these realizations? Are we able to make choices without fetishizing the value of choice and reinscribing the false principles of the liberal ego onto our communitarian selves? We must believe it is possible. Up to our final moments. No matter the odds against us. No matter the uncertainties around the next corner and the next door opening. Like Tony, in the end, we can sit down at the table, a variety of dead animal dishes available on the menu, and instead order a platter of (vegan) onion rings for the table—for all of us, for the family, for a community that won't stop believing . . . it can be better.

NOTES

1. That is, we say we care about family and friendship, values that the "heroes" in the show also espouse, but what happens when those values come up against the realities of "business"? And how, exactly, is Mob life different—if it is different at all—from corporate capitalist life in general? Such questions may be the most easily discernible, arising from the themes of the show that are most direct (the show, in fact, used to advertise that it was about family and "The Family"). For more on this topic, one might confer my "'It's Business; We're Soldiers': *The Sopranos*, Business Ethics and this American Thing of Ours," in *Cutting-Edge Issues in Business Ethics*, ed. Patricia H. Werhane and Mollie Painter-Morland (Berlin: Springer Science + Business Media B. V., 2008), 23–33.

2. *The Sopranos*, season 1, episode 1, "Pilot," dir. David Chase, aired on January 10, 1999, originally released on HBO.

3. Ibid.

4. It will turn out that Big Pussy becomes a major character in the show; but we basically don't hear about Little Pussy again for years—until Uncle Junior's dementia is so bad that he thinks Tony is Little Pussy one night and shoots him, basically putting in action all of the things that happen from that point on until the show's finale.

5. Not the least of which is that there are good reasons for the brothers not to know about Emil's killing at all and thus they shouldn't just dump the body in one of the Kolar brothers' dumpsters (which is far from the ocean and the fishes). This quote is from S01E01.

6. *The Sopranos*, season 1, episode 1, "Pilot," dir. David Chase, aired on January 10, 1999, originally released on HBO.

7. Ibid.

8. Scientists might say that the point is an *emergent* quality. Philosophers, especially phenomenologists who look at the ways in which consciousness is structured and how the Being (and beings) of the world are made manifest, might say that the point of overlap has *ontological* status.

9. *The Sopranos*, season 1, episode 7, "Down Neck," dir. Lorraine Senna, aired on February 21, 1999, originally released on HBO.

10. *The Sopranos*, season 1, episode 9, "Boca," dir. Andy Wolk, aired on March 7, 1999, originally released on HBO.

11. Ibid.

12. *The Sopranos*, season 4, episode 5, "Pie-O-My," dir. Henry Bronchtein, aired on October 13, 2002, originally released on HBO.

13. Usually with the added (psychotic!) understanding that some "invisible hand" will take care of the details as long as they each pursue an individualistic conception of the Good.

14. He tells Dr. Melfi that he admires "Gary Cooper—the strong, silent type" in the pilot episode. *The Sopranos*, season 1, episode 1, "Pilot," dir. David Chase, aired on January 10, 1999, originally released on HBO.

15. *The Sopranos*, season 2, episode 11, "House Arrest," dir. Timothy Van Patten, aired on March 26, 2000, originally released on HBO.

16. *The Sopranos*, season 2, episode 12, "The Knight in White Satin Armor," dir. Allen Coulter, aired on April 12, 2000, originally released on HBO.

17. *The Sopranos*, season 4, episode 6, "Everybody Hurts," dir. Steve Buscemi, aired on October 20, 2002, originally released on HBO.

18. Countless critics and fans see the show operating this way: Tony is heartless toward humans (who do count morally) but compassionate toward animals (who don't count morally). One used to hear the same said of Hitler.

19. *The Sopranos*, season 6, episode 20, "The Blue Comet," dir. Alan Taylor, aired on June 3, 2007, originally released on HBO.

20. *The Sopranos*, season 2, episode 7, "D-Girl," dir. Allen Coulter, aired on February 27, 2000, originally released on HBO.

21. *The Sopranos*, season 4, episode 10, "The Strong, Silent Type," dir. Alan Taylor, aired on November 17, 2002, originally released on HBO.

22. *"The Sopranos* Cast Reveals the Worst Things Their Characters Ever Did," *TV Guide*, accessed June 24, 2020, https://www.tvguide.com/news/the-sopranos-cast -reveals-the-worst-things-their-characters-ever-did/.

23. *"The Sopranos:* What Have the Cast Bada-Been Up to Since?," *The Guardian*, accessed June 26, 2020, https://www.theguardian.com/tv-and-radio/2017/jun/10/the -sopranos-what-have-the-cast-bada-been-up-to-since.

24. "The Pine Barrens," Episode 38 of the podcast "Talking Sopranos" (December 3, 2020), accessed January 7, 2021, https://talkingsopranos.simplecast.com/episodes /episode-37-pine-barrens. (NB: Come for the discussion with Steve Buscemi about this classic episode; stay for the argument between Imperioli and Schirripa about whether or not Schirripa is smarter than a squid.)

25. "The Ups and Downs of the Sopranos Cast," *Amo Mama*, accessed June 26, 2020, https://eng.amomama.com/189796-the-ups-downs-soprano-cast.html#page _number=1.

26. *The Sopranos*, season 1, episode 6, "Pax Soprano," dir. Alan Taylor, aired on February 14, 2000, originally released on HBO.

27. If interested, for more on the animal–communitarian connection one might consult the first three chapters of my *The Thing Themselves: Essays in Applied Phenomenology* (SUNY Press, 2006); the last chapter of my *Founding Community:*

A Phenomenological-Ethical Inquiry (Kluwer, 1998); and my introduction and essay in *Animal Others: On Ethics, Ontology, and Animal Life* (SUNY Press, 1999).

28. In this same episode, Dr. Melfi has a dream about Tony possibly avenging her, and in the dream, Tony appears as a dog.

29. In the first season finale of *The Sopranos,* Tony murders Charles "Chucky" Signore, a soldier in Junior's crew, by pulling a gun out of the mouth of a giant, dead fish—and then takes the body out on his boat to dump it in the sea.

30. One can picture the comedic movie trailer now: "Robert DeNiro is a *capo* who won't eat capocollo, and Billy Crystal is his hired personal chef with a secret in: *Eat This!*" I admit, though, that I think Tony could pull it off. He could have been the first openly vegan Mafioso. The argument to keep his friends from turning on him after coming out could have been: "Look, we live by a code in which violence is unacceptable unless it takes place in a context where everyone involved knows the stakes going in. You, me, we know what this life entails. There are certain innocent people outside the game, though, who are out of bounds. No animal ever did anything wrong to me, anything to warrant my killing him. If one of them did, then I wouldn't have a problem taking him down. But what has a pig ever done to me? They are living their lives and getting by fine. In the same way that I wouldn't go around shooting elementary school kids on the playground, I'm not going to whack a pig in order to get a sausage unless that pig did something to me or my family. It's all about a code. Justice. Honor. Anybody got a problem with that, they'll end up worse than a piece of capocollo!"

31. *The Sopranos,* season 3, episode 3, "Fortunate Son," dir. Henry Bronchtein aired on March 11, 2001, originally released on HBO.

32. *The Sopranos,* season 5, episode 11, "The Test Dream," dir. Allen Coulter, aired on May 16, 2004, originally released on HBO.

33. *The Sopranos,* season 1, episode 9, "Boca," dir. Andy Wolk, aired on March 7, 1999, originally released on HBO.

34. Restrictions of space won't allow for a discussion of the meaning of the bird in the window at Christopher's making ceremony, meat in Christopher's *Cleaver* movie, or the creepy cat in the final episodes who might be able to see Christopher's ghost (or even be Christopher). These and countless other appearances of animality in *The Sopranos* we leave for another day.

35. *The Sopranos,* season 5, episode 1, "Two Tonys," dir. Timothy Van Patten, aired on March 7, 2004, originally released on HBO.

36. It would be interesting to compare this to Tony's daughter, Meadow, who is named for the flora rather than fauna of New Jersey.

37. *The Sopranos,* season 5, episode 12, "Long Term Parking," dir. Timothy Van Patten, aired on May 23, 2004, originally released on HBO.

BIBLIOGRAPHY

Amo Mama. "The Ups and Downs of the Sopranos Cast," accessed 26 June 2020. https://eng.amomama.com/189796-the-ups-downs-soprano-cast.html#page_number=1.

Imperioli, Michael, and Steve Schirripa. "The Pine Barrens." *Talking Sopranos.* Podcast Audio, December 3, 2020. https://talkingsopranos.simplecast.com/episodes/episode-37-pine-barrens.

Steeves, H. Peter. "'It's Business; We're Soldiers': *The Sopranos*, Business Ethics and this American Thing of Ours." In *Cutting-Edge Issues in Business Ethics*, edited by Patricia H. Werhane and Mollie Painter-Morland. Berlin: Springer Science + Business Media B. V., 2008: 23–33.

The Guardian. "*The Sopranos:* What Have the Cast Bada-Been Up to Since?," accessed June 26, 2020. https://www.theguardian.com/tv-and-radio/2017/jun/10/the-sopranos-what-have-the-cast-bada-been-up-to-since.

The Sopranos. Created by David Chase. Aired from January 10, 1999–June 10, 2007. Originally released on HBO.

Chapter 2

The Bigger the Lie, the More They Believe

Morality and Ethics in The Wire

John Hillman

At a time when the emancipatory power of television is, perhaps, far greater than that of cinema, this chapter considers how morality and ethics are not immanent to television shows. They are a reflective apparatus articulating something of the confusion of moral and ethical positions encountered in society, not naturally moral or ethical objects in themselves. There is an antagonism in how a moral or ethical value is implied in the basic structure of a television show itself, yet the opposite is expressed in its form. In order for any television show to be made, a set of non-standard moral and ethical principles need to be met. Morality and ethics can be understood as interventions that impose an external and restricting framework back onto the flexibility of television fiction writing. In reality, writing fiction allows for the expression of almost any position. Such that, from inside any fictional drama there is, potentially, no objective limit to the question of morals and ethics. Fictional dramas can, quite literally, say and do whatever it is they want.

The Wire is an HBO television drama focusing on the police and drug gangs in Baltimore and was first broadcast in 2002. It was conceived as a new form of television, reconfiguring its relationship to both television and cinema. Writer and producer David Simon has repeatedly suggested that with *The Wire*, he created a sixty-hour movie. The five seasons of *The Wire* are not presented through a series of discrete episodes. Instead, each episode and season intertwines with the other, unfolding in a style more familiar in soap operas. The seasons work through a conflict between drug dealers and the police. This is set in place in the first season. The second season, based around the dock, focuses on unions and the working classes. The third season reveals the strategies used by the police to try and solve the conflict. In season

4, the focus is on education and why it has such a limited impact on the situation. Finally, season 5 focuses on the media and the creation of particular narratives. As part of its quest for authenticity, the dialogue and audio can be a challenge to follow. So much so that one recommended way of viewing is to have the sub-titles turned on.

By examining how the series disturbs our moral and ethical expectations, this chapter will consider how sometimes unexpected positions work to sustain one another. It will articulate how the basic premise of *The Wire* is one of remapping shifting moral and ethical positions, in which the behavior of the police and criminals are both interchangeable and somewhat indistinguishable. What this reading of *The Wire* offers is a challenge that problematizes moral and ethical positions. What links each season is how an imperceptible but inevitable gravitational pull of each social group renders truly ethical acts impossible. Such an impossibility is also intrinsic to the overall viewing experience, wherein entertainment appears to offer a kind of validation for its audience that it ultimately cannot actually provide. Perhaps, what an audience actually wants is not to understand a drama as it unfolds but to determine how the drama sees and values the watching audience. It is this proposal that underpins what follows.

The Wire stages psychosocial problems that are partially resolved through each season, but that there are never any particularly clear moral or ethical choices. As a result, *The Wire* offers the viewer little or no chance for any moral or ethical redemption. Its continuously shifting narratives, now more common to the formal structuring of television seasons/series rather than movies, means we never truly achieve a narrative closure.[1] Endings are almost always left with a small opening in order to usher in the potential of another season. Today, the prequel has emerged in order to get around the finality of a season ending (e.g., *Better Call Saul* and *El Camino* are both set before the events in *Breaking Bad* took place, but both were produced after its final season). Thus, in the complex texture of *The Wire*, with its difficult to understand dialogue and its ensemble of flawed characters, viewers are presented with a world where individuals do not have the freedom to make their own ethical and moral choices. The only freedom characters appear to have is the freedom to remain within the social group they are connected to.

All five seasons of *The Wire* combine narratives of different levels of corruption in differing contexts, from the police, politicians, unions, teachers, media, and crime gangs. By doing this, the central themes emerge and evolve through a slowly developing narrative. As Fredric Jameson has noted, the formula shares the characteristics that are more like a Dickens novel than that of the usual freestanding episodes of other television dramas.[2] Furthermore, while the series is usually celebrated for being an example of realist TV, as Slavoj Žižek has suggested, it does not present direct realism, where the topic is presented to its audience in a realistic way. Instead, *The Wire* is structured to present a kind of subject realism, where it appears as if the actual community of Baltimore came together to stage something of their own self representation. Since some of the characters in the series were played by people who actually lived in Baltimore and were not trained actors, there is a sense of self-representation present in the portrayal of the city. Realism is, therefore, not depicted in an authentic way; instead, it is realized through a direct connection to actual people.

The Wire is not realist in a mimetic sense, statically redrawing how things appear in order to entertain.[3] At a formal level, it conveys the "processes of transformation," and the shifting structures situated at the center of the cycles of capitalism.[4] In terms of how it expresses any moral and ethical positions of its characters, it does not resolve them in a way that provides clarity; instead, they are lived in all their confusion and ambiguity and crucially through their limitations.

Throughout the series, *The Wire* repeatedly suggests that in order to achieve anything, one has to, at least in part, break the law or maintain something on the basis of a lie. There are two groups who dominate its narratives: the police and the criminals. What quickly becomes apparent are the similarities, rather than differences, between these two groups. Paradoxically, the police, who are typically understood as the law enforcers, often behave as lawbreakers in order to achieve their goal of upholding the law. Clearly, for the police depicted in *The Wire,* some laws are more important than others. Similarly, the criminals, especially the Barksdale drug gang, and specifically Stringer Bell (played by Idris Elba), aspire to be seen as both respectable businessmen and as tough leaders of the drug gang. In the pursuit of money, Stringer Bell instinctively senses a need to straddle both physical violence and an explicit form of brutal capitalist economics.

There is a certain symmetry to the contradictions of both the police and the criminals; they present a kind of literal mirror to each other. Their behaviors and decisions are constantly challenged and finely balanced between two opposing positions: in order to do the right thing, they also have to do the wrong thing. For the police, it is often about how they interpret the laws that govern the country. But for drug dealers like Stringer Bell, it is about a code of behavior that is entirely unwritten. The relative safety of a clear moral or ethical position is rarely discernible throughout the seasons. *The Wire* does not simply require a judgment to decide where the line that divides behaviors and separates good notions from bad ones is located, but instead forces the viewer to question whether there ever is a line at all.

Due to the intertwined nature of its episodes and seasons, *The Wire* does not contain conventional lead characters. Instead, it could be described as having a number of notable or recurring characters. Thus, its structure challenges the notion of a show needing lead and secondary characters to sustain interest.[5] Its ensemble cast, which grows and unfolds throughout each season, are organized within the interlinking narratives that more closely resembles a soap opera than a television series made up of a set of seasons. With no central character or lead role, it is the institutions and organizations to which people belong that are the cornerstones around which each narrative emerges. These organizations are the police, the drug gangs, the unions, the city government, education, and the media. The fundamental representation of each of these is expressed through the movement of bureaucracy, which at its most efficient operates only to perpetuate itself. When police crime statistics are manipulated, *The Wire* shows how the purpose of an ideal bureaucratic system is, ultimately, to serve itself. Bureaucracy appears outside of any moral or ethical motivation, taking a purely objective position. Within a bureaucracy, people can only do as the system wants them to do; there is no escape from it. Reflecting on this, police lieutenant Cedric Daniels (played by Lance Reddick) expresses his character's frustration with bureaucracy when talking to his team, "The stat games . . . that lie, it's what ruined this department. Shining up shit and calling it gold, so that Majors become Colonels and Mayors become Governors; pretending to do police work while one generation fucking trains the next how not to do the job."[6] Without any irony, *The Wire's* most bureaucratic organization is represented by the police. Policing is continually depicted as an administrative and bureaucratic process peppered with occasional, often lucky, breakthroughs. In many instances, the successes the police enjoy are as a consequence of the failings of the criminals rather than the result of diligent, investigative procedures. Within all of the social groups—police, drug gangs, unions, government, education, and media—it is the procedures and processes that structure how they all, ultimately, fail to function efficiently.

Two unsettling notions emerge from *The Wire*. The first is how the police, and those connected with the work they do, operate both within the law and outside of it. The second is the extent to which the drug gangs are knowingly resigned to their own social status. Barksdale gang leader Stringer Bell makes some attempts to legitimize the drug operation and to use the knowledge he gains from business school to maximize their profits and effectiveness. But he makes no attempt to stop selling drugs and set up a legitimate business; instead, drug money is used for real-estate purchases and to buy shell or front companies. At no point does his ambition appear to be leading out of the environment with which he is so familiar. In this and in many other similar examples, *The Wire* can be read as being fundamentally about class struggle—a struggle between those who have and those who have not. There is a basic narrative of wealth and power which sits beneath each episode. But the series is, of course, also about individual relationships and the frustrations connected to how individuals are forced to live. What we can learn from *The Wire* is how any route to an ethical choice can only be followed if we lose all hope of being able to make such a choice from within ourselves.

The Wire constantly reminds the viewer of class and social structures by how it exposes their inconsistencies and flaws. At the same time, it also presents a narrative of the mundane and overwhelming frustrations of its characters. It renders, in a fictitious form, the underlying truths about society.[7] There is something that feels authentic in how its themes are presented, but this is not simply because many of the storylines are apparently based on real events. Nor can it be because of the visual form of the series or its use of real people from Baltimore in some of the supporting roles. Realism is conveyed through the accurate representation of the trauma of acting ethically or freely.

In the third episode of season 1, D'Angelo Barksdale (played by Larry Gilliard Jr.) explains the rules of chess by referencing the social and power structures of the drug gangs. Barksdale explains the rules by comparing the different roles and responsibilities connected to drug dealing. He sets out how chess is like life in the drug gangs, where each piece on the board has a particular role and can only move in certain ways.[8] This simplified behavioral code, where everyone has a role to play in order to protect the King and win the game, highlights the overarching hierarchy that inherits something from Whiteness, from economics, and from masculinity.[9] What the viewer sees is that if there are rules to be adhered to, then ethics and morality are seemingly collectively fixed and agreed upon and are not so much arbitrary or individual choices. Even though the drug gangs accept they have clearly defined roles within an identifiable hierarchy, the series begins with the police recognizing that they themselves are "wholly ignorant of the structure of the gangs and the very names of the people who control them."[10] Uncovering the individuals behind the drug gangs' structure becomes the principal purpose of the police in season 1. But it is not only a quest to identify and find the people involved, as during the series, the investigation shifts to the commonly cited course of action throughout the series to *follow the money*. The police are then focused on uncovering the economic structure, which is supported by a logistic supply chain. In doing this, they unpack the complexity of the drug gang's operations and reveal how drug operations are intrinsic to many of the social structures depicted in the series. The police are therefore forced to investigate not individual crimes, but a complex social edifice incorporating multiple drug gangs, drug users, politicians, unions, citizens, and even the police themselves. No moral clarity emerges from this; instead, society is depicted to be a homogenous group with porous moral and ethical positions.

While it may appear obvious, what motivates ethics is a drive to do what *seems* ethical. However, in the world of *The Wire*, the question of what seems to be ethical is often confused. The individual demands forced upon the characters, often by a sense of duty, are their essential contact we have with the real of lived reality. As many of their actions have unclear or unintended moral and ethical consequences, what emerges is an underlying chaos and confusion. The response to this is that many characters express how they feel more comfortable returning to a past they did at least partially understand, rather than adapting to a new situation. When Stringer Bell plans to legitimize parts of the drug gangs' operations through corporate structures, the gang leader, Avon Barksdale (played by Wood Harris), tells him "I ain't no suit-wearing businessman like you. I'm just a gangster, I suppose."[11] Barksdale recognizes the symbolic authority of business as ultimately being more powerful than the physical intimidation he uses to control his own drug empire. But, as he states, he is a gangster and he has no sense of how he could ever have been anything else. Similarly, the union leader at the docks, Frank Sobotka (played by Chris Bauer), reflects on the state of the nation and declares "We used to make shit in this country, build shit, now we just put our hand in the next guy's pocket."[12] Sobotka's line is in part self-confessional, as he is acknowledging how he too has had to break his own moral code in the interests of his union members and to protect jobs at the docks. For Sobotka, breaking the law is not about his own ethical or moral choices—any agency he has is bound up into a resigned inevitability. The difference between these two characters is that Sobotka has been forced to change what he does, while Barksdale is resistant to changing despite acknowledging that if he does not, he will ultimately not survive. Despite adapting, Sobotka wants things to be back how they used to be, whereas Barksdale knows things are changing even if he cannot.

The motivations throughout the series—the imperative to make money, to convict criminals, to lie in the face of truth, to protect and defend, and so on—raise all kinds of different ethical questions. What links them is an acknowledgment that there is no universalization of ethics; instead, recognizing its paradoxical inconsistency is the only truly ethical position. Standards of expected behavior are imposed on all the key groups within *The Wire*. Instead of applying an independent standard to how a character behaves to a situation, the viewer sees that ethics and moral behavior are complicated by context. Social behavior is legitimized internally by each of the characters and therefore is less likely to align with what the audience might recognize as universal morals.[13] The multilayering of morality, personal, social, and universal is disrupted because of the pressure social groups place on behaviors. In *The Wire*, behavior that is considered to be outside the norms of a group is punished in some form or other. When Detective Jimmy McNulty (played by Dominic West) appears to follow his own, often questionable moral code by breaking rules simply to do his job, his progress is invariably impeded by those above him whose motivations appear to be bureaucratic or self-serving. Throughout the series, it appears as though the moral codes of criminals are more likely to be adhered to than those of the police. Drug dealing is referred to as a game with fixed rules and codes. Individual moral and ethical positions are, ultimately, always overridden by the institutions, systems, and groups depicted in *The Wire*. Invisible social structures restrain and contain the characters and their decisions, to the extent that what they want to do is really of little consequence. The audience is left to negotiate the tension between individual morality and larger, impersonal institutions that have their own set of rules that add up to a behavioral code, even if that code is morally questionable. For example, for the drug gangs, rules control their actions: they have rules about what phones they can use and where they can have conversations. These are implemented to protect them from police surveillance. They also have rules about where they can sell drugs and the territory they consider to be their own. As stated, drug dealing is considered to be "*the game*," and implicitly, the police, the men working on the docks, the local government, the judiciary, and the media are also playing the game, knowingly or unknowingly. Personal moral positions take a secondary role to the principles of the game. It is a game they are all forced into and ultimately cannot stop playing. Moral ambiguity is explored and articulated extensively in every season, but increasingly we also see how other decisions are simply not possible. The audience can imagine but does not see, a free space for the characters in which they can choose to behave freely or choose to make one moral decision and not another. There is, then, an inevitability that is at the heart of the good and bad decisions that are made. It seems ambiguous moral positions come from there being little opportunity to make radically different decisions.

A standard reading of the series suggests the moral codes for each group are somewhat interchangeable. However, this leads to a universalization of the subject, where no matter what side they are on, they are inevitably forced to behave in a regulated but similar way and would suggest a social determinism that could then be challenged. In an episode where it is revealed that Detective Bunk Moreland (played by Wendell Pierce) and "stick-up man" Omar Little (played by Michael K. Williams) attended the same school, the possibility that each could have, potentially, followed different paths is exposed. But it seems that despite having some similarities, inevitability pulled the characters in their different directions. Neither Bunk nor Omar can really imagine a significantly different life from the one they are already leading. Despite a capacity for reflection, they cannot truly picture themselves in circumstances which are essentially any different from the ones they are currently in. A pervading inevitability must mean any ethical and moral choices matter less to the characters, as no matter what they do, there is no real way out from where they are.

What the audience sees in *The Wire* is a kind of controlled individual passivity where the rules of organization and institutions may be broken, but this makes little or no difference to any wider outcomes. In essence, there are small adjustments to behaviors allowed, but all the real sense in which rules can be freely violated is kept hidden. The characters are therefore locked into a series of highly controlled behaviors organized around their social position. Their personal morals are always overridden by the ethical framework of the social group they find themselves in. More devastatingly, there is no lateral movement across groups. It is as if everyone has a position or role that has been decided at the beginning of the series, after which all the structures remain basically the same.

Along with this sense of inevitability, a theme of resistance emerges throughout *The Wire*. Due to the overriding sense of inevitability, it is always, in some way, pointless to resist. While the characters all have plenty to resist, there is also little reason to hope for anything other than the same outcome. Thus, with resistance comes a weary resignation. The inevitability of a system that is always winning pervades many of the characters' motivations. Police Major William Rawls (played by John Doman) closely controls his crime figures and therefore insists that his detectives solve unsolvable crimes. As a result, there is no relationship between actual crimes and the numbers that are shown on the wall at the Baltimore Police Department HQ. In fact, the numbers are part of the bureaucratic system of control that manages what police have to do rather than what they should do.

Many readings of *The Wire* take as their starting point a communality of disparate institutions and social groups depicted. But there is also something incommensurable about each group in how they are each impenetrable to the other. What the series sets out is a mainly fragmentary engagement between characters, with each trying and failing to understand the different points of view of everyone else. Where universality emerges is in how characters are abstracted from any other way of being. What unites everyone is their individual inability to grasp not only the lives of others but most importantly their own circumstances. There is, then, something within all the characters that is inaccessible to themselves which they recognize by how others are also inextricably disconnected. One should not render the subjectivity of the characters in *The Wire* void simply because they cannot view others as interchangeable with their own circumstances. That they are trapped means they do not seek out in others what resembles themselves. In the world of *The Wire,* symbolic identification operates on a different register. As characters, their subjectivity emerges not from a universal sense of sameness but in the particularity of each individual character. They do not have solidarity because they share moral codes or, ostensibly, all obey similar laws. Instead, what turns them into subjects is their acknowledgment that they each have their own inner particularities, their own fantasies. In other words, it is how they dream their own dreams which define how they live. However, it is not that they are simply a group of existential subjects. It is how, as subjects, they can only properly acknowledge the individuality of others by grasping their *own* detachment from their *own* fantasies. In this way, they understand others by recognizing in themselves their own detachment from their own fantasy and how others occupy a similarly precarious state of illusionary fragility.[14] For its audience, the emancipatory gesture of *The Wire* is in how it formulates the characters and institutions depicted as being, in this way, fundamentally disconnected from each other. In being forced into impossible relations with one another, in a situation where nothing is ever fully resolved, all that can be hoped for is a kind of ethical acceptance of who they are and the life they are leading. At the same time, this also becomes a question for the audience, who are forced to confront their own ethical issues from within a world configured in a way similar to the one depicted in *The Wire*. The paradox being how lived reality is contingent upon the fictions that emerge from within it, all the while remaining stubbornly detached from them.

Characters in *The Wire* express different forms of subjectivity. Over the course of the series, there are portrayals of heroic autonomous characters, those who operate against adversity and make changes for the better. Both Omar and Stringer Bell operate autonomously, striving for a greater good. There are also those who are resigned to the consequences that befall them, both Bubbles and Bunk could be categorized in this way. Finally, there is the narcissistic hero in the form of Detective McNulty, who threads his way through all seasons. These forms of subjectivity relate directly to the three stages of capitalism: liberal, imperialist, and post-industrial. For Stringer Bell, the goal of trying to bring business practice to drug dealing can never be fully realized. It is clear what Bell needs to do in order to reach his goal; his aims are what drives him. But he can never reconcile what he wants, he can only continue to endlessly try and work toward it. In this way, he enacts with precision the basic drive of capital.

With its ensemble cast and numerous settings, *The Wire* could be understood as offering multiple moral and ethical positions. However, it is often interpreted as presenting overlapping positions or similarities in opposing groups. What motivates these is often a level of self-interest. While money connects the interests of all groups, it does not function in the same way for each of them. Trying to locate where the money comes from and where it goes is how the police attempt to trace the drug gangs, whereas for the drug gangs' money underpins a power structure and its continued control. In essence, what oppresses all the characters in the show is the invisible hand of capital. In the world of *The Wire,* the essential form of capital shifts between production and plunder. What is distinctive is an emphasis on distribution rather than production: the drug dealers sell their product while the police are concerned with stopping the spread of criminality with increasingly unorthodox practices.

While there are a number of different modalities of characters in *The Wire*, they still appear to be locked into their own social situation with little chance to absolutely change anything for themselves. Even when Detective McNulty is transferred to the harbor, he still remains within the formal organization of the police. Ultimately, for all of the characters, there is no metalanguage, there is no way for them to observe themselves from the outside of their own situation. This adds to a general feeling of being trapped within predefined social conditions. Even when Stringer Bell attends his university class, his attendance is staged in such a way that he is still clearly an interloper in the domain of education. He is a part-time student who, after class, still has to return to his job of running the drug gangs.

Throughout the series, subjectivity is incorporated into organizational structures. Individuals act, sometimes violently, in what they see as their own best interest. But the overriding sense is that it is also in the interest of the group to which they belong. What encompasses each series is a growing pessimism. Even within Stringer Bell's hopes of transforming the drug business into something that appears more legitimate, there remains an underlying notion that neither he nor the organization can muster enough energy to transform itself. Transformation is not possible since each organization is locked into established ways of operating. The drug gangs legitimize themselves by an implicit stability and this is manifested in the systems and processes imposed upon the gang members who operate within them. Even when these systems are broken and inefficient, they continue to be maintained or adhered to. This then sets in place a basic loyalty that each individual has to the group to which they belong. For the members of the drug gangs, although they see others belonging to other groups, such as the police, there is an acceptance that their circumstances are unchangeable. There can be no shift from group to group, no lateral movement across the social organizations that are defined in the series. The lack of universal contradictions in each group means there is a consistency in things remaining exactly as they are.

The Wire presents most of its characters as having only limited moral agency or choice. Contained within a framework of codes and behaviors, they are prohibited from moving out of where they are to something different. Even when McNulty breaks the law, he does so as a police officer and not as a criminal gang member. It is as though the group to which each character belongs has a gravitational pull keeping each of them in their place. This brings forth the true impossibility of an ethical act. As Žižek notes, the characters are fundamentally limited by the question as to "what can a (relatively) honest individual do in today's conditions."[15] Within these fixed social conditions, there is no possibility for anything redeeming or radically eman-cipatory to happen. As such, the situation for each of them is continuously locked down. The only way they can really break the deadlock is to behave in a way "that somehow violates the Law."[16] This gives rise to a pessimistic conclusion that individuals are unable to elicit any significant social change on their own. Of course, the result of such pessimism is a cynical resignation which appears to prevent anyone acting how they want to act.

There are some characters who appear to bridge different positions. They are motivated by their personal ethical and moral perspectives. For example, throughout the series, Omar Little steals money and drugs from the drug gangs. Although his reputation is already established, what really drives him during season one is revenge for the torture and death of his lover, John Bailey (played by Lance Williams). This is also why he agrees to assist Detectives McNulty and Moreland in their case against one of Barksdale's gang, as well as help solve some other murder cases. Little eventually ends up testifying against the Barksdale drug gang in court, even though his testimony is undoubtedly false. He is one of the few characters who displays a degree of moral integrity.[17] This manifests in how he exercises his own moral code of only pursuing drug dealers. Žižek describes Omar's code as being "only kill those who have the authority to order the deaths of others."[18] In season 2, he even calls the paramedics to attend to a wounded Brother Mouzone (played by Michael Potts), whom he has shot. Omar Little's moral code is distinctly personal; even when he agrees to assist the police he is always, essentially, acting in his own interests and under his own terms. In a scene where Little gives his testimony in court, Barksdale's attorney suggests he is a parasite who feeds off the drug gangs. Little responds by saying, "I've got the shotgun you've got the briefcase,"[19] suggesting there is only a symbolic texture that differentiates him from the defending attorney.

A similar character, who also links different groups together, is heroin addict and informant Bubbles (played by Andre Royo). Connecting the sto-rylines of the gangs with the police (Bubbles is apparently a composite of two real people known to the creator David Simon), he represents the "soul of dope fiendom."[20] The despair Bubbles embodies is expressed at the end of season 3, where he takes on another protégé, attempting to teach him how to scavenge and make money for their next drug fix.[21] Bubbles remains in the background of many seasons and is the connecting tissue between drug users, drug dealers, and police. He is portrayed as having only limited agency, but seems somewhat resigned to this. While it may appear that the police and criminals depicted in *The Wire* share many structural characteristics, the police and drug dealers are really two mutually supporting sides which prop up the overarching but failing social structure of Baltimore. The impossible relationship of the police and the drug dealers is at the heart of *The Wire*.

Clearly, some behaviors of the police are explicitly criminal, while at times the drug dealers appear to uphold a strong moral and ethical code. Bubbles operates at a different register; being a drug user and informant he serves both the police and the drug gangs. He acts not because of some deeper sense of duty or sacrifice, but as an act of self-preservation or even revenge. Omar and Bubbles are situated outside of the institutions that are depicted in the series. In *The Wire's* Baltimore reality, their status is held at the margins, yet they are also two of the most "enduring characters."[22]

What can be seen in the texture of *The Wire* is a mise-en-scène of set ideas and motifs. The idea of a collective class struggle is the most obvious, but on an individual level, there is also an intricate construction and interconnection of moral and ethical questions. In essence, the series is an expression of the social relation between subjects and objects. The problem the series addresses is not how to reconcile these relations but how to express and accept the paradox that such a reconciliation is never possible. In this way, the characters in *The Wire* do not strive for transformation or some form of moral redemption. They are not really trying to move from the social group they are into a better one. Instead, what they are looking for is a kind of confirmation of how the social group they belong to—the drug gangs, the police, the unions, the media, the politicians—actually sees and values them. This self-reflective determinism also translates to how an audience is not simply entertained by a television series or movie but also requires some form of validation back from it. It is only by realizing that such a validation is impossible that the audience is then able to work toward reconciling its own inner tension by knowing that everyone is situated in the same impossible circumstance.

A level of lawlessness can be read in the depictions of the various institutions and social groups. This is most evident in how the police, politicians, and judges behave privately. Throughout the series, it is individuals, not institutions, who are shown as being dishonest. Corruption is part of how they function and, as such, there is no ethical or moral alternative: this is simply how they behave within each of the institutions. In some capacity, corruption appears to be a more effective way of getting things done, even if what is done can be judged to be the wrong things. The police are depicted as being keen to solve crimes, but the police as an institution is more focused on statistics that demonstrate their effectiveness rather than reflecting on how it can be effective. It is as though superfluous, irrational activities drive the day-to-day functioning while solving crimes is a mere sideline activity.

What the audience can take from *The Wire* is how three levels of ethics operate together through a moral framework of behaviors. First, there is a basic morality largely consisting of rules we choose to obey. This manifests itself as to how in society the things we do are usually constrained by laws.

It is the structure of the law that influences how we recognize broadly normal behaviors. Of course, along with crime, the law is an ever-present force in *The Wire,* but it is presented as distinct from an overarching and abstract legal system. The police oscillate between trying to uphold or subvert different aspects of the law. It is social laws, as distinct from actual laws, that formulate the basic conditions of social reality. The law itself is a defined limit, which acts as a disruption of any accepted social reality. It provides an external pressure on how we behave; social law allows individuals a level of freedom from their own internal moral imperative.[23] In other words, we are able to act in accordance with social laws in order to not have to face our own moral decisions. The second level of ethics is the opposite of this formulation of morality: it is the consistent manipulation of the rules. This is best expressed by Detective Jimmy McNulty's character who often breaks the law in order to fight the crimes he wants to tackle. McNulty appears unsettled when dealing with what is happening in his life outside of his work. When his colleague, Lester Freamon (played by Clarke Peters) says "A life, Jimmy, you know what that is? It's what happens while you're waiting for moments that never come,"[24] it is because McNulty's personal life is consistently portrayed as taking second place to his commitment to his job as a detective. The third level of ethics is where the breaking of rules happens out of necessity or where there is little or no option. In season 3, Major Colvin (played by Robert Wisdom) sets up the so-called free zones where drugs can be sold and used without intervention from the police. Following similar lines to the liberal laws in Amsterdam, one of the zones becomes known widely as *Hammsterdam.* Colvin's radical project of legalizing drugs is designed so that police resources can be used elsewhere. For Colvin, the problem had become so complex that it required a drastic and revolutionary strategy. But in *Hammsterdam,* the police effectively lost their purpose, they were no longer needed. This is why it could never legitimately succeed. As a social experiment, it quite literally broke free from the structure that enabled it to exist in the first place.

As stated at the beginning, from inside any fictional drama, there really is no limit to the question of morals and ethics. Fictional dramas can literally say and do whatever it is they want. *The Wire* is a kind of mise-en-abyme, a fictional world unfolding within a real world that increasingly seems also like a work of fiction. In staging the world to itself, *The Wire* appears to have broken free from television entertainment to become a discrete object of study and investigation. With so much written and discussed about it, it is easy to forget how, at the level of spectacle, it confirms something of our own ethical and moral registers. We watch the challenges faced by others not to hide from our own but to confirm that we too are suffering.

NOTES

1. Slavoj Žižek, *The Year of Dreaming Dangerously* (London: Verso, 2012), 100.
2. Fredric Jameson, "Realism Utopia in The Wire," *Criticism* 52, no. 3 (2010): 360.
3. Ibid., 365.
4. Ibid.
5. Ibid., 359.
6. *The Wire,* season 5, episode 10, "-30-," dir. Clark Johnson, aired March 09, 2008, originally released on HBO.
7. See Ruth Penfold-Mounce, David Beer, and Roger Burrows, "The Wire as Social Science—Fiction?" *Sociology* 45, no. 1 (2011): 152–167.
8. Frank Rudy Cooper, "The King Stay the King: Multidimensional Masculinities and Capitalism in The Wire." In *Masculinities and the Law*, ed. Frank Rudy Cooper and Ann C. McGinley. (New York: New York University Press, 2012), 96.
9. Ibid., 97.
10. Jameson, 361.
11. *The Wire,* season 3, episode 6, "Homecoming," dir. Leslie Libman, aired October 31, 2004, originally released on HBO.
12. *The Wire,* season 2, episode 11, "Bad Dreams," dir. Ernest Dickerson, aired August 17, 2003, originally released on HBO.
13. Thomas Wartenburg, "The Wire," Philosophy Now: a magazine of ideas, 2008, https://philosophynow.org/issues/70/The_Wire.
14. Slavoj Žižek, *Looking Awry: An Introduction to Jacques Lacan through Popular Culture* (Cambridge, MA: MIT Press, 1991), 121.
15. Žižek, *Dreaming Dangerously*, 97.
16. Ibid.
17. Wartenburg, para. 15.
18. Žižek, *Dreaming Dangerously*, 99.
19. *The Wire,* season 2, episode 6, "All Prologue," dir. Steve Shill, aired July 6, 2003, originally released on HBO.
20. Linda Williams, "Ethnographic Imaginary: The Genesis and Genius of the Wire," *Critical Inquiry* 38, no. 1 (2011): 218.
21. Ibid., 219.
22. Christopher Hanson, "Some Last Words on The Wire," *Film Quarterly* 62, no. 2 (Winter) (2008): 66–67, 66.
23. Slavoj Žižek, *The Most Sublime Hysteric: Hegel with Lacan* (Cambridge, MA: Polity Press, 2014), 158.
24. *The Wire,* season 3, episode 9, "Slapstick," dir. Alex Zakrzewski, aired November 21, 2004, originally released on HBO.

BIBLIOGRAPHY

Hanson, Christopher. "Some Last Words on *The Wire*." *Film Quarterly* 62, no. 2 (Winter) (2008): 66–67.

Jameson, Fredric. "Realism Utopia in *The Wire*." *Criticism* 52, no. 3 (2010): 359–372.

Penfold-Mounce, Ruth, David Beer, and Roger Burrows. "*The Wire* as Social Science-Fiction?" *Sociology* 45, no. 1 (2011): 152–167.

Rudy Cooper, Frank. "The King Stay the King: Multidimensional Masculinities and Capitalism in *The Wire*." In *Masculinities and the Law*, edited by Frank Rudy Cooper and Ann C. McGinley. New York: New York University Press, 2012.

The Wire. Created by David Simon. Aired from June 2, 2002–March 9, 2008. Originally released on HBO.

Wartenburg, Thomas. "The Wire." Philosophy Now: A Magazine of Ideas, 2008. https://philosophynow.org/issues/70/The_Wire.

Williams, Linda. "Ethnographic Imaginary: The Genesis and Genius of the Wire." *Critical Inquiry* 38, no. 1 (Autumn) (2011): 208–226.

Žižek, Slavoj. *Looking Awry: An Introduction to Jacques Lacan through Popular Culture*. Cambridge, MA: MIT Press, 1991.

Žižek, Slavoj. *The Most Sublime Hysteric: Hegel with Lacan*. Cambridge, MA: Polity Press, 2014.

Žižek Slavoj. *The Year of Dreaming Dangerously*. London: Verso, 2012.

Chapter 3

The Two Walters

Walt Whitman's Poetry and the Moral Vision of Breaking Bad

Douglas Rasmussen

In the AMC television series *Breaking Bad* (2009–2013), there are multiple intertextual references to the American transcendentalist poet Walt Whitman. The series—which deals with a high school chemistry teacher named Walter White (played by Bryan Cranston) who is diagnosed with terminal cancer who decides to use his chemistry skills to produce a strain of methamphetamine called Blue Sky and adopts an alias known only as Heisenberg—is thematically concerned with transformation as the meek and emasculated Walt gradually evolves into a ruthless and violent drug kingpin. The pilot episode establishes that Walt has a Nobel Prize for chemistry, signifying a fall from grace as he is now a middle-aged teacher struggling with medical debt. All this comes crashing down on Walt when his DEA brother-in-law Hank Schrader (played by Dean Norris) finds the inscription in the book *Leaves of Grass* in the episode "Gliding Over All": "To my other favorite W.W. It's an honor working with you, Fondly, G.B."[1] Similarity in handwriting allows Hank to finally discover that Walt is the Blue Sky methamphetamine dealer he has been chasing since the first season. This is far from the first appearance of Walt Whitman, as Walt's one-time lab partner Gale Boetticher (played by David Costabile) quotes the poem "When I Heard the Learn'd Astronomer" in one episode and gifts a copy to Walt of *Leaves of Grass* bearing the inscription, in which Walt can be seen carrying around.

The multiple references to Whitman's poetry establish an important symbolic connection with Walt's love of science and his distortion of democratic principles and notions of individual freedom to serve his own selfish purposes. More than an alliterative connection between Walter White and Walt Whitman, or even the shared name of Walter Whit(e)man, there is the connective tissue between them of both science and perfectionism. Walt Whitman was known to be interested in science, writing columns in the *Brooklyn Daily Eagle* on chemistry and agriculture, and *Leaves of Grass* has a few poems dedicated to scientific thought: about decomposition and the cycle of grass and mulch, for instance, or about attending science lectures. Gary Sloan in his article "Walt Whitman: When Science and Mysticism Collide" comments that Whitman's admiration for science was well-known and that he had "a wide-ranging interest in contemporary science—astronomy, geology, physics, chemistry, biology."[2] Both Walt and Whitman also share a sense of perfectionism. Whitman spent most of his writing career perfecting and revising *Leaves of Grass*, just as Walt on *Breaking Bad* spends much of his time perfecting his Blue Sky methamphetamine formula. So while the two might initially seem to be an odd pairing, they nevertheless share enough in their respective psychological profiles that intertextual references to Whitman on *Breaking Bad* become significant.

Symbolically, the reference to Walt Whitman's *Leaves of Grass* provides the viewer with context to understand the moral compass of the series. While Walt is a sympathetic character who might engender audience sympathy, he is also being juxtaposed against the poetry of Whitman which acts as the moral conscience for the viewer. Whitman represents scientific awe and wonder over the natural universe and democratic principles of freedom, while Walt embodies science as a tool for the pure accumulation of wealth and power. When viewer sympathy veers too much in favor of Walt, Whitman's poetry acts as a signifier that his pursuit of science is a distortion, in that he is using his skills to produce addiction to a dangerous substance rather than to illuminate our knowledge of the world.

Looking at Whitman as a recurring motif in *Breaking Bad*, I posit that his poetry reflects the distorted lens through which Walt views himself. Legitimately or not, Walt does feel like a victim of the same oppressive capitalist forces that Whitman is critical of in his poetry. Walt is undone by the blind pursuit of the American dream and strives to break away from societal constraints through the constant perfection of his work. Walt exists as an inversion of Whitman's democratic and individualistic philosophy. Whereas Whitman extols a transcendentalist and verdant vision, Walt's artistic perfection takes place in the dry and barren New Mexico desert. Whitman was a sensualist in his poetry, and Walt works to perfect an illicit substance that people use to escape from reality which exaggerates, cranks up, and ultimately negates Whitman's sensualism. In this manner, Walt can be viewed as a corruption of individualism for the purpose of satiating his own ego. The connections, I believe, extend beyond the poem "When I Heard the learn'd Astronomer" cited in *Breaking Bad*, and a reading of Whitman's larger *oeuvre* deepens this symbolic connection between the series and the poet.

Through the intertextual references to Walt Whitman *Breaking Bad* is engaging the viewer with morality as a cautionary tale. It is through the rise and fall of Walter White and the methamphetamine empire that the viewer learns how destructive the perversion of an individual's ideals for financial gain contributes to an inevitable psychological and moral collapse as they lose more and more of their core self. Whitman's poetry professes a love of individual freedom and democracy, whereas Walt appropriates those ideals for selfish means and ignores the rules of society, not because they are conforming to him and his scientific ideals but because they are simply inconvenient for his need for power and wealth. In this way, the viewer witnesses the inevitable and terrible consequences of Walt's actions as a cautionary tale.

WALTER WHITE, INDIVIDUALISM, AND SCIENCE

Vince Gilligan explains in *Breaking Bad: The Official Book* how Whitman developed as a key theme: "Walt Whitman is integral to *Breaking Bad* now; in hindsight we did not set out to make it that way."[3] What originated as a reference in one episode when Walt's lab assistant Gale Boetticher, who replaces Jesse Pinkman (played by Aaron Paul) at the insistence of Walt's boss Gus Fring (played by Giancarlo Esposito), recites the poem "When I Heard the Learn'd Astronomer," evolved to become an important symbolic element in *Breaking Bad*. Gale introduces Walt to the poetry of Whitman when he recites the poem "When I Heard the Learn'd Astronomer" (S3E6):

When I heard the learn'd astronomer
When the proofs, the figures, were ranged in columns before me,
When I was shown the charts and diagrams, to add, divide, and measure them,
When I sitting heard the astronomer where he lectured with much applause in the
    lecture- room,
How soon unaccountable I became tired and sick,
Till rising and gliding out I wander'd off by myself
In the mystical moist night-air, and from time to time,
Look'd up in perfect silence to the stars[4]

Gale recites the poem in the episode "Sunset" after being questioned by Walt about his particular path toward criminality, to which Gale responds, "I'm definitely libertarian. Consenting adults want what they want."[5] Gale's libertarian views exemplify the lengths to which a person can rationalize their actions. For the viewer, this speech by Gale is a reflection of how Walt justifies his own brutal actions. Brutal and murderous actions, it should be noted, are commensurate with the emphasis on ruthless competition in the neoliberal economic paradigm and a natural outgrowth of valuing the individual over social support systems. Neoliberalism promotes the accumulation of growth as its end goal to the extent that individuals can exploit an unregulated free market for personal gain. Neoliberalism runs contrary to what Whitman espoused, and by having Gale recite the poem while producing methamphetamine illustrates the cognitive dissonance individuals are capable of.

For Gale, science means doing the public the service of providing a clean and reliable high, and it allows him the opportunity to do the actual lab work required for chemistry rather than having to follow a traditional academic route as a profession. The scene in which Gale recites the poem occurs just after he probes Walt with questions about the unusual dosage and cooking procedures for adding phenylacetic acid to his formula. At this point, Gus is priming Gale to take over Walt's position in the lab, and Walt, becoming more and more suspicious of Gale's constant interrogation about the procedures he uses to create a 98 percent pure strain of methamphetamine, spends a few episodes being as vague as possible so as to prevent his inevitable demise at the hands of Gus once Gale is confident enough to cook on his own. Gale's speech thus has the unintended consequence of ensuring his own death at the hands of Walt (who manipulates Jesse into shooting Gale under the guise of self-protection) in the season 3 episode "Full Measure." Gale is a talented chemist in his own right, and when he relates to Walt his backstory about not wanting to jump through hoops and take orders he naively informs Walt of his own ambitions:

> I was on my way, jumping through all the hoops, kissing the proper behinds, attending to all the non-chemistry that one finds occupied by. You know that world. That is not what I signed on for. I love the lab. Because it's all still magic, you know? Chemistry, I mean, once you lose all that. . . [Walt interjects]: It is. It is still magic. It still is.[6]

Walt, far from desiring freedom in the spiritual sense Whitman describes, only desires absolute control. Freedom for Walt is personal freedom to live according to his own design and selfish desires, and it precludes the potential for any other individual to adhere to freedom in a democratic sense if it interferes with personal financial goals and the fulfillment of his own egoist wishes.

What *Breaking Bad* is depicting is how untrustworthy faith in an unregulated free market truly is. Walt begins the series with the best of intentions, as a victim of circumstance who only wanted to provide for his family. Once removed from the barriers, Walt becomes consumed by greed and the allure of power that degrades his moral center until he fully transforms into the persona of Heisenberg, the alias of his drug kingpin. Neoliberalism and its tangential political ethos of libertarianism strip away the social support systems that would help pay for Walt's cancer treatment, making it an insurmountable task for Walt to prosper until he decides to engage in criminal activities. The catalyst of Walt's initial decision to use his chemistry skills to produce methamphetamine was family and medical debt, but it is an economic system devoid of proper checks and balances that corrodes his sense of self and allows him to become Heisenberg. Without any ethical, moral, or economic constraints, Walt/Heisenberg is able to fully take advantage of neoliberalism's business practices to become a successful drug kingpin. Walt's noble intentions give way to his negative impulses. Or, to use the symbolism of the series, his anger and frustration become like a cancer spreading inside and consuming his entire being.

In much the same way, Whitman rejects the metrical rules of poetry in order to facilitate a new sense of aesthetic and literary democracy, Walt and Gale reject academic rules for a libertarian ethos which produces a better, cleaner, safer high without any added adulterants. The democratic citizen in Whitman's vision, as Patrick Redding contends in the essay "Whitman Unbound: Democracy in Poetic Form 1912–1913," evokes a plain style that "would enable the poet to represent the shared patterns of speech and understanding necessary to a thriving public sphere."[7] Walt by contrast finds magic not in the plain speech of science, or even in the proliferation of science via education, but rather in an undemocratic and elite mastery of the discipline. In fact Walt expresses a distinct embarrassment at being resigned to such a plebeian fate as being a teacher when at a party with his more successful university colleagues in the season 1 episode "Gray Matter." Gale's dubious self-designation as a libertarian is problematic, in that, contrary to Whitman's democratic philosophy, his libertarian ethos leaves a wake of addiction and destruction behind that neither capitalist nor socialist medicine and policing, let alone libertarian medicine or policing, could fix. Much like Walt, Gale is appropriating a politically convenient philosophy to justify his chosen profession in the drug trade. Gale's proposed justification is that at least he is offering methamphetamine users a clean, unadulterated product without any extra toxins, or, rather, toxins that are not natural to the process of making methamphetamine, while ignoring that he is essentially producing a product which requires the disguise of an industrial laundromat to cover up the heavy chemical smell. Gale's rationale proposes individual freedom at the expense of both the larger sociological problems with drug addiction as well as the environmental factor of chemical pollution—an environmental factor, it seems, radically discordant with Whitman's Transcendentalist vision of spiritual naturalism.

For the viewer, it is important to remember that Walt was indeed a legitimate victim, but through the course of the series, they see the gradual unraveling of a family man into a renowned drug kingpin. Walt's own narrative of disenfranchisement is integral to the assuaging of his guilt over his use of excessive violence, even as he is fully in the Heisenberg persona. Walt rationalizes all this to his wife Skyler (played by Anna Gunn) in the episode "I.F.T.":

> I've done a terrible thing, but I've done it for a good reason. I did it for us. That [pointing to a duffel bag full of money] is college tuition for Walter Jr. and Holly, eighteen years down the road. And it's health insurance for you and the kids. For junior's physical therapy, his SAT tutor. It's money for groceries, gas, for birthdays and graduation parties. Skyler, that money is for this roof over your head. The mortgage that you are not going to be able to afford on a part-time bookkeeper's salary when I'm gone.[8]

Walt is trying to validate his actions under the pretense of doing everything for his family while in fact he is more invested in building his criminal empire. The scene, however, shows just how insidious the influence of neoliberal capitalism is and that anyone can fall prey to its machinations, which is what Whitman warns about in his poetry. As Jason Mittell notes in his book *Complex TV: The Poetics of Contemporary Storytelling*, "*Breaking Bad* is a highly moral tale, in which actions have consequences, and thus we expect it is unlikely that Walt emerges from this story as the victorious hero—even though he proclaims 'I won' when he finally kills Gus, we recognize that the cost of that victory is another part of his dwindling morality."[9] Walt's transition to the Heisenberg persona enacts a toll on his psyche that viewers watch slowly unfold over five seasons, wondering at which point Walt goes beyond the point where he can be redeemed. Walt's loss of a moral compass and going beyond the point of redemption are evident in how he misuses science for nefarious ends and is willing to exploit his love of chemistry for pure financial gain, necessitating a tragic end for him.

Both Walt and Gale misuse science for their own selfish needs, whether they are Walt's financial rewards or Gale's desire to pursue life according to his own design. Yet neither can truly be said to be scientific freethinkers in a rationalist sense. Walt's appropriation of the free thinker role in Whitman's poem is evident in the episode ". . . And the Bag's in the River." In this episode, a flashback of a younger Walt during his university years shows him with his first girlfriend Gretchen Schwartz (played by Jessica Hecht), working out the biological composition of the human body and coming up 0.111958 percent shy of a complete chemical profile. Walt and Gretchen ponder what the inexplicable missing element could be, with Gretchen postulating that it could be the soul. Walt rebuffs her: "The soul? There's nothing here but chemistry."[10] This scene places Walt closer on Whitman's spectrum to the stuffy lecturer, comfortable with his columns and measurements, the chemists and geologists Whitman also writes about in "Song of Myself": "Gentlemen, to you the first honors always! / Your facts are useful, and yet they are not my dwelling."[11] According to David S. Reynolds in his book on Walt Whitman, "Whitman also found in science confirmation of his optimistic instincts about the origin and nature of humans and their place in nature."[12] Walt rejects the rules of society because they do not accommodate his individualistic vision, but the rules of science are the profitable means by which he can establish his legacy, not a mystical transcendence in the way Whitman views science. Walt does not fully fit within the conceptual framework of Whitman's democratic ethos and Walt's adoption of Whitman's spiritual democracy is an incorporation of whatever is psychologically convenient for him in his self-rationalizing project of reconstructing his identity.

The poem that entrances Walt when he hears Gale recite it, "When I Heard the Learn'd Astronomer," extols a mystical, navel-gazing view of science that Walt, in his demanding and exacting nature—Walt's condescending attitude toward Jesse in the pilot clearly mark him as the stuffy lecturer obsessed with the charts and diagrams Whitman finds sickening—would not likely abide by. Joseph Beaver in the book *Walt Whitman: Poet of Science* argues, "There is nothing anti-science in Whitman; but he nearly always reserves a higher function for the poet."[13] Beaver's optimistic appraisal, however, is far from consensus. As M. Jimmie Killingsworth puts forth in *Walt Whitman and the Earth*, "Overall, scholars are reluctant to see the poet at odds with the science of his day."[14] Regardless of which aspect of Whitman's approach to science is valid, at the very least it could be argued that Whitman's view of science is unorthodox. So while Whitman's reverence for science unrestrained by the limitations of his profession as a schoolteacher might appeal to Walt, he but ignores that Whitman viewed science as an instrument of poetry. Mark Noble in his essay "Whitman's Atom and the Crisis of Materiality in Early *Leaves of Grass*" writes, "Whitman drew his 'common air' from a popular scientific culture of the 1840s and 1850s in which thinkers were recovering the axioms of a material universe from eighteenth century deism and incorporating them into a progressive consensus regarding humanistic principles."[15] So while Whitman and obviously Walt share a common interest in science, Whitman is arguing for the fusion of poetry, art, and science into a progressive democratic ideal, whereas Walt is manipulating those ideals into a distinctly individualistic and neoliberal philosophy that best benefits his endeavors.

WALT'S PSYCHOLOGICAL COLLAPSE

In Whitman's vision of a spiritually informed democracy, everyone and everything is connected in a larger, somewhat mystical, and collective:

"For every atom belonging to me as good as belongs to you."[16] This belief is an equalizing gesture, one where every aspect of the natural world, regardless of size and scale, has an impact on the rest of the world through interconnectedness. The corollary to everything being interconnected is that "Whoever degrades another degrades me."[17] Walt's subconscious copying of the traits of his victims is an example of the negative consequences of Whitman's collective philosophy of interconnectedness and an absorption of the toxicity of his criminal underworld, as well as emblematic of a power dynamic. Visually, this idea of absorbing the negative aspects of an interconnected world where every atom belongs to everyone is rendered on screen by Walt adopting the traits of the people he has killed, even if he has not witnessed these characteristics personally, such as when he unconsciously imitates Gus' habit of laying out a rolled-up towel at the base of the toilet before vomiting in a later episode titled "Salud." Bryan Cranston identifies this strategy as a deliberate one on his and the writers' parts in the DVD audio commentary when he discusses how to perform for a particular scene:

> Something that you [Vince Gilligan] wrote earlier on, after the demise of Gus, was that Walt was somehow gaining some of his tendencies. And that's why I didn't want to move in this scene. I just wanted to sit there patiently while [Walt's lawyer Saul Goodman] is gesturing and figuring it out.[18]

Walt's calm and detached demeanor in this scene is markedly different from his usual nervous sputtering and resembles more the quiet calm of Gus, who rarely gesticulates, speaks, or even makes movements that are not precise and necessary. This is evident in the season 4 episode "Box Cutter" where Gus kills his own henchman Victor (played by Jeremiah Bitsui). Esposito performs the scene in a very exacting and precise manner, remaining speechless while Walt is gesticulating wildly and talking non-stop in defense of his own life. The imitation of a rival drug dealer like Gus functions as a sign that corruption is starting to take hold of Walt's psyche and that his core identity is eroding as he begins to embody a simulacrum of various personalities. In multiple instances, Walt copies rival drug dealers or individuals he has killed: in the season 3 episode "No Más" he starts cutting the crusts off his sandwich like Krazy-8 (played by Max Arciniega) does; in the season 5 episode "Gliding Over All" he warns another high-level dealer, Lydia Rodarte-Quayle (played by Laura Fraser), to "learn to take yes for an answer," a strikingly similar warning to the one Mike Ehrmantraut (played by Jonathan Banks), Gus Fring's right-hand man, gave Walt in "Thirty-Eight Snub" the previous season; and after killing Mike, he changes his preference for neat scotch to Mike's preference for scotch on the rocks in "Gliding Over All."

Cumulatively, these incidents of copying act as an indicator of how Walt's toxic environment is affecting his character.

Walt conceives of himself as immune to consequences, convinced that he can be involved in the drug trade without any negative effects to him or his family. Walt is essentially appropriating identities of dangerous individuals who he feels occupy a more masculine or authoritative role in society, and very much in contrast to Whitman' spiritual vision of individuality. The loss of self exhibited by Walt is very much a warning signal to the viewer on the risks involved with sacrificing ideals for monetary gain. While monetary gain is not in itself a corruptive factor that distorts Walt's love for chemistry, it is the accumulation of wealth well beyond his needs to alleviate medical debts (Walt eventually has to store his millions in a storage unit), and especially committing murder and manipulating others, that corrode Walt and pervert his love of science. Perhaps because Walt can quite easily rationalize everything as logic, including the human soul or sense of self, he is able to go down this dangerous path without seeing the consequences.

Walt is psychologically adrift and, as such, is beginning to lose his core self, in a sense echoing the "many, many deaths I'll sing" in the episode named after Whitman's poem, "Gliding O'er All."[19] Much like Heisenberg's wave function, the two Walters—the genial family man Walt and the ruthless drug kingpin Heisenberg—cannot co-exist, and as the Heisenberg persona comes more into force, the Walt of previous years disappears. The two halves cannot be observed at the same time. Robert S. Schaible, in the essay "Quantum Mechanics and 'Song of Myself,'" addresses Werner Heisenberg's wave function in connection with Whitman's mystical Self: "Whitman's Self stands to some postulated metaphysical reality in virtually the same fashion as the wave function stands to Heisenberg's pre physical reality, the *potentia*, or potential-for-being."[20] In this case rather than a spiritual self, as in Whitman's poem, Walt's dormant *potentia* is a corroded and decayed self, and once that aspect of Walt's identity comes into full effect, the ordinary self of Walt ceases to exist.

That Walt is losing his core self is evident in the season 4 episode "Crawl Space." The final scene of that episode depicts a harried and frantic Walt rushing home after being threatened by rival drug kingpin Gus in the desert. In fear of his life, Walt contacts lawyer and money launderer Saul Goodman (played by Bob Odenkirk), who in turn employs the services of a professional "disappearer" named Ed (played by Robert Forster) whose skill is in forging new identities, social security numbers, and associated documents. In essence, escaping with the disappearer would constitute a final and complete erasure of the Walter White identity, since he would have to eliminate any familial, professional, or personal contacts other than his immediate family. Walt flees to his home to gather the half a million dollars required to make himself and his family disappear, only to discover a large portion of his money is gone. We see Walt scared, rooting around in the crawl space for the money, and eventually crumpling into a fetal position in tears when he finds a large portion of it is missing (Skyler having given it to her boss Ted Beneke (played by Christopher Cousins) in order to bail him out of back taxes incurred by Ted after he attempted to deceive the Internal Revenue Service), fearing that he will not escape Gus. The soundtrack is that of a heartbeat, as if Walt is connected to a life support machine, figuratively in his death throes, signaling one of the "many deaths I'll sing."[21] Walt changes position and begins to cackle maniacally, and the camera angle shifts to a vantage point looking downward at him as the frame slowly zooms out. The soundtrack has shifted to white noise, the heart monitor flat lining, and consists of a receding shot of Walt surrounded by the black frame of the crawl space. The change in the camera's trajectory from the ground level looking upward to a bird's-eye view looking down on Walt, the change in the soundtrack to indistinct white noise, and Walt's laughing in the face of terror are all emblematic of the dissolution of Walt's old identity and the emergence of Heisenberg. The image evokes a grave, with the square space surrounding Walt resembling a coffin.

By this point in the series, Walt has been degraded to the extent that he is now too far into the Heisenberg persona. Walt has gone too far into a psychological abyss of violence and has given in so much to a lust for power that he has become a false identity, with Heisenberg lurking underneath the thin veneer of normality. That Walt would go to the extent of murder and the ruthless elimination of any rivals signifies a distinct moral collapse in the psyche of Walt. It is inevitable that the two halves of Walt/Heisenberg would eventually merge, blurring the lines between family man and drug kingpin. The viewer can extrapolate from this inevitable merging however justified, such callous acts of violence weigh down on an individual's moral self and corrodes their center of being. Doing so in the name of pure greed only accelerates Walt's eventual decline.

One of the visual indicators foreshadowing this inevitable decline is the painting in the doctor's office in the pilot episode: a Winslow Homer knock-off of a man in a sailboat looking back on his family on the shore, which reappears in the season 5 episode "Gliding Over All." This time, however, the painting is dingy and in the den of the Neo-Nazis that Walt is working with. Its initial appearance in the doctor's office, like the mirrored reflection that signifies the beginnings of the schism, appears here to signify Walt's complete isolation from his family. The appearance of the painting in "Gliding over All" echoes the line in Whitman's poem: "As a ship on the waters advancing / the voyage of the soul—not life alone."[22] Walt might have procured the necessary funds for his family, but Walt's later decision to work with Neo-Nazis—in effect bringing about the full collusion of capitalism with fascism—is a pollution of the soul that contravenes Whitman's promotion of *vox populi* and constitutes a step too far for Walt. For Whitman, democratic commitment is obtained, as Jason Frank states in his essay "Aesthetic Democracy: Walt Whitman and the Poetry of the People," "through the poetic depiction of the people as themselves a sublimely poetic, world-making power."[23] Freedom in Whitman's conceptual framework is about true aesthetic, rather than political, equality, and not about a self-interested notion to do as one pleases according to one's own needs. Now that the impetus for Walt's criminal career is negated by his desire to claim some sort of legacy in a selfish act of hubris, any claims of freedom and disenfranchisement have to be weighed against the violence of his actions and the parties involved in those actions—all without any self-justifying rationalizations.

CONCLUSION

Walt's view of freedom does not accord with Whitman's sense of the term but instead with attempting to gain control of life and direct his own destiny. Walt initially rejects chemotherapy as a method to manage his own fate and control his own death, which in his mind is correlated with ultimate freedom. In the season 3 episode "The Fly," Walt expresses anguish that even his terminal cancer has decided to thwart his control over his mortality by going into an unexpected remission. Not only can Walt not control his own death, but his life with his family and Skyler's reactions to his criminal lifestyle cannot be controlled. The facade of a happy family man forces Walt to subsume his Heisenberg persona and revert back to who he was in the first season. Reverting back to a banal, suburban existence leads to a sense of hubris in which he lets down his guard, convinced that no one can pose a threat to him anymore and that finally now he is in complete control of his fate, which leads to the events that spell his death in a hail of bullets and glory. Hubris and the base desire to enact revenge are what begin Walt's final journey and what end his quest for revenge in the final season of *Breaking Bad*. It becomes apparent that Walt's admiration for the individualism of Whitman is a gross distortion of its democratic ideals in order to support what is essentially a neoliberal project of serving only his own needs.

The multiple references to the poetry of Whitman add insight into how Walt appropriates psychologically convenient explanations for his behavior beyond what can be justified under the rubric of family. When Walt hears the poem "When I Heard the Learn'd Astronomer" he incorporates it into his rationalization for his non-traditional career pursuit as a chemist of illegal substances, identifying with the sense of freedom and autonomy Whitman professes in the poem. Yet by all accounts Walt was a fairly traditional and strict teacher, placing him more in the position of the stuffy lecturer in Whitman's poem than in that of the poet leaving the lecture hall to stare at the stars. Walt truly admires chemistry, and I would even say that he was not lying or distorting the truth when he told Gale that it is still magic, but it has been corroded by his pursuit of power. Much like Heisenberg's wave function, Walt occupies two simultaneous positions as both Walt and Heisenberg, existing as both quanta at once until he decides to occupy the Heisenberg role solely. Walt exists as both wave and particle because until a certain point in the series he could have reformed and truly atoned for his past misdeeds (while he does briefly abandon his career in the methamphetamine business, it was only under duress from Skyler, and even then he was tempted all too easily back into the business). In the end, Walt has to die many deaths, to paraphrase Whitman's poetry, because of the various identities residing in him. Walt's love of chemistry is now a regret for his past love and a realization that he has tainted his one true calling in life with a selfish pursuit of rapid capital growth and the base appeal of exponential wealth.

The duality of family man and drug kingpin is reflected in the alias Walt assigns his criminal persona: Heisenberg. Heisenberg is a reference to physicist Werner Heisenberg who theorized the Heisenberg Uncertainty Principle which proposes that the measurement of a subatomic particle's position or velocity lacks precision because the act of measuring one vector changes the other. Moreover, it is not until the moment of observation that a subatomic particle's reality coheres—the classic example being the photon's simultaneous existence as both a wave and a particle. The division between Walt/ Heisenberg operates in the same ambiguity, as in some instances when the difference between Walt—the beige-colored family man—and Heisenberg— the black-clothed drug kingpin with a porkpie hat—becomes blurred. Walt himself sometimes cannot distinguish between the two halves of his identity. As the series progresses, the two halves become absorbed into each other until they become one singular identity. A merging which is foreshadowed in the episode "The Cat's in the Bag" with Walt's classroom lecture on Chiral molecules:

> So, the term Chiral derives from the Greek word for hand. Now, the concept here being that just as your left hand and your right hand are mirror images of one another, right? Identical, yet opposite. Well, so too, organic compounds can exist as mirror images of one another, all the way down to the molecular level. But though they may look the same, they don't always behave the same.[24]

The schism between Walt and his repressed anger and the merging identity of violence and callousness are mirror reflections of each other. There is the capacity for nobility in Walt, but he allows himself to succumb to the machinations of greed and in the process the two halves merge into one singular identity. The Chirality alluded to in this episode of two mutually co-existing entities becomes more and more difficult to maintain for Walt, and he begins to unravel during the course of the series.

The themes of hubris, greed, and Walter White's naked ambition for total power and control resonate in the series through the intertextual references to the poetry of Walt Whitman, representing a gross distortion of the individualism expressed in *Leaves of Grass*. In this way, the viewer sees the moral message of the series as a warning as to how neoliberalism, which extols an individualism that is selfish and in opposition to the democratic individualism of Whitman, corrupts the self. Without any ethical, legal, or moral constraints, this entitled sense of individualism contributes to a society of greed and ruthless competition where anything and everything is employed in the pursuit of power and wealth. Walt embodies this corrosion of the self, using science to produce a dangerous and addictive substance, and in the process killing numerous rivals who would hinder his path toward violent retribution and wealth. The viewer also sees in Walt how one can rationalize any action, especially if they have been legitimately victimized by the same corrupt system. For a series airing at a time in the American public when the shift toward neoliberal economic principles is increasingly prevalent in politics with continued proposals for deregulation and the healthcare crisis, this is a potent illustration of its negative effects and disastrous consequences. Whitman's poetry, then, as it appears in the series, can also be interpreted as the moral conscience of the viewer, reminding them of how beneficial truly democratic principles would be for everyone.

NOTES

1. *Breaking Bad*, season 5, episode 8, "Gliding Over All," dir. Michelle MacLaren, aired September 2, 2012, originally released on AMC.

2. Gary Sloan, "Walt Whitman: When Science and Mysticism Collide," *Skeptical Inquirer* (2003): 51–54.

3. David Thomson, *Breaking Bad: The Official Book* (New York, NY: Sterling Publishing, 2015), 47.

4. Walt Whitman, *Leaves of Grass* (New York, NY: Bantam Classics, 1892/2004), 228.

5. *Breaking Bad*, season 3, episode 6, "Sunset," dir. John Shiban, aired April 25, 2010, originally released on AMC.

6. *Breaking Bad*, season 3, episode 13, "Full Measure," dir. Vince Gilligan, aired June 13, 2010, originally released on AMC.

7. Patrick Redding, "Whitman Unbound: Democracy in Poetic Form 1912–1913," *New Literary History* 41 (2010): 673.

8. *Breaking Bad*, season 2, episode 3, "Bit by a Dead Bee," dir. Terry McDonough, aired March 22, 2009, originally released on AMC.

9. Jason Mittell, *Complex TV: The Poetics of Contemporary Television Storytelling* (New York, NY: New York University Press, 2015), 162.

10. *Breaking Bad*, season 1, episode 3, "And the Bag's in the River," dir. Adam Bernstein, aired February 10, 2008, originally released on AMC.

11. Whitman, 43.

12. David S. Reynolds, *Walt Whitman* (Oxford: Oxford University Press, 2005), 79.

13. Joseph Beaver, *Walt Whitman: Poet of Science* (New York, NY: King's Crown Press, 1951), 131.

14. M. Jimmie Killingsworth, *Walt Whitman and the Earth: A Study in Ecopoetics* (Iowa City, IA: University of Iowa Press, 2005), 156.

15. Mark Noble, "Whitman's Atom and the Crisis of Materiality in Early Leaves of Grass," *American Literature* 81, no. 2 (2009): 256.

16. Whitman, 24.

17. Whitman, 43.

18. Vince Gilligan, *Breaking Bad: The Complete Series*, performed by Bryan Cranston, Aaron Paul, Anna Gunn, Dean Norris, Giancarlo Esposito, and Jonathan Banks (2008: Sony Home Entertainment, 2014), DVD.

19. Whitman, 232.

20. Robert M. Schaible, "Quantum Mechanics and 'Song of Myself': Getting a Grip on Reality," *Zygon* 38, no. 1 (2003): 25–48, 41.

21. Whitman, 232.

22. Ibid.

23. Jason Frank, "Aesthetic Democracy: Walt Whitman and the Poetry of the People," *The Review of Politics* 69, no. 3 (2007): 403.

24. *Breaking Bad*, season 1, episode 2, "Cat's in the Bag," dir. Adam Bernstein, aired on January 27, 2008, originally released on AMC.

BIBLIOGRAPHY

Beaver, Joseph. *Walt Whitman: Poet of Science*. New York, NY: King's Crown Press, 1951.

Breaking Bad. Created by Vince Gilligan. Aired from January 20, 2008–September 29, 2013. Originally released on AMC.

Frank, Jason. "Aesthetic Democracy: Walt Whitman and the Poetry of the People." *The Review of Politics* 69, no. 3 (2007): 402–430.

Killingsworth, M. Jimmie. *Walt Whitman and the Earth: A Study in Ecopoetics*. Iowa City, IA: University of Iowa Press, 2005.

Mittell, Jason. *Complex TV: The Poetics of Contemporary Television Storytelling*. New York, NY: New York University Press, 2015.

Noble, Mark. "Whitman's Atom and the Crisis of Materiality in Early *Leaves of Grass*." *American Literature* 81, no. 2 (2009): 253–279.

Redding, Patrick. "Whitman Unbound: Democracy in Poetic Form 1912-1913." *New Literary History* 41 (2010): 669–690.

Reynolds, David S. *Walt Whitman*. Oxford: Oxford University Press, 2005.

Schaible, Robert M. "Quantum Mechanics and 'Song of Myself': Getting a Grip on Reality." *Zygon* 38, no. 1 (2003): 25–48.

Sloan, Gary. "Walt Whitman: When Science and Mysticism Collide." *Skeptical Inquirer* (March/April 2003): 51–54.

Thomson, David. *Breaking Bad: The Official Book*. New York, NY: Sterling, 2015.

Whitman, Walt. *Leaves of Grass*. Bantam Classics, 1892/2004.

Chapter 4

Check Your Settings

Change to a Democratic Framework for Feminist Subtitles

Leigh Kellmann Kolb

Since drama has existed as a tool of storytelling and entertainment—from ancient Greek tragedies and medieval morality plays to novels and cable TV shows—these productions have served as moral guideposts, showing us who we are and who we ought to be. For women, the act of both consuming these narratives and living in a society that is reflected by and reflects these narratives has been complicated throughout history.

From the beginning, moral teachings of drama have been deeply embedded in notions of gender and gender roles within a society. None of these teachings or depictions have been favorable to women. In *Women & Power*, Mary Beard points out that our earliest teachings from drama involve demeaning women and relegating the feminine to the private. In Homer's *Odyssey* (~eighth century BCE), Telemachus chastises his mother, Penelope, and tells her that he has the power because he is a man. Beard says it "is a nice demonstration that right where written evidence for Western culture starts, women's voices are not being heard in the public sphere."[1] In *Darkness Now Visible: Patriarchy's Resurgence and Feminist Resistance*, Carol Gilligan and David A. J. Richards point out that the *Oresteia* (fifth century BCE), "the oldest trilogy in the canon of theater, celebrates the founding of Athenian democracy," and that ultimately, "The *Oresteia*—the story of Orestes—links the founding of democracy with the reinstatement of patriarchy."[2] Two thousand and five hundred years later, we still make that mistake—because, as Gilligan and Richards argue in their texts, "the opposite of patriarchy is not matriarchy as many would claim, but democracy which is founded not on hierarchy . . . but on equality."[3] In *Poetics* (fourth century BCE), Aristotle says of characters in drama, "Each kind of character may be effective, for both woman and slave may be effective [or good for dramatic purpose] even though one is perhaps inferior and the other generally base."[4]

Here we have the foundation of Western drama, which has absolutely shaped our understanding of our society and ourselves. Medieval morality plays uplift virtue and Christian teachings. But not all drama supports a patriarchal or misogynistic status quo. Shakespeare's dramas were infused with critical lessons about modern life, and his productions were written and performed for the masses—from peasants to royalty—which certainly created a template for film and television 400 years later. Of course, novels, short stories, poetry, songs—all forms of literary mass communications have served to both reflect and challenge the morality of their times.

Today, we still read the *Odyssey*, observe the monomyth pattern, and read and watch Shakespeare's plays. What drama teaches us—through whose lens, and whose stories—is still an essential piece of our cultural and social (and even political) understanding. While the advent of television in the mid-twentieth century meant that we increasingly consumed our drama at home, we still did so as an audience—people watched shows at the same time, and that experience ensured a kind of collective gaze absorption that shaped our perceptions and conversations.

American film and television is a hegemonic force. Yet our stories are clearly tied to the earliest Greek dramas and patriarchy's influence (sometimes challenged, too often reaffirmed) still dominates. Female audience members have always had to ask, even if their questions have not been heard and responded to: Is this for me? Is this about me? What does this tell me about myself? What does this tell me about the society in which I live? We know how crucial those questions have been when we trace the societal impact of television shows ranging from *Leave it to Beaver* to *The Mary Tyler Moore Show* and from *Julia* to *Roseanne*. TV has always shown us who we are supposed to be and who we are and reinforced our ideas about self and society.

By the twenty-first century, TV had increasingly been elevated as an art form, as premium cable stations were less beholden to advertising dollars and network standards, so they could delve deeper into stories that defined and challenged our times. These shows, which ushered in a new era of Prestige TV, were called "literary" and "Shakespearean," and indeed their narrative roots could be traced to the aforementioned theatrical dramas. And again, female viewers were in a position to navigate their roles as consumers of stories and participants in society, though with more of a voice and more of an opportunity to raise questions about representation in a public and substantial way.

"Difficult Men" ruled the screen in this latest Golden Age of television. The antihero reigned. One could take a compulsory look at the shows from this era and see a celebration of (mostly white) male criminals. However, nothing is ever that simple. Focusing on series like *Breaking Bad* and *Sons of Anarchy* helps us see that these TV dramas were challenging our idea of patriarchy and the masculine/feminine dichotomy that has so long shaped our cultural and sociopolitical realities.

In a 2013 article, critic Alyssa Rosenberg looked at the post-Prestige landscape of television, and how showrunners and executives (*Orange Is the New Black*'s Jenji Kohan and Showtime President David Nevins, respectively) used the term "Trojan Horse" to talk about pulling in audiences and keeping them. Kohan said, "You're not going to go into a network and sell a show on really fascinating tales of black women, and Latina women, and old women and criminals. But if you take this white girl, this sort of fish out of water, and you follow her in, you can then expand your world and tell all of those other stories."[5] Preceding these comments, it seemed clear that shows like *Breaking Bad* and *Sons of Anarchy* had done something similar—pulled us in with compelling antiheroes, and then revealed themselves to be morality dramas—elevating the feminist ethic of care and showing that the violence and individualism of patriarchy were not only not sustainable but were destructive as well. Since we too often see writers' rooms and stories that still adhere to Aristotle's ideas about characters, it can be useful to have white men be the Trojan Horse that delivers feminist messages. Culling these messages from the narratives, however, demands a deeper, more active viewing on the part of the audience.

When they aired, I wrote extensively about the feminism of these two shows. As we watched them (*Breaking Bad*: 2008–2013, *Sons of Anarchy*: 2008–2014), we were also in a great transition as a society. In 2008, these shows premiered. When we look back on 2008, we might see a transition to a more open, more multiracial, multiethnic, society even as we know that it was also the beginning of a simmering white, patriarchal backlash that exploded in 2016 and again in 2020. In 2008, a feminist, African American man was elected president of the United States. The Democratic primary frontrunners for president had been a woman and an African American man. Barack Obama was elected and built a diverse administration. It felt as if there was a tectonic shift beneath our feet.

Just as American society was in transition in 2008, so was television: while the antihero protagonists pulled audiences in, the shows unfolded to reveal not only complex female characters but also feminist themes of care, compassion, and empathy being the values that most characters embodied (male and female). The familiar, "heroic" masculine pulled us in, but the feminine was exposed as, if not the ideal, then a necessary correction to the violence of white masculinity.

By the early 2000s, but certainly by the late 2010s, there was a change in the ways that television was consumed. Prior to the VCR, television was appointment viewing: people were tied to the broadcast schedule. The VCR, then DVR, allowed people to pick when they watched a program and also allowed them to create their own archive of favorite shows. The rise of streaming services fundamentally changed how people experience TV: they could watch on their own schedule; revisit old programs; and most importantly, consume mass quantities of a program in a single viewing. At the same time, there was still something collective about the way television was consumed. Despite streaming and binging, there was still a sense that we watched and discussed television together. We watched these shows through a democratic framework; the sociopolitical context and viewing habits supported notions of progressive, collective inclusivity and an advancement of feminist ideals across platforms both fictional and real. The proliferation of streaming channels and networks gave space for more programming and with that, more feminist visions. Feminist viewers felt emboldened to read these series as feminist texts, or reread older series and mine them for feminist themes and values, and felt justified in doing so.

However, there was a backlash, and the lead up to the 2016 presidential election shifted our gaze away from the blossoming of a polyvocal and inclusive television universe to something that felt all too familiar: we were thrust back into a patriarchal framework. While the backlash was occurring politically and socially, *how* we watch television was also dramatically transformed. Instead of TV being a communal experience (so much so that research has shown that stock markets dip after a beloved series ends), it was more individualized.[6] Independent streaming at one's own pace has replaced the communal experience of watching a show at the same time as millions of other people. What had been democratic and communal consumption shifted back to patriarchal/individualized consumption. What these shows meant, which themes rose to the surface, and what people were getting from them ebbed and flowed with the cultural and political shifts of the late 2010s and early 2020s. Rewatching *Breaking Bad* and *Sons of Anarchy* in this framework feels markedly different—when there was hope, it was more possible to read against the patriarchy and misogyny of the show and main characters; as American culture and politics took a darker turn, it became more difficult to see the feminist interpretation. One felt that as patriarchy and misogyny became culturally and politically ascendant, then that would also be the dominant themes and interpretations of these television shows. The voices of women that had surfaced had been silenced again.

The doubling-down of the patriarchal framework coupled with audience fragmentation has resulted in TV being less and less of a site of moral learning and conversation. Gilligan and Richards argue that one of the functions of patriarchy is that it disrupts relationships. In a democratic framework, these shows were consumed in a more communal space, and their roles as moral artifacts were heightened because the audience was watching, learning, and analyzing together. The political and technological landscape has severed those relationships in the years after the series finales.

In *Why Does Patriarchy Persist?* Carol Gilligan and Naomi Snider consider why patriarchy continues to grip us, even as broad strides are made to move more toward a democratic social order. In providing a context for the definition of patriarchy (beyond a society or household ruled by a father), they say:

> We define patriarchy as a culture based on a gender binary and hierarchy, a framework or lens that:
>
> 1. Leads us to see human capacities as either "masculine" or "feminine" and to privilege the masculine.
> 2. Elevates some men over other men and all men over women.
> 3. Forces a split between the self and relationships so that in effect men have selves, whereas women are selfless, and women have relationships, which surreptitiously serve men's needs.[7]

Carol Gilligan, whose 1982 *In a Different Voice* is a landmark text in understanding justice and morality in gendered ways, is still a leading feminist voice in ethics and psychology. She has collaborated with David Richards (a law professor and her colleague at New York University), and delved deeply into the history and prominence of patriarchy in our society, and how it is a threat to democracy. *The Deepening Darkness: Patriarchy, Resistance, and Democracy's Future* (2008) and *Darkness Now Visible: Patriarchy's Resurgence and Feminist Resistance* (2018) are bookends to a decade of transition—progress and backlash—as it pertains to feminism, democracy, and the threat of patriarchy. In an interview, Gilligan defines the feminist ethic of care as

> an ethic of resistance to the injustices inherent in patriarchy (the association of care and caring with women rather than with humans, the feminization of care work, the rendering of care as subsidiary to justice—a matter of special obligations or interpersonal relationships). A feminist ethic of care guides the historic struggle to free democracy from patriarchy; it is the ethic of a democratic society, it transcends the gender binaries and hierarchies that structure patriarchal institutions and cultures. An ethics of care is key to human survival and also to the realization of a global society.[8]

Looking closely at the first and final episodes of *Breaking Bad* and *Sons of Anarchy* reinforces the argument that these shows had clear messages about masculinity, patriarchy, and the feminist ethic of care, as well as who we were and are as a society. These hallmarks of Prestige TV are moral beacons and relics of their time. Through a democratic framework, their messages were clear. As patriarchy has persisted, the morality becomes cloudier.

BREAKING BAD

In the first episode of *Breaking Bad* we meet Walter White (played by Bryan Cranston), who appears to be a vulnerable, pitiful man in crisis: he's scrambling around the desert in his underwear, and leaves an emotional, love-soaked message to his wife, son, and unborn child. Then, he snaps into action, a look of conviction flashes over him, and he confidently wields a gun and points it at the oncoming sirens. The cold, steely look he gives after he hangs up is important foreshadowing. As the show goes back in time, Walt is waking up on his 50th birthday; he exercises on a cheap stepper while looking at a plaque that recognized his Nobel Prize-adjacent research in a room that is being converted to a baby's room. His wife, Skyler, serves him veggie bacon. His son, Walt Jr. (played by RJ Mitte), who is disabled, struggles to get out of the car in the high school parking lot, and Walt doesn't pause to help. He summons some passion in front of the high school chemistry class he teaches, but the students are apathetic. He has to work at a car wash after school to make ends meet. At his surprise birthday party, he's contrasted with his brother-in-law Hank, a DEA agent who is loud and comfortably wields a gun, which makes Walt uncomfortable. Skyler (played by Anna Gunn) bothers him, and his mild birthday handjob does nothing. Then, he is diagnosed with lung cancer.

We get it, right? He's weak and emasculated at every turn. It's only after hearing he has a fatal illness that he claims power: beating up a bully, cursing out his carwash boss, requesting a ride-a-long with Hank and negotiating a new drug business, picking up and pointing a gun, and having domineering sex with his wife. Walt has broken bad and he is now *a man*. We understand this narrative because it's deeply embedded in our culture. The instinct is to have deep pity for this man, whose cancer diagnosis is the final straw to all of the other injustices he has to face (a strong wife, children who need him, a career with little status or compensation). Our reactions to Walt echoes reactions to the widening fractures in patriarchal systems—our level of sympathy with him likely accompanied our own feelings about what it means to be a man in America, and how sad it must feel to not be one.

In *Darkness Now Visible*, Gilligan and Richards refer to Virginia Woolf's *Three Guineas*, which she wrote in 1938 as fascism took hold in Europe. They point out that Woolf's central thesis is that "The violence of fascism was rooted in humiliated manhood."[9] This is evident on the national and international stage, of course, but is also evident in *Breaking Bad*. The premise of the show is often touted as a high school teacher who starts selling meth to support his family. While the financial need is a reality (itself a critique on American healthcare costs), the first episode presents a much deeper tension rooted in "humiliated manhood," which resulted in violence, greed, and empire-building.

But that look he gives after hanging up from his emotional voicemail is distinct. Walt is often depicted as delving further and further into greed and crime—as if we are also to pity his descent. However, if we look closely, it was always there. Is he "breaking bad," or is he just *bad*? The final episode reveals what we know to be true if we look hard enough. He didn't break. He tells Skyler, "All the things that I did," and she interrupts him: "If I have to hear one more time that you did this for the family" He stops her. "I did it for me. I liked it. I was alive."[10] Even at the end, when Walt is tying up all of the loose ends, and caring as best he knows how—leaving millions for his children, and a get-out-of-jail-free card for Skyler—he is still using fear and violence to get there.

When watching the series in real time, it was fairly clear that the true hero, the one who embodied a kind of new anti-patriarchal manhood, who consistently displayed a feminist ethic of care, was Jesse Pinkman (played by Aaron Paul). In *Philosophy and Breaking Bad*, I wrote extensively about how Jesse embodies what feminist manhood can be, and how the show consistently uplifted him as the most compassionate and sympathetic character.[11] Feminist viewers could recognize Jesse as a foil to Walt's toxic masculinity. His ultimate survival—literally and figuratively breaking free from not only Walt but also white supremacists—indicates that we are to see his way of being as the way forward for men. Looking beneath the surface (which good fiction demands of us), we see that his compassion, his vulnerability, his focus on relationships over self, and his capacity for emotional expression are what will drive men into the future. It seems no accident that the defeated villains in that final episode, besides megalomaniac Walt, are white supremacists, yet another strain of toxic masculinity that we felt for a time was beginning to be defeated.

However, the world was changing between 2008 and 2013. When Todd arrived on the scene in the final season, there was a growing shift in perception from many audience members. *New Yorker* critic Emily Nussbaum wrote about the "bad fans" of the series, and followed up with an article titled "The Great Divide," which delves into the history of the "bad fan" through a historical retelling of Archie Bunker's appeal in *All in the Family*. She says:

> This sort of audience divide, not between those who love a show and those who hate it but between those who love it in very different ways, has become

a familiar schism in the past fifteen years, during the rise of—oh, God, that phrase again—Golden Age television. This is particularly true of the much lauded stream of cable "dark dramas," whose protagonists shimmer between the repulsive and the magnetic. As anyone who has ever read the comments on a recap can tell you, there has always been a less ambivalent way of regarding an antihero: as a hero. . . . More recently, a subset of viewers cheered for Walter White on "Breaking Bad," growling threats at anyone who nagged him to stop selling meth. In a blog post about that brilliant series, I labelled these viewers "bad fans," and the responses I got made me feel as if I'd poured a bucket of oil onto a flame war from the parapets of my snobby critical castle.[12]

The "bad fans" increasingly aligned themselves with Walt and saw him as a hero (going so far as having a #TeamWalt hashtag). The lionization of Walt brought with it the villainization of Skyler .

As the hatred for Skyler (and Gunn herself) reached a fever pitch online, Gunn broke the fourth wall and penned an op-ed in the *New York Times* titled "I Have a Character Issue," published as the series was coming to an end. She says:

My character, to judge from the popularity of Web sites and Facebook pages devoted to hating her, has become a flashpoint for many people's feelings about strong, nonsubmissive, ill-treated women. As the hatred of Skyler blurred into loathing for me as a person, I saw glimpses of an anger that, at first, simply bewildered me.[13]

She acknowledges how Walt being a sympathetic character is understandable and a credit to the excellent writing, also saying how showrunner Vince Gilligan was purposeful in writing Skyler as a strong and three-dimensional woman. She ends by saying:

But I finally realized that most people's hatred of Skyler had little to do with me and a lot to do with their own perception of women and wives. Because Skyler didn't conform to a comfortable ideal of the archetypical female, she had become a kind of Rorschach test for society, a measure of our attitudes toward gender . . . I'm glad that this discussion has happened, that it has taken place in public and that it has illuminated some of the dark and murky corners that we often ignore or pretend aren't still there in our everyday lives.[14]

At the time, it seemed almost radical that there was a need for her to write this in a public forum. Now, the most radical part of the story is that we still thought these sentiments were relegated to "dark and murky corners."

For those of us feminist viewers and critics who saw a deeper potential of *Breaking Bad* to teach moral lessons about the ultimate downfalls of toxic masculinity, these reactions to Skyler were horrifying but not completely surprising. How we see these characters and storylines is indeed a Rorschach test for audiences. Certainly everyone knows Walt is not a hero, we assume. And yet—the "bad fans" kept getting louder in lockstep with the backlash in society against an increasingly feminist-friendly government and media. Life reflects art, and life also responds to art based on social changes.

When we revisit the series, the idealization of Jesse is perhaps harder to see, because we have been presented with an era in which Jesses do not win. That version of manhood has not been presented as a good alternative, since we were thrust back into a patriarchal framework of understanding. Skyler's beleaguered role as a woman who should stay out of Walt's way still feels achingly familiar, however.

Prestige TV is "prestigious" because, in large part, it's so well-written. Like the difference between literary and commercial fiction (which of course is a contentious debate in itself), "literary" TV demands more of us—we are asked to analyze and think deeply and critically about what we are seeing. It was easy to feel as if these "bad fans" were watching an entirely different show. However, when we think about a show as a moral artifact, and the question about what framework we are approaching it from, the stark contrast becomes clearer. From a democratic framework, it was natural to see Walt as an antihero and understand that he was showing us the worst of patriarchy. For viewers who did analyze from that perspective, Walt was not a villain.

The fever pitch of the Walt fandom increased as the backlash to an increasingly anti-patriarchal society took hold. The framework from which we view shapes the power of the moral message of the text. Rewatching *Breaking Bad* from a feminist perspective in 2020 feels like revisiting a time when we felt much more sure about the role of toxic masculinity in our society. From a democratic framework, *Breaking Bad* exists and succeeds as a feminist text. Watching from a patriarchal framework, the morality is grayer; we perhaps focus more on the unrepairable damage Walt has done instead of Jesse's triumph. We see ourselves in a society full of "bad fans" instead of thoughtful ones.

SONS OF ANARCHY

In the first episode of *Sons of Anarchy* we meet Jax (played by Charlie Hunnam), the protagonist of the series and the "Hamlet" role of the show's "Hamlet on Harleys" nickname. Jax looks lovingly at a children's book in a gas station and buys condoms, engaging in friendly conversation with the young female clerk. In the first episode, we see Jax in contrast to Clay (played by Ron Perlman)—the club's patriarch—especially, and also some of the toxic masculine culture of the club. He's visibly disturbed by the death of innocent immigrants (a woman and child); he doesn't react to homophobic jokes; he encourages Opie to choose his family; he hesitates to shoot an enemy; he cries when he sees his newborn son.[15]

While *Breaking Bad*'s moral lessons about toxic masculinity were tied to Walt as an individual, *Sons of Anarchy* showed Jax attempting to embody the feminine qualities of compassion and inclusiveness, but he was too intertwined with the patriarchal structure of the Sons of Anarchy. Walt ran headfirst into patriarchy. Jax tried to escape. Neither survived.

In *Sons of Anarchy*, women who attempt to navigate the patriarchal world by playing its own game are embodied in Gemma (played by Katey Sagal), Jax's mother. Instead of embodying the feminist ethic of care that we see Jax and Tara (played by Maggie Siff) display in the first episode, Gemma cares about power and family—and keeping that structure by any means necessary.

Sons of Anarchy drew lines between the feminist ethic of care and the masculine ideals of justice and power. These lines are not drawn between women and men, which makes for compelling storytelling—and perhaps even more effective presentation of moral lessons. The villains—both Clay and Gemma—are interested in power and upholding and codifying patriarchal systems. Clay also upholds the white supremacy of the long-standing segregation of the motorcycle clubs. Their allegiance to patriarchal systems and justice over care makes them destructive villains (even though they are complex and at times sympathetic characters, especially Gemma).

Jax attempts to upend this system, but he cannot fully disentangle himself from the chains of patriarchy, so he sacrifices himself for the sake of the club and his sons, whom he does not want to know or live in "this life of chaos." However, the only way forward that Jax can understand or move toward is to lean heavily into justice in the hopes that care can lead the way after he is gone. Gemma (whom the district attorney refers to as "the matriarch," which Gilligan and Richards remind us is not the opposite of patriarchy) has killed Tara, who pushed too hard for the democratic ideals of care (her role as a doctor and a healer was established from the first episode). Jax kills Gemma when he learns the truth and spends his final days establishing an order of things that he believes will allow the club to move away from the white patriarchal "chaos" of the past into a new era.

Jax oversees the installation of an African American member of the club, their first after a history of brutal segregation. Abel (Jax and Wendy's son) and Thomas (Jax and Tara's son) are left in the care of Wendy (played by Drea de Matteo) and Nero (played by Jimmy Smits), who have proven themselves as caring and compassionate parental figures. Jax's father, J. T. Teller, hoped Jax could totally reform the club; Jax didn't want his sons to be saddled with the same impossibility.

In the first shot of the series, the audience is introduced to Jax. He is riding his motorcycle and looks to be at peace and free. Two crows munch on trash on the road. In the final scene of the series, Jax—leading a long line of police—dies by suicide by driving into a tractor-trailer, arms outstretched to his side in a Christ-like gesture. Two crows are on the road again; this time, there's a piece of wine-soaked bread, and Jax's blood slowly spreads toward the feast. The sacrifice, the body, the blood; the "communion" referenced in the final shot connects us not only to the morality play inherent in the show but also the fact that we as an audience were experiencing it together—it was a communal experience. Even if we were not watching together, the idea of Jax making a Christ-like sacrifice of himself in front of the viewer, for the viewer, suggests both communion and community. The viewer has been with Jax on his first and last ride.

In *Sons of Anarchy and Philosophy* and a follow-up at andphilosophy.com, I wrote about Gilligan's research and assertions about traditionally "feminine" approaches to care (connectedness and care are uplifted over individualism and justice).[16] In *Sons of Anarchy*, Wendy and Nero—who exemplify this care ethic—survive at the end and prioritize parenting children far away from Charming. They want to raise their sons away from individualistic, vengeful patriarchy. They are both also recovering addicts, and this recovery and renewal point to a better way of living.

Keeping with the moral structure of many Shakespearean tragedies, women must die so men will learn. Jax is ultimately a tragic hero because he realizes that care, not justice, will heal and raise his children. But the tragedy of masculine justice and violent revenge results in Tara's gruesome death by Gemma's hand, and Gemma's death at Jax's hand. He participates in, and knows he is too far gone to be redeemed from, the toxicity of patriarchal violence.

"DIFFICULT MEN" AND THE
PERSISTENCE OF PATRIARCHY

If this all sounds familiar—not just Shakespearean but also biblical—of course it does. These tropes permeate human history and serve as parables about us in our own times. In *Darkness Now Visible*, Gilligan and Richards point out that in Shakespeare's four great tragedies (all bearing men's names as their titles—*Othello*, *King Lear*, *Hamlet*, *Macbeth*), the protagonists are

> distinguished by their sensitivity, their humanity, by being the noblest, the most loyal, the most sensitive and poetic, the most generous, become caught in the grip of a manhood that will lead to their destruction. Men who become caught

in the demands of patriarchy . . . All are chewed up in the struggle, which yields some of Shakespeare's most emotionally taught and evocative poetry.[17]

Shakespeare also was writing at a time of great transition in England. Gilligan and Richards say:

> Thus it makes sense that at times of transition, such as our own, when the cultural framework is shifting and becoming more democratic or less rigidly patriarchal, the frailties of manhood would surface. Shaming would be in the air—heightening the potential for violence, especially among white men, and also the awareness of the price men have paid for what is now recognized as toxic masculinity.[18]

It was powerful and possible for the audience to watch these shows and see clearly their moral lessons that persuaded the viewer to look at patriarchy and toxic masculinity as violent, destructive paths for individuals and institutions. Through a democratic lens, that message is clear. While "bad fans" existed when they aired, would it be possible to see them as similar moral artifacts now? Patriarchy has persisted, and it is difficult to not see the world through that lens since the 2016 election. In addition, we are watching differently—instead of the communal experience of watching "together," we are stream-ing independently, bingeing, watching erratically and alone. In the article "5 Ways Streaming Changed Television Forever in the Last Decade," Toni Fitzgerald describes binging and niche content as two of the top changes.[19] The space for television to be a beacon of moral learning is and will continue to be fractured by fragmented viewership.

Also noteworthy on re-watch is the fact that unequivocal villains in both *Breaking Bad* and *Sons of Anarchy* were white supremacists. While our heroes (antiheroes) were villainous and complicated, written so well that sympathy was often inevitable, there seemed to be a collective understanding that white supremacists were absolutely villains. How quaint, we think now, that it was not so long ago we felt comfortable in a democratic framework assuming such collective understanding of villainy.

Audiences cannot expect to derive moral messages from TV by seeing the medium as a form of passive entertainment. Being able to consider the moral-ity of drama—whether Shakespeare or Prestige TV—relies upon critical thinking and analysis skills. The lack of this ability threatens the audience's ability to actually understand the messages presented in drama.

For example, Ron Perlman (the actor who played Clay in *Sons of Anarchy*) is a vocal progressive on Twitter, constantly antagonizing conservative ideas and politicians. In a stunning display of audience ignorance in 2020, an angered U.S. Representative tweeted back at him, "This racial justice warrior had no problem in Hollywood portraying the White Supremacist leader of a motorcycle gang. #SOA."[20] What ensued was a ludicrous back-and-forth that included a U.S. Senator challenging Perlman to fight another U.S. Representative. It was a remarkable display of not only media illiteracy, but toxic masculinity. We can turn to Gilligan and Richards for an explanation, as they analyzed the recent resurgence of patriarchy: "Once again, only patriarchy can account for this darkening of ethical and political intelligence."[21]

In *Darkness Now Visible*, Gilligan and Richards spend a chapter delving into the classic American novels *The Scarlet Letter* by Nathaniel Hawthorne (1850) and *Moby Dick* by Herman Melville (1851). They posit that the novels are prophetic, and truly show "the toll patriarchy takes on American manhood."[22] They say, "It counters the assumption that in privileging men and giving them power, patriarchy is in men's interest. Instead, we are shown how it destroys them."[23] *Breaking Bad* and *Sons of Anarchy* showed the same.

In the series finale of both shows, the protagonists admitted that they could not change. Walt's admission to Skyler that he did everything he did *because he liked it*, and Jax's admission that he cannot change, that he's "not a good man," suggested they were too far gone to be redeemed. Watching in real time, the endings left hope that Jesse was victorious, and Wendy and Nero's compassion would raise a new generation.

However, when we revisit the shows years later through a patriarchal lens, were Walt and Jax instead presenting a hopeless future of American patriarchy?

In "How aristocrats ate prestige TV" (2019), Aaron Bady discusses how the shift in "prestige TV" in recent years has echoed the shift in political power. He writes of dramas like *Breaking Bad*: "Auteur-driven and obsessed with crumbling masculinity and violence and America, these shows can retroactively blend together into one continuous thing, one feel, one attitude."[24] "Put differently," he says, "capitalized American History haunted them with the conviction that they were living at the end of American men, at the point at which it was no longer possible to be and live the way you had always thought it was your birthright to be and live, and that winning, inexplicably, had turned out to be losing."[25]

For feminist viewers between 2008 and 2013, this message seemed to clearly bubble right beneath the surface of these TV shows. As a feminist female viewer, I felt exhilarated at the prospect of both being comfortably in the "boys club" of fans of these shows while also seeing how they conveyed a feminist message that felt in line with the changes and movements in society. It felt like I was not alone in seeing it all through a democratic framework. However, for us to meaningfully glean morality from TV and live differently, there must be some social and collective understanding of heroism and villainy, which was readjusted when we entered into a new era of reinforced patriarchal framework and, at the same time, more individualistic TV viewing habits.

Bady writes that "the 'him' that Walter couldn't imagine losing was the particular self-image that all of those shows endlessly reiterated, the prospect of (white) power and (masculine) self-sufficiency, of individual greatness, independence, and American empire-building."[26] He points out that the shows of this era were ultimately about consequences and that the post-Prestige landscape is riddled with people in power who face no consequences, thus the dearth of the same kind of drama. His question: "How do you make drama in a world without consequences or history?" resonates when we think about how differently audiences might read *Breaking Bad* and *Sons of Anarchy* outside of a democratic framework.

FOCUSING THROUGH A DEMOCRATIC LENS

The morality that audiences understand from a TV show can be a kind of Rorschach test, as Anna Gunn suggested in her *New York Times* column. What we see about ourselves, others, and our society drastically changes depending on the framework from which we are viewing. Fragmentation and patriarchy (itself a kind of fragmentation) threaten the ability for us to meaningfully view TV shows as moral artifacts. What happens when the Trojan Horse empties to an empty castle?

In the final season of *Breaking Bad*, one of the final episodes (season 5 episode 14) was titled "Ozymandias." The title refers to Percy Bysshe Shelley's 1818 poem "Ozymandias." Ozymandias was the Greek name for the Egyptian pharaoh Ramesses II. The poem (which Bryan Cranston read in promos for the episode) describes a destroyed monument and wasteland that used to be an empire. The meaning is clear: empires fall, monuments crumble, rule of kings is not sustainable. These were not hidden messages about Walter White. His was a masculine heroism that was destined to fall—after destroying so many in his path (including, of course, the alternative masculinity embodied by Gale, who loved another American proponent of alternative masculinity, Walt Whitman). A viewer could skip over all of this, opting for passive entertainment instead of challenging themselves with critical analysis. But then all meaning and morality is lost. One could argue, of course, that this choice to consume passively is what pulled us back into the patriarchal framework we had been working to move past.

So also did *Sons of Anarchy* ideally demand more of its audience; showrunner Kurt Sutter was heavily influenced by literary tradition, and the show's Shakespearean parallels do not end with the Hamlet-esque storyline. Shakespeare's plays were commercial hits for the masses. There was bawdiness, violence, and humor, but there was also deep cultural commentary (and criticism) about power, gender, and indeed, the tragedy of what we now know as toxic masculinity. *Sons of Anarchy* appealed to many different types of viewers, and it felt incredibly hopeful to be a feminist fan, because these TV shows brought together a collective cultural experience. Nussbaum says:

> The best series rattle us and wake us up; the worst are numbing agents. Sometimes, a divided audience is a result of mixed messages, an incoherent text; sometimes, it's a sign of a bold experiment that we are still learning how to watch. But there's a lot to be said for a show that is potent without being perfect, or maybe simply perfect for its moment: storytelling that alters the audience by demanding that viewers do more than just watch.[27]

But we must do more than just watch.

In *Darkness Now Visible*, Gilligan and Richards say, "The displacement of a democratic by a patriarchal framework in the 2016 election has not only been profoundly disorienting and destabilizing. The shift in frame has contributed to the breakdown of public discourse because we literally cannot agree on what we are seeing."[28] True debate relies on some semblance of agreement of truth; there is no desire for unquestioned agreement, for only one way of seeing, particularly in a democratic framework. For us to individually and collectively engage with TV as a moral agent in society, there needs to be some common vision. And that feels increasingly difficult. TV then can be individually transformative, but less so for the collective, democratic whole.

The fragmentation of TV audiences is illustrative of the fragmentation of our sense of a shared truth or reality about our society and our place in it. The struggle to arrive at a shared truth—or shared morality—in a society is nothing new, as early drama reminds us. Upholding or challenging patriarchal ideals has often been central to both the storytelling and the audience's understanding. The difference now is that the dissonant volume of the surround-sound system is louder than ever. Our ability to share a sense of shared morality through TV has eroded as the channels, platforms, and streaming options multiply. There is much more art to consume, but we are not consuming it together.

The power of watching shows like *Breaking Bad* and *Sons of Anarchy* through a feminist lens relied on being able to say, "Let's look at this closer. Let's analyze and make meaning together." That kind of analysis relies on collective, democratic viewership—and some common agreement on what makes a villain, for example. Prestige TV existed in a moment when TV was both increasingly literary, and arguably increasingly feminist. The sociopolitical backlash that came next was accompanied by dramatically different viewing habits—habits that can intensify the patriarchal framework.

Gilligan and Richards say in regard to morality, that "patriarchy both undermines democracy and subverts moral character."[29] Although there is currently no dearth of feminist TV shows that uplift an ethic of care or push back against patriarchal ideals, the collective gaze has faded. We may individually find truth and meaning in TV, but if we are doing so in a fragmented way, how then can TV be a transformative medium on a societal level? Hegemony persists if morality is independent, and not collective. The patriarchal lens distorts the possibilities.

If we can continue to check our settings and search for meaning, individualized morality can deepen and spread. With greater widespread media literacy and analytical skills, generations of viewers can have some level of agreement upon what they are seeing together, which can ultimately lead to a shared, more democratic view of humanity.

NOTES

1. Mary Beard, *Women & Power: A Manifesto* (New York, NY: Liveright Publishing Corporation, 2018), 4.

2. Carol Gilligan and David A.J. Richards, *Darkness Now Visible: Patriarchy's Resurgence and Feminist Resistance* (Cambridge: Cambridge University Press, 2018), 10–11.

3. Ibid., 12.

4. Aristotle, *Poetics*, trans. Kenneth A. Telford (Chicago, IL: Henry Regnery Company, 1961), 27.

5. Alyssa Rosenberg, "'Ray Donovan,' 'Orange Is the New Black,' and the Rise of Trojan Horse Television," *ThinkProgress*, September 3, 2013, https://archive.thinkprogress.org/ray-donovan-orange-is-the-new-black-and-the-rise-of-tro-jan-horse-television-174365cf40a4/.

6. Tom Jacobs, "Hit TV Show Ends; Stock Market Goes Down," Pacific Standard, February 20, 2015, https://psmag.com/tag/stock-market.

7. Carol Gilligan and Naomi Snider, *Why Does Patriarchy Persist?* (Cambridge: Polity Press, 2018), 6.

8. "Carol Gilligan: Interview," Care Ethicists Network, *Ethics of Care*, June 21, 2011, https://ethicsofcare.org/carol-gilligan/.

9. Gilligan and Richards, 13.

10. *Breaking Bad*, season 5, episode 16, "Felina," dir. Vince Gilligan, aired on September 29, 2013, originally released on AMC.

11. Leigh Kolb, "The Crumbling Patriarchy and Triumphant Feminist Ethic of Care in *Breaking Bad*," in *Philosophy and Breaking Bad*, ed. Kevin S. Decker, David R. Koepsel, and Robert Arp (Cham (Switzerland): Springer International Publishing, 2017), 109–121.

12. Emily Nussbaum, "Fandom's Great Divide," *The New Yorker*, March 31, 2014, https://www.newyorker.com/magazine/2014/04/07/the-great-divide-emily-nussbaum.

13. Anna Gunn, "I Have a Character Issue," *The New York Times*, August 24, 2013, https://www.nytimes.com/2013/08/24/opinion/i-have-a-character-issue.html.

14. Ibid.

15. *Sons of Anarchy*, season 1, episode 1, "Pilot," dir. Allen Coulter and Michael Dinner, aired on September 3, 2008, originally released on FX.

16. Leigh Kolb, "Sons of Anarchy and Philosophy: Female Violence, Feminist Care," *AndPhilosophy.com*, December 17, 2014, https://andphilosophy.com/2014/12/16/sons-of-anarchy-and-philosophy-3/.

17. Gilligan and Richards, 76.

18. Ibid., 75.

19. Toni Fitzgerald, "5 Ways Streaming Changed Television Forever in the Last Decade," *Forbes*, December 24, 2019, https://www.forbes.com/sites/tonifitzgerald/2019/12/24/5-ways-streaming-changed-television-forever-in-the-last-decade/.

20. Aris Folley, "Ron Perlman, Matt Gaetz Get into Back-and-Forth on Twitter," *The Hill*, June 15, 2020, https://thehill.com/blogs/in-the-know/in-the-know/502692-ron-perlman-matt-gaetz-get-into-back-and-forth-on-twitter.

21. Gilligan and Richards, 48.

22. Ibid., 95.

23. Ibid., 96.

24. Aaron Bady, "How Aristocrats Ate Prestige TV," *The Week*, October 29, 2019, https://theweek.com/articles/874740/how-aristocrats-ate-prestige-tv.

25. Ibid.

26. Ibid.

27. Nussbaum, 2014.

28. Gilligan and Richards, 6.

29. Ibid.

BIBLIOGRAPHY

Aristotle. *Poetics*. Translated by Kenneth A. Telford. Chicago: Henry Regnery Company, 1961.

Bady, Aaron. "How Aristocrats Ate Prestige TV." *The Week*, October 29, 2019. https://theweek.com/articles/874740/how-aristocrats-ate-prestige-tv.

Beard, Mary. *Women & Power: A Manifesto*. New York, NY: Liveright Publishing Corporation, 2018.

Breaking Bad. Created by Vince Gilligan. Aired from January 20, 2008–September 29, 2013. Originally released on AMC.

"Carol Gilligan: Interview." Ethics of Care, July 21, 2011. https://ethicsofcare.org/carol-gilligan/.

Fitzgerald, Toni. "5 Ways Streaming Changed Television Forever in the Last Decade." *Forbes,* December 24, 2019. https://www.forbes.com/sites/tonifitzgerald /2019/12/24/5-ways-streaming-changed-television-forever-in-the-last-decade/.

Folley, Aris. "Ron Perlman, Matt Gaetz Get into Back-and-Forth on Twitter." *The Hill*, June 15, 2020. https://thehill.com/blogs/in-the-know/in-the-know/502692-ron -perlman-matt-gaetz-get-into-back-and-forth-on-twitter.

Gilligan, Carol, and David A.J. Richards. *Darkness Now Visible: Patriarchy's Resurgence and Feminist Resistance.* Cambridge: Cambridge University Press, 2018.

Gilligan, Carol, and David A.J. Richards. *The Deepening Darkness: Patriarchy, Resistance, & Democracy's Future.* Cambridge: Cambridge University Press, 2009.

Gilligan, Carol, and Naomi Snider. *Why Does Patriarchy Persist?* Cambridge: Polity Press, 2018.

Gunn, Anna. "I Have a Character Issue." *The New York Times*, August 24, 2013. https://www.nytimes.com/2013/08/24/opinion/i-have-a-character-issue.html.

Jacobs, Tom. "Hit TV Show Ends; Stock Market Goes Down." Pacific Standard, February 20, 2015. https://psmag.com/tag/stock-market.

Kolb, Leigh. "Mothers of Anarchy: Power, Control, and Care in the Feminine Sphere." In *Sons of Anarchy and Philosophy: Brains before Bullets*, edited by William Irwin, George A. Dunn, and Jason T. Eberl. West Sussex: Wiley Blackwell, 2013.

Kolb, Leigh. "Sons of Anarchy and Philosophy: Female Violence, Feminist Care." The Blackwell Philosophy and Pop Culture Series, December 17, 2014. https:// andphilosophy.com/2014/12/16/sons-of-anarchy-and-philosophy-3/.

Kolb, Leigh. "The Crumbling Patriarchy and Triumphant Feminist Ethic of Care in *Breaking Bad.*" In *Philosophy and Breaking Bad*, edited by Kevin S. Decker, David R. Koepsel, and Robert Arp. Cham (Switzerland): Springer International Publishing, 2017.

Nussbaum, Emily. "Fandom's Great Divide." *The New Yorker*, March 31, 2014. https:// www.newyorker.com/magazine/2014/04/07/the-great-divide-emily-nussbaum.

Rosenberg, Alyssa. "'Ray Donovan,' 'Orange Is the New Black,' and the Rise of Trojan Horse Television." ThinkProgress, September 3, 2013. https://archive .thinkprogress.org/ray-donovan-orange-is-the-new-black-and-the-rise-of-trojan -horse-television-174365cf40a4/.

Sons of Anarchy. Created by Kurt Sutter. Aired from September 3, 2008–December 9, 2014. Originally released on FX.

Chapter 5

"The Lord of War and Thunder"

The Morality of Nemesis and Retributive Justice within Justified

James L. Shelton

Through analyzing the FX television series *Justified*, this chapter will iden-tify how a structuralist interpretation of the Western genre can be utilized to discuss the moral constraints of retributive justice.[1] Retributive justice is in this case first categorized as only action limited to being a response to past transgressions or imminent threats and second that it is a form of justice that focuses on punishment instead of rehabilitation. These constraints are placed front and center within the opening moments of the series; within the first scene, the protagonist, U.S. Marshal Raylan Givens (played by Timothy Olyphant), meets with a "Miami Gun Thug," Tommy Bucks. Givens has recently given Bucks an ultimatum.

Tommy Bucks: You, you're a character. I was telling my friends this morning how yesterday you come to me and, "You don't get out of town in 24 hours, I'm gonna shoot you on sight!" Come on, what is that. They thought it was a joke. They started laughing.
Raylan Givens: You tell them about the man you killed? The way you did it? Because I found nothing funny in that.[2]

As the conversation between Bucks and Givens continues, the countdown to the conclusion of the 24-hour period elapses; Bucks draws a pistol from his lap and Givens shoots him dead. The shooting was justified because Bucks drew first, creating a requirement for retribution. The circumstances of the situation are questioned in the next scene, though, which covers a conversa-tion between Raylan and his superior, Chief Deputy U.S. Marshal Dan Grant, who raises the issue of coercion:

Dan Grant: They might think that you cornered him, didn't give him a choice.
Raylan Givens: Oh, he had a choice.[3]

Although set in the modern day, *Justified* adopts the generic conventions of the Western to investigate the application of morality from a different era to the present time. Through self-reflexiveness and hybridity, the series questions many of the moral attributes of the Western genre. At the same time, *Justified* maintains a commitment to a key feature of the Western narrative in resolving many episodes or season-long narratives through the climactic "showdown": the idea that narrative resolution must be made concrete through the death of the antagonist, usually one-on-one in a test of who draws and shoots first. This chapter will question the morality of this justice, especially where it is seen as retributive. In doing so, this chapter will focus on the concept of retributive framing within narratives from the Western genre, and in doing so will present a framework for potential further inquiry into representations of retributivism as a theory of punishment in media.

Justified self-reflexively engages with this debate (the scene previously highlighted has Grant later ask Givens "You do now that we're not allowed to shoot people on sight anymore?").[4] The opening statement of the series is that justification for violent action can be predicated on complex moral questions. Givens's ultimatum to Bucks was justified because of the actions Bucks took in their shared history; this later legitimizes issuing the ultimatum, and Bucks's unwillingness to meet this ultimatum leads to his attempt to shoot first, therefore justifying Givens's action as retaliation. These complex moral justifications are key to an understanding of the righteous nature of the showdown between protagonist and antagonist—but, at the same time, the showdown also forms a key mechanism for resolving narratives in the Western genre. In this way, a degree of circularity inevitably exists; on a moral level, all the actions of the cycle are predicated by the implications of violence. As a concluding action to the cycle, however, the final violence of the showdown is viewed as having moral justification; to draw from the Christian Bible (Matthew, 26:52) violence against those who commit acts of violence is in part justified, "[. . .] for all who draw the sword will die by the sword."[5] What is of paramount importance, here, is the moral justification for retributive violence. The Western hero, per Warshow, must be unquestioning in knowing their decision to shoot is right.

There is no suggestion, however, that he draws the gun reluctantly. The Westerner could not fulfil himself if the moment did not finally come when he can shoot his enemy down. But because that moment is so thoroughly the expression of his being, it must be kept pure.[6]

My argument within this chapter is that the showdown, in its capacity as the climactic shootout between protagonist/hero and antagonist/villain, represents not only a narrative mechanic but also a representation of a form of retributive justice whose morality can be interrogated. The framework for this potential questioning is designed to bring together two specific elements. In the first instance, I will interpret the narrative function of the showdown within *Justified* by reference to the structuralist narrative analysis put forward by Todorov, specifically drawing from the idea of narrative equilibrium.

> The minimal complete plot can be seen as the shift from one equilibrium to another. This term "equilibrium," [. . .] is a social law, a rule of the game, a particular system of exchange. The two moments of equilibrium, similar and different, are separated by a period of imbalance, which is composed of a process of degeneration and a process of improvement.[7]

From Todorov, I suggest that the showdown can be analyzed as a narrative mechanism that can form part of the "process of improvement"—the move toward a new and different equilibrium. At the same time, in order to analyze the morality of the showdown within the series (and the wider context of the Western genre), I will also make reference to the concept of nemesis. Although through lexical drift nemesis has come to be used as a synonym for "villain," the original definition of the term refers to the Greek Goddess Nemesis (Νέμεσις)—the Goddess of retribution who "saw to it that justice and luck were evenly distributed in human life and who meted out due punishments for misdeeds and arrogance (hubris)."[8] As such, retributive justice forms a key narrative mechanic of the Western genre in terms of both moral and narrative discussions. The climactic shootout between protagonist/ hero and antagonist/villain represents a mechanism by which the period of destabilization can be resolved into a new state of equilibrium within a narrative. This structuralist approach to *Justified* and the Western genre will also acknowledge the prior scholarship of Wright in highlighting the specific relationship of the generic conventions of the Western to narrative structure.[9] The attraction of the Western structure as evidenced in the narratives of *Justified* is the tendency for, to paraphrase Theodore Parker, the moral arc of the series bend toward justice. As this analysis will explore, however, it is the adherence to the strictest idea of justice that motivates Raylan Givens as a character, governs the transition between narrative equilibrium states, but that also dictates the outcomes for the personal narrative arcs of characters in ways that do not conform to a more traditional "happy ending." The central tenet of *Justified*—arguably the concept that makes it attractive to viewers—is that what a person *wants* and what a person *deserves* are fundamentally different.

Because of this, within *Justified* there are multiple opportunities for investigating specific moral issues related to the portrayal of retributive justice. Nemesis is relevant to both a structuralist and moral analysis of this precisely because the mythology sets out precise guidelines for the retribution the goddess was said to mete out. Equally, as Shuster puts it,

> Westerns are conceived of as having a sort of 'mythological' status, in the robust sense that Greek myths are considered to have been operative. With its own invocations of the past [. . .], *Justified* engages with this understanding of the Western, but it refuses to embrace it completely.[10]

I am suggesting that, while relating Westerns to the narratives of mythology is something that has been previously undertaken, the possibility exists to relate the guidelines set out by Nemesis to narrative analysis. This will in turn lead to an analysis of the morality of the depictions of retributive justice provided in *Justified*. From a perspective informed by prior narrative analysis research, while Campbell[11] only makes passing reference to the idea of nemesis, Booker finds nemesis to be important to narrative analysis precisely because the concept represents a method by which equilibrium is reset after it has been disturbed—specifically, in this case, by hubris,[12] wherein

> The inevitable consequence of hubris was nemesis, from the root *nemein,* to "allot a due portion," the same root from which sprang *nomos,* "law." Literally, nemesis was the "due portion" required to restore the equilibrium of the cosmic order.[13]

The narrative of *Justified* follows the return of U.S. Marshal Raylan Givens to Harlan County after his own act of hubris: a "stepping over of the bounds" usually interpreted as "a form of overweening pride, a reckless arrogance" which in this case is the killing of Tommy Bucks.[14] The series then goes on to explore multiple ideas related to the morality of retributive justice. In this fashion, then, rather than utilizing violence for narrative or entertainment purposes, *Justified* explores the moral reasoning for, and consequences of, violence. *Justified* can be read as an examination of the place of violence within the narrative and what it means to be able to commit justified acts of violence; per Rivette:

> Violence has no other purpose, once the ruins of conventions are reduced to dust, than to establish a state of grace, a void, in the midst of which the heroes, completely unfettered by any arbitrary constraints, are free to pursue a process of self-interrogation, and to delve deep into their destiny.[15]

Justified attempts to include both the self-interrogation of the protagonist over both their inherent violent nature and a discussion of the wider effects of retribution and retributive justice. My argument is that the series does so with a conscious recognition of the impact of violence on the narrative progression from disturbed equilibrium to new equilibrium state. For Raylan Givens, the desire for justice is ingrained; it acts as a bulwark against becoming like his father Arlo (played by Raymond J. Barry), who Raylan despises for his abusive nature and Arlo's criminality. The first step to the refutation of Arlo's criminal and genetic heritage for Raylan was to join the U.S. Marshals; to maintain this stance, however, requires that Raylan maintains both his personal moral framework and a commitment to the upholding of the law at all times. This maintenance is then further complicated by its operation within a complex framework of moral obligations, family ties, promises, and debts. On returning to Harlan, Raylan Givens has to determine his place within a complex web of family, society, and history—both the foreign country of his personal past and the wider past of Harlan County, a place historically defined by clashes between coal mining unions and the attempts by power companies to oppress them (as documented by Kopple and Portelli, 2012).[16] Returning to Harlan places Raylan at the center of a number of intersections, which in turn have a noticeable impact on the moral nature of his interactions with other characters with whom he has prior associations. An instance of this is witnessed in the first episode of the third season.[17] At the conclusion of the previous season, Boyd Crowder (played by Walton Goggins) rescues Raylan from a potentially fatal beating by Dickie Bennett (played by Jeremy Davies), who Boyd wishes to kill for Bennett's earlier assault on Ava Crowder (played by Joelle Carter), Boyd's lover. Having rescued Raylan, Boyd allows Raylan to leave with Dickie on the understanding that the latter would be rendered back to him for justice—likely fatal—at a later date. Following the conclusion of this encounter, Dickie is subsequently arrested and processed and placed outside of Boyd's vengeful reach. This is then addressed during a seemingly innocuous meeting between Boyd and Raylan in season 3, episode 1:

Boyd Crowder: I want you to apologise. [. . .] By the time I got out to Wade Messer's house, Dickie Bennett was tuning you up like it was his birthday and you was his piñata, only I don't think there would have been candy pouring out.

Raylan Givens: You're saying you saved my life.

Boyd Crowder: Are you saying I didn't?

Raylan Givens: I would respectfully suggest what you're looking for is a thank you, not an apology.

Boyd Crowder: Well now follow my logic, Raylan. I had my own plans for Dickie, on account of his shooting Ava, but you said you needed him, so I let you have

him under the condition that you would return him to me once his services had
been rendered.

Raylan Givens: I'm sorry, did you see a creek out in the lobby? Some pretty green
trees and cut off mountains? Do you think we're in the Holler? I am a Deputy
US Marshal, Boyd

Boyd Crowder: You're a Givens, Raylan.

Raylan Givens: And you think I'm going to hand a man over to you to be murdered, like he's what, a pig I borrowed from you.

Boyd Crowder: You gave me your *word.*[18]

This exchange is then followed by a fistfight between Raylan and Boyd,
which crashes, in the style of a tavern brawl, through the glass paneling into
the office next door.

The characterization of Raylan—as the stoic lawman for whom justice
is a pursuit that must be maintained at all times as a barricade against slip-
ping into criminality or amorality—is not only a central pillar of this chapter
but also something that clearly resonated with audiences, to the level where
not only could a devoted fan purchase branded blankets from the FX shop
("Keep yourself warm with the cool indifference of Raylan Givens") but to
the degree that the 88th volume of the *Popular Culture and Philosophy* series
was devoted to the series.

Although *Justified and Philosophy* is designed to appeal to a wider—rather
than purely academic—audience, the chapter by Cotton and Palazzo offers
a useful starting point for discussion of the morality of retributive justice in
proposing a framework based on the philosophy of Kant.[19] Where the initial question of retributive justice relates to the morality of the mechanism
by which it is apportioned, retributivism may offer a complementary view.
According to Hill, the Kantian view of retributive justice states that

> [. . .] although retributivists grant that, theology aside, it is a contingent question
> whether wrong doers are actually likely to suffer for their misdeeds, they see it
> as a moral necessity, independently of the consequences, that wrongdoers ought
> to be made to suffer in proportion to their offenses.[20]

This forms part of a "darker, less attractive picture of moral agents" where

> Law, for example, is not to rely on citizens' respect for the legal system. Explicit
> sanctions for nonconformity, appealing to nonmoral motives, must be included
> in the laws. Kant even suggests at one point the law should be designed so that
> a race of devils could live in peace under it.[21]

The issue with the assertion by Cotton and Palazzo that the justice portrayed
in *Justified* is retributive in nature is that this offers an incomplete picture.

The question is raised by this discussion of whether violence—especially fatal violence—can truly constitute morally acceptable retributive justice.[22] This is something that Shuster further highlights with reference to the Kantian perspective that *Justified* has on the law, whereby

> [T]he law requires particular consequences, demands them, and that falling short of them is to mistreat both the law *and* particular agents of and to the law, including, importantly, the criminal.[23]

Shuster positions *Justified* between this Kantian perspective—where it can be said that action against the criminal by the law is demanded, therefore justifying taking action in an appropriate fashion or at an appropriate level—and a Hegelian perspective of the social interpretation of the law, which—in broad terms—states that applications of the law are based on "shared values"—so rather than a set of universal laws, a Hegelian approach

> [. . .] underlines that every person thinking about justice is herself situated in specific circumstances, and that hence the particularity of any viewpoint cannot be eliminated but should be recognized.[24]

In narrative terms, however, where both the episodic and serial narratives of *Justified* are often resolved through a showdown, the reestablishment of narrative equilibrium usually (although not always) follows the death of a perpetrator. This resolution is problematic in that the "particular consequences" central to Shuster's application of a Kantian view on the law potentially define the threshold of hubris—the threshold that triggers this form of retributive action (killing)—which has been seemingly justified when it is portrayed as being reached by the final actions of an antagonist. When a "villain" may have gained unfair material advantage or evidenced overwhelming arrogance through criminal actions, this justifies the intervention of the lawman; the final arrogance leads to the situation where a villain has the hubris to believe they can outdraw the lawman and win the showdown. This is where references to Kantian retributive justice can be seen to split between retributive justice and narrative justice, where both forms have different structural functions within the narrative of *Justified.* Although initially similar, the two forms of retributive justice are divisible along the lines highlighted by Tunick, where "the punishment for a being who is guided by moral standards is retributive, but punishment for the violation of (pragmatic) law is imposed to reform or deter."[25] In this sense:

> All punishments imposed by sovereigns and governments are pragmatic. They are designed either to correct or to make an example. Ruling authorities do not

punish because a crime has been committed, but in order that crimes should not be committed. . . . Contrary to what Dolinko suggests, Kant does not think we legally punish for the sake of giving lawbreakers their just deserts. Legal punishment is not an end in itself; rather, on Kant's view, legal punishment is justified as a useful social practice. One way the practice is useful is by deterring actions which would upset a society of ordered liberty. For Kant, we legally punish to preserve and enforce rights we have by nature.[26]

Tunick notes that punishment through retribution is complex primarily because retribution is a problematic term, citing the statement within the 1972 Model Sentencing Act that "sentencing should not be based on revenge and retribution," lest retribution be confused with vindictiveness.[27] Similarly, Scheid highlights that Kant's conception of retributivism requires that "to be just, the punishment must be proportionate to the crime committed;" the punishment is not just if the punishment is disproportionate.[28] In this respect, the criminals killed by Raylan Givens receive the ultimate sanction apportioned at the moment of the showdown and justified by their inability to give up and risk incarceration.

It is therefore possible to question the nature of retributive justice in *Justified* primarily because of the generic conventions the series follows from the Western genre. This is something multiple prior scholars in this area have attempted to address through subcategorizing or identifying additional hybrid elements within the series.

Zinder, for example, identifies *Justified* as a "9/11 Western" or a "post-Western" where particular narrative elements of the series are informed by the media production conditions and cultural conditions following the attacks of September 11th, 2001.[29] By defining the show in this way, Zinder represents the first of several attempts at interrogating *Justified* by generically reframing the series. Barrett, by contrast, frames an analysis of *Justified* through analyzing the series' intertextuality, referencing potential similarities between Olyphant and Clint Eastwood, stating that "he [Olyphant] was not only aware of the associations with Eastwood but actively invested in them."[30] This complexifies the idea put forward by Turnbull in that such intertextuality can suggest a "range of potential pleasures" for the viewer:

> These include the recognition of a familiar face, the construction of a fantasy relationship with the character, and other forms of "identification" is a complex one [. . .]. Within this fictional world the hero performs the role of guide, equipped with a usually reliable moral compass, who "takes" the viewer on a weekly excursion into the world of crime [. . .][31]

Because of this, Olyphant-as-Givens seemingly embodies the guide in the role of, per Barrett, a "trustworthy, paternalistic hero."[32] The issue recognized by Barrett can also be contextualized with reference to the prior work of Crossley in highlighting that *Justified* includes generic conventions from other genres, notably the Gangster genre—something Crossley classifies as genre hybridity.[33] The example Barrett gives in relation to this hybridity is that Olyphant can both reference the iconicism of Eastwood within, for example, the *Dollars* trilogy, while also referring to the iconic intertextual potential of Eastwood within the *Dirty Harry* films. This hybridity potentially strengthens the representation of Givens as a screen lawman by trading on what is, Barrett argues (quoting Tudor), "media-derived nostalgia."[34] At the same time, this hybridity can also inform the expectations of the audience in relation to the taking of violent action while at the same time placing these expectations within the multiple contexts that *Justified* evidences—contexts that form the backdrop to many aspects of discussion within this chapter. Through the situation of expressions of violence within a complex set of contexts, audiences for the series are encouraged to consider the complicated situations from which this violence arises—and how this violence will impact upon the equilibrium of the narrative. These contexts and ideas can in turn be tied to the structuralist interpretation put forward by Fiske that a character within a series is a "textual device constructed [. . .] from discourse."

> On television the physical presence of the player is used, not to authenticate the individual self, but to embody (literally) discourse and ideology. In the structuralist inflection of this pose, a character cannot be understood as an individual existing in his or her own right, but only as a series of textual (and intertextual) positions.[35]

Justified, in presenting viewers with a hybridized agglomeration of Western tropes can be analyzed through the idea that hybridized genres potentially have the function of offering further opportunities to "interrogate the actual and media history of the West."[36] The issue here is that the "traditional Western," for Crossley, has a "focus on ritualistic killings that sanitize the reality of violence."[37]

This sanctioned, sanitized violence is problematic in terms of both retributive justice and morality. Raylan Givens is listed during the sixty-five episodes of the series as having killed twenty-one antagonists directly along with five "proxy killings"—deaths in which Givens plays a part but does not directly enact. This is something Joyce identifies as an issue precisely because *Justified* evidences not only hybridity of genre but is also subject to the generic shifts of its own base genre.[38] Initially, *Justified* requires little interpretation as the protagonist wears a white hat and justice at the conclusion of an episode is often apportioned through a climactic showdown. For Joyce, however, this simplicity complexifies a generic analysis of *Justified* precisely because it is anachronistic in nature. Joyce identifies the issue that "the thematic and ideological tenets of the Western are not just profoundly influential, but also widely diffuse in American culture"; because of this, the understanding of genre conventions by viewers potentially influences their perception of retributive justice.[39] Joyce ties this analysis to one of gun culture and self-defense, in that even while positioning the series within the Western framework, Joyce categorizes Raylan Givens

> as a mediator between opposing social forces, a reconciler of violent inclina-
> tions with democratic values, and a laconic protagonist made heroic by killing
> only in self-defence despite his vengeful tendencies, Raylan Givens is, however,
> clearly a protagonist cut from the old Western cloth.[40]

If, by this logic, Givens can be seen as what Fiske refers to as a "paradigmatic set of values" or an "embodied ideology," this ideological representation is therefore problematic.[41] The question returns to Warshow's concept of purity—that there can be no suggestion of reluctance in the pursuit of righteous belief—but for Joyce, the only reason Givens is "heroic" is because he acts out of "self-defense." The "vengeful tendencies," however, complicate this issue. Within the narrative of *Justified,* for example, Raylan Givens's character traits are portrayed as stemming from family issues, with a sense that these issues may explain a proclivity toward violence. The relationship between Raylan and his father, Arlo Givens, is shown as antagonistic; Arlo Givens is a career criminal with a thoroughly vindictive personality. Within S01E05 ("The Lord of War and Thunder"), the viewer is shown that Raylan's choice of career stemmed from this fact; Arlo, however, notes that his own father was "no picnic."

> Arlo Givens: [He] was a preacher when I was a boy. A real old-time religion
> man. His god was the Lord of war and thunder. That house was nothing but fear.
> And I rebelled, as boys do, chose a path I knew would aggravate, and it did,
> which is why you barely saw him. He didn't much approve.[42]

Raylan's character is therefore related to the need to rebel against his father's criminal tendencies, which was in turn related to his grandfather's authoritarian ways.[43] The depth of resentment between Arlo and Raylan is such that when Arlo is given the opportunity, on his deathbed, to offer Raylan key information on an important case that his last words to his son are, simply, "Kiss my ass."[44] In narrative terms, this complexifies Raylan's devotional adherence to justice, as within the narrative of the series it is never as simple as having, as Miller states, a "white-hatted hero and black-hatted, moustached villain."[45] The purity of the decision to draw, fire, and kill the villain is complicated by whether it constitutes retribution, retaliation, or revenge. Where retaliation can simply constitute "an action taken in return for an injury or offense" by contrast[46]

> [. . .] what justifies retribution is not any supposed good consequences, such as deterring similar acts in the future, but simply that the guilty party has done wrong and deserves to pay. From the point of view of retribution, it doesn't matter if any further good comes of punishment; punishing the guilty is inherently right and just, and that's all it needs to be.[47]

Raylan Givens's behavior is motivated by his conception of what is "inherently right and just," but it is not a vengeful justice; even in cases with which he maintains a personal connection, Givens does not evidence "the desire to punish criminal offenders"—"to retaliate a past wrong by making the offender suffer."[48] The distinction is important because of the meaning conferred. While revenge is a key generic feature of the Western (according to Kitses) the action of revenge is "both gratuitous and essential" and simultaneously "meaningless"

> yet it is necessary because it is evidence of a way of life that the hero embodies: "Some things a man can't ride around." This stoicism arms the character with a grace that forms an impenetrable armour against the temptations and threats of life.[49]

Were *Justified* to operate strictly within the generic conventions of the classical Western, the morality of the situation *should* be clear; per Batty and Waldeback,

> The antagonist of the Western is often somebody who has let personal greed or power overrule their moral conduct. Even in more modern Westerns with so-called anti-heroes, where the antagonist can be somebody of high social and seemingly respectable standing, the battle is often over moral ground, and the protagonist embodies the values that belong to the land (at times wilderness), whereas the antagonist carries the potential corruptive influences of civilization.[50]

Justified, however, has a complex relationship with the narrative of the moral high ground. The process of generational refutation—the idea that sons in the Givens family take up careers in opposition to their fathers—forms a subtext for the way by which the show frames characters as not only a "series of textual positions" but also a series of familial relations. This has been previously analyzed in terms of the way by which *Justified* intertwines familial relationships, narrative, and agency.[51] Between season 1 and season 5, *Justified* introduces multiple family units (often referred to as "'clans'"); the Givens family, the Crowder family, the Bennett family, and the Crowe family. Of these family units, none of the patriarchal or matriarchal figures of the previous generation are alive by the end of the series, and the majority of these units are reduced to between one and two characters. In the case of the Givens, Crowder, and Crowe families, the family unit loses its second-generation patriarchs to varying degrees—death (Crowe), incarceration (Crowder), and separation (Givens, although this is portrayed as amicable). Outside of the family unity, the representatives of organized crime from Detroit portrayed in the show experience a high mortality rate; the majority—four of seven primary characters—are dead by the conclusion of the narrative and one is imprisoned. By the conclusion of the series, to borrow a concept from social justice, *Justified* begins to represent a "violence of hopelessness"—a form of violence bred by problematic social conditions and disconnection from community leaders or "patriarchs."[52]

Violence intrudes on the moral and ethical framework of the series in more than just straightforward ways; a second moral issue found within *Justified* relates to a death-by-proxy. The placement of violence at even one remove brings into question the justified nature of said violence—especially within the context of the fourth season of the show. The narrative of the fourth season is centered on the identity of Drew Thompson, a fictional interpretation of the hijacker D. B. Cooper.[53] The fate of Cooper—who, in 1971, hijacked a Northwest Orient Airlines flight, successfully demanding and receiving $200,000 and subsequently parachuting out of the hijacked flight "somewhere between Seattle and Reno"— has never been established.[54] *Justified* reinterprets Cooper as Thompson—a character with ties to the Detroit Mafia. It is established that Thompson witnessed a crime committed by Theo Tonin (played by Adam Arkin)—the current head of the Detroit Mafia—and subsequently fled, bailing out of a plane over Harlan County with a sizeable quantity of cocaine which he trades to Arlo Givens and Bo Crowder for safety and a new identity.[55] The story arc of season 4 follows the attempts by the U.S. Marshalls, the Detroit Mafia (the 'Tonin Family') and local interests to locate Thompson—later revealed to be the character of Shelby Parlow—to satisfy their various ends. Toward the conclusion of this story arc, Givens's pregnant ex-wife, Winona Hawkins (played by Natalie Zea), is held hostage by three men from the Detroit Mafia who threaten to kill her if Givens does not give the location of Thompson. Although Givens and Hawkins manage to kill their assailants, the threat still remains in the form of Nicky Augustine (played by Mike O'Malley), an ambitious underboss within the criminal organization. Givens later meets with Augustine and offers a choice:

Raylan Givens: I want you to turn yourself in, confess to murder, racketeering, obstruction, whatever other horrible things you done.

Augustine: Is that all?
Raylan Givens: I want you to swear you'll leave my family be.
Augustine: Or?
Raylan Givens: Or you'll die here in this limo.[56]

Augustine refuses the offer, stating that he does not believe Givens would "execute" him—especially as Augustine is unarmed, meaning Raylan would not be justified in shooting and killing him. Augustine goes on to state that he is planning to kill the son of the head of the organization, Sammy Tonin (played by Max Perlich), and assume his place. As part of this discussion, Augustine in turn attempts to justify the necessity of his actions:

Augustine: I don't have a badge, so all I got is my word. So if I say I'm gonna kill your family, I'm gonna kill your family. Because these animals out here, they think they can get one over on me, they'll tear me to pieces.[57]

Givens does not "execute" Augustine, instead choosing to exit the limousine within which the discussion has taken place. The viewer then sees a private jet taxiing toward the limousine, from which Sammy Tonin emerges with several armed men. Tonin thanks Givens for "reaching out" and Givens appraises Tonin of Augustine's intentions. Tonin checks whether Givens would intervene if he witnessed a crime being committed, to which Givens simply responds "I'm suspended"—which, in terms of his legal role as a Marshal, is correct at that specific time. Tonin's men then murder Augustine (in the limo) while Givens walks away.

The death of Augustine is not "pure" by Warshow's definition, for the simple reason that the protagonist—the "Westerner"—does not draw his weapon or take direct responsibility for the necessary action. Augustine's death is, however, justified within the internal logic of the series because of the threats made toward Givens's family. Per Batty and Waldeback (above), Augustine represents the "potential corruptive influences of civilization"; the "moral high ground," however, is much more difficult to establish in this instance.[58] Givens comes perilously close to becoming a "revenger," per Maus:

Revengers are driven to their bloody task because a ruler has failed to punish injustice properly, usually because he himself or members of his family are implicated in the wrongdoing. Most conspicuously, revengers assault the body of the sovereign or the bodies of his close kin. Less obviously, the revenger's outlaw legalism commandeers the monarch's exclusive prerogative over the prosecution of felonies [. . .].[59]

The parallels between the revenge tragedies and this narrative come to the surface of the analysis when the morality of the Westerners' actions loses their Warshowian purity. In structuralist terms, Augustine's death represents the move toward the new, post-season 4 narrative equilibrium; in narrative terms, the sword of Damocles cannot be left hanging over Givens as it is anathema to his personal set of values. At the same time, Givens cannot "execute" Augustine despite the seriousness of the threat. Augustine reaches a threshold of hubris through this threat—in threatening not only Givens but also his family Augustine suggests a disdain for law and morality that exceeds the typical posturing of criminals in the series. It is because of this that Augustine must receive his due; his threat at this level cannot go unpunished, and he must receive his due. The moral issue, however, is that Givens cannot be directly responsible, as this would strip away—as raised earlier—his purity of purpose. The solution, however—to delegate Augustine's death—still strips Givens of a layer of his righteousness, leading to confrontations with his superior later within the series.

This moral question stems from the issue of genre hybridity, per Barrett (above). The inclusion of the Detroit Mafia/Tonin Family into the narrative represents a hybridization of the Gangster and Western genres within the narrative of the series. This is by no means unique within the Western genre; the question, however, is what this hybridity brings to the narrative of the series. For Slotkin, "borrowing elements" is a method used to "aggrandize a Western," in that

> The basic premise of the gangster film had been to question the easy equation of material and moral progress and to see corruption as the necessary adjunct of America's rise to the economic heights. Shifting the setting of the social critique from the modern city to the Old West "softens" the critique by setting its objectives at a distance. But at the same time it widens the scope of the critique to include mainstream industries and businesses whose "progressive" and respectable character the gangster film never challenged.[60]

Harlan is not precisely the "Old West," although *Justified* may often attempt to represent it as such. The argument here, however, is that hybridization compromises the morality and purity of the nature of justification within the series. There is no doubt that Augustine reaches and exceeds the threshold of hubris or that Givens offers him a bloodless way out of the situation. To abrogate responsibility to Tonin, however, compromises Givens's moral authority in absolute terms as, per John Stuart Mill, "bad men need nothing more to compass their ends, than that good men should look on and do nothing."[61]

The last example of representations of morality within *Justified* that I will highlight for discussion is drawn from the sixth season and is found within the final five episodes of the series as a whole. The narrative of the sixth season follows an attempt by the gangster/businessman Avery Markham (played by Sam Neil)—again representing a "mainstream industry" in this capacity as the owner of a marijuana empire in Colorado—to buy up land in Harlan County in preparation for potential legalization. This process of acquisition is facilitated by Markham's own men—a group of private military contractors—but when they fail and are killed, the character of Boon (played by Jonathan Tucker) enters the narrative as Markham's new "right-hand man."

Boon is used to directly represent the dark opposite of Givens and, in doing so, casts into relief the moral statements made within the series. Where Givens lives by the code of Warshow's "Westerner" with the associated ideas of purity, Boon offers a reflection—in the words of Hale—"whose emulation of movie gunslingers was both code and psychopathy."[62]

This psychopathy manifests itself within a warped mimicry of Givens characteristics. In terms of iconography where Givens justification for his white hat is that "I tried it on one time, and it fit" Boon, by contrast, intimidates a diner employee into giving up a dark hat. Where Givens has a surrogate fatherly relationship with the teenage character of Loretta McCready (played by Kaitlyn Dever), Boon sexualizes his interactions with her. For Givens, the gun is a tool and work dress is plain; Boon contrasts this by wearing multiple large rings and carrying a larger gun. Even the iconography of firearms becomes important here; Givens is shown to carry a standard law-enforcement issue Glock 17 pistol, while Boon carries a Colt Single Action Army revolver.[63] The latter demonstrates the commitment of the narrative to the representation of Boon as Givens's corrupt reflection: where Givens represents an updating of "cowboy" archetypes to modern law enforcement, Boon comes to represent a throwback to the amoral frontier. The final point of contrast is that Givens repeatedly evidences reluctance to kill unless it is justified; Boon has no such compunctions. Boon says of the burdens of conscience:

Boon: Always seemed to me, as far as conscience goes, the sweet spot is you either be poor enough you can't afford to have one or rich enough you can afford to hire someone to carry the weight.[64]

Where throughout the series Givens has represented the moral face of retributive justice—barring the situations discussed above—Boon represents a flawed nemesis for Givens, in that he is intended to punish Givens's hubris for daring to face the faceless behemoth of organized crime. During the final showdown between the two Givens follows his training and aims for the heart, while Boon aims (symbolically) for Givens white hat. While he only succeeds in grazing Givens's temple, the white hat is destroyed. Boon is the last person Givens kills during the series, but probably not the last person he kills in his career as a U.S. Marshal; having slain a darker reflection of himself, Givens then moves on to his next posting, one that allows him to be closer to his daughter.

As this chapter has demonstrated, a moral analysis of *Justified* is complicated by multiple issues. The intertextual references discussed by Barrett
place the series within a specific context where morality is influenced by the
prior work of Eastwood, in turn informed by the prior work of John Wayne.
At the same time, the hybridity suggested by Crossley means that the series
attempts to portray the application of the moral tropes applied by the traditional generic Western while simultaneously contrasting them against generic
elements drawn from the Gangster genre. The morality of retributive justice
is therefore complicated by generic and intertextual concerns—"Moral judge-
ments," per French, "are not so easily arrived at" in the interpretation and
classification of the Western genre.[65] Key to this is the portrayal of violence,
in that

> [. . .] for filmmakers and moviegoers alike the staging and viewing of violent
> spectacles are among the genre's prime attractions. Where this is the only
> motive [. . .] there is perhaps a cause for censure . . . The trouble with western
> violence lies not with the inflexibility of the genre's metaphor or the audience's
> ability to interpret it, but with its immutability. [. . .] The most immediate and
> continuously topical accusation against the western is the role it plays in sustain-
> ing an outdated and dangerous pattern of behaviour [. . .].[66]

This chapter has highlighted how the expression of the morality of the
Western can be found through the purity of violent action by the hero. This
violent action must never be petty and must always be justified—in moral
terms that the viewer can understand and accept. The showdown therefore
represents the narrative mechanism by which both those guilty of criminal
hubris can be allotted their due portion in death and by which the new equilibrium can start. The problem with this mechanism is that, per Prince

> [. . .] this aesthetic, when it becomes the chief means for representing violent
> death, as it all too often has been, is an insufficient means for probing the mean-
> ing and consequences of violence, should those be a filmmakers' intentions.[67]

The "meaning and consequences" are therefore found through the way in
which the narrative frames the results of violent action. The agency to take
violent action therefore represents an empowerment of the protagonist to
become, per Todorov "dynamic motif"—a motif which, Todorov states (quoting Tomashevsky) is one which changes "the situation" of the narrative (in
opposition to static motifs, which do not).[68] The "meaning and consequences"
of Raylan's actions are expressed within the way in which the narrative of
the series concludes, in that the state of new equilibrium is based on justice

and not on personal satisfaction. Because of this, in each case Ava, Boyd, and Raylan reach states of new equilibrium that parallel their initial states, albeit with changes in each case. Because of the desire for justice Raylan resists the impulse toward a violent showdown with Boyd Crowder, instead arresting and incarcerating him. Ava Crowder survives with her and Boyd's child— whose existence Ava and Raylan elect to conceal from Boyd as they believe he would stop at nothing to find and take the child. Without this knowledge Boyd returns to his prior state of equilibrium—that of a preacher—albeit in a new carceral setting. Raylan returns to Miami, resuming something analogous to the posting he occupied at the start of the series—albeit now with access to his daughter and a seemingly amicable relationship with his ex-wife and her partner. The new state of equilibrium is dictated by the commitment of Raylan to his idea of justice, not by an idea of karma; the characters receive their due portion, and not, necessarily, what they deserve.

The morality of *Justified* is complex precisely because it is predicated on interpreting the generic conventions of the Western within a hybridized, modern setting. The predications of the show rely on the portrayal of retributive justice, where criminal hubris brings fatal downfall. At the same time, the hybridization offered by the series means that the purity of the Western can be simultaneously portrayed, interrogated, and placed against the "corruptive" influences of civilization. In the final analysis, it is worth noting two elements, both relating to the conclusion of the final episode of the series. In the first instance, when clearing out his desk prior to leaving for Florida, Givens finds a book. It is not a book of Western stories, as might be expected, but *The Friends of Eddie Coyle*—a novel by George Higgins from 1970 centered on the interactions between criminals, with the titular character attempting to establish who he can sell out to lower his upcoming potential custodial sentence.

In the second instance having shared the series narrative for six seasons the final episode of the series—"The Promise" leads to the final showdown between Raylan Givens and Boyd Crowder.[69] During the verbal prelude to this final showdown, Crowder makes it clear that if he is sent to jail, he will kill both Givens and Ava Crowder, Boyd's partner (albeit one who has informed on him to, in turn, ameliorate her own jail sentence *a la* Coyle). After Boyd's statement, the tension builds toward a potential—and likely fatal—showdown only to subvert this expectation by having the next scene show Boyd in handcuffs being led away. In some respects, this represents the new equilibrium for Givens, in that even with justification he chooses *not* to shoot; the decision represents the character's new equilibrium following the journey from shooting Tommy Bucks in the show's first episode to *not* shooting Boyd Crowder in the show's finale. At the same time, the decision is a moral one based on Givens's pre-existing relationship with Crowder as, prior to the series, they had worked alongside each other. Givens chooses not to shoot Crowder at least in part, as the series makes clear, because of the significance of this relationship. The series and Leonard's short story, *Fire in the Hole*, share the reasoning behind this;

"He have any last words?"
"He said I'd killed him."
Raylan paused. "I told him I was sorry, but he had called it."
Art was frowning now. "You're sorry you killed him?"
"I thought I explained it to you," Raylan said in his quiet voice.
"Boyd and I dug coal together."[70]

Retributive justice—whether righteous and/or justified—is portrayed as alternatingly complex (with a base in personal history, familial relations, or societal factors) and simple (the requirement of retribution for acts of hubris) within *Justified*. For many of the antagonists—both either native to the county or who arrive from outside—it becomes true, as the refrain of the song used to close several of the seasons of the show states that they will never leave Harlan alive.[71] It is when this moment does *not* occur, however, that the situation becomes more complex. The final hubris of the criminal—the belief that they can outdraw the lawman and everything he represents—justifies their being shot down in the purity of the moment. As this chapter has demonstrated, where the genre becomes hybridized or the generic conventions are altered for narrative purposes the justifications falter, and the purity wavers. In either case, however, the new equilibrium state at the end of the narrative is reached through a transformative event predicated on violent intervention—with all the moral complexity that this brings.

NOTES

1. Graham Yost, dir., *Justified*, performed by Timothy Olyphant, Nick Searcy, and Joelle Carter (2010; Dallas, TX: FX Productions).
2. *Justified*, season 1, episode 1, "Fire in the Hole," dir. Michael Dinner, aired March 16, 2010, originally released on the FX Network.
3. Ibid.
4. Ibid.
5. Matthew, 26:52 (NIV).
6. Robert Warshow, *The Immediate Experience* (Chicago, IL: Harvard University Press, 2002), 110.
7. Tzvetan Todorov and Arnold Weinstein, "Structural Analysis of Narrative," *NOVEL: A Forum on Fiction* 3, no. 1 (1969): 75.

8. Manfred Lurker, *The Routledge Dictionary of Gods and Goddesses, Devils and Demons* (London: Routledge, 2004), 134.

9. Will Wright, *Sixguns & Society: A Structural Study of the Western* (London: University of California Press Ltd., 1975).

10. Martin Shuster, *New Television: The Aesthetics and Politics of a Genre* (London: The University of Chicago Press, Ltd., 2017), 179.

11. Joseph Campbell, *The Hero with a Thousand Faces* (Novato, CA: New World Library, 2008, 3rd Ed.), 12.

12. Christopher Booker, *The Seven Basic Plots: Why We Tell Stories* (London: Continuum, 2004), 329.

13. Ibid.

14. Ibid.

15. Jacques Rivette, "Notes on a Revolution." Originally appeared in *Cahiers du cinema* 54 (Christmas 1955), 17–21. Reprinted in Jim Hillier, ed., *Cahiers du cinema: The 1950s,* (Harvard, 1985) [94–98].

16. See Barbara Kopple, dir., *Harlan County, USA,* (Documentary), Cabin Creek Films, 1976 and Alessandro Portelli, *They Say In Harlan County: An Oral History* (Oxford: Oxford University Press, 2012).

17. *Justified*, season 3, episode 1, "The Gunfighter," dir. Michael Dinner, aired January 17, 2012, originally released on the FX Network.

18. Ibid.

19. Christian Cotton and Anthony Palazzo, "I Did What I Had To Do," in *Justified and Philosophy: Shoot First, Think Later,* ed. Rod Carveth and Robert Arp (Chicago, IL: Open Court Publishing Company, 2014), 93–109.

20. Thomas E. Hill, "Kant on Wrongdoing, Desert, and Punishment," *Law and Philosophy* 18, no. 4 (1999): 409.

21. Ibid., 408.

22. Cotton and Palazzo, 105.

23. Shuster, 175–176.

24. Dana Schmalz, "Social Freedom in a Global World: Axel Honneth's and Seyla Benhabib's Reconsiderations of a Hegelian Perspective on Justice," *Constellations* 26, no. 2 (2019): 302.

25. Mark Tunick, *Punishment: Theory and Practice* (Berkeley, CA: University of California Press, 1992), 62.

26. Mark Tunick, "Is Kant a Retributivist?" *History of Political Thought* 17, no. 1 (1996): 63.

27. Ibid., 67.

28. Don E. Scheid, "Kant's Retributivism," *Ethics* 93, no. 2 (1983): 263.

29. Paul Zinder, "Osama Bin Laden Ain't Here: *Justified* as a 9/11 Western," in *Contemporary Westerns: Film and Television since 1990,* ed. Andrew Patrick Nelson (Plymouth: The Scarecrow Press Inc., 2013), 119–134.

30. Jenny Barrett, "'A Cop in a Cowboy Hat: Timothy Olyphant, a Postmodern Eastwood in *Justified*," in *Critical Perspectives on the Western: From a Fistful of Dollars to Django Unchained,* ed. Lee Broughton (Lanham, MD: Rowman and Littlefield, 2016), 91–92.

31. Sue Turnbull, *The TV Crime Drama* (Edinburgh: Edinburgh University Press, 2014), 98.

32. Barrett, 91.

33. Laura Crossley, "Ganstagrass: Hybridity and Popular Culture in *Justified*," *Journal of Popular Television* 2, no. 1 (2014): 57–75.

34. Barrett, 97.

35. John Fiske, *Television Culture* (London: Routledge, 1987), 151.

36. Crossley, 60.

37. Ibid.

38. Justin A. Joyce, *Gunslinging Justice: The American Culture of Gun Violence in Westerns and the Law* (Manchester: Manchester University Press, 2018), 2.

39. Ibid.

40. Ibid., 207.

41. Fiske, 160.

42. *Justified*, season 1, episode 5, "The Lord of War and Thunder," dir. Adam Arkin, aired April 6, 2010, originally released on the FX Network.

43. Paul Zinder, in Rod Carveth and Robert Arp (ed.), *Justified and Philosophy: Shoot First, Think Later* (Chicago, IL: Carus Publishing Company, 2015), 159–160.

44. *Justified,* season 4, episode 8, "Outlaw," dir. John Dahl, aired February 26, 2013, originally released on the FX Network.

45. William Miller, *Screenwriting for Narrative Film and Television* (London: Columbus Books Ltd., 1980), 147.

46. J. C. Huefner and H. K. Hunt, "Consumer Retaliation as a Response to Dissatisfaction," *Journal of Consumer Satisfaction, Dissatisfaction and Complaining Behaviour* 13 (2000): 61–82.

47. Judith Lichtenburg, "The Ethics of Retaliation," *Philosophy and Public Policy Quarterly* 21, no. 4 (2001): 4.

48. Monica M. Gerber and Johnathan Jackson, "Retribution as Revenge and Retribution as Just Deserts," *Social Justice Research* 26 (2013):61.

49. Jim Kitses, *Horizons West: Directing the Western from John Ford to Clint Eastwood* (London: Bloomsbury/BFIm, 2004), 179.

50. Craig Batty and Zara Waldeback, *Writing for the Screen: Creative and Critical Approaches* (Basingstoke: Palgrave MacMillan, 2008), 86.

51. James Shelton, *"We Dug Coal Together": The Complexity of Antagonism within Justified* (Conference paper presentation: Current Thinking on the Western III), 2015.

52. Dee Cook, *Criminal and Social Justice* (London: Sage Publications Ltd., 2006), 157.

53. Ed Grossweiler, "Hijacker Bails Out Without Loot," *The Free Lance-Star* (Fredericksburg, VA), November 26, 1971; Geoffrey Gray, "Unmasking American Legend D.B. Cooper, Who Got Away with Hijacking a Plane," *New York Magazine*, October 18, 2007, https://nymag.com/news/features/39593/.

54. FBI.GOV, *D.B. Cooper Hijacking*, accessed online July 2021 via https://www.fbi.gov/history/famous-cases/db-cooper-hijacking.

55. Matt Zoller Seitz, "Jim Beaver on Last Night's Justified and the Odds of a Deadwood Reunion," *Vulture*, March 27, 2013, https://www.vulture.com/2013/03/justified-jim-beaver-interview.html.

56. *Justified*, season 4, episode 13, "Ghosts," dir. Bill Johnson, aired April 2, 2013, originally released on the FX Network.

57. Ibid.

58. Batty and Waldeback, 86.

59. Maus, "Revenge Strategy," in *Revenge Tragedy: Contemporary Critical Essays*, ed. Steve Simkin (Basingstoke: Palgrave MacMillan, 2001), 88–89.

60. Richard Slotkin, *Gunfighter Nation: The Myth of the Frontier in Twentieth Century America* (New York: HarperCollins, 1992), 295.

61. John Stuart Mill, *Inaugural Address Delivered to the University of St. Andrews* (London: Longmans, Green, Reader and Dyer, 1867).

62. Mike Hale, "Review: 'Justified' Finale on FX Ends Show's 6-Year Run," *The New York Times*, April 15, 2015, https://www.nytimes.com/2015/04/15/arts/television/review-justified-finale-on-fx-ends-shows-6-year-run.html.

63. Internet Movie Firearm Database.

64. *Justified*, season 6, episode 10, "Trust," dir. Adam Arkin, aired March 24, 2015, originally released on the FX Network.

65. Philip French, *Westerns* (Manchester: Carcanet Press Limited, 2005), 72.

66. Ibid., 72–74.

67. Stephen Prince, *Screening Violence* (New Brunswick, NJ: Rutgers University Press, 2000), 200.

68. Tzvetan Todorov, *The Poetics of Prose*, trans. Richard Howard (USA: Vail-Ballou Press, 1977), 219–221.

69. *Justified*, season 6, episode 13, "The Promise," dir. Adam Arkin, aired April 14, 2015, originally released on the FX Network.

70. Elmore Leonard, *Fire in the Hole and Other Stories* (USA: William Morrow Ltd., 2012), 112.

71. Jessica Blankenship, "Darrell Scott Explains the Story Behind *You'll Never Leave Harlan Alive*," Kentucky Country Music, October 29, 2020, https://kentuckycountrymusic.com/2020/10/darrell-scott-harlan.html.

BIBLIOGRAPHY

Batty, Craig, and Zara Waldeback. *Writing for the Screen: Creative and Critical Approaches*. Basingstoke: Palgrave MacMillan, 2008.

Blankenship, Jessica. "Darrell Scott Explains the Story Behind *You'll Never Leave Harlan Alive*," Kentucky Country Music, October 29, 2020. https://kentuckycountrymusic.com/2020/10/darrell-scott-harlan.html.

Booker, Christopher. *The Seven Basic Plots: Why We Tell Stories*. London: Continuum, 2004.

Broughton, Lee. *Critical Perspectives on the Western: From a Fistful of Dollars to Django Unchained*. Lanham, MD: Rowan and Littlefield, 2016.

Campbell, Joseph. *The Hero with a Thousand Faces.* Novato, CA: New World Library, 2008.

Carveth, Rod, and Robert Arp. *Justified and Philosophy: Shoot First, Think Later.* Chicago, IL: Carus Publishing Company, 2015.

Cavarero, Adriana. *Retelling Narratives: Storytelling and Selfhood.* Abingdon: Routledge, 2000.

Cook, Dee. *Criminal and Social Justice.* London: Sage Publications Ltd., 2006.

Crossley, Laura. "Ganstagrass: Hybridity and Popular Culture in Justified." *Journal of Popular Television* 1, no. 1 (2014): 57–75.

Elsaesser, Thomas, and Warren Buckland. *Studying Contemporary American Film: A Guide to Analysis.* London: Bloomsbury Academic, 2002.

FBI.GOV, *D.B. Cooper Hijacking*, accessed online July 2021 via https://www .fbi.gov/history/famous-cases/db-cooper-hijacking, various authors, updated regularly.

Fiske, John. *Television Culture.* London: Routledge, 1987.

French, Philip. *Westerns.* Manchester: Carcanet Press Limited, 1973; 2005.

Gray, Geoffrey. "Unmasking American Legend D.B. Cooper, Who Got Away with Hijacking a Plane." *New York Magazine*, October 18, 2007. https://nymag.com/news/features/39593/.

Gerber, Monica M., and Johnathan Jackson. "Retribution as Revenge and Retribution as Just Deserts." *Social Justice Research* 26 (2013): 61–80.

Grossweiler, Ed. "Hijacker bails out without loot." *The Free Lance-Star* (Fredericksburg, VA), November 26, 1971.

Hale, Mike. "Review: 'Justified' Finale on FX Ends Show's 6-Year Run." *The New York Times*, April 15, 2015. https://www.nytimes.com/2015/04/15/arts/television/review-justified-finale-on-fx-ends-shows-6-year-run.html.

Higgins, George V. *The Friends of Eddie Coyle.* USA: MacMillan Publishing, 1970.

Hill, T.E. "Kant on Wrongdoing, Desert, and Punishment." *Law and Philosophy* 18 (1999): 407–441.

Huefner, J.C., and H.K. Hunt. "Consumer Retaliation as a Response to Dissatisfaction." *Journal of Consumer Satisfaction, Dissatisfaction and Complaining Behaviour* 13 (2000): 61–82. Internet Movie Firearm Database.

Justified. Created by Graham Yost. Aired from March 16, 2010–April 14, 2015. Originally released on FX.

Kitses, Jim. *Horizons West: Directing the Western from John Ford to Clint Eastwood.* London: Bloomsbury/BFI, 2004.

Kopple, Barbara, dir. *Harlan County, USA.* 1976; New York, NY: Cabin Creek Films/Artefact Films, 2009. DVD.

Leonard, Elmore. *Fire in the Hole and Other Stories*, USA: HarperCollins, 2002.

Lichtenburg, Judith, "The Ethics of Retaliation," *Philosophy and Public Policy Quarterly* 21, no. 4 (2001): 4–8.

Lurker, Manfred. *The Routledge Dictionary of Gods and Goddesses, Devils and Demons.* London: Routledge, 2004.

May, Todd. *A Decent Life: Morality for the Rest of Us.* London: The University of Chicago Press, Ltd., 2019.

Mill, John Stuart. *Inaugural Address Delivered to the University of St. Andrews*. London: Longmans, Green, Reader and Dyer, 1867.

Miller, William. *Screenwriting for Narrative Film and Television*. London: Columbus Books Ltd., 1980.

Nelson, Andrew Patrick. *Contemporary Westerns: Film and Television since 1990*. Plymouth: The Scarecrow Press Inc., 2013.

Portelli, Alessandro. *They Say In Harlan County: An Oral History*. Oxford: Oxford University Press, 2012.

Prince, Stephen. *Screening Violence*. New Brunswick, NJ: Rutgers University Press, 2000.

Ratcliffe, Susan. *Oxford Essential Quotations*, 5 Ed. Oxford: Oxford University Press, 2017.

Rivette, Jacques. "Notes on a Revolution." *Cahiers du cinema* 54 (Christmas 1955): 17–21. Reprinted from *Cahiers du cinema: The 1950s*, edited by Jim Hillier (Cambridge, MA; Harvard, 1985). Translated by Liz Heron.

Scheid, Don E. "Kant's Retributivism." *Ethics* 93, no. 2 (1983): 262–282.

Schmalz, Dana. "Social Freedom in a Global World: Axel Honneth's and Seyla Benhabib's Reconsiderations of a Hegelian Perspective on Justice." *Constellations* 26, no. 2 (2019): 301–317.

Seitz, Matt Zoller. "Jim Beaver on Last Night's Justified and the Odds of a Deadwood Reunion." *Vulture*, March 27, 2013. https://www.vulture.com/2013/03/justified -jim-beaver-interview.html.

Shelton, James. *"We Dug Coal Together": The Complexity of Antagonism within Justified*. Presentation at Current Thinking on the Western III, Bradford, UK, July 14–15, 2016.

Shuster, Martin. *New Television: The Aesthetics and Politics of a Genre*. London: The University of Chicago Press, Ltd., 2017.

Simkin, Steve. *Revenge Strategy: Contemporary Critical Essays*. Basingstoke: Palgrave MacMillan, 2001.

Slotkin, Richard. *Gunfighter Nation: The Myth of the Frontier in Twentieth Century America*. New York: HarperCollins, 1992.

Todorov, Tzvetan. *The Poetics of Prose*. Translated by Richard Howard. United States of America: Vail-Ballou Press, 1977.

Todorov, Tzvetan, and A. Weinstein. "Structural Analysis of Narrative." *Novel: A Forum on Fiction* 3, no. 1 (1969): 70–76.

Tunick, Mark. "Is Kant a Retributivist?" *History of Political Thought* 17, no. 1 (1996): 60–78.

Turnbull, Sue. *The TV Crime Drama*. Edinburgh: Edinburgh University Press, 2014.

Warshow, Robert. *The Immediate Experience*. USA: Harvard College, 1946.

Wright, Will. *Sixguns & Society: A Structural Study of the Western*. London: University of California Press Ltd., 1975.

Chapter 6

Law and Loyalty in *Hellcats*

Matt Hummel

Granting that the era of Peak and Prestige TV begins in 2011, then producers Kevin Murphy and Tom Welling's singular season of *Hellcats* (September 2010 to May 2011) sits squarely at its dawn. Fittingly, the series showcases the transition to the era's emphasized themes of community over individuality and connection over self-actualization. It is a show about competitive college cheerleading, so the "teamwork" component is nigh inevitable. If the cheerleading aspect was the only thing the show boasted, which a cursory glance of reviews of the show and even its own description on CW Seed where it currently streams would heavily suggest, then it would not and indeed should not be as noteworthy as it is. And yet, from its debut episode, *Hellcats* promises a captivating and valuable through-line to the messages making it worthy of consideration as a moral artifact. In brief, the main character Marti Perkins (played by Ali Michalka) is a pre-law student. She knows what she wants to be and is fully invested in becoming a lawyer, because it will provide the answer to achieving the life she wants: living on her own, creating her own success story tethered to no one. In a way, Marti has a kind of tunnel vision about what the law will do for her, obscuring the fact that she, alone, has to work tirelessly to get there and with no guarantee. That tunnel vision carries over when, after a sudden financial setback, she joins the cheer squad purely as a way to pay her college tuition and continue her pre-law studies. The show's writers could have given the character literally any professional academic major if their only intention was to make a wacky juxtaposition between budding professional and bubbly cheerleader, à la *Legally Blonde*. Instead, they create a binary between an individualist, friendless world of law and the communal, embracing world of cheerleading. Time and again, the answers to Marti's problems or those of the friends she makes in the cheer squad are better solved through community than through individual action.

Then as Marti tries to navigate the central conflict of the show, the audience is led to reconsider an often misplaced devotion to law as a guide for right and wrong in favor of the power of relying on a loyal community.

Loyalty dominates as a guiding theme in *Hellcats*. Faithfulness to the cheer squad is treated as paramount. The show extends that theme out as moral questions. Is total devotion to a team truly valuable? Is loyalty to family unquestionable? And ultimately, is there something greater than loyalty? Cue the classic utilitarian argument—at what point does ensuring the good of many trump the rights of the individual? Each of the primary characters grapples with loyalty over the course of the show and ultimately develops the prevalence of community for the dawning age of Peak and Prestige TV.

THE ROUTINE: *HELLCATS'* STORY

To ask the *AV Club* reviewer of the *Hellcats* series debut, it's "terrible . . . an endlessly, strangely watchable terrible."[1] The same words resonate among the more positive reviews the show received on *Rotten Tomatoes*: it is "watchable," "a guilty pleasure," and it "has potential."[2] For all the suggestions of value to come, not one critic glanced back at the series after its debut. To say this drama is easily overlooked is an understatement. Its Nielsen rating and viewership steadily declined over the course of its run on The CW.[3] It could be, and apparently was for some, very easy to dismiss the production for what it seemed to be on its surface—a show about competitive college cheerleading. It had name recognition in Michalka and Ashley Tisdale, who audiences would be excited to see in more mature roles outside of the Disney Channel where they started. And it boasted visual appeal with its high-flying cheerleaders in skin-baring uniforms, workout gear, and cosplay. It was ten years too early to generate the audience response of Netflix's docuseries *Cheer*, a show which arguably presented the world of Kate Torgovnick's *Cheer!: Inside the Secret World of College Cheerleaders* (the inspiration for *Hellcats*) better than *Hellcats* did. But while showcasing the dramatic world of competitive college cheerleading may have been best served through documentary, *Hellcats'* dramatization still opened it up for story and moralization. It just wasn't billed that way.

The show's first couple of episodes do not do it any favors. Other than mentioning Marti's major, not one critic goes into any detail about it, because there is no detail to get into. The debut episode presents Marti's first dilemma as finding a way to stay enrolled at Lancer University when her scholarship through her mother's university employment is cut. Graduating and going on to be a lawyer is Marti's dream so she can get out of Memphis and be her own person away from home. She resolves her problem almost immediately by getting onto the Hellcats squad. From there, it's off to the races as Marti quickly becomes a coach favorite due to her improvisational dance technique, gymnastic prowess, and potential as a flyer. The pilot episode closes as Marti leads the squad with cheer captain Savannah Monroe (played by Ashley Tisdale) walking toward the arena for her first big cheer competition. It is clear the show is not going to be about learning to be a cheerleader and rising to stardom. The central thesis of the episode, which carries through the series, is that cheerleading is a serious athletic feat. But it is not quite clear actually what the show is supposed to be from its pilot episode, only that it is going to be character-driven.

Episode 2 is spent developing the show's other core characters. Savannah's character as a former student and cheerleader at Memphis Christian University is tested when her sister suffers an accident. Savannah is shown to be estranged from her family, especially her mother, by choosing to transfer to a secular school. She and Marti bond over their complicated relationships with their mothers, Marti's having been too overbearing for her liking and also too irresponsible to keep her own life and finances in order. The two become best friends quickly and end up sharing a room at the co-ed "Cheertown" residence for squad members. The third major character, Alice Verdura (played by Heather Hemmens), serves as a rival for Marti as she takes Alice's place after her injury in the pilot. The show pivots around these three key figures, as well as the Hellcats coach Vanessa Lodge (played by Sharon Leal). Vanessa's storylines understandably contrast with the other three and tend to follow a standard love triangle drama between her current boyfriend and back-in-town ex-boyfriend from her own college days at the university where she now works. By the end of episode 2, characters and storylines are centrally placed, all except for Marti's. Again, the audience surrogate does not yet have anywhere to go beyond juggling life on a demanding competitive team and attending college classes. Then, episode 3 opens things up.

Episode 3 introduces Marti's law professor Julian Parrish (played by Gale Harold), and for the first time the show introduces a moral point of view. Marti is excited to learn under Parrish since he is a renowned, still-working lawyer. He presents to the class his personal project to repeal the state's three strikes law. He enlists several students to join his project outside of class, and of course Marti earns a spot. In an instant, the show reveals a story path for its lead character and invests the audience in moral stakes vis-à-vis the fallibility of law. As Marti the student is tasked with critiquing the law, *Hellcats* asks its audience to do the same. The show heralded as a "watchable guilty pleasure" makes good on its potential by creating an avenue for moral discussion seeded in the very first critic reviews: she's a law student who enters the world of cheerleading.

THE STUNT: LAW IN *HELLCATS*

Television loves law. That is because law is a conflict generator. Law makes good drama, and good drama fills stories. Consider how legal philosopher John Austin defines law: "a rule laid down for the guidance of an intelligent being by an intelligent being having power over him."[4] There is inherent conflict in law's imposition: it casts at least two groups in opposition and establishes a duty to obey.[5] A law enforcement officer then is an extension of a holder of power, a lawmaker, while a citizen is one guided by that officer to obey the law or face consequences as set forth by the law(maker). The nature of the law or rule is important to the dynamic of the two groups, but the rule itself is simply a point around which tension manifests. Law itself does nothing, it just is.

Now, it is not to suggest that law *just is* without any intention behind it. The law is not a naturally occurring thing, but for the purposes of television, it might as well be. The origin of the law, that is, lawmakers are rarely characters in any real sense, notwithstanding shows with characters inhabiting that world like *House of Cards* or *The Politician*. Even there, the focus is gaining access and surviving within the American political world, not necessarily the craft of lawmaking. It is the political realm itself where much, if not all, of the drama takes place, cueing the question as to what actually drives a story in which law has a significant presence. The answer is morality. Grappling with moral choices is a good plot driver. In a procedural drama, for instance, morality motivates the action, not the law itself. To obey the law or not or to enforce it or not and how are all identifiable through the moral intentions of a character, ones which translate easily in television stories through examination of a character's loyalties. Its use in *Hellcats* seems to reflect and expand on that tension between law and morality by having its main character literally study the law and witness its inability to help her deal with problems.

Legal accuracy is not the point of bringing up the three strikes law in *Hellcats*. The temptation to let *Hellcats'* real setting in Memphis, Tennessee, lead the discussion of its implementation of law is strong. Tennessee does have a "Three strikes" provision in its state code.[6] It provides guidance for determining what criminal convictions apply to a designation of "repeat violent offender" which itself is a separate criminal charge that may enhance a defendant's sentence for a new offense in accordance with Tennessee's sentencing statute.[7] In "Papa, Oh Papa," Travis Guthrie (played by Robbie Jones), the client in Professor Parrish's pet case for overturning the three strikes law, admits his two prior felony convictions were for "drunk and disorderly" and "resisting arrest," neither of which are listed for designation as a repeat violent offender in the Tennessee statute—nor would they likely be considered felonies.[8] One could accept it as a research error, per its addition on the IMDb page for the episode, and leave it there.[9] That would be focusing on the law more as a character or a setting, that it is not being portrayed *correctly*. But again, law is not a character, it is a conflict generator. It is more appropriate to look at the "error" as contextual grounding for the larger point of bringing criminal sentencing reform up in the first place, which has nothing to do with the law and everything to do with character conflict. In short, based solely on his simple convictions, Travis is not that bad of a guy. Professor Parrish however, by virtue of Travis's case, is effectively using Travis as a means to an end. Marti is torn by the notion of leaving Travis's potential innocence of his third offense unchecked in order to pursue the larger goal of overturning the law. It is a classic utilitarian conflict and point of moral debate not just for Marti's law class storyline but for the show as a whole: where should loyalties most lie and to what degree?

THE SPOTTER: MARTI'S DILEMMA

Marti's law student arc and her position on Julian's three strike's student task force reveal the rawest vulnerability the cheer squad has. Her investigation into Travis's innocence exposes a larger conspiracy at Lancer University to cover up misdeeds by its student athletes in order to promote illegal fund transfers among players, football backers, and former alumni. The athletic program, which oversees the Hellcats, is already on probation for such illegal activity, and the program stands to be shut down entirely if it is caught again. As it turns out, the crime for which Travis faces three strikes legislation was a hazing-instigated robbery-turned-unintentional-murder committed by none other than the football team's star quarterback, Jake, during his freshman year. Lancer's athletic department, spearheaded by athletic director Bill Marsh (played by Aaron Douglas), had covered up the crime and framed Travis, a drunken nobody. Enter Marti's classic utilitarian dilemma: disclose the truth and risk the demise of the athletic department, the Hellcats, and all of their scholarships or stay quiet and permit Travis's unjust condemnation. The needs of the many versus the rights of the few—here, one. The show's writing brings to the forefront the big question the audience would have been anticipating at this mid-season climax: isn't loyalty limited when it comes to moral decision-making if the group to which one is loyal isn't good, or at the very least abstains from good?

In answer to that question, the show keeps pace with itself and continues to push for community over individual problem-solving. Rather than purely focus on Marti's inner struggle, the show devotes an entire episode to bearing down on the stakes of Marti's decision. "Remember When" features Alice feigning the importance of "formally initiating" Marti into the Hellcats as a front for forcing Marti to learn what the team means for her closest friends.[10] It is revealed that the Hellcats is as much a life-changing haven as it is a competitive cheer squad. For Savannah, joining the Hellcats meant a new start in a world without her family; for Lewis, Marti's base and romance interest, a way to stay an athlete without the pressure of Lancer's unethical financial scheme; for Alice, a literal life saver before she turned down a path of self-destruction. Even Vanessa, a former Hellcat herself, was able to rejoin as coach when life after Lancer became listless and degrading. By fleshing out the characters in such a focal way—their relation to Marti as a Hellcat—it counterbalances all the time Marti spent getting to know Travis.

The writing through the first half of the episode seems to argue that greater weight in the utilitarian dilemma comes down to loyalty and then exposes the problem of conceiving of loyalty in that way. Alice knows how much time Marti has devoted to Travis's case; she even assisted Marti at the climax of the investigation and discovers that her boyfriend Jake is the true culprit. She therefore understands Marti's loyalty to do right by Travis. So, at the initiation, she is the one to prod each individual to share their stories to even the utilitarian odds. As she says to Marti, "[i]f you're determined to put a bullet in the Hellcats, I'm going to make you look us in the eye when you pull the trigger."[11] For Alice, loyalty is the pinnacle to the moral dilemma; it is just a matter of how much. Alice's tact here is itself a demonstration of loyalty, however backhanded. Her development up to "Remember When" shows a progression from loyalty as a veil for self-interest to genuine trust.

THE FLYER: ALICE AND THE ETHICS OF REVENGE

Though billed as the rival, Alice is not an antagonist. At the series start, she comes off as someone who would sell out another for her own gain. She emits narcissism and engages with her teammates passive-aggressively, but Alice is not an island unto herself. She seeks a leadership role on the squad, or at least to hold onto her position after figuratively and literally falling from it in the pilot episode. She believes herself the most capable to lead the Hellcats to victory, especially when it calls for tough decision-making. Alice is also fully aware of her own vulnerability. Her injury in the pilot incites the whole story of community in *Hellcats* with all of the primary characters reacting to her fall. Savannah is right there showing great concern, as is Marti, who, not even affiliated with the squad at the time, witnesses the fall and reprimands her friend Dan for making a joke of it. Alice does not have a moment of reaction, and in her next appearance, she is in the gym with the rest of her squad. She shows some angst at Savannah for what she believes is blind optimism and then zeroes in on Lewis, the base for her cheer stunts and former boyfriend.

Her comments to him indicate a vague, unearned feeling of betrayal by him. And so begins Alice's lessons on the ethics of revenge.

At the outset, it is important to distinguish revenge or vengeance from retributive justice. Robert Nozick clarified the distinction as a difference between the personal and the impersonal, of gaining pleasure over another's suffering versus pleasure of justice carried out.[12] Even that distinction, though, does not seem to clearly draw a line of separation, but for story purposes, a character pursuing vengeance without the buffer of retributive justice is a psycho seeking gratification while the alternative seeks a better world. Alice, in the gym with Lewis, seeks personal satisfaction. There is already bitter history between the two, and the suggestion that he dropped her is dubious at best—she fell from a pyramid stunt, so plenty of room for error. Alice's insult that he's clumsy is not meant to right any wrongs. Still, it is wrong to view the gym scene as introducing Alice as the school bully, a characterization that only feeds into the one-and-done reviews of the pilot. It is a glimpse into the way Alice views reality. Harm to her and what she cares about must be returned. Moreover, it must be returned *by her.*

Though separate, revenge and retributive justice have the same sentiment: fairness. The difference, again, is the perspective. In revenge, fairness is understood personally. Retributive justice would judge fairness systemically. Alice demands fairness. A weightier example than the very short gym scene comes in the whole of "Ragged Old Flag."[13] The Lancer volleyball team intrudes on the Hellcats' practice, taking over the space. The volleyball captain, Carol, spars with Alice after throwing the ball at her during a stunt, causing her to fall and almost suffer another serious injury. Vanessa threatens to report Carol, but Alice waves her off. Once the person of legitimate— a.k.a. "legal"—authority is gone, Alice pushes the issue, and Carol reveals her true grief is that the Hellcats do not deserve the status the school gives them because cheerleaders are not athletes. She even quotes the NCAA, which continues to not recognize cheerleading as a varsity sport to this day.[14] At this point, Alice has been assaulted physically and disrespected personally, but only after her team is disrespected does she respond formally. No passive-aggression, just a straight assertion that cheerleaders are athletes, better athletes even than volleyball players. It is a motivating moment that carries the thesis of the show only to be quickly dumped when Alice accepts, without thought, a challenge to prove her team's athleticism. Her pride in this moment is actually Alice's penchant for vengeance, to attain fair recompense for a grievance by her own terms. And it is not even vengeance for herself, though her piercing gaze at the initial confrontation suggests she is personally excited to rain punishment on her offender. She seeks revenge for the Hellcats, for the sake of loyalty, albeit that similar misplaced sense of loyalty to which she will return in "Remember When." Again, an audience can recognize a knee-jerk move to defend one's group or seek revenge for a slight against it.

The writers keep setting that familiarity up for audiences in order to push a fresher take on loyalty by highlighting how revenge in defense of one's group diminishes the moral value of that group. They show that revenge is in fact still personal, best ascertained by considering the grievance in the form of a question. Are cheerleaders athletes? From a systemic point of fairness, proof of that may lie in NCAA terminology or a campaign to amend the NCAA's consideration of the term athlete. Alice's response, according to her personal terms of fairness, is "cheerleaders are such good athletes that they can beat other athletes at their own game." Her answer is personal and addresses a sense of fairness imbalanced by Carol's attitude and behavior. It is also completely indicative of nothing because, should the Hellcats lose the challenge, it will not have sincerely addressed the issue of their athleticism. It would simply be an unsuccessful attempt at revenge. And Alice seems to know this. She is aware that her team could lose. If it were truly about proving the Hellcats as serious athletic contenders, then accepting the challenge would be unnecessary. It is the personal that gets in the way, and since she wrapped her team up in her personal campaign for vengeance, she feels responsible for it. So she cheats.

Since revenge is rooted in the person, the feeling of being wronged, and the need for fairness on one's own terms, the view from outside of that perspective is always going to be critical. Perhaps one could support the notion of revenge, but certainly not to the same degree or in the same way. Seeing Alice accept Carol's challenge to a flag football match without input from the Hellcats is like watching proverbial "suicide," as Marti puts it. It is Alice puffing out her chest at an imposing opponent. But rather than call off the challenge, the squad falls in line with Alice and, under Lewis' coaching, practices to beat the volleyball team. It is another instance of loyalty, this time of the Hellcats to Alice. But that kind of loyalty escapes Alice; it is sacrificial and demands trust. So despite the team's rallying and proof of cohesion, Alice takes it upon herself to ensure victory by stealing the opposing team's playbook, an act which itself demeans the pride she's vying to avenge. She commits herself to a night of sex with Jake, who volunteered to coach the volleyball team, and snaps photos of the playbook at his place. Only when Savannah points out the fault of her revenge—that winning by cheating does not prove anything and that it does not address the question of the grievance—is she forced to face the price of real loyalty. She must sacrifice guaranteed revenge and trust her team. And it pays off in a big way. She trusts Lewis to come up with new plays and he, in turn, throws off Jake, who secretly knew Alice had stolen his plays. The Hellcats win her the revenge she was seeking, preserving her pride and demonstrating the promise of community.

Alice shows more willingness to trust larger, communal answers to her grievances. In "Pledging My Love," after nude pictures of her leak online,

Alice tracks down the culprit.[15] He is a football player, and though he apologizes for his behavior, he leans on the corruption of the athletic department to ensure he will face no consequences. So at first, Alice goes the revenge route. She learns the player is secretly gay, and she tries to secure video of him with another male in his room, but she is caught in the act. Vanessa outright asks her, "if stopping a monster means becoming a monster yourself, was it worth it?"[16] A torn Alice, shamed and denied her revenge, asks what she can do, if there is a proper way to right the wrong. The show's writing then takes a bit of an outdated, victim-blaming stance against women who have had nudes leaked—the show aired about four years prior to the major iCloud leaks of private celebrity photos which prompted a national discussion about online privacy and online sexual abuse. But it settles on some community-based "frontier" justice, referring to the practice of extra-judicial punishment to satisfy grievances where law provides no remedy. It sounds like revenge, and as Alice presents the terms of her settlement to the football player, it certainly seems like it. She demands he enroll in classes on the exploitation of women and the ethics of privacy, as well as serve as a nude model for a figure studies art class, where his body will be looked at but not in shame. Then, as the player relents, Alice promises that the two will be "bonded." She comes closer to terms with the power of systemic answers to grievances through retributive justice. She is more trusting of a community to help her claim such justice. She may still have an antagonist in the football player, but her remedy promises the potential for growth.

Thus, Alice reveals what she has learned about revenge ethics when she confronts Marti, albeit underhandedly, at Marti's initiation. Even though it seems like she has backslid into vengeful ways, it is important to recall how she phrased her plan to Marti, to make Marti "look [them] in the eye." She's not plotting around Marti or vying to undermine her. She is forcing Marti to face the stakes of her utilitarian decision. Alice is trusting Marti to hold loyalty to the Hellcats above loyalty to Travis. It is as if she is asking Marti to choose family over strangers. And if things were left there, the idea of loyalty as a worthy guide to moral decision-making would fail. In order to not revert back to that simplistic vision of loyalty as blind defense of one's group, the group has to stand for something more in relation to the individual. It must be self-actualizing.

THE CAPTAIN: SAVANNAH'S FAMILY
AND SELF-ACTUALIZATION

As captain of the Hellcats, Savannah cues the show's initial theory about loyalty. She exudes team spirit and competitive drive, and it is important to see her character in the role as captain consistently being sniped at by the initially vengeful Alice as her second. While Alice's character arc teaches of the moral reward of loyalty compared with individual pursuits, Savannah's showcases loyalty tested and refined. Savannah has conviction as a captain yet leads innately with an ear for her team. There is little to suggest she has ever tested her convictions though, such as the "no negativity zone" she demands in the gym after catching Alice and Lewis bickering. Savannah does not hold out her "positive-outcomes-only" mantra as a rigorously examined method of team cohesion. The squad nevertheless seems to favor Savannah's outlook because her convictions come from a genuine place. That's why it is so surprising to learn early on that she is estranged from her family. For Savannah to contend with a broken family relationship when she does not readily test her convictions is significant and vastly instructive as a moral storyline about what loyalty is and should be.

Meeting Savannah, a leader figure, after she has already severed ties with her family makes for a kind of mystery storytelling. "I Say a Little Prayer" is all about opening up that mystery.[17] Vanessa drops a clue that Savannah used to attend the school with the team to beat at regional qualifiers, Memphis Christian University. Immediately afterward, Savannah shares a tense conversation with one of their cheerleaders. The "MemChris" cheerleader is cold and dismissive, leaving Savannah jarred although she presses on. Vanessa seems to know the girl, asking how "Charlotte" is. Later, Savannah watches with pride as MemChris performs a stunning routine, only to run on the floor when Charlotte (played by Emma Lahana) is knocked unconscious after a major fall. As Charlotte is loaded into the ambulance, Savannah hesitates to join her. Vanessa vows to deal with the consequences of Savannah leaving to be with Charlotte, and the mystery is suddenly solved for the audience. Only family is ever permitted to ride along in ambulances, and Vanessa confirms the answer as the screen cuts to black—Charlotte is Savannah's sister.

The mystery is the driving force of the beginning of the episode, but it carries the complex question of loyalty throughout. The top starts with Vanessa giving a rousing inspiration to her team, laying the stakes of qualifying out plain. They must place at nationals or lose their competitive program and scholarships. Then the mystery begins, as do the questions. Why is Savannah wishing good luck to the enemy? Why is she watching their lead flyer with pride, and why is she the first at her side when she falls? The mystery peaks when Vanessa, who had just warned that the program will end if the Hellcats do not win, openly suggests Savannah go with Charlotte; it demands an explanation. Finally, ending the scene revealing that the two are family closes the mystery but leaves the commercial break for the audience to ponder the moral question: Does loyalty to family truly come first, and why? Or, at least, that is the familiar part of the question. The show writers, even as early as episode two, are preparing the audience to find a familiar moral point of view in order to explore an expanded vision of loyalty and to justify it.

Wrestling with Savannah's leaving the regional qualifier despite the stakes is an exercise in justifying an expanded vision of loyalty. Standing merely on a "family comes first" morale is a position that begs the same question. Does family come first in relation to duty, as an obligation, as a merit, or something else? To compare, it is helpful to consider that Vanessa's permission for her to leave is itself an act of loyalty. She has a whole squad to look after, yet she potentially sacrifices their futures at Lancer for Savannah. Is she duty bound to tend to her athletes in such a particular way as Savannah's situation warrants? Has Savannah earned the loyalty of her coach? Or is Vanessa's loyalty driven by something else? Perhaps Vanessa is just confident in her ability to assuage the situation favorably for the Hellcats, as she indeed does by getting their qualifying routine bumped to a later date. Vanessa's choice does at least highlight an important facet of loyalty: that it is testable by action that presents a detriment to the loyal figure. With these pieces in mind, it may be possible to track why Savannah still shows loyalty for her family even in the face of their disdain.

Savannah and her family seem most at odds over their terms of loyalty, of what is valued and therefore on the chopping block to test it. She enters Charlotte's room in the hospital, and her mother gives her a cold greeting, similar to the way Charlotte did. Savannah wonders aloud that it had been a year since she had shared the same room with her family, happy to at least see her mother and almost grateful that, despite the circumstances, they could be together. Charlotte then shuts her down, chastising Savannah for perceiving Charlotte's injury as a positive moment for herself. Though Charlotte's point is well-made, the audience is primed to feel for Savannah as she then puts on a brave face for her coach and teammates. Savannah's "positive-outcomes-only" attitude seems to fall on deaf ears with her family. In a later exchange with her mother, Savannah alights at the opportunity for reconciliation by attending a healing prayer service for Charlotte. But she has to attempt a compromise when she learns the service will take place at the same time as the Hellcats' newly scheduled qualifier. She tries to show balancing justifications for loyalty. Savannah's team made a sacrifice for her in a moment of crisis, so she could not very well ask that of them again for anything less than a crisis. Her mother retorts, falsely equivocating Charlotte's fall and MemChris's subsequent loss at regionals to Savannah and the Hellcats' decision to postpone their routine. Attending the prayer service is a test of Savannah's loyalty to her family *on her family's terms*. Savannah's compromise to show up to the service later than it starts, to still be present in support, shows a willingness to be loyal on her terms. The mystery of Savannah's estrangement is resolved a bit more while the complexity of family loyalty grows.

Further in the episode, Savannah fully opens up to Marti about her family, sacrificing the mystery storyline for character bonding. But, in so doing, she articulates the grounds for which she committed herself to being estranged. She left her family's legacy school for the sake of personal flourishment, a reason which falls in line with Kleinig's assessment of one of the justifications of loyalty.[18] Savannah felt herself, a vibrant social being with leadership potential, being stifled by the dictates of her family at a school she considered shut off from engagement with the world. Leaving the school and remaining loyal to her family were equally plausible, simply expanding her terms of family and the loyalty it inspires. Her willingness to compromise with her mother on the prayer service is expressive of her expanded form of loyalty, addressing conflicts through consideration rather than on default terms. The show's writing then argues in favor of Savannah's justification, showing Savannah committing herself to her family by praying for her sister prior to the Hellcats' performance. Though she still is not sacrificing on family terms, she dedicates herself to that moment without the possibility of reward vis-à-vis reunification with her family.

For Savannah, loyalty is at once associative and contemplative. In this way, she becomes the linchpin for the moral perspective developed in *Hellcats*. She herself is not the moral center of the show—she is not a guru or sage. Rather, she embodies a necessary element for the show's expanded view of loyalty, that is, that loyalty should flow out of and simultaneously empower the self. Savannah surrounds herself with diverse social groupings and pledges loyalty to them all. She negotiates conflicts with reason, putting her at odds with her closed-minded family. The estrangement was not her doing, and she longs to reconcile but not at the cost of loyalty to her greater pursuit of self-actualization. And since her sense of self is so ingrained in being a cheerleader—a Hellcat—loyalty to that very sense of self encompasses loyalty to her team. Moreover, Savannah's Hellcat loyalty is enriched by her willingness to express it, not through sacrificial testing but through devotion to her inner principles of reason, compromise, and "positive-outcomes-only" attitude.

LAW AND LOYALTY

At the end of "Remember When," Marti must complete her initiation by falling from the height of the Hellcats' practice space to a dark and silent floor below. She must trust that her squad mates will be there to catch her without seeing it. The whole thing is hyper-dramatized, but it brings home key ideas each of the main characters bring to focus. Marti has to make a choice, Alice has to trust her teammate to be loyal in making that decision, and Savannah has to help all of them parse the terms of loyalty in deciding what the right decision is. She jumps, the Hellcats catch her, and it seems like she intends to choose the Hellcats over Travis. In keeping with what she has learned of systemic justice, Alice simply asks Marti what she intends to do; she does not gloat or demand Marti fall in line. Then, Marti receives a call that Travis has been severely brutalized while in prison. Savannah drives Marti out to see him. They both witness his injuries, and it's heavily implied that the offenders were put to the task by people in the athletic department trying to keep the truth from coming out. It is then that Savannah reveals it is the first time she has ever seen Travis. She sees Marti distraught and presses Marti to reveal everything to her. This is important as Savannah is now fully aware of the other side of Marti's dilemma that saving Travis and revealing his innocence could mean the end of the Hellcats. The scene then cuts to Marti and Savannah, likely at Savannah's urging, revealing the dilemma to all of the Hellcats. Once the story is out, Savannah is the first in the circle to declare their path forward—they will risk losing the program, their scholarships, and their sense of identity to save Travis.

To its credit, the show presents no debate among the Hellcats. It needs no debate. By revealing the dilemma to Savannah alone first, it leaves her act of leadership as a surrogate for the debate and its resolution. As with her conviction to come to Lancer, to be shunned by her family, Savannah vies for personal flourishment through social self-actualization. She has seen Travis's suffering first hand, so to turn her back on that suffering when she can do something to correct it would be a detriment to her personal sense of justice. It is not that the law has the answers; it is clearly incapable of determining justice without people standing up for it. It is not about whether it is right to let the many suffer for one. And it is not even about loyalty to one group versus another. Through Savannah, loyalty to the Hellcats means embracing justice together. The Hellcats are loyal to each other even as they pursue a path that might end them, to sacrifice for and because of each other. They are more than good athletes; they are good people. Alice, the last hold-out, accepts this to be true as well.

With the decision made, the story then turns back to law. Good and loyal people may have to stand up for what is right, but the law still has rules. "God Must Have My Fortune Laid Away" sees Marti reconvene with Julian to go over what she has ascertained in her investigation into Travis's case.[19] In good faith, she presents him with a winnable case to get Travis's conviction overturned, but she demands not an exchange but rather another round of brainstorming. Marti intends to broaden the social circle and diversify the group of good people, something in line with the ideals of Savannah's self-actualization through association. They align with the uncorrupt coach of the football team, Red Raymond, who is himself aligned with Vanessa as a friend and romantic partner. Marti states outright, "Vanessa trusts him and that's good enough for me . . . Lancer stands to lose a lot of good people."[20] Julian, inspired by her determination, agrees.

What follows is a drawn-out heist-style story as the group works together to pressure Bill Marsh into implicating himself and to make Jake turn himself in. Just as the plan seems to be working flawlessly, it crumbles as Jake, feeling abandoned, asserts he will bring the system down because "a lot of people did wrong here, it's not fair that [he's] the one that's supposed to suffer."[21] He has a strong point because, while his initial crime only implicates him, the cover-up would constitute a criminal conspiracy. Justice, legally speaking, would see culprits face judgment for that conspiracy, so for Jake, being loyal, at least at that instant, is personally disadvantageous and irrational. In trying to bring Jake under the loyalty fold, Marti appeals to Jake's personal sense of right and wrong, but she fails to actually embrace him, to make him feel trusted, and so he lashes out. The story then falls to Alice saving the day, bringing her ethics of revenge lessons to a close as she leads Jake to higher moral ground and a promise to stay loyal to him even after he goes to prison. Their scene closes with the second display of prayer of the episode, the first being Savannah struggling with her decision to lead the Hellcats to possible destruction. Jake endures the same strife but is assured, as he takes Alice's hand, that he is not alone in his decision. The show resolves with Jake confessing publicly, and Marti faces the hard truth that truth is always going to be skewed publicly. She watches, dismayed, as reporters hail Jake a hero without any mention of Travis. Her discomforted face suggests she understands now that doing the right and loyal thing is always going to be hard. Still, as Bob Marley's "Redemption Song," sung by Marti and the absolved Travis, plays over the action, the sentiment rings out that the right thing will always be worth pursuing and best achieved together.

OVERLOOKED AND CONCLUDED

Series producer Tom Welling believes it was a regime change at The CW that did *Hellcats* in.[22] He mentioned a cult following could be bringing it back, but that was four years ago.[23] The show just never held enough appeal. Seven episodes followed its climactic "God Must Have My Fortune Laid Away." The show seemed to anticipate another season as it tried to set up more storylines for Marti, developing a relationship between her and Julian and a budding one with her newly found sister. The singular season closed out on a major rift between the sisters that would have tied in with Savannah suffering a huge family breakdown, fodder for a new season to explore the ideas of loyalty after betrayal and learning to forgive. But, as the reviews demonstrate, a big bang right from the start is crucial; otherwise, no one will follow through. When the series ended, the media landscape was already one-month deep into the critically acclaimed *Game of Thrones. Hellcats* did not pave a path forward but nonetheless heralded new endeavors for storytelling in the era of Peak and Prestige TV. The show is fascinating because it did not have to dive so headfirst into a legal narrative that really does not fit the aesthetic of the show, further evidencing its importance as a sign of things to come in the new television era.

Perhaps its one-off life amounts to the public denying a spin on *Hellcats'* own thesis, that a TV show about cheerleaders is just as morally insightful and can grapple with uneasy questions as effectively as any other show.

NOTES

1. Emily VanDerWuff, *"Hellcats –* 'A World Full of Strangers,'" *AV Club,* September 8, 2010, https://tv.avclub.com/hellcats-a-world-full-of-strangers -1798165865.

2. "Hellcats: Season 1 Reviews," *Rotten Tomatoes,* accessed June 1, 2020, https://www.rottentomatoes.com/tv/hellcats/s01/reviews/.

3. Trevor Kimball, *"Hellcats:* CW TV Series Cancelled; No Season Two," *TV Series Finale,* May 18, 2011, https://tvseriesfinale.com/tv-show/hellcats-canceled -season-two/.

4. John Austin, *The Province of Jurisprudence, Determined* (London: Weidenfeld & Nicholson, 1954), 18.

5. Ibid., 19.

6. "Repeat violent offenders 'Three strikes,'" Tennessee Code 40-35-120.

7. "Imposition of sentence; Evidence to be considered; Presumptive sentence; Sentence explanation," Tennessee Code 40-35-210.

8. *Hellcats,* season 1, episode 12, "Papa, Oh Papa," dir. Andy Wolk, aired January 25, 2011, digitally released on CW Seed.

9. "Goofs—*Hellcats,* 'Papa, Oh Papa' (2011)," *IMDb,* accessed June 3, 2020, https://www.imdb.com/title/tt1755329/goofs/.

10. *Hellcats,* season 1, episode 14, "Remember When," dir. Omar Madha, aired February 8, 2011, digitally released on CW Seed.

11. Ibid.

12. Robert Nozick, *Philosophical Explanations* (Cambridge, MA: Harvard University Press, 1981), 367.

13. *Hellcats,* season 1, episode 6, "Ragged Old Flag," dir. Kevin Flair, aired October 10, 2010, digitally released on CW Seed.

14. Rachel E. Greenspan, *"Cheer* Shows Competitive Cheerleading Is Almost as Dangerous as Football. So Why Isn't It Officially Considered a Sport?," *Time,* originally published March 4, 2020, updated March 10, 2020, https://time.com/5782136/ cheer-netflix-cheerleading-dangers/.

15. *Hellcats,* season 1, episode 10, "Pledging My Love," dir. Debbie Allen, aired November 17, 2010, digitally released on CW Seed.

16. Ibid.

17. *Hellcats*, season 1, episode 2, "I Say a Little Prayer," dir. Allan Arkush, aired September 15, 2010, digitally released on CW Seed.

18. John Kleinig, "Loyalty," *Stanford Encyclopedia of Philosophy*, published August 21, 2007, revised October 16, 2017, https://plato.stanford.edu/entries/loyalty/.

19. *Hellcats*, season 1, episode 15, "God Must Have My Fortune Laid Away," dir. John Behring, aired February 15, 2011, digitally released on CW Seed.

20. Ibid.

21. Ibid.

22. Rachel Ellenbogen, "'Hellcats' Is Coming Back, Producer Tom Welling Reveals Cancelation Reason," *International Business Times*, September 12, 2017, https://www.ibtimes.com/hellcats-coming-back-producer-tom-welling-reveals-cancelation-reason.

23. Ibid.

BIBLIOGRAPHY

Austin, John. *The Province of Jurisprudence, Determined.* London: Weidenfeld & Nicholson, 1954.

Ellenbogen, Rachel. "'Hellcats' Is Coming Back, Producer Tom Welling Reveals Cancelation Reason." *International Business Times*, September 12, 2017. https://www.ibtimes.com/hellcats-coming-back-producer-tom-welling-reveals-cancelation-reason.

Greenspan, Rachel E. "*Cheer* Shows Competitive Cheerleading Is Almost as Dangerous as Football: So Why Isn't It Officially Considered a Sport?" *Time*, originally published March 4, 2020, updated March 10, 2020. https://time.com/5782136/cheer-netflix-cheerleading-dangers/.

Hellcats, created by Kevin Murphy. Aired from September 8, 2010–May 17, 2011. Originally released on CW Seed.

IMDb. "Goofs—*Hellcats*, 'Papa, Oh Papa' (2011)." Accessed June 3, 2020. https://www.imdb.com/title/tt1755329/goofs/.

Kimball, Trevor. "*Hellcats:* CW TV Series Cancelled; No Season Two." *TV Series Finale*, May 18, 2011. https://tvseriesfinale.com/tv-show/hellcats-canceled-season-two/.

Kleinig, John. "Loyalty." *Stanford Encyclopedia of Philosophy*, published August 21, 2007. revised October 16, 2017, https://plato.stanford.edu/entries/loyalty/.

Nozick, Robert. *Philosophical Explanations.* Cambridge, MA: Harvard University Press, 1981.

Rotten Tomatoes. "Hellcats: Season 1 Reviews." Accessed June 1, 2020. https://www.rottentomatoes.com/tv/hellcats/s01/reviews/.

VanDerWuff, Emily. "*Hellcats* – 'A World Full of Strangers.'" *AV Club*, September 8, 2010. https://tv.avclub.com/hellcats-a-world-full-of-strangers-1798165865.

Chapter 7

Justice Is Served

Bryan Fuller's Hannibal *and the Evolution of Cultural Morality*

Douglas L. Howard

There is a compelling moment at the end of season 1 of Bryan Fuller's *Hannibal* where the cannibalistic psychiatrist and the insightful former FBI investigator Will Graham (played by Hugh Dancy) meet one last time in the Baltimore State Hospital for the Criminally Insane. After psychologically (or "psychically") driving Will toward the brink of madness and handily framing him for his own grisly Chesapeake Ripper murders, the manipulative Lecter (played by Mads Mikkelsen), intent on seeing the results of his work, goes to visit Graham, now incarcerated in a maximum-security ward.[1] As he confidently walks the hallway toward Will's cell, the operatic voices from Patrick Cassidy's "Vide Cor Meum," initially used to great effect in Ridley Scott's 2001 film *Hannibal*, soar in the background.[2] "Hello, Will," the impeccably dressed Lecter says. "Hello, Dr. Lecter," Will, in patient fatigues, responds knowingly, as they face each other, separated only by the steel bars that should keep the deranged killer in and the sane captor out. Within the framework of the season, this scene is a fitting end to the fine meal that Fuller has prepared because, while Will has been able to solve bizarre murder after bizarre murder for the FBI, he has been unable to see his enemy, often appearing in surreal dream sequences on the show as a "Ravenstag man," standing next to him until this final episode.[3] Although he has fallen prey to the doctor's insidious machinations and been disgraced and discredited to all who know him, Will now knows his enemy, a critical juncture in their complex relationship, one that dramatically sets the rest of the series in motion.[4] But, in restaging what amounts to be a pivotal scene in Lecter lore and repurposing the characters for this moment on television and in television history, Fuller forces the audience to think about what they were, what they meant to us, and

what they still mean to us, the audience, as we continue to (re)evaluate heroism and villainy on TV. Not only does the scene ultimately reveal the moral
instability that has always been at the heart of the Hannibal Lecter mythology
itself, but it contextually speaks to the instability that is now a regular part
of our television dramas as well as to our shaken faith in those institutions of
justice and order.

A MOMENT OF SILENCE

For starters, Will's confrontation with Hannibal at the end of the season
immediately works as a call-back to the beginning of Jonathan Demme's celebrated 1991 film *The Silence of the Lambs*, when Lecter (played by Anthony
Hopkins) is first questioned by Clarice Starling (played by Jodie Foster), with
Graham even wearing the same kind of prison uniform and being isolated in
the same kind of ward under Dr. Chilton's care.[5] The scene, however, is not
exactly the same, and we are meant to notice the differences, both subtle and
not-so-subtle. From the foreboding Howard Shore score to the ominous pre-
cautions that Clarice gets from both Jack Crawford (played by Scott Glenn),
the head of the Behavioral Science Unit of the FBI, and Dr. Chilton, chief
of staff at the Baltimore State Forensic Hospital, to the unsettling glimpses
of those other inmates (like Multiple Miggs) that we see in Lecter's ward,
Clarice's long walk down the dimly lit hallway in *Silence* seems more like
a trip through a haunted house, with Lecter as the main attraction. Where
Will has bars on his cell in *Hannibal*, in the movie Lecter stands behind a
glass wall, a design decision on Demme's part to create a "sense of intimacy
between Lecter and Starling."[6] And, as the visitor, Clarice is clearly appre-
hensive about making that walk, yet she repeatedly, ambitiously, heroically
makes it, to take on what seems to be a career opportunity from Crawford
and, in her own words, "to learn from [Lecter]" about the twisted world that
will lead her to the serial killer Buffalo Bill and his intended victim, Catherine
Martin. She is an innocent on the outside of the glass looking in and the character that the audience immediately sympathizes with. She is also the figure
of justice and morality in the film, the one who puts herself at risk, as we
learn, to save a lamb from the slaughterhouse as a child and to save Catherine
as an adult; she, too, is the one who is rightly horrified when Lecter, during
their first interview, famously describes how he ate a census taker's "liver
with some fava beans and a nice Chianti."[7] Lecter himself, on the other hand,
is, as Crawford and Chilton tell her, "a monster," a cold-blooded serial murderer who rejects law and order in favor of his own orally aggressive desires,
a socially transgressive figure who takes a not-so-secret glee in plumbing the
depths of Clarice's childhood traumas or obscenely referring to the phantom

pain that Senator Martin might feel if Buffalo Bill kills her daughter. But, though he is incarcerated, Lecter behind the glass is also the authority and the power; subject to Dr. Chilton's "petty torments," he paradoxically holds the keys to Buffalo Bill's disturbing psychology and, ironically, Catherine Martin's imprisonment.[8] According to a note on *IMDb*, Jonathan Demme wanted Anthony Hopkins to "look directly at the camera as it panned into his line of sight [so that] Lecter [appeared] as 'knowing everything.'"[9] As the film plays this relationship out, if Clarice can withstand Lecter's scrutiny to gain some of that knowledge, then she can save "poor Catherine" and, perhaps, exorcise the demons from her own past.

While we might be ready to side with the justice system in these efforts, however, *Silence* frequently challenges our faith in that system, as the people who uphold and work for it are often revealed as flawed, corrupt, and, on some level, immoral or criminal themselves. Connecting "Jame Gumb's 'use' of female bodies and the FBI's cold 'use' of Clarice," Linda Mizejewski believes that Clarice becomes a "target of male institutions and contempt for women."[10] Crawford exploits her as much for her beauty as for her intelligence by sending her to Lecter's cell in the first place, and he later uses her femininity to get around a local sheriff by suggesting that the details of "this type of sex crime" would be too much for her. Crawford's mistaken belief in Gumb's whereabouts is, in many ways, also what puts Clarice alone in the dark in the killer's basement. Moreover, as Mizejewski argues, the "psychological violence" that she suffers when Miggs throws his semen at her is "enabled by the very institutions (the Baltimore State Hospital and the FBI) that both protect her from Miggs and set her up for abuse."[11] As Lecter's jailor, Chilton should be studying him for the greater good, to help the FBI learn about and catch other serial killers, yet he is quick to abandon his job for his own self-interests, hitting on Clarice moments after he meets her and exposing the FBI's "Plum Island" ploy so that he can negotiate his own deal with Hannibal and Senator Martin, with "a few conditions for his own benefit."[12] Although he is no killer, Chilton, in his smarminess, becomes so alienated from the audience that Lecter is nearly heroic or "almost benign," in the words of Cynthia Freeland, by contrast. As she points out, the film encourages "viewers [to] root for Lecter even after his horrific murder of his guards" and as he eyes a panicked Chilton during his final phone call with Clarice; she reports, moreover, that, during two separate screenings, audiences "were clearly and vocally on Lecter's side [at the end]."[13]

I must also agree with Thomas Elsaesser and Warren Buckland's view of Lecter in the film as "part of the FBI machinery, [. . .] the 'obscene enjoyment' (as [Slavoj] Žižek would say) of the system, the uncanny database intelligence of the modern administrative government."[14] He provides information and "expertise" that the Bureau relies on, and, while the FBI might be just as reluctant to acknowledge his contributions as it would be to admit Chilton's pomposity or its own misogyny, he is just as important to the overall function of the machine. Though he may be othered and separated from Clarice—both physically in his cell and morally in his mindset—he is also perhaps just as much a mentor and teacher to her as Crawford is and could be included in both the best and worst assessments of the FBI.

In *Hannibal*, Lecter's visit to Will's cell is about an altogether different kind of horror, a horror that exposes just how broken the machine is and how off-kilter the moral compass of this world is. Lecter certainly is not warned about Will in the way that Clarice is warned about Lecter in *Silence*, with off-putting photographs and stern directions, and, even if he was, we would see through the dramatic irony of those instructions. As the jail door closes behind him, he momentarily closes his eyes, more at peace with his triumph than in fear at what he might see, almost as if he, too, is enjoying the Cassidy music in the background. If this visit is about power—and it clearly is, since Lecter has orchestrated Will's imprisonment—it is not as much about knowledge or, at least, the kind of knowledge that Clarice is looking for. Will may not stare at the camera as it comes into view—and now we follow Hannibal's point of view as opposed to Clarice's—and appear to know everything, but, having seen so many gruesome crime scenes and reimagined so many dark fantasies, he already knows this world.[15] (In season 2, he is able to manipulate the serial killer Matthew Brown into making an attempt on Hannibal's life, just as he gets his friend Chiyoh to kill the prisoner in Hannibal's mansion in season 3; as Chiyoh tells him, these are the kind of manipulations that Hannibal himself would "be proud of").[16] Rather, inasmuch as he represents the figure of justice and morality on the show, if not innocence, Will's incarceration and this role reversal from *Silence* instead lead the audience to question and fear just exactly what the world of the show and its moral/judicial framework are.

For all of the flaws in the justice system, *Silence* still maintains a worldview where some people, like Clarice, want to do good as much for the sake of doing good as for personal satisfaction, to see the guilty punished and the innocent spared, and where these people somehow make the system work. The seeds of discontent about that system and the moral order in that film give way to the show's chaotic inversion, where the serial killer enjoys his freedom and observes from the safety beyond the cell, while the hero pays for his crimes behind those "less intimate" metal bars. Not only have Lecter and Graham been brought together by Jack Crawford (played by Laurence Fishburne on the TV show) and the FBI, but Lecter works for the very system that he undermines and rejects, just as Will has been punished by it, essentially for doing his job.

Although we may come to the show with the idea that Lecter, as a desta-bilizing figure, will be/should be caught and punished, appropriately, by the forces of law and order, *Hannibal* frustrates that expectation and is, perhaps, as difficult to categorize and pin down as the eponymous cannibal himself. Since we know that Will is not the Ripper, that he has been arrested and charged with Hannibal's crimes seems like a wrong that the series must address/redress. Instead, it becomes, for the viewer, one of many significant turns that reveal the illusion of both law and order on the show and challenge our understanding of Will as hero and Hannibal as villain.

DUNGEONS AND RED DRAGONS

In its intertextuality, the scene at the end of season 1 also plays off of other portrayals of Graham on film and in Thomas Harris's first Hannibal Lecter novel, *Red Dragon*. In a *CSTonline* essay on *Hannibal* from 2013, I called Harris's Graham "an F.B.I. Christ" for good reason; his mind and body bear the scars of his sacrifices for the Bureau and, on a larger level, for mankind in hunting down these psychopaths.[17] (Being manipulated by Crawford and "punished" for his "talents" seem to be regular parts of Graham's story.) In Freddy Lounds's *Tattler* article on the Tooth Fairy murders in Harris's novel, we are told that Will was institutionalized for "deep depression" after killing Garrett Jacob Hobbs and then gutted with a linoleum knife after he identified Lecter as a serial killer. Catching Francis Dolarhyde also leaves him facially disfigured and may even cost him his wife and stepson.[18] As he realizes at the end of the book, he, too, "contain[s] all the elements to make murder" and shares an unsettling kinship with the monsters that he hunts, a kinship that director Michael Mann uses to develop his character in the 1986 film *Manhunter*.[19]

Mann and actor William Petersen portray Will Graham in that film as a man on the edge, as someone struggling to deny the appeal of such homicidal fantasies and impulses in his pursuit of another killer. Graham's behavior during the film's prison scene works as a good case in point. Although Will is free and "Lecktor" is behind bars in this version of the story—and, rightly so, as Will's assertion that Lecktor is "insane" goes unchallenged—Will, dressed in dark clothing, appears more "monstrous," anxious, and uncertain in Lecktor's stark white cell, while Lecktor, also in white, looks paradoxi-cally angelic and seems more in control.[20] At times, the camera angle changes to Lecktor's view, which makes Will seem like he is behind bars, an intrigu-ing visual device that Fuller similarly makes use of in season 3 of *Hannibal*. Panicked by Lecktor's suggestion that they are "just alike," Will sprints from the cell, down to the lobby, and out of the hospital, physically trying to escape the truth (his own psychological imprisonment), that Lecktor, in his assessment of him, is right.[21]

Mann cut an interesting scene from the theatrical version of *Manhunter*, where a bruised and scarred Graham, fresh from his final encounter with the Tooth Fairy, frightens "Dollarhyde's" next intended victims, the Shermans, a family that Will goes to check on and has been able to identify as the killer's next targets largely through his ability to adopt the killer's way of thinking.[22] In this regard, critic Kendall Phillips rightly wonders if Graham, in this moment, "is [. . .] still struggling with the empathetic mindset of Dollarhyde [and] his desire to see the family [is] of an altogether different nature."[23] For 1980s' audiences that had seen Paul Kersey take revenge on more street criminals in *Death Wish II* (1982), Harry Callahan apply his own brand of justice to a murder/vigilante case in *Sudden Impact* (1983), and ultra-violent Marion "Cobra" Cobretti rid society of the "disease" of crime in *Cobra* (1985), though, the scene's removal seems to make sense. In the same way that those figures bent, if not broke, the law to maintain domestic order, Will dances with these devils and adopts the serial killer mindset so that families like the Shermans or even his own can go about their lives; like Kersey, Callahan, and Cobra, he should not pose a threat to them.[24] Without this scene, we and the original audience can trust that he will, in the end, pull back from the dark side (like Luke Skywalker did in 1983's *Return of the Jedi*) and that the walk that he takes with his family out on that beach in Florida is a sunny sign of things to come.

Brett Ratner's take on Graham is different in 2002's *Red Dragon*, as sandy-haired Edward Norton interprets Will Graham more like the ace investigator that Clarice is trying to become in *Silence* than the monster that Lecktor/Lecter is in these versions of the novel. When he makes that walk down that all-too-familiar hallway toward Lecter's cell—a walk that, in the chronological framework of the Lecter narrative, precedes Clarice's in *Silence*—we have a better sense of what is waiting for him, and Graham seems a little more steely-eyed in making the trip. Rather than standing omnisciently with eyes wide open, Lecter rests on his bunk, and, again, Will stops him with the assertion that he is insane. (Lecter himself even admits, in his letter to Will, that "any rational society would either kill me or put me to some use.")[25] And, although Lecter goads Will with the notion of their similarity, we never get the sense that this investigator is one bad meal away from a facial restraint and straightjacket. Where Petersen's Graham walks through a crime scene and describes the Tooth Fairy's actions as his own, not unlike Will in *Hannibal*, Norton's FBI protagonist, clean-shaven and neatly dressed, appears, both physically and metaphorically, on the outside looking in, in search of clues as opposed to potential victims.[26] As he tosses Lecter's final note, with all of its barbs about his scars and dreams, into the ocean to go sailing with his family, his ordeal, his sacrifices, and any abuses that he has suffered at the hands of the system appear to be over. In the film's final scene, however, Chilton tempts Lecter with an interview request from Clarice Starling, "a young woman," in his decidedly creepy estimation, who seems "far too pretty" to be from the FBI.[27] Not only does this odd collaboration between Chilton and Lecter tie Ratner's film to Demme's, but it, too, points to the system as a devourer, as the jailer and the criminal conspire to heap future abuses upon a different victim.

Again, as I mentioned in my *CST* piece, with *Hannibal*, Bryan Fuller moves Graham "somewhat closer to Petersen's interpretation, with [actor Hugh] Dancy looking over the edge and beyond."[28] His Graham does not inhabit what should be Lecter's cell by accident. Will suffers from blackouts and seizures, he has a tenuous grip on reality, and he is emotionally unstable. As he insightfully envisions the crimes that he investigates from week to week, he always sees himself in the role of the killer, actively committing the murders and creating the design of the crime scenes. Jeff Casey keenly notes that, during Will's interview with Beverly Katz in season 2's "Kaiseki," which also "mirrors [the prison scene] from the novel *Red Dragon* and its two film adaptations" and includes "dialogue verbatim," he is given "Lecter's lines," the lines of the villain and serial murderer.[29] (Consulting on a murder case with the FBI in the same episode, Hannibal, in turn, tells Bedelia Du Maurier that he "got to be Will Graham today").[30] And, in the second season episode "Mukozuke," he even dons a version of the iconic Lecter face mask and straightjacket during the investigation of Beverly Katz's murder, yet another call-back to *Silence* (*see Figure 7.1.*). The advertising and the DVD cover for season 2 also show a rather menacing-looking Graham dressed this way—it is the only season, in fact, that uses images of Dancy's Graham, as opposed to pictures of Mads Mikkelsen's Lecter, to promote the series—and viewers coming to the show for the first time might well think, under these circumstances, that he was the titular cannibal. In addition to working as a call for viewers, the tagline for the second season, "Embrace the Madness," could be read as an endorsement of Will as Hannibal or as encouraging the audience to follow Will into instability. Both troubled and troubling, this is Will Graham, the "hero" on the show and in the mythology, and how he is now presented.

Fuller uses the source material to expand on the extent of Will's relationship with Lecter, and the series addresses the question of justice and morality by mining this gray area. In Harris's novel and Mann's film, Graham does not have a great deal to do with Hannibal before the doctor attacks him. We only hear about the incident and how Graham identified Lecter as a killer after seeing a book or an illustration about war wounds on his shelf as backstory and a dramatic illustration of how Will's keen understanding of the evidence informs his insight and intuition. "I looked up at some very old medical books

Figure 7.1   Hugh Dancy's Graham in a Straightjacket and Face Mask on *Hannibal*. *Hannibal*, season 2, episode 5, "Mukozuke," dir. by Michael Rymer, aired March 28, 2014, originally released on NBC.

on the shelf above his head," Will tells the Atlanta Chief of Detectives in the novel; "And I knew it was him."[31] Ratner actually fleshes this story out a little more at the beginning of *Red Dragon*; instead of simply questioning Lecter about a series of murders, we find out that Norton's Graham has been consulting with him on the case—just as he had worked with him previously, we later learn, on the Hobbs case—and they have worked out a profile together, a profile that Graham now realizes is completely wrong. "He's not collecting body parts," Will explains; "He's eating them."[32] When Lecter leaves the room, Will flips through a cookbook on his shelf and has his epiphany just before the doctor stabs him. Hopkins's Lecter calls it the end of a "game" when he attacks, but his failed attempt to mislead and deceive Graham pales in comparison to the often surreal cat-and-mouse gymnastics that Lecter and Will go through on Fuller's *Hannibal*, gymnastics that continue to complicate their roles and our perception of them in the narrative.

THE NOVEL APPROACH

The nod to Ridley Scott's film in the prison scene from "Savoureux" is key because it, too, refers to how the portrayal of Lecter and the binaries of hero/villain and good/evil have changed over time. Given the critical and financial success of *The Silence of the Lambs*—not only did the film win the five major awards at the 1992 Oscars, but it was one of the highest grossing horror movies of all time—readers and movie-goers alike had high hopes for Harris's next novel, *Hannibal*, and the film adaptation that would certainly come thereafter.[33] Rather than following the author's notorious cannibal through a thrilling manhunt that would lead to his arrest or death, however, Harris decided to go in an entirely different and ultimately more unsettling direction. Disenchanted with the Bureau, Clarice Starling seeks Lecter out to save him from a disfigured, vengeful Mason Verger, only to be saved by him, and then to dine with him on sleazy Justice Department official Paul Krendler's brain.[34] Describing their relationship at the end of the novel, Harris says, "Sometimes [they dance] at dinnertime. Sometimes they do not finish dinner [. . .]. Sex is a splendid structure they add to every day."[35] In his essay "Deposing an American Cultural Totem," critic Stephen Fuller notes "that many American readers" responded to this ending with a "profound sense of outrage and betrayal," but that Harris's intention was to purposefully thwart the cultural distinctions between hero and villain.[36] "Having installed Clarice with all of the required qualities of a conventional American hero and having ingratiated her with his fans," he explains, "Harris punishes his audience for their shallow idolatry."[37]

Be that as it may, readers, actors, and filmmakers were not ready for such a postmodern assault on their value systems. As plans for a *Hannibal* movie got underway, *Silence* star Jodie Foster was unable to reprise her role in the sequel because she was busy with another project. According to an article in the *Daily Mail*, however, she actually opted out because she "found the ending of the book [. . .] unacceptable and disturbing."[38] *Silence* director Jonathan Demme similarly "refused to work on the [project], claiming that [the novel] was unfilmable."[39] While Julianne Moore signed on in place of Foster and Ridley Scott took over for Demme, the producers still called for a rewrite, and Scott and writer Steve Zaillian reworked an original David Mamet draft into the version that was shot.[40] The completed pre-9/11 2001 film, which received an "R" rating, still includes a dinner scene with Paul Krendler's brain—a drugged Starling does not try the entrée—but it leaves out what must be the greater obscenity, steamy love scenes between Hannibal Lecter and Clarice Starling. Instead, when Hannibal has her restrained against a refrigerator in the film's closing moments and wonders if Clarice would ask him to stop "for love," her reaction is, perhaps, the reaction of so many *Silence* audiences and Clarice fans: "not in a thousand years."[41] Lecter may love Clarice enough to cut off his own hand, but those feelings are not mutual; when Hannibal escapes to feed brains to a young boy on a plane, he does so by himself. Moreover, if Graham is Christ-like in Harris's novel, Hannibal, in this film, is connected to Christ on more than one occasion, including in a scene where he is restrained in a crucifixion pose as a meal for Verger's pigs.[42] Nevertheless, for all that the movie might make him out to be, as the

lesser evil to figures like the sadistic pedophile Verger or the vulgar misogynist Krendler or as the proponent of some new code of propriety, the thought
of literally embracing the villain and "the madness" was simply too much for
Scott and the writers to stomach, just as it seemed contrary to Foster's moving
portrayal of Clarice in *Silence*. In order to preserve her heroism and dedication, however, they also deny what Linnie Blake calls the novel's interrogation of "the judicial machinery of the state"; instead, at the end of the film,
she remains tied, even handcuffed, to the "politically and judicially corrupt
nation whose institutions exist only to further the interests of the class-bound,
racist, sexist and sexually perverted economic elite."[43]

If the Cassidy music that comes from the opera scene and that plays
through the closing credits in Scott's film is the theme of a free Hannibal—he
is enjoying all that life has to offer in his new identity in Italy when we first
hear it, and he is still on the loose when we hear it again at the end of the
movie—it is more than apropos for the end of Fuller's "Savoureux" as an
exclamation point to Lecter's master plan. Where the films frequently show
Lecter physically behind bars and contained, the series drives home the point
that Jessica Balanzategui, Naja Later, and Tara Lomax make about the character historically, that "Lecter's serial violence [. . .] cannot be effectively
[. . .] contained," just as Lecter himself cannot be effectively contained.[44] On
Hannibal, in one way or another, he is always free. It is his choice to give
himself up in the season 3 episode "Digestivo," so that Will can find him,
and he has just as much influence on the world of the show in captivity as he
does outside of it. Lecter exerts control through his contact with Dolarhyde
(played by Richard Armitage) and his pointed conversations with Chilton
(played by Raul Esparza), Crawford, Alana Bloom, and, of course, Will.
(After speaking with him for the first time in the episode "...And the Woman
Clothed with the Sun," Will even has "the absurd feeling that [Hannibal]
walked out with [him]," a feeling that Alana Bloom immediately relates
to.)[45] But this Hannibal is more than just free; he is loved, beloved, idolized,
and worshipped. He enthralls and manipulates virtually everyone who comes
into contact with him, from potential victims to the FBI, the very symbols
of morality and order. Foster or Julianne Moore's Clarice might not be able
to think about Hannibal in any kind of romantic or sexual way, but, through
the course of the series, Will has an intricate "bromance" of sorts with him,
with all kinds of homoerotic overtones, seasoned psychiatrist Alana Bloom
sleeps with him, FBI Director Jack Crawford eagerly comes to his house for
gourmet meals largely made from the choice cuts of his victims, traumatized
Abigail Hobbs kills for him, and victimized therapist Bedelia Du Maurier
lives with him overseas and meticulously prepares the meal of her own leg for
him in the series finale.[46] The title of Fuller's show itself, like Scott's movie,
pays tribute to Hannibal, and that, too, reflects a change of sorts. When he

Figure 7.2 **William Petersen's Graham Investigating a Crime Scene in** *Manhunter.*
Michael Mann, Manhunter, dir. Michael Mann (1986; Los Angeles, CA: DEG/Shout!
Factory, 2016), DVD.

adapted *Red Dragon* in the 1980s, Michael Mann gave us a story called *Manhunter*; so much of the advertising for the film even centered around Graham as investigator and hero, flashlight in hand, on the trail of the killer (see Figure 7.2.). Almost thirty years later, Fuller, for all of his focus on Will and even in those season 2 ads that include him, makes it clear that his series is really about the serial killer, *Hannibal*.

OF DEATH AND CANCELLATION

A little more than halfway through season 3, in "The Great Red Dragon," the prison scene from "Savoureux" is again replayed, but, this time, the moral order appears to be restored, as Will greets Lecter behind an intimate, more *Silence*-like glass wall and Lecter a few episodes later wears the facial restraint and straightjacket. That appearance, however, like the "Ravenstag" or the dragon's billowing wings, is yet another illusion for us to see through. As I mentioned, the perspectives in Lecter's cell often change in these episodes—again recalling Graham's interview with Lecktor in *Manhunter*—so that we can never be sure if Will is the investigator or the prisoner. And given what we have seen him do by this point in the series, the functionality of Will's moral compass has clearly spun out of control. Not only has he tried to manipulate people into killing, but he has killed several people himself. Realizing how far he has gone (or how far gone he is) by the end of the season, Will wonders, appropriately enough, if he will be able to "save [himself]."[47] After he teams up with Lecter to destroy the Red Dragon, in one of the bloodiest fight scenes ever to air on broadcast television, he takes the step that Clarice never could in Scott's film and embraces Hannibal (and the madness), as they admire the terrible beauty of what they have done. Figuratively and literally, he goes over the edge, carrying them both to their apparent deaths somewhere at the bottom of the cliffs and into cancellation.[48] But, if this is Will's sacrifice, we would be hard-pressed to say that he makes it, like Clarice in the films, out of dedication to Jack Crawford and the FBI, or for the love that he feels for Molly and her son, or even for domestic order, like those other versions of Graham in film or in print. Do Will and Hannibal "fall for each other" out of fatigue and exhaustion? Or is it some kind of romantic murder-suicide, the culminating coup-de-grâce of what Siouxsie Sioux musically calls a "Love Crime" at the end of the episode?

If they are really gone—and Fuller has expressed interest in reviving the show ever since it went off the air—and Will sees this as some kind of atonement for all that he has done, that Christ and the devil die together, it is a strange kind of justice or redemption.[49] Unlike Christ, Will has not just died for the sins of mankind; he has committed them, psychologically, as well as physically. So how do we, as the audience, invest in this hero, if he is one? Regardless of how damaged the other FBI agents are in their dealings with Hannibal Lecter and how broken the Bureau is in those other films, there is the suggestion, through Will or Clarice, that someone is out there who is aware of the line between good and evil, right and wrong, sanity and insanity. While they may cross from one side to the other in the name of justice, they reaffirm that order (or the illusion of it) in the end, as the killers are stopped, the victims are saved, Will goes back to his family, and Clarice returns to the Bureau. The heroes do not become sociopaths or psychotics once the job is done.

In the closing moments of *Hannibal*, though, "things fall apart" for the audience, in Yeats's words, and the moral "centre cannot hold."[50] To catch Hannibal, this Will, the FBI investigator, becomes what he has beheld, a becoming that seems difficult to swallow and digest, if this has been a story about, among other things, law and order and justice. But then, if it has, nearly all of the players involved in this enterprise—Graham, Crawford, Chilton, Bloom, Du Maurier, and even Lecter himself—have paid for their part in this system, for being, as Crawford puts it, "in this stew together," and are, in one way or another, maimed, scarred, traumatized, compromised, and corrupted as a result.[51] In the end, the system itself becomes the real cannibal, chewing up those within it, spitting what is left out and over those cliffs, and leaving us with only victims and survivors. And the series narrative leaves us—perhaps for good, if it never returns—in this very dark place, a place of instability, chaos, disorder, and madness.

REACHING THE PEAK

There is another moment that is left out of some versions of Mann's *Manhunter*, just before Graham realizes that Dollarhyde has seen the films of the families, when he admits to Crawford that he feels sorry for the killer:

> My heart bleeds for him as a child. Someone took a kid and manufactured a monster. At the same time, as an adult, he's irredeemable. He butchers whole families to pursue trivial fantasies. As an adult, someone should blow the sick fuck out of his socks. Do you think that's a contradiction, Jack? Does this kind of understanding make you uncomfortable?[52]

In response, Crawford takes a step back, adjusts his tie, and changes the subject; the paradox of accepting the killer as an abused child and rejecting him as a remorseless adult is obviously too much for him. That Graham is watching TV sets while making this comment is somewhat ironic and ultimately prophetic because, in the years since the film was released, television has become the place for such complex characterizations/contradictions and such complicated justice narratives. The medium's most recent Golden Age, in fact, was grounded in antihero studies that reflected what L. H. M. Ling has described as a general distrust in "the public sector's supposed institutions of law and order, rationality and science."[53] Unapologetically hypocritical, the characters from these compelling dramas—*The Sopranos*, *The Shield*, *Dexter*, *Breaking Bad*, and *Mad Men*, to name just a few—contributed to society even as they undermined it, breaking some laws as they enforced others and often subscribing to their own codes after more legal, political, and social ones had failed them. As Amanda D. Lotz notes, these figures—Tony Soprano, Vic Mackey, Dexter Morgan, Walter White, and Don Draper—"[were] obviously 'bad' men by dominant social and legal, if not moral, norms. Yet most of the series also probe[d] the circumstances and conditions that [. . .] led them to transgress the bounds of propriety," circumstances and conditions not unlike the uncomfortable understanding that Graham posits in *Manhunter*.[54]

Amid this smorgasbord of ethically challenged antiheroes, Hannibal Lecter became an appetizing addition, as his bloody backstory in both the 2006 novel and the 2007 film *Hannibal Rising* portrayed him simultaneously as a traumatized victim and merciless killer, paving the way for Fuller's 2013 reimagining, with Hannibal as the bloody center of the series.[55] If he was something of a well-mannered monster in the pre-9/11 world and through Anthony Hopkins's enticing performance in *Silence* and *Red Dragon*, post-9/11 audiences could no longer dismiss his "otherness" from a moral high ground without consciously admitting the reductive nature of that perspective, without denying their complicity in supporting an ongoing Hannibal franchise of novels, movies, and television shows, and without acknowledging the glaring flaws in those institutions that would identify his criminality and, as a result, destabilize any definitions of heroism and villainy. The character of Lecter, as a result, could no longer be restricted and restrained, a creature to be oddly stared at from behind a glass wall or a set of iron bars, the epitome of disorder and immorality. Conversely, Will Graham, as the agent of an FBI that often failed to maintain order and serve the greater good, could not be portrayed solely as the "hero" and Lecter's moral counterpart, especially when he was influenced by and acted upon the selfsame "villainous" impulses and desires.[56] To put it simply, the table was set for Hannibal/*Hannibal*.[57]

The Peak TV era has not so much dismissed or rejected what these characters and the series stood for, but, if anything, it has offered a larger menu, with even more opportunities for the disorder and destabilization that brought the Fannibals home for dinner in the first place. In many ways, *Killing Eve*, for example, is *Hannibal*'s stylish sister, a British crime drama developed around the dangerous attraction between an American MI-6 agent, Eve Polastri, and a sociopathic Russian assassin, Villanelle. As the two repeatedly circle one another in the series, their respective organizations conspire and unabashedly collaborate, clearly proving that moral ambiguity is not restricted to just one side of the Atlantic. Although Netflix's *Mindhunter* takes viewers back to the past to offer a glimpse at the beginning of FBI profiling, ambitious agent Holden Ford—whose character is, incidentally, inspired by the same FBI profiler who inspired "Jack Crawford in the novels *Red Dragon* and *The Silence of the Lambs*, as well as Bryan Fuller's take on Will Graham"—is soon caught up in the morbid allure of talking to serial murderers in prison, conducting Graham/Starling-like interviews to gain valuable insights into their crimes and minds.[58] Again suffering for the system, Ford nearly loses his mind after receiving a hug from one of his interview subjects, while his partner Bill Tench tries to balance his job responsibilities with his concerns about his adopted son Brian, who may be as disturbed as the killers themselves. If *Killing Eve* is *Hannibal*'s sister, then *Prodigal Son* is more like its deranged younger brother, as the series liberally takes several pages, if not whole chapters, from the *Hannibal* cookbook. On this show, though, former FBI profiler Malcolm Bright solves strange murder cases for the NYPD, often with a little help from his father Martin Whitly, an imprisoned serial killer also known as "The Surgeon." In the same way that Lecter torments Graham with their similarity, Bright is repeatedly haunted by his father's suggestion that they are "the same."[59] And, again, the legal system that recruits him is also the one that abuses and fails him—repeatedly putting him next to both his father and other killers, housing Whitly as a source of knowledge in the service of justice, and offering Bright up, both physically and psychologically, as another sacrifice for that illusory ideal.[60]

In addition, although Fuller had been trying to add Clarice Starling to his global plans for the *Hannibal* storyline (See n48), CBS recently created a series around the character, aptly called *Clarice*. Where Fuller chose to focus on the Graham–Lecter relationship and the events prior to *Silence* as an artsy psychological nightmare, *Clarice* returns us to a post-*Silence* 1990s and picks up on the dysfunctionality of the FBI from the Demme film, as Starling and her co-workers repeatedly have to deal with racism and misogyny while investigating a conspiracy that involves and implicates the agency, big pharma, and the attorney general's office. Even Clarice's father, the lawman whose death figured so prominently in her backstory from *Silence*, is revealed as having exploited her and risked her life. While she, too, is threatened, attacked, and even tortured through her work and in her desire to solve cases on her own, *Clarice* tries to bring us back to a narrative with an obvious heroine. Surrounded by the light in the opening credits, she even appears angelic. In her dedication and commitment to justice, though, does she demonstrate that goodness and morality can still exist and survive through the experience of the corrupted world, or is she, too, a pawn of that "politically and judicially corrupt nation" that Blake identifies in her reading of Scott's *Hannibal* film?[61]

Hannibal may have only given us three seasons, but this line-up of thrillers and killers pointedly illustrate its profound influence and that our appetite for such compromised characters and their moral dilemmas is still alive and well, as is the interest in and support for the show itself. Amid the onslaught of Peak programming and even through the viewing possibilities of our recent quarantine, the series continues to benefit from a thriving fan base, widespread critical admiration, and enthusiastic word-of-mouth, to the point where streaming powerhouse Netflix even added it to the service in June 2020. Not only was *Vulture*'s Matt Zoller Seitz, a long-time fan of the show, quick to make it required viewing for homebound audiences in light of this news—"*Hannibal*," he told readers, "deserves to be placed in that canon [of landmark series]"— but the move has refueled talk of a restart, and, for new viewers, makes the series, contextually, something of a Peak broadcast.[62] While our political circumstances and the television medium itself may have changed since the show first aired and first asked us to compare Will's innocence with Hannibal's guilt, the series' underlying critique of our legal and moral sources of order remains timely and relevant—like the clues, perhaps, to one of the show's many crimes scenes—as Trump's impeachments, the 2020 presidential election, the Capitol riot, the #MeToo Movement and pronounced responses to gender inequalities and patriarchal abuses, public concerns about the handling of the coronavirus outbreak, the death of George Floyd and the Chauvin trial, and the ongoing growth of the Black Lives Matter movement have only added to our questions about authority and the foundational institutions of our society. Who are the heroes and the villains in the narratives that we read about in the news or that we tell ourselves, and would our neighbors be inclined to agree?

In this regard, the Graham/Lecter reversal in season 1 and the Graham-Lecter cliff-dive in season 3 seem like more than just an end to a season or a series; they seem like uncomfortably familiar, chaotic signs of the times and symbols of a culture in search of itself, of a culture transforming, of a culture becoming. They refer to our changing perspectives and our evolving perception of what is right and just, to what we continue to see when we look out at the world, when we look into our phones and flat-screen televisions, when we stare into the design. So, whether the show is over or not, it has still left us with more to chew on.

NOTES

1. After endorsing Dr. Chilton's use of psychic driving in his treatment of killer Abel Gideon in "Entrée" (S01E06), Lecter similarly guides Will toward the belief that he is the Chesapeake Ripper in the remaining episodes of the season. "If you followed the urges you kept down for so long, cultivated them as the inspirations they are," Lecter tells him in "Savoureux," "you'd become someone other than yourself" *Hannibal*, season 1, episode 13, "Savoureux," dir. David Slade, aired June 20, 2013, originally released on NBC.

2. The title, translated as "Look into My Heart," easily refers to Lecter's passion; on a more ghoulish note, it also has something to do with his cannibalism, as the aria is inspired by a dream vision from Dante's *La Vita Nuova* "about eating the heart." The song comes from the opera scene in the Scott film, when Lecter turns to face a conspiring Inspector Pazzi, and musically conveys "the uneasy idea of the debonair cannibal giving his heart to Clarice Starling" (David Crow, "How the Passion of Hannibal Lecter Inspired a New Opera About Dante," *Den of Geek*, February 17, 2021, https://www.denofgeek.com/movies/hannibal-lecter-passion-inspired-opera -dante/). As it plays in the episode, does it now suggest that Hannibal, in his own devious way, is making the same offer to Will?

3. In the pilot, the serial killer Garret Jacob Hobbs is connected to deer and birds, leading Will to envision an animal, a "Ravenstag," that is a combination of them both. As he begins to suspect and later realizes that Hannibal is the Chesapeake Ripper, Will sees him in his imagination as the embodiment of this animal, a "Ravenstag man." *Hannibal*, season 1, episode 13, "Savoureux," dir. David Slade, aired June 20, 2013, originally released on NBC.

4. Jeff Casey agrees that Will's arrest may be "the most important inversion [on the show]" (Jeff Casey, "Queer Cannibals and Deviant Detectives: Subversion and Homosocial Desire in NBC's *Hannibal*," *Quarterly Review of Film and Video* 32, no. 6 (2015): 554).

5. The scene from the film is also recalled several episodes earlier, in "Entrée" (S01E06), when Will and Alana Bloom go to question Abel Gideon in a similar cell at the hospital for the Chesapeake Ripper murders. Not only does their visit prefigure Will's situation at the end of the season, but, in both cases, the wrong man is accused of the crimes.

6. *IMDb*, "*The Silence of the Lambs* (1991): Trivia," accessed October 22, 2016. http://www.imdb.com/title/tt0102926/trivia.

7. Jonathan Demme, *The Silence of the Lambs*, dir. Jonathan Demme (1991; New York, NY: Strong Heart Productions/Orion Pictures, 2007), DVD.

8. Ibid.

9. *IMDb*, 2016.

10. Linda Mizejewski, "Picturing the Female Dick: *The Silence of the Lambs* and *Blue Steel*," *Journal of Film and Video* 45, no. 2/3 (1993): 15.

11. Miggs's "attack" on Clarice, which Mizejewski elsewhere describes as "a symbolic rape" (2004, 158), takes place during her first meeting with Lecter, and this "discourtesy" is what prompts Lecter to help her with the Buffalo Bill case. Mizejewski, 15.

12. Demme, 1991.

13. According to *Silence* screenwriter Ted Tally, the original ending for the film was even darker. After finishing his phone call, Lecter, with a "paring knife in hand," turns to Chilton, who "is trussed up in a chair across from him [in] the same method of restraints the doctor used on [him] earlier in the movie," and says, "Shall we begin?" As ingratiating and unappealing as Chilton is, however, director Jonathan Demme found this conclusion to the film to be "just [. . .] too squirmy" (Mike Fleming, Jr., "Jonathan Demme and Untold '*Silence Of The Lambs*' Tales: Hannibal, Clarice, Tally, Hackman, and a Discarded Scary Ending," *Deadline*, April 26, 2017, http://deadline.com/2017/04/the-silence-of-the-lambs-25th-anniversary-untold-tales -jonathan-demme-ted-tally-hannibal-lecter-clarice-starling-1201703981/). Fuller, of course, has no such qualms on *Hannibal*, as the poor doctor has his organs rearranged by Abel Gideon, is shot in the face by a traumatized Miriam Lass, and has his lips chewed off and is set on fire by Francis Dolarhyde. (Cynthia A. Freeland, *The Naked and the Undead: Evil and the Appeal of Horror* (Boulder, CO: Westview, 2000), 209.)

14. As Elsaesser and Buckland play out their Foucaultian reading of the film, Gumb becomes "heroic [in his] self-sacrifice" and his "refusal of normative heterosexuality." (Thomas Elsaesser and Warren Buckland, *Studying Contemporary American Film: A Guide to Movie Analysis* (New York, NY: Oxford University Press, 2002), 274–275.)

15. Where detectives were once, according to Casey, "normalizing figure[s] who restore[d] the social order when it [was] disrupted by a crime," Will is part of a new breed of detectives, like Ryan Hardy in *The Following* or Stella Gibson in *The Fall*,

who "connect the world of normalcy to the world of deviancy" (Casey, 561). Of course, while these contexts constitute unique "worlds" for the people/figures who perceive and experience them as such, they coexist/conflict in the same physical space and are part of the same "world." As Mark Knopfler puts it in "Brothers in Arms," "We have just one world, / But we live in different ones" (Dire Straits, "Brothers in Arms," May 13, 1985, track #9 on *Brothers in Arms*, Warner Bros. Records, 1985, CD).

16. Right after Graham puts this plan in motion, he begins to grow antlers in his jail cell, as his descent into murder turns him into the Ravenstag man. As Casey explains, it is almost "as if Lecter's personality is growing inside Graham and bursting out like a butterfly from its chrysalis" (Casey, 559.); (*Hannibal*, season 2, episode 5, "Mukozuke," dir. Michael Rymer, aired March 28, 2014, originally released on NBC.) (*Hannibal*, season 3, episode 3, "Secondo," dir. Vincenzo Natali, aired June 18, 2015, originally released on NBC.)

17. Douglas L. Howard, "Good Eats: NBC's *Hannibal* as Food for Thought," *CSTonline*, June 12, 2013, https://cstonline.net/good-eats-nbcs-hannibal-as-food-for -thought-by-douglas-howard/.

18. Will's wife, Molly, clearly blames Crawford for his injuries. When Jack comes to visit him in the hospital, she coldly asks him if he is there "to give [Will] a face transplant" (Thomas Harris, *Red Dragon* (New York, NY: Dell, 1981), 348). Although she encourages Will's involvement on the Tooth Fairy case, Molly also blames Crawford on the series after Dolarhyde shoots her; *Hannibal*, season 3, episode 11, "...And the Beast from the Sea," dir. Michael Rymer, aired August 15, 2015, originally released on NBC.

19. Harris, *Red Dragon*, 354.

20. Both the films and the television show take unique liberties with Harris's characters, including Lecter himself. For example, in the *Silence* novel, Harris describes Lecter as having "six fingers on his left hand, yet the films and the series have never made this a part of the character's portrayal. (Thomas Harris, *The Silence of the Lambs* (New York, NY: St. Martin's, 1988), 15.) In Mann's film, his name is also spelled "Lecktor" instead of "Lecter," as it appears in Harris's novels. When Will makes the point about his insanity in the novel, he lists Lecter's "disadvantages" as both "passion" and insanity (Harris, *Red Dragon*, 65.)

21. Michael Mann, *Manhunter*, dir. Michael Mann (1986; Los Angeles, CA: DEG/ Shout! Factory, 2016), DVD.

22. Dolarhyde thinks about his plans for the Shermans in the novel, and Crawford correctly concludes that they "were probably on his itinerary" (Harris, *Red Dragon*, 343.)

23. Kendall R. Phillips, "Redeeming the Visual: Aesthetic Questions in Michael Mann's *Manhunter*," *Literature/Film Quarterly* 31, no. 1 (2003): 14.

24. As Jonathan Rayner notes, however, Will's job is precisely what puts his family at risk, hence his dilemma: "in order to save the families of strangers he must risk his life and the safety of his own family" (Jonathan Rayner, *The Cinema of Michael Mann: Vice and Vindication* (London: Wallflower Press, 2013), 96.

25. In his letter to Will in the novel, Lecter states that "any rational society would either kill me or give me my books" (Harris, *Red Dragon*, 349); (Brett Ratner, *Red Dragon*, dir. Brett Ratner (2002; Universal City, CA: Universal Studios, 2003), DVD.)

26. "The house is mine," Will states, as he makes his way through the Leeds' kitchen. (Mann, 1986.)

27. Ratner, 2002.

28. Howard, 2013.

29. (Casey, 555); Will is not the only one on the show to adopt Lecter's lines or language, a further illustration of the moral chaos on the show. In an intratextual moment, Crawford, feeling responsible for Will's apparent breakdown and incarceration, uses Lecter's description of how another killer "is driven" and sees "those in the world around him [as] a means to an end" to describe himself. (*Hannibal*, season 2, episode 2, "Sakizuke," dir. Tim Hunter, aired March 7, 2014, originally released on NBC.)

30. *Hannibal*, season 2, episode 1, "Kaiseki," dir. Tim Hunter, aired February 28, 2014, originally released on NBC.

31. Miriam Lass, a Starling-like FBI trainee, realizes the Lecter is the Chesapeake Ripper in nearly the same way. After interviewing him about a former patient, she notices his *Wound Man* drawing on his desk in season 1's "Entrée," although she is not lucky enough to get help or get away. (Harris, *Red Dragon*, 55.)

32. Ratner, 2003.

33. In discussing the film's unique place in Oscar history, Mike Fleming Jr. notes that "[it is] the first and only Best Picture-winning horror film; the last film to win Oscars in the five key categories [Best Picture, Best Actor, Best Actress, Best Director, and Best Adapted Screenplay]; and the only modern-era film to win Best Picture despite being released over a year before its Oscar night triumph" (Fleming, 2017). In fact, both *Silence* and *Hannibal* made Alex Aronson's list of "The 20 Highest Grossing Horror Movies of All Time." (Alex Aronson, "The 20 Highest Grossing Horror Movies of All Time," *Redbook*, September 25, 2019, https://www.redbookmag.com/life/g29148346/highest-grossing-horror-movies/?slide=12.)

34. Referring to her disenchantment in more psychoanalytic terms, Gill Plain believes that Clarice has been "betrayed by her adopted 'father'—the institutional patriarch of the FBI" and that Lecter, through the course of the novel, becomes both "surrogate father" and "mother," a force of truth," to her. (Gill Plain, *Twentieth-Century Crime Fiction: Gender, Sexuality and the Body* (Chicago, IL: Fitzroy Dearborn, 2001), 230.)

35. Harris, *The Silence of the Lambs*, 483.

36. Stephen M. Fuller, "Deposing an American Cultural Totem: Clarice Starling and Postmodern Heroism in Thomas Harris's *Red Dragon, The Silence of the Lambs*, and *Hannibal*," *Journal of Popular Culture* 38, no. 5 (2005): 819. Stephen Fuller is not related to *Hannibal* creator Bryan Fuller.

37. Ibid.

38. Alison Boshoff, "Why Julianne Took on *Hannibal*," *Mail Online.com.,* February 6, 2001, http://www.dailymail.co.uk/tvshowbiz/article-20838/Why-Julianne-took-Hannibal.html.

39. Ibid.

40. *Silence* writer Ted Tally passed on the project, too, as did Zaillian himself initially, "until the ending was resolved." (Jill Bernstein, "'But Dino, I Don't Want

to Make a Film about Elephants. . . .'" *Guardian*, February 8, 2001, https://www.the-guardian.com/film/2001/feb/09/culture.features.) According to Mizejewski, although there were "at least three different endings for this film, all of them [veered] dramatically away from the ending of Harris's novel." (Linda Mizejewski, *Hardboiled and High Heeled: The Woman Detective in Popular Culture* (New York: Routledge, 2004), 171.)

41. Ridley Scott, *Hannibal*, dir. Scott Ridley (2001; Beverly Hills, CA: MGM, 2007), DVD.

42. Along these lines and considering the role of religion and religious symbolism in Fuller's *Hannibal*, Geoff Klock adds that "many characters come to occupy the placeholders labeled God, Jesus, Judas, and the Devil" (Geoff Klock, *Aestheticism, Evil, Homosexuality, and Hannibal: If Oscar Wilde Ate People* (Lanham, MD: Lexington Books, 2017), 76).

43. Linnie Blake, *The Wounds of Nations: Horror Cinema, Historical Trauma and National Identity* (Manchester: Manchester University Press, 2008), 115–116.

44. As Balanzategui, Later, and Lomax define his challenge both to the FBI and to narrative, "Lecter resists profiling and containment [. . . and] embodies the perpetual threat that serial murder and thus serial narratives cannot ultimately be contained." (Jessica Balanzategui, Naja Later, and Tara Lomax, "Hannibal Lecter's Monstrous Return: *The Horror of Seriality in Bryan Fuller's* Hannibal," in *Becoming: Genre, Queerness, and Transformation in NBC's Hannibal,*" ed. Kavita Mudan Finn and EJ Nielsen (Syracuse: Syracuse University Press, 2019), 33–34.)

45. *Hannibal*, season 3, episode 09, "...And the Woman Clothed in Sun," dir. John Dahl, aired August 1, 2015, originally released on NBC.

46. Fuller has described the relationship on multiple occasions with this term. In a 2015 interview with *Collider*, for example, he said that, in creating the series, his intention was "to recontextualize the mythology of *Hannibal* into this bromance." (Christina Radish, "Bryan Fuller on 'Hannibal', Still Wanting to Do 'Silence of the Lambs', and That Final Scene," *Collider*, December 11, 2015, http://collider .com/bryan-fuller-hannibal-silence-of-the-lambs-interview/.) As Richard Logsdon explains, Fuller uses this relationship to refer back to the tension between Hannibal and Will. When Hannibal sleeps with Alana Bloom and Will sleeps with Margot Verger in "Naka-Choko" (2.10), the visual juxtaposition [of the couples] points to the two men's desire to enjoy each other—and [carries] over to a scene in which [they] appear to be sharing [Alana] in a *manage a trois*." (Richard Logsdon, "Merging with Darkness: An Examination of the Aesthetics of Collusion in NBC's *Hannibal*," *Journal of American Culture* 40, no. 1 (2017): 55.)

47. *Hannibal*, season 3, episode 13, "The Wrath of the Lamb," dir. Michael Rymer, aired August 29, 2015, originally released on NBC.

48. The show was cancelled not long after the third season started in June 2015. While it struggled in the ratings, though—according to the *Hollywood Reporter*'s Lesley Goldberg, the second episode of the season posted a "series low [of] 1.66 million [viewers]"—the network's decision to cancel it may have been motivated by other factors and did not necessarily mean the end of the series. Goldberg suggests that Fuller and the show's producers "may have been [dealing with] a rights issue"

over the introduction of Clarice Starling, the character from the *Silence* and *Hannibal* novels and films. (Lesley Goldberg, "NBC's 'Hannibal' Canceled After Three Seasons," *Hollywood Reporter*, June 22, 2015, https://www.hollywoodreporter.com/live-feed/hannibal-canceled-at-nbc-804239.) Moreover, as Matt Zoller Seitz points out in an interview with Fuller, *Hannibal* was largely "funded through a variety of other sources" (2015), so NBC's decision did not prevent another network from picking it up. (Fuller, 819–833.)

49. In a 2019 tweet, he affirmed, "I want to do it, the cast wants to do it and [executive producer] Martha [De Laurentis] wants to do it. We just need a network or a streaming service that wants to do it, too. I don't feel there's a clock on it or an expiration date for the idea. We just need someone to bite." (Bryan Fuller, Twitter Post, May 27, 2019, 3:30 p.m., https://twitter.com/bryanfuller/status/1133093208211091456?lang=en.)

50. William Butler Yeats, *Selected Poems and Three Plays of William Butler Yeats* (New York, NY: Collier Books, 1987), 89.

51. *Hannibal*, season 3, episode 9, ". . . And the Woman Clothed with the Sun," dir. John Dahl, aired August 1, 2015, originally released on NBC; As a sign of just how much they have changed, in the season 3 finale, Crawford, Bloom, and Graham all conspire to kill both Dolarhyde and Lecter.

52. According to *IMDb*, this conversation is "missing from both Anchor Bay DVD versions [of the film]" ("*Manhunter*_(1986): Alternate Versions"). It does appear, though, in the Shout! Factory's theatrical version.

53. Anticipating the moral complexity of the series, Ling specifically considers how Hannibal's "alternative code of ethics" (2004, 394), as they appear in Harris's novels, "offers true justice and morality" to a troubled post-9/11 world. (L.H.M. Ling, "The Monster Within: What Fu Manchu and Hannibal Lecter Can Tell Us about Terror and Desire in a Post-9/11 World," *Positions: East Asia Cultures Critique* 12, no. 1 (2004): 393–394.) Douglas Kellner sees the same kind of response in films like 2004's *Batman Begins*, where Batman's vigilantism is set against "an almost totally corrupt legal system, dominated by corporate and criminal powers, an analogue to the Bush-Cheney partisan evisceration of the political and legal system." (Douglas Kellner, *Cinema Wars: Hollywood Film and Politics in the Bush-Cheney Era* (Malden, MA: Wiley-Blackwell, 2010), 10.)

54. Lotz insightfully explores the connection between criminality and gender here: "This turn to illegality may be assumed to be a reaction against fading patriarchal power, but the intricately constructed characters and their stories reveal a far more complicated engagement with changing gender roles and social norms than might be presumed." (Amanda D. Lotz, *Cable Guys: Television and Masculinities in the 21st Century* (New York: New York University Press, 2014), 63, 83–84.)

55. Harris's novel was released not long after *Dexter* began on Showtime.

56. Alexandra Carroll agrees that the series "allude[s] to a certain ineptitude on the part of the FBI to protect and defend American citizens against threats of violence and terrorism." (Alexandra Carroll, "'We're Just *Alike*': Will Graham, Hannibal Lecter, and the Monstrous-Human," *Studies in Popular Culture* 38, no. 1 (2015): 58.)

57. Klock believes that "*Hannibal* emerge[d] as [an] experimental, violent, poetic, arty, and aesthetic triumph" from "this context" and through "the rise of prestige television." (Klock, 1.)

58. Brian Tallerico, "The Real FBI Agents and Serial Killers Who Inspired Netflix's *Mindhunter*," *Vulture*, October 17, 2017, http://www.vulture.com/2017/10/mindhunter-netflix-real-serial-killers.html.

59. *Prodigal Son*, season 1, episode 1, "Pilot," dir. Lee Toland Krieger, aired September 23, 2019, originally released on the FX Network.

60. In a delicious bit of irony that epitomizes/symbolizes this general sense of moral confusion and corruption in the legal system, the serial killer in the pilot is played by the same actor who plays Holden's FBI supervisor on *Mindhunter*, Michael Cerveris.

61. Blake, 116.

62. Matt Zoller Seitz, "*Hannibal* Is Your Next Great Binge-Watch," *Vulture*, June 16, 2020, https://www.vulture.com/2020/06/hannibal-tv-show-netflix.html. Mads Mikkelsen has openly added to this talk. As Shannon Carlin reports, "Mikkelsen even got his Instagram followers riled up with a loaded question: '*Hannibal* hits Netflix in June: Is *Hannibal* season 4 on the way?'" Shannon Carlin, "*Hannibal* Was Cancelled In 2015, But Netflix Has Given Fans New Hope," *Refinery29*, June 12, 2020, https://www.refinery29.com/en-us/2020/06/9846462/will-netflix-renew-hannibal-season-4-movie.

BIBLIOGRAPHY

Aronson, Alex. "The 20 Highest Grossing Horror Movies of All Time." *Redbook*, September 25, 2019. https://www.redbookmag.com/life/g29148346/highest-grossing-horror-movies/?slide=12.

Balanzategui, Jessica, Naja Later, and Tara Lomax. "Hannibal Lecter's Monstrous Return: The Horror of Seriality in Bryan Fuller's *Hannibal*." In *Becoming: Genre, Queerness, and Transformation in NBC's Hannibal*," edited by Kavita Mudan Finn and EJ Nielsen, 27–53. Syracuse: Syracuse University Press, 2019.

Bernstein, Jill. "'But Dino, I Don't Want to Make a Film about Elephants....'" *Guardian*, February 8, 2001. https://www.theguardian.com/film/2001/feb/09/culture.features.

Blake, Linnie. *The Wounds of Nations: Horror Cinema, Historical Trauma and National Identity*. Manchester: Manchester University Press, 2008.

Boshoff, Alison. "Why Julianne took on Hannibal." *Mail Online.com.*, February 6, 2001. http://www.dailymail.co.uk/tvshowbiz/article-20838/Why-Julianne-took-Hannibal.html.

Carlin, Shannon. "*Hannibal* Was Cancelled In 2015, But Netflix Has Given Fans New Hope." *Refinery29*, June 12, 2020. https://www.refinery29.com/en-us/2020/06/9846462/will-netflix-renew-hannibal-season-4-movie.

Carroll, Alexandra. "'We're Just *Alike*': Will Graham, Hannibal Lecter, and the Monstrous-Human." *Studies in Popular Culture* 38, no. 1 (2015): 41–63.

Casey, Jeff. "Queer Cannibals and Deviant Detectives: Subversion and Homosocial Desire in NBC's *Hannibal*." *Quarterly Review of Film and Video* 32, no. 6 (2015): 550–567.

Crow, David. "How the Passion of Hannibal Lecter Inspired a New Opera About Dante." *Den of Geek*, February 17, 2021. https://www.denofgeek.com/movies/hannibal-lecter-passion-inspired-opera-dante/.

Demme, Jonathan, dir. *The Silence of the Lambs*. 1991; Beverly Hills, CA: Orion/MGM, 2006. DVD.

Dire Straits. "Brothers in Arms." Released in October 1985. Written by Mark Knopfler, produced by Neil Dorfsman and Mark Knopfler. Track number 9 on *Brothers in Arms*. Warner Bros., CD, vinyl, and cassette.

Elsaesser, Thomas, and Warren Buckland. *Studying Contemporary American Film: A Guide to Movie Analysis*. New York, NY: Oxford University Press, 2002.

Fedak, Chris, and Sam Slaver, creators. *Prodigal Son*. September 23, 2019–May 18, 2021. Originally released on Fox.

Fleming, Mike, Jr. "Jonathan Demme and Untold '*Silence Of The Lambs*' Tales: Hannibal, Clarice, Tally, Hackman, and a Discarded Scary Ending." *Deadline*, April 26, 2017. http://deadline.com/2017/04/the-silence-of-the-lambs-25th-anniversary-untold-tales-jonathan-demme-ted-tally-hannibal-lecter-clarice-starling-1201703981/.

Freeland, Cynthia A. *The Naked and the Undead: Evil and the Appeal of Horror*. Boulder, CO: Westview, 2000.

Fuller, Bryan, creator. *Hannibal*. Aired from April 4, 2013–August 29, 2015. Originally released on NBC.

———. Twitter post. May 27, 2019, 3:30 p.m. https://twitter.com/bryanfuller/status/1133093208211091456?lang=en.

Fuller, Stephen M. "Deposing an American Cultural Totem: Clarice Starling and Postmodern Heroism in Thomas Harris's *Red Dragon, The Silence of the Lambs*, and *Hannibal*." *Journal of Popular Culture* 38, no. 5 (2005): 819–833.

Gentle, Sally Woodward, executive producer. *Killing Eve*. Aired from April 8, 2018–Present. Originally released on BBC America.

Goldberg, Lesley. "NBC's '*Hannibal*' Canceled After Three Seasons." *Hollywood Reporter*, June 22, 2015. https://www.hollywoodreporter.com/live-feed/hannibal-canceled-at-nbc-804239.

Harris, Thomas. *Hannibal*. New York, NY: Delacorte, 1999.

———. *Hannibal Rising*. New York, NY: Dell, 2007.

———. *Red Dragon*. New York, NY: Dell, 1981.

———. *The Silence of the Lambs*. New York, NY: St. Martin's, 1988.

Howard, Douglas L. "Good Eats: NBC's *Hannibal* as Food for Thought." *CStonline*, 12 June 12, 2013. https://cstonline.net/good-eats-nbcs-hannibal-as-food-for-thought-by-douglas-howard/.

Kellner, Douglas. *Cinema Wars: Hollywood Film and Politics in the Bush-Cheney Era*. Malden, MA: Wiley-Blackwell, 2010.

Klock, Geoff. *Aestheticism, Evil, Homosexuality, and Hannibal: If Oscar Wilde Ate People*. Lanham, MD: Lexington Books, 2017.

Kurtzman, Alex, and Jenny Lumet, creators. *Clarice.* Aired February 11–June 24, 2021. Originally released on CBS.

Ling, L.H.M. "The Monster Within: What Fu Manchu and Hannibal Lecter Can Tell Us About Terror and Desire in a Post-9/11 World." *Positions: East Asia Cultures Critique* 12, no. 1 (2004): 377–400.

Logsdon, Richard. "Merging with Darkness: An Examination of the Aesthetics of Collusion in NBC's *Hannibal.*" *Journal of American Culture* 40, no. 1 (2017): 50–65.

Lotz, Amanda D. *Cable Guys: Television and Masculinities in the 21st Century.* New York, NY: New York University Press, 2014.

"*Manhunter* (1986): Alternate Versions." N.d. *IMDb.* Accessed November 21, 2017. http://www.imdb.com/title/tt0091474/alternateversions.

Mann, Michael, dir. *Manhunter.* 1986; Los Angeles, CA: Shout! Factory 2016. DVD.

Mizejewski, Linda. *Hardboiled and High Heeled: The Woman Detective in Popular Culture.* New York, NY: Routledge, 2004.

———. "Picturing the Female Dick: *The Silence of the Lambs* and *Blue Steel.*" *Journal of Film and Video* 45, no. 2/3 (1993): 6–23.

Penhall, Joe, creator. *Mindhunter.* Aired from October 13, 2017–August 16, 2019. Digitally released on Netflix.

Phillips, Kendall R. "Redeeming the Visual: Aesthetic Questions in Michael Mann's *Manhunter.*" *Literature/Film Quarterly* 31, no. 1 (2003): 10–16.

Plain, Gill. *Twentieth-Century Crime Fiction: Gender, Sexuality and the Body.* Chicago, IL: Fitzroy Dearborn, 2001.

Radish, Christina. "Bryan Fuller on '*Hannibal*', Still Wanting to Do '*Silence of the Lambs*', and That Final Scene." *Collider*, December 11, 2015. http://collider.com/bryan-fuller-hannibal-silence-of-the-lambs-interview/.

Ratner, Brett, dir. *Red Dragon.* 2002; Universal City, CA: Universal, 2003. DVD.

Rayner, Jonathan. *The Cinema of Michael Mann: Vice and Vindication.* London: Wallflower Press, 2013.

Scott, Ridley, dir. *Hannibal.* 2001; Beverly Hills, CA: MGM, 2007. DVD.

Seitz, Matt Zoller. "Bryan Fuller on *Hannibal*'s 'Cancellation' and Where He Wants to Take the Show in Season 4." *Vulture*, June 25, 2015. http://www.vulture.com/2015/06/bryan-fuller-on-hannibals-cancellation-season-four.html.

———. "*Hannibal* Is Your Next Great Binge-Watch." *Vulture*, June 16, 2020. https://www.vulture.com/2020/06/hannibal-tv-show-netflix.html.

Tallerico, Brian. "The Real FBI Agents and Serial Killers Who Inspired Netflix's *Mindhunter.*" *Vulture*, October 17, 2017. http://www.vulture.com/2017/10/mindhunter-netflix-real-serial-killers.html.

"*The Silence of the Lambs* (1991): Trivia." N.d. *IMDb.* Accessed October 22, 2016. http://www.imdb.com/title/tt0102926/trivia.

Webber, Peter, dir. *Hannibal Rising.* 2007; Santa Monica, CA: The Weinstein Company, 2007. DVD.

Yeats, William Butler. "The Second Coming." In *Selected Poems and Three Plays of William Butler Yeats*, edited by M.L. Rosenthal, 3rd Ed., 89–90. New York: Collier Books, 1986.

Chapter 8

What Made the Devil Do It?

Matilde Accurso Liotta and Martina Vanzo

INTRODUCTION

The purpose of this chapter is to focus on the ethical aspects of self-determination and individualism that are woven through the Fox and Netflix TV series *Lucifer*, specifically through the two main supernatural characters: Lucifer Morningstar (the Devil, played by Tom Ellis) and Amenadiel (the Angel, played by D. B. Woodside). *Lucifer*'s narrative construction presents an ethos in which the dichotomy between good and evil is no longer absolutized in the opposition between angel and devil. Instead, this dichotomy is explored in how individuals choose to behave and define themselves through their behavior. Therefore, the goal of each character is to construct a sense of self through the exercise of their agency and autonomy over and against how they have been determined by the role assigned to them in the larger cosmic battle between good and evil.

Where other television shows can address good, evil, free will, and determinism through metaphor, *Lucifer* does so explicitly and literally. For that reason, it is an interesting and useful example of a show that could stimulate the audience to reflect upon these themes and draw connections to their own lives. For Gill and Adams, a serial television show, as a form of mass media, contains and communicates ideologies to the audience that they use to build their world.[1] In this case, the audience is asked to identify with the main character, Lucifer, as he is the point of view character who frames how the audience ought to relate to other characters and events. Identification with this type of main character—one who is morally ambiguous—puts a great deal of power in the hands of the producers, first, and more generally, in those who use mass media to perpetuate the values of the United States. Though the United States does not exert the power and influence it once did in terms

of influencing global geopolitical fortunes, America still has a role in influencing world cultural production through global distribution of mass media
television shows like *Lucifer*.[2] One power that mass media has demonstrated,
and this is true of serialized television produced in America, is the ability
to desacralize the world and depict a secularized society. In a secularized
society, the necessary tools to interpret the world, to give us the answers to
the great questions of life, are no longer conveyed by the ancient institutions
in charge, such as the Roman Catholic Church.[3] A TV series like *Lucifer* is
therefore interesting because it intertwines two different tensions. Studies on
religious phenomena and secularization underline a persistence of religion
in the United States in opposition to a progressive secularization of Europe.
However, this is incorrect for both of the regions.[4] If, on the one hand, Europe
proves to be more religious than it appears, then, on the other hand, television
has become the main source of answers to existential questions in America,
showing a profound weakening of the institutional churches in favor of less
conventional actors, including new religious movements. As opposed to the
process of secularization, there is a process of re-enchantment of the world.[5]

Things have changed since Weber declared the disenchantment of the
Western world between 1918 and 1919.[6] A goal of modernity was the rationalization of reality, leaving no place for magic and the sacred. However,
where secularization has failed, there has been a turn back toward the religious, though in some instances this turn has taken the form of a rejection
of liberal democracy and led to violence. Today, magic and the sacred have
returned to permeate the world and it is not out of bounds for people to
think that the Devil and angels also walk among humans. Since the 1960s, a
time when new religious movements were established and flourished, there
have been efforts to find replacements and substitutes for the disappearance
of values caused by the decline in social and political authority from traditional—religious—institutions. Those movements tended to be organized
in non-hierarchical groups and focused on developing and empowering
the self-placing spirituality at the center.[7] Generally, secularization and the
disenchantment of the world robbed religious organizations of their moral
authority. Lacking a place to find meaning outside of oneself, there is a rise
in relativism, and the individual is thrown back on themselves to determine
the meaning of their own lives.

One could account for the success of overtly religiously themed shows on
mainstream television networks (e.g., *Highway to Heaven* or *Touched by an
Angel*) or shows that borrowed from the good/evil binary (*Buffy the Vampire
Slayer* and *Angel*) by the need to fill the void left by the decline of traditional
sources of moral authority; this could explain why *Lucifer* has been so successful. Broadcast on Fox for the first three seasons, and then on Netflix for
an additional, though shorter, three seasons, *Lucifer* is adapted from the DC

comic created by Neil Gaiman and published by Vertigo as a spin-off of the graphic novel *Sandman*.[8] The plot explores the changes to Lucifer who, after becoming tired of ruling Hell, decides to move to Los Angeles where he ends up fighting crimes in collaboration with Detective Chloe Decker (played by Lauren German). The relationship between Decker and Lucifer becomes one of the main points of the show: unlike other women who come into his orbit, she is not sensitive to Lucifer's charms and power. At the same time, Lucifer begins to visit psychotherapist Linda Martin (played by Rachel Harris) in order to understand the new world he is living in. Things get complicated when the Angel Amenadiel, with whom Lucifer has a brotherly bond, is sent to Earth with the task of returning Lucifer to Hell.

This chapter looks at how the different characters relate to ideas associated with free will, determinism, and moral responsibility and then analyzes whether these different approaches how the ethics of *Lucifer* are represented and the possible impact on the society that benefits from the final product.

LUCIFER MORNINGSTAR

The main character of the series is the Devil himself, Lucifer Morningstar, the perfect antihero. That he is—literally—the Devil means that the audience will bring certain preconceived notions about him and his motivations to their viewing of the show; however, because he is the point of view character, the audience must trust him and his perspective, at least a little.[9] On the show, Lucifer is depicted as handsome, rich, and elegant; he possesses the power to reveal the most secret desires of the human heart. The audience enters into a sympathetic relationship with the character, feeling something like sympathy for the devil, and is able to identify with his desires and plight.[10] According to Cohen, identification occurs when the audience takes the perspective of the character, sees the world, and assigns meaning to events, from the perspective of that character.[11] Furthermore, identification is not understood to be a binary variable, but rather a continuous variable, with various levels of identification possible. When strongly identifying with a particular character, the audience takes the character's point of view, shares the character's knowledge of the events in the narrative, and understands the character's motivations and goals. Normally, preference for a character is expressed as liking or disliking that character; viewers monitor a character's actions and assign a moral value to them.[12] Characters who act justly are judged more favorably, whereas characters who act reprehensibly are judged more harshly. Support for dispositional approaches to understanding perceptions of characters has received wide-scale support across a variety of media content, though this original conceptualization of disposition theory seems to have a difficult time explaining how antiheroes would enjoy popular appeal.[13] However, extensions and reconceptualizations of the original formulation of disposition theory provide various avenues to understand the role of perceived morality on viewers' liking of media characters and of antiheroes or morally ambiguous characters specifically.[14]

Some explanations for audience preference, or even affection, for antiheroes focus on the importance of forgoing constant moral monitoring. According to Raney's extension of the original formulation of disposition theory notes that when individuals begin a narrative, they frequently have some indication of whether or not they should like a given character.[15] For example, perhaps prior publicity or early scenes suggest that a character is a protagonist. Under these circumstances, viewers may begin a narrative with a favorable disposition toward a character already in place and then forego monitoring of the character's moral (or immoral) behavior. On *Lucifer*, even if the main character is a rebel (his first action on screen is to corrupt a policeman for petty reasons), he is presented as more attractive than the men around him and women are attracted to him. The character's social success is indubitable, which is one of the most important tools for identification building. Lucifer is financially successful: he owns a club called Lux, where he is depicted as confident and popular. On the show, Lucifer is someone that the audience could aspire to be or would want to spend time with even if, upon reflection, it might not be in their best interests to do so.

Lucifer lives at Lux with his most loyal demon, Mazikeen (played by Lesley-Ann Brandt). Both Lucifer and Mazikeen are depicted as treating humans as if they were pleasurable pets. Lux is a mild transposition of Hell on Earth: it is the physical place where Lucifer does favors in exchange for future repayments, though those repayments do not involve the soul of those he contracts with. This is a rewriting of the traditional version of "the deal with the Devil," in which people obtain something in exchange for eternal damnation. While it is true that Lucifer does favors for people in exchange for something, he is never shown as exchanging a favor for a soul; people are not eternally harmed in the exchange. Additionally, Lucifer does not corrupt humans as much as he encourages or forces them to reveal their deepest desires to themselves and to anyone else who is listening. Getting people to speak their own truth creates moral distance between Lucifer and that truth: the evil they confess is not in him but is in human beings. Lucifer is merely the occasion for the evil part of humanity to reveal itself. Lucifer is not bad, and he never was.

On *Lucifer*, the Devil is a scapegoat; this is the first important reversal of the audience's expectations about him. Lucifer's original sin goes back to something that happened between him and God. The audience is never told what exactly happened, but it is clear that Lucifer did something that angered

God. Vague hints are given that the behavior can be likened to a son acting out against his father or doing something to harm his family. For this, Lucifer was banished from Heaven and sent to rule Hell; he was charged with punishing those who did evil.

Throughout the series, the focus of the show is on Lucifer and his growing self-understanding. Through his interviews with his psychotherapist, Dr. Linda, the audience tries to gain a better understanding of Lucifer's motivations; as they do, they come to see Lucifer as a more rounded character. According to Forster, a round character is more complicated and harder to understand than a flat one.[16] A round character is not a *topos*, is unconventional, and their multifacetedness makes it difficult to identify them; a round character is a character who demands attention in order to be understood. The character's complex nature draws the audience to him, but it is also true that common narrative techniques are used to make the audience empathize with Lucifer. Both contribute to Lucifer being a good antihero: he is selfish and disobeys most social customs and rules. If it is true that he starts helping Decker for altruistic reasons—to find the murderer of a girl whom he used to know—it is also true that he continues to collaborate with her for his own reasons, not only from a sense of justice. One reason that an audience might identify with him is that even though he is the Devil, there is the possibility of his redemption. That Lucifer is both a round and dynamic character, and is on some kind of quest to understand who he is, can be summarized with the last bit of dialogue in the first episode:

Lucifer: I sense your disapproval, Maze. What is it?
Maze: I just can't understand why you would save a human life.
Lucifer: Well, there's . . . something different about her that I don't quite understand, and it vexes me.
Maze: Maybe it's not her that is different.
Lucifer: Is this where I'm supposed to ask, "whatever do you mean?"
Maze: I'm worried the humans are rubbing off on you. Stop caring. You are the Devil.
Lucifer: Yes I am.[17]

AMENADIEL

Amenadiel is the eldest brother of all the angels, and he has been tasked by God to bring Lucifer back to Hell. He is chosen to come to Earth because he is the most trustworthy angel in Silver City, the angels' home. Amenadiel is depicted as the mirror opposite of Lucifer: he is obedient to their father. As God's messenger, he is fully aware of the importance of his task.[18] Similar to

Lucifer, though, he is alienated from humanity: his point of view is radically different from the human one and for that reason he possesses a different set of moral values and priorities. In a scene where Lucifer has defended to Mazikeen his right not to fulfill his responsibilities, Amenadiel tries to, first, convince him of the importance of his role. When Lucifer is unmoved by this argument, Amenadiel becomes violent.[19] To show the viewer that Amenadiel is a threat to Lucifer, the scene is filmed in a way that shows Lucifer as vulnerable and Amenadiel as aggressive. The audience identifies with Lucifer and feels empathy for him because of his vulnerability. Furthermore, the audience can relate to Lucifer: he does not want a task that has been assigned to him; he wants to choose his own destiny. Where Lucifer appears open and reasonable, Amenadiel appears authoritarian, deaf to his brother's reasons, and much more distant from humanity. He is not interested in Lucifer's inner growth, but instead in a greater good.

Amenadiel: I've been watching you, Lucifer.
Lucifer: You, perv.
Amenadiel: And I'm not sure I like what I see. You're showing restraint, mercy.
Lucifer: You're scared I'm turning my back on the dark side, bro?
Amenadiel: Lucifer, there is a balance here that we must maintain.[20]

Despite his fidelity to God and his task in the early episodes, Amenadiel changes over the course of the series. In the first season, he commits actions that go against his own moral code in order to convince Lucifer to go back home: he has sex with the demon Mazikeen, he brings a soul back from Hell, and he lies and takes advantage of a human by using his fears against him. Worst, he makes an attempt on Decker's life. Amenadiel is moved by the idea of his duty and a greater good, but when he becomes aware of his sins, he loses his power and his wings, the symbol of his angelic being. He realizes his need to atone when he understands how much he hurt Linda Martin, Lucifer's analyst, by pretending to be her colleague and using her to manipulate Lucifer.[21] Gradually, loving his brother becomes his true mission. He falls in love with Linda Martin and starts to have doubts and more human-like feelings.

CHLOE DECKER

It is obvious to the audience that Chloe Decker, the main female lead, is a police detective. She is introduced at a crime scene, her badge is clearly visible, and she acts in a determined and competent way. Her first meeting with Lucifer is significant in several ways. First, perhaps surprisingly, Lucifer is absolutely honest with her about everything: he declares his real name, his immortality, and lets Chloe know that he is not human; Chloe does not believe him. At the same time, Lucifer shows no respect for her reputation or social convention: he asks Chloe if they have ever had sex, though not with an offensive intention, but because he is trying to understand where he has seen her before. His difference from humanity becomes clear in the relationship with Decker. For Decker, Lucifer's difference is literally other-worldly; she asks him "and, uh, what planet are you from . . . London?"[22] Despite their many differences, what they have in common is a concern for justice. In this dialogue, we also see what really makes him the Lord of Hell: he wants the responsible punished.

Lucifer: What will your little corrupt organization do about this?
Chloe: Excuse me?
Lucifer: Will you find the person responsible? Will they be punished? Will this be a priority for you? Because it is for me . . . Someone there needs to be punished! We are not done!
Chloe: Yeah, yeah we are.[23]

More than everything else, Lucifer is a punisher concerned that people get what they deserve. Decker helps him better understand this part of himself.

The audience sees Decker again in the same episode when she raids the house of a famous hip-hop singer and gangster; Lucifer is already there, having gone to ask him about the victim. The audience's perception of her as someone assertive, competent, and professional is reinforced by the way she manages the situation: confidently and without hesitation. Decker is undermined when one of the people at the scene recognizes her as an actress from a soft-core porn teen-movie, *Hot Tub High-School*; Lucifer suddenly remembers where he knows her from. From this juxtaposition between a competent police officer and former actress, Decker is revealed to be a more complex character. Additionally, when she eventually arrests Lucifer, she provides justifications that are not professional: "You are interfering with a police investigation, you have broken I can't even count how many laws, and you pissed me off."[24] But the most interesting thing about Decker is that she is entirely unaffected by Lucifer's power. When he tries to demonstrate his skills to her, she simply doesn't understand:

Lucifer: Tell me, detective, what do you desire more than anything else in this life?
Chloe: This is it? Your big trick?[25]

And then, she teases him:

Chloe: I guess, when I was a little girl, I . . . always wanted to be a cop like my
     daddy, so that . . . that one day I could help people and, and be taken seriously
     when I say to shut up and get in the damn car.[26]

It is interesting that she is joking, but she is also telling the truth: Chloe did
become a police officer because of her father, and she does desire to be taken
seriously. Though it might seem like she is responding to Lucifer's power to
get people to confess their desires, she is consistently shown as immune to it:

Lucifer: That's interesting, 'cause . . . you don't look at me that way.
Chloe: What way?
Lucifer: With carnal fascination.
Chloe: That's 'cause it doesn't exist.
Lucifer: No, you see, that's just it . . . with most women it does. I tend to appeal
     to the dark mischievous hearts in all of you, but you, detective, you seem oddly
     immune to my charms.
Chloe: Referring to them as "charms," I think is a bit of a stretch. Truth be told, I
     find you repulsive, like on a chemical level.
Lucifer: That's fascinating.[27]

In the rest of the episode, the audience learns that Chloe is a young mother
with an ex-husband (also a policeman) who does not take her seriously and
acts in a condescending manner toward her. At the end of the first episode,
Lucifer saves Decker (he does so repeatedly throughout the series). Through
Decker, Lucifer learns to care for another person; through his feelings for her,
he discovers love and the good inside of him.

LINDA MARTIN

The last character that the audience meets is Dr. Linda Martin. She is juxtaposed to Decker by the way that she responds to Lucifer: where Decker can
resist Lucifer's charms, Dr. Martin cannot. Where it is later revealed that
Chloe is a miracle from God, hence her lack of response to Lucifer's powers,
Dr. Martin is depicted as thoroughly human. When she first meets Lucifer,
she is completely charmed by him; she agrees, at his request, to begin a professional and sexual relationship with him. Dr. Martin tries to help Lucifer
with his family problems but she does not understand that he is being sincere
when he speaks about divine entities. She interprets everything Lucifer says
as metaphors until Lucifer shows her his devil face.[28] During the series, she
starts a close, sisterly friendship with Maze, Chloe, and Ella, while also trying
to be helpful by analyzing her friends. Dr. Martin's insights drive the plot and

become a way that the audience learns more about the characters, especially Lucifer.

FREE WILL AND THE BLURRED BORDER BETWEEN GOOD AND EVIL

Lucifer's world is a place with a far and silent God. For those who do not see or experience the world as disenchanted, the world of *Lucifer* is a mirror to ours. The audience might be intrigued by this world because they wish to know how the characters are dealing with similar questions and doubts about meaning and morality: in the show, there are few strong believers in the great and modern city of Los Angeles; most of the characters on the show are thoroughly secular. What makes *Lucifer* unique is that it places at the center of the narrative divine creatures who question the meaning and presence of God. The absence of God is such that not only are the heavenly persons not sure of the will of God, but they suffer from feeling abandoned. Lucifer expresses this feeling when he agonizes over having to make a decision about his mother's destiny:

> Everyone thinks they know what He wants! Amenadiel did when he first got here and now Uriel does. Human wars have been waged because of it. Dad showed me an open door. Does that mean I was meant to take you back to Hell or was he insinuating that Hell was getting drafty? Nobody bloody knows because the selfish bastard won't just tell us! I'm sick of it. No more.[29]

In the absence of God, or disagreeing with what God wants, the angels need to find their own meaning in their life. Whereas humans are born with free will and learn to accept it or wrestle with its meaning, angels and all the divine entities are born to obey their destiny, so they have to learn how to manage the free will they find on Earth. Amenadiel and Lucifer represent the two possibilities for how supernatural beings relate to free will: if Lucifer is the ultimate rebel who embraces it, Amenadiel thinks himself as the obedient soldier who performs the will of God. For this reason, Amenadiel—because of his mission—is the villain of the first season and remains a foil to Lucifer. The audience can relate to Amenadiel when he suffers a crisis of faith and meaning and is forced to reckon with the meaning of free will.

Different from Amenadiel, Lucifer wants to be released from his destiny and wants free will. However, he finds that free will is not easy to live with. When Lucifer asks Amenadiel for help in finding his lost wings, he answers: "You wanted free will, you wanted accountability. Well . . . fix your own damn mess, for once."[30] Lucifer himself recognizes free will as the key to his story and his damnation. After a fight with Amenadiel, Chloe asks him what happened and he answers:

> Well, where do I begin? With the grandest fall in the history of time? Or per-
> haps the far more agonizing punishment that followed? To be blamed for every
> morsel of evil humanity endured, every atrocity committed in my name? As
> though I wanted people to suffer. All I ever wanted was to be my own man
> here. To be judged for my own doing, and for that I've been shown how truly
> powerless I am, that even the people I trusted, the one person, you, could use
> to hurt me.[31]

Lucifer's search for free will is an integral part of the construction of his character, because of the way that it dramatizes many theories about the existence and meaning of evil. In the modern era, the idea that evil existed as a metaphysical force was replaced by the belief that scientific and technological progress could improve the world to the point where evil was no longer a meaningful problem. However, the wars of the twentieth century and the Holocaust ended any hope that evil had been removed from the world. In *Lucifer*, God is back in the world, but God is not entirely good and the Devil is walking around Los Angeles trying to make meaning in a modern, but fallen, world.

The challenge is to depict God as both wholly perfect, which would imply that God is wholly good. In *Lucifer*, God does not make mistakes; God has collaborators that God made, and they make mistakes. Creation and the created are not perfect, and there are actions and events that go against God's will, but not God's knowledge because God, in *Lucifer*, is omniscient. Those actions seem evil, but they are not; rather, the human perspective cannot grasp the vastness of God's decisions. It is in this perspective that Lucifer and his desire to escape from Hell exist. Lucifer does not understand his destiny and fights against it in order to discover that he had the most onerous and important task of all: to maintain universal balance.[32]

There is a connection between free will and identity: to reject determinism and/or predestination is to embrace the idea that one is free to choose one's self. This belief makes evil a choice (though one can choose otherwise) but should one choose evil, one is ultimately responsible for having done so. In a world where moral values are no longer absolute, but relative and so the evil is redeemable and forgivable, the question on the table is the freedom of choice.[33] On *Lucifer,* wings symbolize the characters' willingness to adhere to their destiny or their rebellious choice to follow their own path. Upon arriving on Earth, Lucifer cuts off his own wings. Both angels, Lucifer and Amenadiel, are forced to make decisions and end up making many mistakes on their way to becoming who they want to be. We first meet this problem thanks to Linda, when Lucifer talks to her about the theft of his wings by a criminal in the sixth episode of the first season:

Linda: This loss brings up an issue that we've been skirting since we began our work together.
Lucifer: Right.
Linda: Your identity.
Lucifer: (wry laugh) It's still the Devil, darling.
Linda: Yes, but who are you trying so hard to become?
Lucifer: Nobody. I'm completely unbecoming.
Linda: And yet you keep trying on many hats to hide your horns. Playboy, cop, club owner . . .
Lucifer: Yes, you forgot "master of all things tongue-related."
   [. . .]
Linda: One of the hardest things we ever do is learn to be ourselves. I want you to tell me who you believe is the real you.
Lucifer: I . . . I am second-guessing your skills as a therapist.[34]

The fourth season opens with a significant scene that furthers this point. Lucifer is shown sitting at his piano, singing:

> When you were here before, couldn't look you in the eye, you're just like an angel. Your skin makes me cry. You float like a feather in a beautiful world. Oh I wish I was special, you're so very special. But I'm a creep. I'm weirdo, what the hell am I doing here? I don't belong. She's running.[35]

Lucifer's clothes change multiple times, indicating he has been singing this song at Lux over and over again; his facial features show that he is becoming more upset as he is singing. Then, a gun is placed up against his head and Lucifer says, "Have I played this song too much? I have, haven't I?"[36] Lucifer is distraught because of the deterioration of his relationship with Decker, who has seen his true face. Having seen his true face, Lucifer is forced to confront who he really is. Decker has always been able to resist Lucifer's powers and his charm. Her ability to resist him is directly linked to her emancipation from the role usually assigned to women in culture: either mother/virgin or monster/whore. In this regard, Decker is juxtaposed to Mazikeen who is depicted as being more overtly sexual. Decker is emancipated enough to free herself from submission to Lucifer, her natural master, and to look for her own identity.[37] But for Lucifer, it is Decker's freedom, specifically her freedom from him, which causes Lucifer to think about his own identity. When Lucifer shows Decker his true face, she runs away and he goes through an identity crisis which is clarified in a dialogue with Lee, the man holding a gun to his head. Lucifer takes out his confusion and frustration on Lee and several other gunmen who had planned on robbing Lux:

Lucifer: What if she's decided that I am evil incarnate? And what if she's right?
Lee: Don't kill me man . . . please . . . I'm just a thief! That's all.
Lucifer: That's not true.
Lee: Excuse me?
Lucifer: That's not all you are.[38]

The scene suddenly changes and the camera shows us a treasure of gold while Lucifer says:

> Don't get me wrong, you are indeed a thief, but perhaps you deserve a chance to prove to people that's not all you are. Hm? Right, there you go. Money to cover any debts that you owe, pay your friends downstairs medical bills, and have a chance of a new life. A chance for people to see you in a different way.[39]

Lucifer's desire to be seen differently is revealed in the opportunity he gives Lee. This tension inside Lucifer between his God-given identity as the Devil and the person he is trying to become is further explored in the juxtaposition between Eve and Decker. Eve (played by Inbar Lavi) is introduced early in season 4; she is Lucifer's ex-girlfriend, and as her name implies, based on the Biblical character. Eve, the audience is told, left Adam because she wanted to experience a new kind of life; she does this through her relationship with Lucifer. Like the other characters on the show, Eve is trying to find herself:

Eve: I always felt like something was missing. People always forget I didn't choose Adam. I was created for him. Turns out an arranged existence kind of takes the spark out of things. We got along just fine, but I don't think he ever really loved me. The real me, you know?
Lucifer: It hurts to not be accepted for who you are. I . . . I would imagine.[40]

By the end of the season, Eve will understand that she cannot define herself through a relationship, but that she needs to find her true self.[41] On the other hand, Decker always tries to make Lucifer better. She inspires Lucifer to be less selfish and criticizes his antisocial, irresponsible behavior.[42] The difference between Eve and Decker is that Eve represents the choice (if it is a choice) to accept oneself for who one is. Decker represents the possibility of becoming someone that you are not. On the one hand, accepting who you are can be defeating because you are accepting that there is no other way for you to be. Alternatively, accepting who you are can be liberating because it releases the pressure to be something that you are not. The benefit of Decker motivating Lucifer to become a better person is that there is the freedom to be other than one is; the ability to change is proof that one is free to author one's own destiny. However, the downside to believing that change is possible is that one is solely responsible for making that change happen. If that change does not occur, or does not occur as quickly as one would like it to, then there is no one to blame but oneself. In choosing between Eve and Decker, Lucifer is choosing between two different ways of understanding the relationship between his destiny and the future he wants for himself.

Amenadiel is the other mirror of Lucifer's behavior. Like his brother, he has been dealing with the notion of free will since leaving Heaven. Amenadiel is first introduced as being committed to the common good and playing the role that has been assigned to him. His internal struggle about freedom and obligation begins during his relationship with Mazikeen. When Mazikeen is tasked by Lucifer with killing Amenadiel and sending him back to Heaven, Amenadiel confesses how conflicted he is about his feelings for Maze and for what he has been tasked by God to do. What frightens Amenadiel is the possibility of returning to God as a failure and so he feels that he must do what he has been ordered to do. He becomes a more complex character when he begins to admit that there is the possibility that he could fail or choose not to complete his assigned task. When Amenadiel sees that he has options and it is his responsibility to choose between them. At the end of the first season, Lucifer is ready to go back to Hell, but Amenadiel refuses to take him:

Lucifer: You don't want to take me back to Hell? The one bloody thing you have wanted this entire time. Did I punch you in the head too hard?
Amenadiel: Maze was right, Luci. We used her. And Malcolm. People have died because of us . . . Brother, somehow I lost sight of the biggest picture, of the cost of my actions, and just how truly selfish they were. But, Luci, my eyes are wide open now, and I need to make this right . . . I need to find Malcolm, and I need to send him back to Hell. Will you help me brother?[43]

The characters on *Lucifer* come at free will differently than the audience: it is likely that the audience assumes that they have free will and may at some point in their lives encounter theologies, philosophies, or situations that make them question whether free will exists at all or if it comes in varying degrees. The divine characters on *Lucifer* begin knowing that they do not have free will because everything is part of some cosmic plan or they have been ordered to act a certain way by God. For that reason, the divine characters on *Lucifer* have to learn how to deal with free will and what it means for their sense of self and moral identities. Because humans have always operated with the belief that they possess something like free will, they prove to be better guides for the divine characters.

The question of free will versus determinism posed by the divine charac-ters is kept in tension with the moral concerns of the human characters. If everything is part of a plan, then all morality is relative to that plan. Good and bad things are on the same moral level as long as they are part of the plan. From the human perspective, morality matters a great deal. The lack of knowledge by the humans about the divine plan makes them feel that something important is at stake in every situation. Additionally, the divine characters know that there is a God and that there is meaning in the universe. The human characters are confronting a rationalized, secularized, and disen-chanted world and are struggling to make meaning in a seemingly meaning-less universe. This perspective forces one to be alone with the responsibility of building one's own moral code. The lack of clarity about whether an action or event is part of, or contributes to, something larger than oneself is what makes the antihero compelling. The antihero reflects the ambiguity and frus-tration of living in a world where the values one is supposed to adhere to are random, arbitrary, and do not point to anything beyond themselves. Without the certainty of truth, the complex ambiguity of the world opens a space for main characters who doubt morality to confront questions that the audience might not be able to or lack a vocabulary for.[44] Lucifer, as the Devil, upends audience expectations about how someone could think about good, evil, pre-destination, and free will. Perhaps more than any other character in Western literature, the Devil should have very clear, unambiguous stances on these topics. On the show, Lucifer questions both evil and good, and in doing so reveals himself to be more human than divine. The situations he finds himself in and the relationships he has with the other characters positions Lucifer as an antihero that the audience can empathize with: he is both in control of his own destiny and the victim of fate, a situation that it is easy to see oneself in. As his relationships with his father, mother, brothers, lovers, and others become more complex, those relationships become more human, and so does Lucifer. At his core, Lucifer is a son trying to break free from the control of his father and be his own person. Moreover, in contrast to a lot of other antiheroes, he never hurts innocent people or does something unquestionably evil; he is more like a capricious baby who does not accept authority and chooses to live for his pleasure principle. The fact that he is harmless and wants to help makes it safe to identify with Lucifer and root for his success.

CONCLUSION

The way that *Lucifer* deconstructs the binary between good and evil, and also free will and determinism, creates a new, more complex, landscape of choice for the audience. Because the human characters are depicted as faring better with free will, the show sends the message that even in a secularized or disenchanted world, humans can be trusted to construct a viable and meaningful morality. Ironically, it is the divine beings who struggle to make meaning in this sort of world. It is for this reason that the divine beings are thrown into existential crisis when meaning is no longer certain. The audience is able to position themselves between the divine beings who are asking important questions about the meaning of life and the human characters who, even if they are not entirely certain in their answers, have a better grasp of the situation and are able to function in the world. Amenadiel and Lucifer come from a dimension in which good and evil are clearly defined and differentiated. When they arrive on Earth, the border separating the two begins to crumble. While the divine characters stumble, the human characters are shown as being able to balance themselves more easily. In the end, therefore, the human being, imperfect and far from God, proves to be better and more suitable to act in the world. So, the identification by the audience with the human characters, against the alienation felt by the divine beings, helps to see humans, even humans living in a secularlized or disenchanted world, as better from a moral point of view. Obviously, humans can also choose evil, as that is what drives the plot of the show, but that choice shows how important and impressive it is when humans choose good: they could have chosen otherwise.

Lucifer's relevance is that, similar to other shows in the era of Peak TV, it is obvious in that it is asking questions about morality and values. Though it is not the first show to have a divine figure as a moral guide, nor is it the first show to have characters that are supposed to be evil (or, determined by their nature to be evil) explore the complexity of the human condition, using the Devil as a moral guide, and to depict the Devil on a hero's journey as he struggles for redemption and salvation, might be a first. Or, it might be a continuation of the process started by Marino in *La morte degli innocenti*, and refined by Milton in *Paradise Lost*, that culminates in a new version of the Devil who can be the main character in a contemporary morality play.[45] Considering Lukács's point of view, it's easy to see a strong link between this narrative construction and the complexity of a postmodern morality.[46] Given the complexity of contemporary society and the resurgence of nondenominational religion, it will be interesting to see how depictions of the Devil and his relationship to humanity continue to evolve.

NOTES

1. David Gill and Bridget Adams, *ABC of Communication Studies* (Nashville: HarperCollins, 1998), 86.

2. Dominique Moisi, *La géopolitique des séries, ou Le triomphe de la peur: essai* (Paris: Flammarion, 2017), *foreword*.

3. Mary Talbot, *Media Discourse: Representation and Interaction* (Edinburgh: Edinburgh University Press, 2017), 3.

4. Cf. Peter Berger, Grace Davie, and Effie Fokas, *America religiosa, Europa Laica? Perché il secolarismo europeo è un'eccezione* [Religious America, Secular Europe? A Theme and Variations] (Bologna: Il Mulino, 2010).

5. Christopher Partridge, *The Re-Enchantment of the West* (London: T&T Clark, 2005), 44.

6. Cf. Max Weber, *La scienza come professione* [Wissenschaft als Beruf (Science as a Profession)] (Roma: Armando Editore, 1997).

7. The distinction between religion and spirituality is not easy to make because clearly defining what "religion" is puts at stake possibilities difficult to control, being that "religion" might be a category that allows access to political and economic benefits.

8. It is not the first time that the Devil has been illustrated in a comic or graphic novel. Cf. Fredrik Stromberg, *The Comics Go to Hell: A Visual History of the Devil in Comics* (College Park, MD: Fantagraphics Books, 2005); Neil Gaiman, *The Sandman* (Burbank, CA: DC, 1989–1996).

9. We are using the idea of *topos* in a way similar to the notion of flat character proposed by E. M. Forster, *Aspetti del Romanzo* [Aspects of the Novel], trans. Corrado Pavolini (Milano: Garzanti, 1991).

10. Cf. Alexander Todorov and James S. Uleman, "Spontaneous Trait Inferences Are Bound to Actors' Faces: Evidence from a False Recognition Paradigm," *Journal of Personality and Social Psychology* 83, no. 5: 1051–1065.

11. Cf. Jonathan Cohen, "Audience Identification with Media Characters," in *The Psychology of Entertainment*, ed. Jennings Bryant and Peter Vorderer (Mahwah, NJ: Erlbaum, 2006), 183–197.

12. Cf. Arthur A. Raney, "Expanding Disposition Theory: Reconsidering Character Liking, Moral Evaluations, and Enjoyment," *Communication Theory* 14, no. 4 (November 1, 2004): 348–369.

13. For a review of how dispositional approaches shape audience understanding, see Raney 2006.

14. K. Maja Krakowiak and Mary Beth Oliver, "When Good Characters Do Bad Things: Examining the Effect of Moral Ambiguity on Enjoyment," *Journal of Communication* 62, no. 1 (2021): 117–135.

15. Cf. Raney, 348–369 and Raney, "The Psychology of Disposition-Based Theories of Media Enjoyment," *Psychology of Entertainment* (2006): 137–150.

16. Forster, 58–62.

17. *Lucifer*, season 1, episode 1, "Pilot," dir. Len Wiseman, aired January 25, 2016, originally released on Fox.

18. Ibid.

19. Ibid.

20. Ibid.

21. *Lucifer*, season 2, episode 2, "Liar, Liar, Slutty Pants on Fire," dir. Louis Shaw Milito, aired October 3, 2016, originally released on Fox.

22. *Lucifer*, season 1, episode 1, "Pilot," dir. Len Wiseman, aired January 25, 2016, originally released on Fox.

23. Ibid.

24. Ibid.

25. Ibid.

26. Ibid.

27. Ibid.

28. *Lucifer*, season 1, episode 2, "Lucifer, Stay. Good Devil," dir. Nathan Hope, aired February 1, 2016, originally released on Fox. *Lucifer*, season 2, episode 6, "Monster," dir. Eagle Egilsson, aired October 31, 2016, originally released on Fox.

29. Lucifer's mother, God's wife, was cast to Hell by God. When Lucifer asks God to save Decker, God shows Lucifer that his mother's cell in Hell is empty. Lucifer reads this as a sign that God has granted his request as long as he brings his mother back to Hell. But when he met his mother, despite his fear for Decker's life, Lucifer and Amenadiel choose to stand up for their mother, and Uriel is sent to Earth to bring her back to Hell. *Lucifer*, season 2, episode 5, "Weaponizer," dir. Karen Gaviola, aired October 24, 2016, originally released on Fox.

30. *Lucifer*, season 1, episode 7, "Wingman," dir. Eriq La Salle, aired March 7, 2016, originally released on Fox.

31. *Lucifer*, season 1, episode 12, "#TeamLucifer," dir. Greg Beeman, aired April 18, 2016, originally released on Fox.

32. *Lucifer*, season 4, episode 10, "Who's da New King of Hell?," dir. Eagle Egilsson, released digitally May 18, 2019, on Netflix.

33. As the important novel of Victor Hugo, *La fin de Satan* (France, 1886), has already pointed out.

34. *Lucifer*, season 1, episode 6, "Favorite Son," dir. David Paymer, aired February 29, 2016, originally released on Fox.

35. *Lucifer*, season 4, episode 1, "Everything's Okay," dir. Sherwin Shilati, released digitally May 8, 2019, on Netflix.

36. Ibid.

37. *Lucifer*, season 1, episode 12, "#TeamLucifer," dir. Greg Beeman, aired April 18, 2016, originally released on Fox.

38. *Lucifer*, season 4, episode 1, "Everything's Okay," dir. Sherwin Shilati, released digitally May 8, 2019, on Netflix.

39. Ibid.

40. *Lucifer*, season 4, episode 4, "All About Eve," dir. Sherwin Shilati, released digitally May 8, 2019, on Netflix.

41. *Lucifer*, season 4, episode 10, "Who's da New King of Hell?," dir. by Eagle Egilsson, released digitally May 8, 2019, on Netflix.

42. *Lucifer*, season 1, episode 2, "Lucifer, Stay. Good Devil," dir. Nathan Hope, aired February 1, 2016, originally released on Fox.

43. *Lucifer*, season 1, episode 13, "Take Me Back to Hell," dir. Nathan Hope, aired April 25, 2016, originally released on Fox.

44. Cf. Andrea Bernardelli, ed., *Il trionfo dell'antieroe nelle serie televisive* (Perugia: Morlacchi, 2012).

45. Mario Praz, *La carne, la morte e il diavolo nella letteratura romantica* (Firenze: Sansoni, 1996), 56.
46. György Lukács, "La fisionomia intellettuale dei personaggi artistici," in *Il marxismo e la critica letteraria* (Torino: Einaudi, 1953), 332–387.

BIBLIOGRAPHY

Bakhtin, Mikhail. *Tvorchevsto Fransua Rable* [Rabelais and His World]. Moscow: Kuhdozvestennia literatura, 1965.

Berger, Peter, Grace Davie, and Effie Fokas. *America religiosa, Europa Laica? Perché il secolarismo europeo è un'eccezione* [Religious America, Secular Europe? A Theme and Variations]. Bologna: Il Mulino, 2010.

Bernardelli, Andrea, ed. *Il trionfo dell'antieroe nelle serie televisive*. Perugia: Morlacchi, 2012.

Cohen, Jonathan. "Audience Identification with Media Characters." In *The Psychology of Entertainment*, edited by Jennings Bryant and Peter Vorderer, 183–197. Mahwah, NJ: Erlbaum, 2006.

Dawson, Lorne L. *I Nuovi Movimenti religiosi* [Comprehending Cults. The Sociology of New Religious Movements]. Bologna: Il Mulino, 2005.

Di Prazza, Bianca. *Un tesoro di diavolo: perché gli antieroi seriali sono i nostri protagonisti preferiti. Comparatismi*, vol. 3, 2018: 153–163.

Forster E. M. *Aspetti del Romanzo* [Aspects of the Novel]. Translated by Corrado Pavolini. Milano: Garzanti, 1991.

Gill, David, and Bridget Adams. *ABC of Communication Studies*. Walton-on-Thames: Nelson, 1998.

Heelas, Paul, and Linda Woodhead, Benjamin Seel Bronislaw Szerszynski, and Karin Tusting. *The Spiritual Revolution: Why Religion Is Giving Way to Spirituality*. Oxford: Wiley-Blackwell, 2005.

Krakowiak, K. Maja, and Mary Beth Oliver. "When Good Characters Do Bad Things: Examining the Effect of Moral Ambiguity on Enjoyment." *Journal of Communication* 62, no. 1 (2021): 117–35.

Lucifer. Created by Tom Kapinos. Aired from January 25, 2016–September 10, 2021. Originally released on Fox (seasons 1–3); seasons 4–6 released on Netflix.

Lukács, György. "La fisionomia intellettuale dei personaggi artistici." In *Il marxismo e la critica letteraria*. Torino: Einaudi, 1953.

Moisi, Dominique. *La géopolitique des séries, ou Le triomphe de la peur: essai*. Paris: Flammarion, 2017.

Partridge, Christopher. *The Re-Enchantment of the West*. London: T&T Clark, 2005.

Praz, Rio. *La carne, la morte e il diavolo nella letteratura romantica*. Firenze: Sansoni, 1996.

Raney, Arthur A. "Expanding Disposition Theory: Reconsidering Character Liking, Moral Evaluations, and Enjoyment." *Communication Theory* 14, Issue 4 (November 2004): 348–369.

————. "The Psychology of Disposition-Based Theories of Media Enjoyment." In J. Bryant and P. Vorderer, eds., *Psychology of Entertainment* (Mahwah, NJ: Lawrence Erlbaum Associates Publishers 2006): 137–150.

Snyder C.R., and Shane J. Lopez. *Positive Psychology*. Thousand Oaks, CA: Sage Publications, 2007.

Talbot, Mary. *Media Discourse: Representation and Interaction*. Edinburgh: Edinburgh University Press, 2017.

Todorov Alexander, and James S. Uleman. "Spontaneous Trait Inferences Are Bound to Actors' Faces: Evidence From a False Recognition Paradigm." *Journal of Personality and Social Psychology* 83, no. 5: 1051–1065.

Warner, Marina. *Sola fra le donne: mito e culto di Maria Vergne* [Alone in All Her Sex: The Myth an Cult of the Virgin Mary]. Palermo: Sellerio, 1999.

Weber, Max. *La scienza come professione* [Wissenschaft als Beruf (Science as a Profession)]. Roma: Armando Editore, 1997.

Zillman, Dolf, and Peter Vorderer, eds. *Media Entertainment: The Psychology of Its Appeal*. New York: Routledge, 2000.

Chapter 9

Letterkenny

Tolerance Meets Tradition

Dutton Kearney

If tolerance becomes a tradition, is it no longer tolerance?[1] *Letterkenny*, Jared Keeso's breakout comedy show—premiered first on the Canadian streaming service Crave in 2016 and streams on Hulu—looks at that question from a multitude of perspectives before offering its answer: No. Tolerance and tradition can coexist, and do so in a way that allows for a variety of individuals to live within a reasonable balance of freedom and restraint. *Letterkenny* is set in the fictional town of Letterkenny, Ontario, population 5,000. Each episode features a different set of "problems" that the community resolves. The community is broken up into different groups: Hicks, Ags, Skids, Hockey Players, Christians, and Natives. This ensemble cast is led by the Hicks, that is, those who own and work on a farm. Wayne (played by Jared Keeso) and his sister Katy (played by Michelle Mylett) are Hicks; they inherited their farm from their parents. They and their friends Daryl (played by Nathan Dales) and Dan (played by K. Trevor Wilson)—when they are not working the farm—are often in front of the local produce stand drinking countless Puppers lager while making observations about life. The farming community expands somewhat into town where the Ag Community is stationed. Also in town is Gail (played by Lisa Condrington), who manages Modean's, the local bar, Bonnie McMurray (played by Melanie Scrofano), who works at the Dollar Store and Modean's, and the Skids. Stewart leads the Skids in meth-fueled marathon dancing in the Dollar Store parking lot; their other base of operations is in Stewart's (played by Tyler Johnston) mother's basement. Additionally, there are the hockey players, Reilly (played by Dylan Playfair) and Jonesy (played by Andrew Herr), whose chronically livid coach lives a life of mourning for his wife when he is not apoplectically screaming and kicking trash cans in response to another lost game. The hockey community is expanded in later seasons as Reilly and Jonesy join the senior hockey team and choose to become coaches for the women's hockey team. The Christians are led by Glen (played by Jacob Tierney), the effeminate pastor of the Grace Fellowship Church. Finally, there are the Tanis-led Natives, who, as members of the First Nation, live on a reservation just outside of town. There are several other characters in the show, but these are the main subgroups of the larger group we will call Letterkenny. These diverse groups all live in harmony in the town of Letterkenny, combining tolerance with tradition.

Letterkenny reviewers often point to the idiosyncratic slang of the show, where subgroups known as the Hicks, Skids, Christians, Hockey Players, Natives, and Mennonites all vie for peaceful co-existence in a fictional town within Ontario. There are some groups hostile to the communities in Letterkenny: Degens from Up Country, Freaks Acting Krayzee United (F.A.K.U.), Hard Right Jay (played by Jay Baruchel), and big city snobs, among others. The language of the show is offensive, most of the characters seem to have severe drinking problems, and still others have issues with drug addiction and crime. In general, the rarely faithful sexual relationships are often not so much expressions of intimacy as they are used for stress release and personal satisfaction. Furthermore, there is constant violence, whether physical and/or verbal, be it threatened or actual. There is no pressing need to be responsible: children, the middle-aged, and the elderly are nowhere to be found; the one pregnancy in the series ends with an abortion, and, while the local bar burns down every two seasons, there is always a place to gather and drink, usually to excess. An objective list of the vices in the show makes it sound similar to the dark comedies mentioned below. However, the characters of *Letterkenny* see their behavior as having lasting consequences to themselves and to their community. And within this community, a sense of permanence is formed. There are traditions that are rigorously celebrated every year. There are unbreakable moral codes: "When a friend asks for help, you help them." Fidelity is the highest virtue. There is a high privileging of fidelity, either in dating or in marital relationships, even if it is not always fulfilled. And ultimately, there is the widest berth given to the show's highest virtue: tolerance.

While we are still experiencing the phenomenon known as Peak TV (John Landgraf's term for the overwhelming number of shows available on television, and very good shows at that), shows that portray morality positively without becoming trite and cliché are far and few between. The dark comedies of the past decade (*You're the Worst*, *It's Always Sunny in Philadelphia*, and *Bojack Horseman,* among others) are about variations of sociopathology rather than actual morality. In other words, morality in those shows serves as a foil for the protagonists. Far from being a guide, morality is something to fight as individual characters wreak havoc on a community striving for order. The order of the community is subjected to continuous mockery. However, in *Letterkenny,* the community is an essential arbiter of individual behavior, and it tolerates individual transgressions until the community is threatened. The main value of the community is conservative in nature: tradition. While tradition is not so flexible as to accommodate a transgression that would subvert the community, it is flexible enough to accommodate a reasonable modification: tolerance. *Letterkenny* roots its characters in something higher than the individuals who make up the community, while still embracing the same sort of tolerance that marks most contemporary liberal democracies. Its success is directly related to its ability to hold tolerance and tradition in tension with one another.

What is so interesting is that this tension between tolerance and tradition is the exact same tension that we find in the dramatic structure of any situational comedy (sitcom). Tradition demands that the characters in a sitcom behave in a familiar manner: certain characters repeat their signature lines, a light plot complication be introduced, and the show's plot coming to more or less of a resolution at the episode's conclusion, which allows for the next episode to repeat the structural sequence with very few structural changes. Over the course of a season, perhaps someone gets a new job, or a new dating partner might appear, but the end of a season is very close to a complete plot reset, which is then repeated the next season.[2]

Through a synthesis of Herbert Marcuse's "Repressive Tolerance" and Immanuel Kant's Categorical Imperative, the characters on the show allow any sort of behavior except when it is self-destructive (at least repeatedly), or behavior which violates previous oaths.[3] For example, pre-existing annual activities like Daryl's Super Soft Birthday Party, or Wayne and Katy's annual penny drive, must take place. When Daryl tries to avoid the former and Wayne the latter, other characters push against this rebellion and force the dissenters to participate. Their main weapon is appeals to conscience. Conscience absolutely requires a moral universe. In contrast, moral situations such as violence, abortion, faith, atheism, teetotalling, alcoholism, seduction, et cetera, are all treated as being value-neutral. Thus, all characters are encouraged to follow their consciences, and their consciences are formed by fulfilling what the tradition requires and tolerating what the tradition is silent about. When these tolerations come into conflict with one another, the underlying drama of the series emerges in the form of communal conscience versus individual will. Because the show is a comedy, the pattern is that individuals choose to change and embrace the communal value; in a tragedy, of course, the individual does not conform and is destroyed by the limitation they sought to escape or transcend. There is no one set formula for judging whether tolerance or tradition will be the deciding factor in each moral situation. Appeals to conscience allow for experience, tradition, and toleration all to sort themselves out in individual minds. If moral situations were resolved using ideology, there would be no need for any deliberations, which would lead to greater intolerance and close-mindedness. Hence, conservatives as well as liberals love this show.

Sitcoms are wholly dependent upon pattern recognition and repetition. Viewer delight depends on the audience expecting and recognizing typical sitcom patterns: catchphrases, returns to normalcy, and adventures that tease at the edges of change but stop just before delivering on that change. Unfortunately, the very thing that contributes to a sitcom's popularity also leads to its demise. What was once clever and original can become trite and boring, resulting in cancellation. After eight seasons, Jared Keeso's *Letterkenny* has largely avoided these pitfalls, even while it is as—or, perhaps even more—dependent upon catchphrases, repetition, set pieces, and narrative structures as any other sitcom. The show has maintained its freshness through two very traditional entertainment methods. First, its reliance upon the classical rhetorical trope of *copia* (the style of abundance). One of the great charms of *Letterkenny* is its focus on variation. Familiarity and surprise constantly play off of one another. The variations on the foundational patterns make each season seem simultaneously fresh yet familiar. Also, the language comes at viewers so quickly that it is almost impossible to catch every phrase, pun, and metaphor the first time an episode is viewed.

The structure of the show's narrative depends upon its moral framework. In fact, it may seem odd to speak of morality when so much of the show is either decidedly hostile to moral judgment or is flat out amoral. The Christians are depicted as ineffective, the Mennonites are used as opportunities for escapist sexual innuendo, McMurray (played by Dan Petronijevic) and Mrs. McMurray (the one married couple in the show, who ought to provide an example for others) take polyamory to such extremes that the other characters become either uncomfortable or shocked by their behavior, abortion is spoken of with nonchalance, one season ends with an extravagant same-sex wedding,[4] heavy drinking up to the point of "spitting" is a common occurrence, drug use is as casual as the continuous cigarette most of the characters have in the corner of their mouths, no major conflict is settled without a fistfight—and that is just a quick overview. The show avoids becoming a sum of its parts through tradition, habit, and a couple of inviolable bedrock morals. It is this moral foundation that allows for all of the variations from standard sitcom tropes. Without comic variations from behaviors that tradition would enforce or suggest, the show would have played itself out and not lasted as long.

One of the reasons for the show's success—that is, after its unique lexicon—has been the ways in which it subverts audience expectations. Every moment of the show is somehow a familiar surprise. The technical rhetorical term for these variations is *copia*, which is a rhetorical style characterized by abundance. Interestingly, a figure from the Renaissance who would find himself very comfortable with this show's technique (but probably not its content) is Erasmus of Rotterdam. A humanist who sought to bring Roman and Greek classics to bear on contemporary learning, Erasmus found himself collecting and commenting upon books of classical rhetoric as he wrote his own books. Borrowing from and building on Quintillian and Cicero, Erasmus' work *De Copia* argues for the development of writing and speaking skills that lead to an apparent overabundance of variety.[5] One common rhetorical exercise in school during this time was to write a common phrase such as "thank you for your letter" in fifty uniquely different ways. If you try it yourself, you will find that the first fifteen come to mind very easily, the next twenty come with some difficulty, and the last fifteen come to mind with great difficulty. However, these last fifteen will be the richest and best variations, just as the first fifteen will tend to be predictable clichés. Sitcoms with lazy writing reveal an impoverished imagination, while a show like *Letterkenny* revels in abundance. The show avoids situational repetition and clichés through this sort of linguistic innovation. The show is full of received wisdom delivered through short adages which are more than solely practical; they are also prudent, moral, and they might serve as a substitute for the spiritual. Instead of saying the obvious moral truth in a standard and familiar way, moral wisdom is communicated in unique, short adages. The foundation of all of these adages is that they are communal, and preserving community may well be the most important value on *Letterkenny*.[6] For example, these adages drive the work ethic at the farm and guide behavior in other locales:

"More hands mean less work."
"It's a great day for hay."
"Pitter patter."
"Back to chorin'."
"Sundays are for picking stones."
"You don't fuck with tradition."
"Bad gas travels fast in a small town."
"It's impolite to kiss and tell."
"When a friend asks for help, you help them."
"If they cheat, it's over."

At the level of plot and language, *Letterkenny* is grounded in the familiar and traditional but grows from that to include difference—different ways of speaking, thinking, and behaving—that others tolerate because they share the same fundamental principles and vocabulary.

Abundance is comedy's natural habitat.[7] However, the wild variety found in abundance requires a stable foundation from which those variations spring; otherwise, without structure, there cannot be any variations. A firm center is required. What is that central structure in *Letterkenny*? It is not easily discovered. In most shows, morality tends to be their organizing principle—good behavior is rewarded, bad behavior is punished. Even in a television show that subverts traditional morality and celebrates bad behavior, an extended moral universe still judges characters whom audiences have been habituated to liking and defending.[8] However, with *Letterkenny*, traditional morality is not an organizing principle. It exists, yes, but characters are pre-defined against it, rather than by it. Premarital sex, group sex, polyamory, abortion, drug use, and chronic excessive drinking—these are just a few of the normalized behaviors that demonstrate *Letterkenny's* commitment to tolerance. Its moral center resides elsewhere. Many behaviors and opinions are tolerated, but only insofar as they do not subvert the authority of the community as a whole. For a community to function properly, there has to be enough trust in the other people to create a sense of safety and comfort so that one can freely be oneself. Hence, fidelity is one of the cardinal virtues in this show and those who violate it are punished severely.

Letterkenny has seized upon a formula that has worked for eight seasons and will work for as long as the show lasts.[9] Each season has had a trajectory of character development which allows the audience to learn a little bit more about individual characters. For example, season 1, episode 1 ("Ain't No Reason to Get Excited") opens with Wayne having recently broken up with his girlfriend of five years, Angie, and her presence hangs over this first season's episodes like a shadow. Reminders of her keep him from moving forward. He slowly regains his emotional footing with each victory over challengers to his title of the "Toughest Guy in Letterkenny." In season 2, Angie and Wayne get back together for a quick rendezvous in his truck, and by the end of that season Wayne must decide between three love interests: Angie, Rosie, and Tanis. He develops from hapless to confident over the course of the first two seasons.

There can be no tradition without a community to express that tradition within, and since everything within *Letterkenny* can be understood as a participation within, or a reaction against its own tradition, the city of Letterkenny may well be the most important character in the series. Season 7, the lowest rated season, demonstrates the importance of community and the disintegration that occurs when one strays too far from it.[10] Viewers had already seen the consequences of going to the subaltern communities of the Dark Web in season 5. Hard Right Jay tried to import his version of community into Letterkenny and was rejected. Those who have ostracized themselves from Letterkenny (such as the Skids) are still recognized as integral to it, much to their surprise, which we see in the touching conclusion to season 4, episode 6 "Great Day for Thunder Bay." This episode brings the Hicks together with the Skids as the Bay Brothers hug Stewart, and they all drink a beer together.[11] Threats from outside of the community are dealt with privately, such as the big city wedding guests in season 5, episode one "We Don't Fight at Weddings" who insult the lifestyles of the people who live in Letterkenny and are met with a violent defense.[12]

Season 7, episode 1 ("Crack an Ag") is essential to the series because it clearly demonstrates the role of community and its importance to the show, but adds the idea that community is defined by both emotional and spatial proximity. When we think about the city of Letterkenny, we tend to picture the core group in front of the produce stand (Wayne, Katy, Dan, and Daryl) and we limit the core community to these four, who drink Puppers and talk with one another. What the "Crack An Ag" storyline does is expand the participation of the produce stand into the wider community, by taking what is essentially a private moment and making it public. What is impressive about the season opener, "A Fuss at the Ag Hall," is Wayne's deep familiarity with the extended community. He knows *everybody* who calls in to his cable access show (named "Crack and Ag") and his knowledge is far from superficial. He knows specific details about each caller, and the majority of each call is spent "catching up" rather than with dispensing advice. The cable access show is intimate, personal, and full of inside jokes. However, as the season progresses, the geographical radius of the callers increases, two beers per episode become seven or eight, and "Crack An Ag" shifts from being a proxy participation in a friendly conversation in front of the produce stand to becoming an actual burden. A clever parallel within season 7, episode 4, "Letterkenny vs. Penny" shows the irony inherent in creating a community for the sake of creating community—it turns out to be no community at all.[13] The title of the episode suggests that one must choose between the city of Letterkenny and a false version of it that can generate pennies. In this episode, Wayne and Katy have their annual contest to collect the most pennies for hockey broadcaster Don Cherry's Pet Rescue Foundation. In order to obtain these pennies, both have to go out into the community and engage in small talk for the sole purpose of adding pennies to a jar. It is a fake version of a real community, and Wayne punctuates each encounter with a catchphrase: "So much fun." Clearly, it is not fun, but it is the fake phrase that drives the donations up. *Letterkenny* is definitely not about meaningless clichés and empty encounters.

The same pattern establishes itself in the "Crack an Ag" season. While the community in "Crack an Ag" never becomes a plastic façade, it does grow too large, which causes Wayne, Daryl, and Dan to lose interest in it and cancel the show. This season's trajectory goes from Wayne knowing each and every caller in the first episode to fielding questions from "half a dozen townships" in the fifth episode, and as result, the show ceases to be local.[14] Rather than helping friends and improving the town of Letterkenny, the cable access show becomes a general advice show. The nature of the advice also changes. Agricultural experts are now called upon to give advice concerning relationships, and Crack An Ag loses its sharpness as Wayne, Daryl, and Dan all get too drunk to answer questions effectively. Not only do they lose contact with the city of Letterkenny, they also lose contact with one of their own: Daryl. Wayne, Katy, and Dan have all decided to let Daryl travel up to Quebec by himself to fight for a relationship that is already over. It is a fight that he will lose, both physically and emotionally. When hapless McMurray enters the studio to drink beers with the gang during the last show, the show has already aired. Wayne, Katy, and Dan are so far removed from what had made them a core team that it takes McMurray to remind them that they should never have abandoned Daryl. McMurray is the one who delivers the proverb heard so many times on this show: "When a friend asks for help, you help him." McMurray has to repeat it to get a reaction. Wayne, Katy, and Dan lose their focus when they help strangers instead of friends. They learn that a small town community is not something that can be expanded into a wider realm or audience, and the fact that the news comes from McMurray—a man these characters do not respect—is humbling.

Another failed community revolves around a parody of Facebook called Fartbook. This artificial community founded upon recordings of flatulence has as much longevity and substance as its name—light, airy, quickly experienced, and just as quickly forgotten. However, its popularity skyrockets; that is, until Devon the Skid seeks to monetize the platform. Interest wanes as more rules are applied and enforced, and Gail is banned while Katy receives a warning. Community in Letterkenny is dependent upon individualism, not conformity. These groups (Hicks, Skids, Hockey Players, Christians) should be held in tension with one another; Fartbook requires everyone to act exactly the same, and so it fails. The basic formula for Fartbook is then appropriated by Glen (for Christian Fart Mingle) who calls it "taking advantage of a growing trend" and points out that "fart culture" and the technology of social media has been appropriated by many others (Plenty of Farts, Fart Filter, a site devoted to gluten-free farts).[15] The point here is that there are plenty of attempts to create synthetic communities in Letterkenny which, contrasted against organic communities, cannot help but fall flat because of their inauthenticity. Community, in order to be a community, requires the sameness that comes from tradition as well as the difference that requires tolerance. The relevance and importance of tradition is derived in deviation from it. Without deviation from tradition there is nothing to come back to. Attempts to flatten and eliminate difference also threaten tradition. *Letterkenny* demonstrates that only in lived communities where people have to be around each other can tradition ground common, moral values and, at the same time, tolerance for difference.

Nevertheless, communities are not important in and of themselves. For Jared Keeso's generation, the traditional sources of the moral stability that creates communities—church, family, government—have all abdicated their authority and their rights to guide this generation. That being said, the show is far from being amoral, and most reviewers of the show identify the existence of a moral framework in the show even if they cannot fully articulate its content. Cintra Wilson identifies a "moral decency at its core" that is based upon Karl Popper's "paradox of tolerance," which is toleration of everything except intolerance.[16] Caitlin Wolper tries to locate this moral decency in the show's female characters.[17] There definitely is a moral decency at the core of the show, but it is not located in the women of Letterkenny. Rather, it is located in the traditions of Letterkenny, about which the women often remind the men, but as the conclusion of season 7 demonstrates (see above), women can forget the moral foundations of life just as easily as the men. The show posits a fascinating tension between liberalism and conservatism. On the one hand, one of the highest virtues on the show is the tolerance that is advocated by thinkers such as Popper and Herbert Marcuse. On the other hand, the virtues of tradition and natural justice as advocated by thinkers such as Russell Kirk and Wendell Berry seem to be as important as tolerance.

Herbert Marcuse's essay "Repressive Tolerance" could very well be a blueprint for how tolerance is understood in the twenty-first century.[18] According to Marcuse, pure or abstract tolerance does not exist because such tolerance is utopian. It is impossible to allow all perspectives all the time. Tolerance by its very nature is liberal because it expands freedom; conservatism, properly understood, is not opposed to freedom, however, its emphasis upon preserving pre-existing traditions necessarily contrasts with liberalism's desire to transcend pre-existing traditions, either through modifying them or doing away with them. Marcuse's conclusion is that tolerance as a liberal value must exclude conservatism because, inevitably, it will be perceived and experienced as being oppressive. What is interesting about *Letterkenny* is that within the show, the expansiveness of tolerance is willingly limited by tradition, loyalty, and natural justice.

Taking up these three virtues (tradition, loyalty, and natural justice) against the virtue of tolerance, we see how the tension between these virtues accounts for the show's wide appeal across liberal, conservative, and libertarian lines. Marcuse notes that a tolerant city is a utopia, but only because it is next to impossible to reconcile the freedom of an individual with the freedom of a community. Either the individual or the city must make an identity-compromising concession. However, he suggests that a city possibly could be founded upon these ideals, and if an entire community could agree on particular limits for human behavior, then such a community could exist. Letterkenny might be that community. In Marcuse's words,

> the problem of making possible such a harmony between every individual liberty and the other is not that of finding a compromise between competitors, or between freedom and law, between general and individual interest, common and private welfare in an *established* society, but of *creating* the society in which man is no longer enslaved by institutions which vitiate self-determination from

the beginning. In other words, freedom is still to be created even for the freest of the existing societies. [emphasis in the original][19]

In Letterkenny, there are no children and there are no elders. There are only the twentysomethings who have problems that are discussed on the show. They have come to an understanding about what institutions and self-determination require. In this way, though, *Letterkenny* transcends the limitation of having to endlessly expand freedoms because reason puts limits upon tolerance. Tradition gives a community its identity, loyalty maintains the integral wholeness of that community, and natural justice keeps the community rooted in the realm of the actual instead of the speculative—Marcuse's impossible utopianism.

Each subgroup is given the space to judge for themselves what they will and will not tolerate. As long as it is not a threat to Letterkenny, then that behavior or idea is tolerated. The episode featuring Hard Right Jay begins with the problematic of intersectionality: there is no strict equality when it comes to being oppressed. Who has it the worst? White women? Black women? The disabled? War amputees? And so on. Dan recounts a controversy on Twitter about this very question. To make matters worse, this Twitter discussion took place when some of these groups were requested not to post on Twitter for a day. The expanding intersectional outrage and infighting never would have happened had people respected the request not to Tweet. It is this overstepping that Wayne and Katy object to; if there is a hierarchy, it is whatever is conducive to order.

Take, for example, Hard Right Jay and his crusade to keep the name of the junior soccer team, the Letterkenny Chiefs in season 5, episode 3, "Hard Right Jay." The team has decided to change its name to something less offensive. As far as who has the authority to make a change and decision about the name, priority is going to be given to the communities within Letterkenny most directly affected by the change and to reason; if the First Nation does not want the title for the team, that is fine. It is their choice. Hard Right Jay wants to protest the name change in the name of tradition. However, the tradition that allowed the tolerant change is the tradition of the First Nation. The First Nation is part of Letterkenny. If a member community makes a change that does not subvert the larger community, that change is always tolerated. Hard Right Jay's version of tradition is incompatible with the First Nations' and Letterkenny's traditions because Hard Right Jay's "tradition" is based on ideology, not on the needs and the wills of the individuals who live there, who play on the Chiefs, and who have named the Chiefs. Hard Right Jay is offensive because he is a threat to the stability and integrity and tradition of the town.[20] He makes the case for being a proponent of tradition because he wants to maintain the name of "Chiefs," but it is not the tradition of Letterkenny.

Letterkenny's traditions are more substantial than name changes. The Hicks are not indifferent to the change, but they also would not have forced it to come about because the First Nation should be allowed to make its own decisions about what to tolerate and what not to tolerate. "The only constant in life is change, as they say," Katy tells us. These adjustments are a normal part of life, and the responses to her are immediate and abundant:

"Sounds about right."
"They had a good run."
"Probably for the best."[21]

This situation is something for the First Nation to act upon, which the various groups in Letterkenny will support. In that way, the autonomy of each subgroup is balanced with the loose heteronomy of the town's authority. Hard Right Jay's politics are distasteful to the groups in the town (he has a Confederate flag sticker on his SUV, and we hear in the series' very first episode that Wayne threw an egg at pickup truck that has a Confederate flag on its back windshield), but the reason why he and his groups are expelled is because of the threat they pose to Letterkenny's unity.[22] There is no tradition that is compatible with Hard Right Jay's perspective or activity. Even Stewart, whose Dark Web activity brings Jay into the Letterkenny fold, has no idea who the Letterkenny Chiefs are (and Roald asks what even is a junior soccer team, before asking, "Who cares if a soccer team changes its name?"). When Hard Right Jay asks, "What about the history? The tradition?" he is asking a question that is not his to ask.[23] It is not *his* history; it is not *his* tradition. Besides, the Skids are self-proclaimed anarchists. Because their particular brand of anarchy is so well-ordered, they are tolerated within Letterkenny, never actually threatening it. Hard Right Jay, however, is a threat to the city's order.

Here is where Marcuse's ideas on toleration break down and where Russell Kirk is helpful.[24] If Hard Right Jay was instead Hard Left Jay, he would still be rejected by Letterkenny because he introduces chaos to an accepted and stable order. However, in response to Hard Left Jay, Marcuse would say that the order of the town and its traditions have become oppressive and need to be overcome. Kirk would say that the focus on liberalism is a focus on ideology (which he dismisses as "theoretic dogma") over practicality. The wisdom from practicality comes to us from history and from tradition. Not Hard Right Jay's history and tradition, but Letterkenny's history and tradition.

Often men may not realize the meaning of their immemorial prejudices and customs—indeed, even the most intelligent of men cannot hope to understand all the secrets of traditional morals and social arrangements; but we may be sure that Providence, acting through the medium of human trial and error, has developed every hoary habit for some important purpose. The greatest of prudence is required when man must accommodate this inherited mass of opinion to the exigencies of new times. For prejudice is not bigotry or superstition, although prejudice sometimes may degenerate into these. Prejudice is prejudgment, the answer with which intuition and ancestral consensus of opinion supply a man when he lacks either time or knowledge to arrive at a decision predicated upon pure reason.[25]

Excluding Kirk's dependence upon Providence, this passage accurately captures the *Letterkenny* ethos. Characters often forget what a particular tradition is, and sometimes seek to evade its demands (Daryl asks to opt out of his Super Soft Birthday celebration, but Wayne and Katy assert tradition; Joint Boy offers a handshake instead of a fight, and Katy asserts tradition to Wayne; Wayne seeks to avoid this year's Super Hard Easter Egg Hunt, which Katy will not allow, and so on), but, in the words of the show, "you don't fuck with tradition."[26] Kirk's mention of "trial and error" emphasizes the role of prudence in the establishment of any tradition. Simply put, you go with what works. Ideology is speculative knowledge; tradition is practical knowledge. An agricultural community looks to tradition for its practical knowledge, which is reflected in the various adages of the show. When Kirk says, "for prejudice is not bigotry or superstition, although prejudice sometimes may degenerate into these," he means that a tradition pre-judges every situation, and prudence can provide the answer to a problem before the problem has manifested itself. Through prudence, tradition has its own voice and therefore influence. When he speaks of "intuition and ancestral consensus of opinion," Kirk is talking about the role of tradition and its reasonable suggestions. A farm is not going to increase in its liberalism. An attitude toward the name of a sports team might (and probably will).

Hard Right Jay acts from a place of ideology, which is why he is a threat to the community. He adopts the vocabulary of the alt-right, and when he divides men into Alphas and Betas, he means that one becomes an Alpha by being "based," that is, having the correct understanding (i.e., sharing Hard Right Jay's understanding) about the situation with the junior soccer team. The irony is that, in a community rooted in prudence and natural justice, Alphas are true Alphas, and Betas are true Betas. In other words, actual strength and actual leadership will win this conflict, not having the "right" thoughts. Jay seeks out Dan, Daryl, and Wayne as "salt of the earth Alphas," who are "the stewards of traditional morals, traditional values."[27] Jay uses the rhetoric of traditional conservatism to express his far-right ideology, but he is talking about something completely different than the conservatism of Russell Kirk or of Letterkenny. The conversation reaches an interesting conclusion. Hard

Right Jay asks, "Why is keeping the name the Chiefs important to you?" To which all four answer in unison, "It isn't," while the bartender, Bonnie McMurray, yawns.[28] Dan sees no reason to fight the Left; his understanding of tradition does not come in conflict with liberalism because he sees the decision about the name change as being made within a different subgroup in Letterkenny than the Hicks. The Hicks do not have the same level of author- ity on this issue as the Natives; part of Hard Right Jay's misguidedness is that he is usurping the authority of the only group that is qualified to decide whether or not the name should be changed at all. Jay asks them if they will accompany him and, after conferring, Wayne says that they will, but that Jay has to fight Wayne for it. We already know from season 1 that Wayne is "the toughest guy in Letterkenny." What is clear is that ideology is being pitted against natural justice; Wayne would definitely win this fight. Later, even the slow-witted hockey player, Reilly, is able to see that Hard Right Jay is just a "goof." Interestingly, the girl's hockey team begins to argue and fight over a name change for their own team, the Shamrockettes. Hard Right Jay has created a schism in the community and Reilly says, "you're fucking up our progress dude. Just get out of here."[29] If an idea is imported into Letterkenny rather than developed through experience and reason within Letterkenny, not only does the idea not belong, but it will not survive in strong subgroups, and it will cause dissension in weaker subgroups.

In this way, tradition is strongly linked to natural justice. Either something is or it is not: either Wayne is the toughest guy in Letterkenny, or he is not. That title is determined by fighting everyone who thinks the title is theirs. Natural justice puts limits on the characters' possibilities. If Stewart the Skid has a severe drug problem, he has no choice but to go to rehab. The citizens of Letterkenny expect the Skids to consume methamphetamine, but not at Stewart's unhealthy rate. He does not have the freedom to consume as much as he wants, and the community will not tolerate it because it damages rela- tionships in Letterkenny, thus damaging the city itself; preserving the good of the city is one of the few moral absolutes in this show.[30] Tanis and the First Nation are there in the snow to fight over the name change. Hard Right Jay says, "We are an inclusive movement. I think you should join us."[31] This demonstrates what was argued above: Letterkenny should be subsumed by this ideology so that it can become something else. What happens instead is that the foreign object is rejected. He points out their commonalities like he did with the Hicks. "We both pride ourselves on traditional values, traditional morals. We share a very anti-immigration stance." And then, just like the problem that Reilly and Jonesy had with the Shamrockettes, we see that Hard Right Jay has caused division with his promise of unity. Tanis says, "Hey, no one had a problem with this. No one had a problem until you's came to town." To which Jay responds, "That's it. The Hard Right, coming to a town near you." This is the threat that must be removed. So, in the end, the alt-right interlopers are beaten up by the First Nation and the Hicks: Two subgroups unite to deliver natural justice for the benefit of the larger group, namely, Letterkenny itself.

If toleration is the highest good in the town of Letterkenny, then that toleration must be at the service of something higher than itself. Virtues do not exist in a vacuum. There is no upper limit to love or being good or kind. Love, goodness, and kindness all point to something beyond themselves, namely, the beneficiary of those virtues. Applying the same notion to the show, who or what benefits most from the virtue of toleration? Letterkenny itself. Thus, toleration is at the service of—and thus limited by—tradition. The entire show can be interpreted in light of this hermeneutic; this chapter merely lays the groundwork for a fruitful reading of *Letterkenny.*

In the 1950s, people learned how to resolve moral conflicts through shows such as *Father Knows Best.* Is it better not to gossip? Not to take advantage of others? Not to try and get ahead in the insurance business by any means necessary? Jim Anderson often did not know if his "old-fashioned" advice would actually work in the new world of 1955, but he counseled his children to act accordingly, and even though it was difficult, he also did it himself. Our times are just difficult. On any news show today, we seem to be split into unalterable camps, with liberals, conservatives, and libertarians unable to communicate, much less compromise with one another, as each group thinks that the other two groups are manipulative and morally bankrupt. Because these types of programs thrive upon unresolved conflict, audiences must turn to television show such as *Letterkenny* to learn that resolution is even possible.

Each of these political traditions has been developed over a long time. Drama has its own lengthy tradition, too, and all drama has the exact same formula: Conflict and subsequent resolution. *Letterkenny* puts these traditions into conflict with one another again and again, allowing for complexity over facile dichotomy. The show searches out the limits of toleration in its conflict resolution: How much can one group tolerate from another group without sacrificing its identity or its autonomy? Each episode of the show revisits the moral limits of each group. Toleration is not some ever-expanding limitless concept. Instead, what we see is that characters respond to other characters, to their uniqueness and to their unrepeatability, not to their ideology. If there is a conflict that cannot be solved with toleration because toleration would destroy or fundamentally redefine the community, then tradition necessarily asserts itself. Most conflicts in the show are resolved by characters discovering that, fundamentally, there is not an inherent conflict between the two groups in question, but rather only differing points of view. There is always enough elasticity in the city of Letterkenny to accommodate differing points of view. As a particular tradition is tolerated over time, it settles in with other established traditions, and the result is what we might call balanced pluralism. The traditions are not held in tension with one another, at least not permanently; there is a harmony between all of them. When that balanced pluralism interacts with a new tradition, the conflict that emerges is either reinforced or resolved. What determines the main outcomes seems to be whether or not the new tradition expresses an ideology or a personalism.[32] Ideology allows people to conduct a conversation without ever speaking to one another; their conversation is dependent upon ideological differences. Personhood requires people to listen to one another and to adjust one's beliefs and preconceptions in order to accommodate the individuality of the interlocutor. If the new tradition is an ideology first and a personalism second, it will not be accommodated into the community. However, if that new tradition is a personalism first, and an ideology second, there is a high probability that the tradition will be accommodated into the community. In addition to ideology, disloyalty is not tolerated, automatically and permanently ostracizing an individual in *Letterkenny*. Thus, rather than merely alleging a harmony between tradition and tolerance, *Letterkenny* enacts and models an active harmony, one that both Kirk and Marcuse would enthusiastically approve of.

NOTES

1. In this chapter, an italicized Letterkenny denotes the television show, while a non-italicized Letterkenny denotes the town itself.

2. Season 8's *Miss Fire* is a deliberate wink at sitcom formulae; *Letterkenny* is a very smart show.

3. Simply put, Kant's Categorical Imperative states that one can do what one wants, as long as it does no harm to another person. Theft and murder, for example, are excluded from allowable behavior.

4. Although it is later revealed to be more for tax benefits than for love.

5. Desiderius Erasmus, *On Copia of Words and Ideas,* trans. Donald B. King and H. David Rix (Milwaukee: Marquette University Press, 2005).

6. The foundational value of community is essential to understanding and defending the importance of season 7 ("Crack an Ag"), the most improperEly maligned seasons of the show, as we will see later in this chapter.

7. Conversely, scarcity is tragedy's habitat.

8. For example, in "Dad-Not-Dad," from season 4 episode 10, Jimmy is revealed to be a boorish rube who is nothing like he perceives himself to be. Rather than relying upon an extended moral universe, *Letterkenny* handles all of its morality in-house, as it were.

9. Jared Keeso's current contract with Hulu will take the show to fourteen seasons, each season consisting of six episodes.

10. Official ratings have never been released, but on internet sites such as Reddit, Ranker, and Ratingraph, season 7 is at the bottom of each ranking of seasons 1 through 8.

11. *Letterkenny,* season 4, episode 6, "Great Day for Thunder Bay," dir. Jacob Tierney, released December 25, 2017, available on Hulu.

12. *Letterkenny,* season 5, episode 1, "We Don't Fight at Weddings," dir. Jacob Tierney, released June 29, 2018, available on Hulu.

13. *Letterkenny*, season 7, episode 4, "Letterkenny vs. Penny," dir. Jacob Tierney, released October 11, 2019, available on Hulu.

14. *Letterkenny*, season 7, episode 5, "W's Talk, Baby," dir. Jacob Tierney released October 11, 2019, available on Hulu.

15. *Letterkenny,* season 1, episode 3, "Fartbook," dir. Jacob Tierney, released on February 7, 2016, available on Hulu.

16. Cintra Wilson, "The Brutally Funny, Radically Moral World of *Letterkenny,*" *New York Review of Books Daily,* published July 24, 2020, https://www.nybooks.com /daily/2020/07/24/the-brutally-funny-radically-moral-world-of-letterkenny/.

17. Caitlin Wolper, "Women Secretly Run the Town of *Letterkenny,*" *Vice,* Published October 19, 2019, https://www.vice.com/en_ca/article/evjqg4/women -secretly-run-the-town-of-letterkenny.

18. Herbert Marcuse, "Repressive Tolerance," in *A Critique of Pure Tolerance*, ed. Robert Paul Wolff, Barrington Moore, Jr., and Herbert Marcuse (Boston, MA: Beacon Press, 1965), 81–117.

19. Ibid., 87.

20. Of course, his views are offensive, but Letterkenny responds to his actions, not necessarily his words and beliefs.

21. *Letterkenny*, season 5, episode 3, "Hard Right Jay," dir. Jacob Tierney, released on June 29, 2018, available on Hulu.

22. *Letterkenny*, season 1, episode 1, "Ain't No Reason to Get Excited," dir. Jacob Tierney released on February 7, 2016, available on Hulu.

23. Hilariously, Roald tells Hard Right Jay that he self-identifies as a wood nymph. *Letterkenny*, season 5, episode 3, "Hard Right Jay," dir. Jacob Tierney, released on June 29, 2018, available on Hulu.

24. Wendell Berry and his essays on a rural sense of place are also helpful. See his book *The Gift of Good Land: Further Essays Cultural and Agricultural* in particular.

25. Russell Kirk, *The Conservative Mind, from Burke to Santayana* (Chicago, IL: Henry Regnery, 1953), 42.

26. Season 1, episode 2, "Super Soft Birthday," dir. Jacob Tierney, released on February 7, 2016, available on Hulu.

27. Op cit, season 5, episode 3. When Hard Right Jay asks the hockey players to join him, Riley tells him, "The Chiefs is kinda not PC there, buddy," and Jonesy says, "We try to keep it like, kind of in touch there."

28. Ibid.

29. Ibid.

30. Again, see Wendell Berry's essays for thoughts about cities and culture that transcends ideology.

31. Op cit, season 5, episode 3.

32. By "ideology," I mean that the group identity and agenda are more important than the people who make up the group, and by "personalism," I mean the opposite of that, namely that the group is made up of individuals first, and the ideas they share in common are secondary to individual identity.

BIBLIOGRAPHY

Erasmus, Desiderius. *On Copia of Words and Ideas.* Translated by Donald B. King and H. David Rix. Milwaukee: Marquette University Press, 2005.

Kirk, Russell. *The Conservative Mind, from Burke to Santayana.* Chicago, IL: Henry Regnery, 1953.

Letterkenny, created by Jared Keeso and Jacob Tierney, aired from February 7, 2016–present. Originally released on Hulu.

Marcuse, Herbert. "Repressive Tolerance." In *A Critique of Pure Tolerance*, edited by Robert Paul Wolff, Barrington Moore, Jr., and Herbert Marcuse, 81–117. Boston, MA: Beacon Press, 1965.

Wilson, Cintra. "The Brutally Funny, Radically Moral World of 'Letterkenny.'" The New York Review of Books, October 19, 2020. https://www.nybooks.com/daily/2020/07/24/the-brutally-funny-radically-moral-world-of-letterkenny/.

Wolper, Caitlin. "Women Secretly Run the Town of 'Letterkenny'." VICE, October 19, 2019. https://www.vice.com/en_ca/article/evjqg4/women-secretly-run-the-town-of-letterkenny.

Chapter 10

Morality versus Mortality

The Meaning of (After)Life in The Good Place

Jill B. Delston

The series finale of Michael Schur's *The Good Place* seemed to present walking through "the door" as a choice that gave meaning to the eternal souls ensconced in the Good Place.[1] It suggested choosing the door as a decision that was appropriate, good, or beautiful for the characters who made it. In this chapter, I argue against that interpretation of the finale, which I will call the "happy interpretation." I instead defend a view that going through the door is problematic as the show presented it. According to this tragic interpretation, only when the characters lost sight of the show's true message of "what we owe to each other" did non-existence look like an attractive option. That is, only when they devoted their lives to an inwardly directed, hedonist goal did they conclude existence had lost meaning. Thus, the show does not endorse the characters' actions, and if it did, doing so would be a potentially problematic treatment of themes associated with suicide. In advancing this argument, I defend a virtue ethicist interpretation of the point system leading to the Good Place. I also conclude that this interpretation of the finale and not the happy interpretation best situates *The Good Place* within the ethos of the Peak TV era. The tragic interpretation of the finale that I endorse is the only one that fits with the show from moral, philosophical, literary, medical, and cultural perspectives.

THE HAPPY INTERPRETATION

On the happy interpretation of the series finale, the show presents a lovely, if bittersweet, ending for its protagonists in which the door was the right and good decision for Jason Mendoza (played by Manny Jacinto), Chidi Anagonye (played by William Jackson Harper), and Eleanor Shellstrop (played by Kristen Bell).[2] "But it was perfect," Ted Danson says. "It was a perfect ending to our story. . . . It was sad but uplifting and kind and gentle and sweet."[3] In this understanding of the finale, mortality is necessary to give meaning to any existence in the afterlife; choosing to return one's essence to the fabric of the universe and, in the process, eliminating any conscious self is an appropriate response to a certain sort of self-actualization or self-improvement. The audience is, of course, sad to say goodbye to beloved characters, but the door is presented as an alternative to a horrific ending in which the characters might lose their memories, concept of self, and greater understandings of the world, as Hypatia (or "Patty," played by Lisa Kudrow) does when her mind turns to mush.

But is this ending as happy as we are led to believe? To answer this question, I first need to offer a moral theoretical foundation of the show. Eleanor and Jason know that they have done more wrong than right in their lives and are never convinced that they belong in the Good Place. However, the other half of the "Soul Squad," Tahani (played by Jameela Jamil) and Chidi, believe that their lives on Earth merited them a heavenly reward. Why they fall short, and how the point system lands them there provides the overarching moral framework of the show.

A MORAL THEORY OF *THE GOOD PLACE*

In season 1, when Michael (played by Ted Danson) explains the point system to the souls who believe they are in the Good Place, he focuses on the consequences of actions. "During your time on earth, every one of your actions had a positive or negative value, depending on how much good or bad that action put into the universe," Michael says in explanation.[4] The numeric evaluation of acts, the scope of moral action, the lack of morally neutral actions, as well as a system which is maximizing, consequentialist, and impartial all point to utilitarianism as the moral underpinning of the show.

In fact, in season 4, one of the two major reasons the Soul Squad objects to the point system is a commonly understood objection to utilitarianism. They reference the divide between "objective" and "subjective" interpretations of utilitarianism, where subjective utilitarianism refers to what consequences an individual could reasonably expect their actions to have, and objective utilitarianism refers only to what consequences an action really does have.[5] The Squad objects that the infinite indirect consequences of actions are such that, in a complex and interconnected world, no action can achieve a positive output. Thus, while their actions might be subjectively good, since they have reason to believe they would create positive output, the infinite and unpredictable consequences mean they can never achieve objectively positive point values.[6]

In addition, utilitarianism does not place emphasis on the motivation or intention of an act, which explains why someone like Chidi could end up in the Bad Place. Chidi, a strict deontologist, had the best intentions and was motivated by the appropriate Kantian duty in his actions. However, since he was indecisive and ineffectual, his actions often led to bad consequences. The point system disregards his desire to be good and focuses only on the consequences of his well-intentioned but poorly executed actions. Chidi is the embodiment of the dictum, "the road to hell is paved with good intentions."

So, utilitarianism explains Chidi's arrival in the Bad Place. However, utilitarianism cannot explain Tahani's. On a utilitarian interpretation of the point system, Tahani's bad motives in her philanthropy, benevolence, and altruism should not count against her actions. With millions of dollars at her disposal to do good in the world and a life devoted to philanthropic aims, Tahani most certainly created a great amount of good in the world. And, since the point system places greater emphasis on actions with greater impact, the status, privilege, and scope of her action should make it that much easier to land in the Good Place. Despite this, she does not. Unlike Chidi, her actions were motivated by jealousy, spite, desire for attention and approval, and competition. While on a purely consequentialist interpretation of the point system, she might have been able to reach the threshold of points needed for the Good Place, she was not able to rack up any points due to her motivations. While Chidi's deontology is incomplete, so too is Tahani's utilitarianism.[7]

A more accurate interpretation of the point system is virtue ethicist. Michael begins his speech on the point system in season 1 by saying, "You were all, simply put, good people."[8] In other words, character matters. I argue that goodness requires aiming at the bullseye of an Aristotelian target. Actions which are not the expression of the character virtues, or which coincide with virtue but are not virtuous, fail to earn points. To earn points, individuals need to perform virtuous acts as the expression of virtuous characters.

For example, actions like Chidi's, which originate from good intentions but fail to reliably bring about good consequences, as well as actions like Tahani's, which reliably bring about good consequences but do not proceed from a good character, fail to achieve positive moral status or earn any points. This virtue ethicist view of the point system can also explain the arrival of Eleanor and Jason in the Bad Place: both Eleanor, who pursues vice with knowledge, as well as Jason, who pursues vice without knowledge, end up in the same place. Mindy St. Claire (played by Maribeth Monroe), who both created an influential charity and did so with some level of self-sacrifice (intending to use her life's savings) and motivation (wanting to do good in the world), also hit the Aristotelian bullseye and offsets her mostly bad life in such a way that neither deontology nor utilitarianism can fully explain.[9]

Eleanor, who desires to be good, uses philosophy to train her rational capacity and aims not only to hit the mark in acting virtuously but also to be well off with regard to feelings and pleasures.[10] The explanation of how to achieve this state through knowledge and practice, with habituation as a key component in character development, shows how virtue ethics can explain characters' activities, goals, desires, and successes. Precisely because the characters habituated goodness for so many lifetimes as Michael rebooted the neighborhood over and over again, they actually started to achieve goodness. This shift upset the idea of the afterlife as a retributive theory of punishment based on desert rather than a rehabilitative theory based on improvement. Helping others through virtue, as the characters each aim to do in varying capacities, is the central driving mission of the characters' pursuits and the plot of the show.

THE TRAGIC INTERPRETATION: THE SERIES FINALE AS A TRAGIC END FOR JASON, CHIDI, AND ELEANOR

The members of the Soul Squad who chose the door had already happily spent thousands of Jeremy Bearimies in the Good Place. However, they also improved morally in that time: Jason became less impulsive, Chidi less indecisive, and Eleanor less selfish. Only when they considered existence to be the perfection of the virtues of intellect or artistry did the characters seek to end their conscious existences. Jason completed the perfect Madden game; Chidi completed his work in philosophy; Tahani mastered skills like woodwork and driveway paving; Eleanor finished her copy of Scanlon's *What We Owe To Each Other* as a purely armchair exercise of rationality with no practical application. These pursuits of self-improvement and skill, while valuable, are incomplete versions of self-actualization if they do not also include obligations to improve the lot of others.

The penultimate episode of season 4 was a literary return to the first season. The Soul Squad find themselves in the actual Good Place, not a Potemkin village or simulacrum as in season 1. By creating a path to the Good Place for every human, they have created so much good in the world and performed this act with such selfless motivation that the action tips the balance of points in their favor. In fact, that action was so large and meaningful that they earned a spot in the Good Place despite not achieving complete virtue. They have done more good than any other human being in all of existence. Yet, they remain imperfect. In fact, almost immediately after demonstrating the way the afterlife will work, Tahani fails a test to measure her goodness when she is unable to give a toast to her sister.[11] This test, and her failure, demonstrates that while they deserve to be in the Good Place, they still have a lot of work to do to become truly good.

In season 1, Eleanor's realization that she did not earn her spot in the Good Place prompts her to try to become as good as possible. This sets the pieces in motion for the ensuing three seasons of the show. In season 4, however, the same realization does not prompt her to try to improve. Instead, she and the others allow their virtues to languish, taking the hedonist existence the Good Place offers without reflection. Condemning themselves to a hedonist reward, amid a non-hedonist worldview in the show, seals their fate. On the happy interpretation, there is no callback or allusion to the first season, but the tragic interpretation gives literary meaning to this series of events.

For the entirety of the show and for many lifetimes in each individual character's timeline, acting virtuously and doing so as the expression of a virtuous character—not accidentally or selfishly—was the unifying mission and sole measure of each person. Had the characters achieved their goal, they would have embodied a well-off state with respect to their feelings and pleasures that would make the continuation of virtuous acts not only desirable but also pleasurable.[12] Truly virtuous individuals are probably not very interesting from an entertainment perspective, and so the choice to put them in the Good Place without achieving complete virtue—much like Mindy St. Claire's arrival in the Medium Place while retaining her vice—makes for great comedy. However, it presents a problem in need of resolution, and that resolution does not come.

For each character, a last-minute consideration of what they owe to others delayed their decision to go through the door, but also raised the specter of the door as the wrong choice for them and helping others as the right choice. Had they realized in time that they could have continued to help others—that doing so would revive their habituations to goodness, would give them greater pleasure than partying and honing skills, and could have further developed their characters to true virtue—they could have continued their existence.

Jason decided to walk through the door, but happily waited a thousand Jeremy Bearimies when he realized that he was not able to give Janet the necklace he made for her. A gift for someone else, looking outside his own hedonistic pleasures, gave Jason enough motivation and purpose to exist happily for countless eternities, even after choosing the door.

Chidi changed his mind about going through the door when Eleanor begged him not to abandon her. This selfless act on his part gave him the motivation and purpose to continue in his existence just as Jason's altruism gave him the motivation to live on.

Eleanor decided to use the door but later realized that she could help Michael and Mindy St. Claire find happiness, meaning, and virtue. Giving them the chance to fulfill their dreams meant that the last two hopeless rational beings were now on the path to a greater future. By delaying her desire to go through the door, Eleanor displayed selflessness. Once again, the narrative arc of the show tells us that what gives life meaning, purpose, value, goodness, and happiness is helping others.

Eleanor's choice marks the end of the protagonists who went through the door. But others considered it and similarly delayed it for altruistic reasons. The difference is, their delays became eternal. Like the others, Tahani decided to go through the door when she had achieved a loving relationship with her sister and parents, something that showed character development and psychological improvement. This relationship she developed with her family demonstrates not just intellectual achievement, achievement in art, or achievement in skill, but true virtue. Unlike Jason's mastery of impulsivity and Chidi's mastery of indecision—neither of which have negative consequences anymore— Tahani makes the afterlives of her family better. In fact, since we have a clue about what test she would have had to pass to express the kind of soul that would earn a spot in the Good Place—give a toast to her sister—we know that by achieving this relationship, she would have been able to pass the test. Even more than the others, she was able to look beyond her own selfish desires and hedonistic pursuits to approximate an Aristotelian eudaimonia through virtuous self-improvement. When she reached this state of virtue, she considered going through the door. However, she changed her mind when it occurred to her that she could help others reach the Good Place by becoming an architect. Her last-minute diversion is eternal, since she is helping countless strangers, rather than short-lived, like Jason, Chidi, and Eleanor's, who only help one or two loved ones. Happiness is an activity that requires constant action, not a state one can achieve and then be done, and Tahani demonstrates this point.[13]

In fact, choices like Tahani's speak volumes about Jason, Chidi, and Eleanor's. Tahani did not have to continue helping others. She did not seek an eternal reward; she gave one up. She was not compelled to help others as a punishment; she chose to do so freely. And, she did not need mortality to give meaning or happiness to her life; she rejected mortality. By finding meaning without mortality, and by finding meaning with morality, Tahani demonstrates that the door is neither necessary nor sufficient for finding meaning and happiness. Furthermore, when we check in with her later, she is flourishing in her new role as an architect. Helping others is not a skill like woodwork that one can just master and move on. Helping others is a lifelong mission that, when an expression of an ordered soul, can provide happiness and meaning for eternity. The eudaemonists were right: virtues benefit their possessor.

The last protagonist to consider the door but not take it is Michael. Unlike the others, who have second thoughts and delay their passage through the door, Michael finds out he is no longer needed to help others and walks right through it. When he discovers he still exists after walking through it, he realizes he needs a new purpose. He does not consider that helping others is what brought him so far and instead suggests opening up a repair shop. It takes Eleanor to suggest that his seasons' long obsession with humans—their ways, their things, and their Earth—is what could give his life meaning and purpose, with the understanding that he has to rack up enough points to return. Eleanor states, "You're gonna live down there for like, some amount of time, you'll die, really die, then you'll enter an afterlife test, be judged on what you did, the whole deal."[14] In other words, Michael knows that his human life will have to be about being a good person and expressing good character through virtuous acts. Importantly, the existence of the door or his own mortality never brought Michael meaning. Although eternal beings have no door, they do have "retirement" in which, according to Michael, "my essence would be scooped out of my body with a flaming ladle and every molecule of my body would be placed on the surface of a different sun."[15] So, the idea of ending eternity or being mortal and finite does not bring Michael meaning. When we return to Michael's storyline later in the episode, we find him happy, engaged, and loving life. And, like Tahani, he had to leave the Good Place to reach that point.

What Tahani and Michael's stories have in common is not just that they consider the door and choose life, nor that they both leave the Good Place. Another common thread between their paths is that they remember the overarching message of the show: what we owe to each other. They remember the message that they have been studying, acting on, and exhorting others to consider for the last four seasons: to express their virtuous characters through virtuous acts. Tahani and Michael did not just make different choices than Jason, Chidi, and Eleanor; they made better ones.

Countless eternal beings, including Michael, found existences that did not lack purpose, lead to loss of enjoyment of the activities that once brought them pleasure, turn their brains to "mush," or make them seek non-existence, even after billions of years. Every angel and demon achieves this existence but does so by pursuing what they owe to others. These counterexamples speak against the idea that mortality is either necessary or sufficient to give meaning to eternal existence. It is not necessary, because eternal beings manage to accomplish it without an existential crisis. For example, Vicky Sengupta (played by Tiya Sicar), Shawn (played by Marc Evan Jackson), Janet (played by D'Arcy Carden), and Derek Hofstetler (played by Jason Mantzoukas) are some of the many rational beings we encounter who are not mortal and are eternal but do have meaning in their lives. It is not sufficient, because many mortal beings, who are aware of their own mortality, still lack purpose and meaning. For example, Jason, Chidi, and Eleanor, as well as countless beings on Earth who struggle through life are acutely aware of their mortality without this fact giving them meaning. If morality is both necessary and sufficient, but mortality is not, then it looks as though what we owe to each other—not the door—is the central motivator of the show.

I argue that morality is necessary and sufficient for meaning. First, helping others and performing virtuous acts as the expression of a virtuous soul is sufficient for happiness, flourishing, and living out a life without seeking death. Everyone who settles on it finds the sort of peace, contentment, and long-term flourishing that indicates meaning, purpose, and happiness. It brings Tahani and Michael meaning and flourishing. It also brings Jason, Chidi, and Eleanor meaning and flourishing as long as they choose to pursue it. Morality also looks to be necessary, since so many eternal beings devote their lives to helping others and find meaning doing so. We do not know for sure that it is necessary, because the show leaves open whether some souls will remain happy in the Good Place forever without using the door. However, the show strongly implies that nobody will be able to stay in the Good Place forever. So, we can merely state that it is consistent with the trappings of the show that virtue is both necessary and sufficient for happiness and meaning, while mortality is not.

But, if morality and not mortality is what brings meaning to our lives, then Jason, Chidi, and Eleanor made the wrong choice. They choose to end their lives rather than pursue virtue. Or rather, they choose to stop pursuing virtue, and thus end their lives. The tragic end is the only one consistent with the moral and philosophical understanding of the show.

PARADISE LOST: JUSTIFYING THE WAYS
OF HUMAN BEINGS TO THE DIVINE

At the end of the series finale, some protagonists have chosen the door, and some have not. However, all of them had to leave the Good Place to find happiness and meaning. I argue this fact is not an accident. Tahani did not accidentally leave the Good Place to become an architect and fulfill her mission to help others. Michael did not accidentally leave the Good Place to move beyond being an architect. Jason, Chidi, and Eleanor did not accidentally leave the Good Place, literally taking a door out of it. The Good Place is incompatible with flourishing, and every being must leave it behind to live out their fullest self. In this section, I consider what the view of meaning, morality, and eudaimonia I defend above entails for a virtuous person in the afterlife, and how the Good Place almost definitionally fails to achieve it.

Goodness requires the sort of eudaimonia, or flourishing, which could not exist in the Good Place, where no individual has needs. The often-cited prerequisites for the conditions of justice include features simply not present in the Good Place: moderate scarcity and limited altruism.[16] Moderate scarcity is required because if scarcity is too great, people will be too desperate to survive to allow room for justice, and if there is no scarcity, there will be no need for justice. Similarly, limited altruism is required because if there is no altruism, no one would pursue justice, and if everyone perfectly adheres to impartial judgments to help others with no special regard for their own pursuits, justice would not be necessary. The Good Place as it is presented to the audience meets neither condition of justice. The inhabitants cannot help each other because the Janets meet their every whim and desire. Additionally, since everyone present in the Good Place has achieved an ordered soul, no personal development can be possible there either.

What makes the Good Place good? When Michael arrives there in season 4, episode 12, unsure of how he will be received and is suddenly in charge, he stumbles upon a whiteboard full of ideas for how to make the Good Place better. The sign reads:

Ideas for Improving the Good Place

- Music you can eat
- Get more chocolate in chocolate
- More hoverboards
- Wait until Beyoncé gets here, ask her to fix it
- Fewer hoverboards somehow?
- Giant Mini-Donuts (not just regular donuts—Dave will explain)
- P[illegible][17]

As the viewer encounters this list, it reads like a funny and fun way to spend one's time: come up with new and creative ways to fulfill every wish and whim, without even the laws of physics to constrain the possibilities. However, in light of the later events in the episode, in which we discover along with the characters that inhabitants of the Good Place are trapped in an endless charade of empty pursuits which chip away at their minds and identities, we revisit the list as the desperate and hopeless plea for help that it is. It looks instead like a tragic and fatal misunderstanding of what the Good Place should be. It is no longer comic; it is comically misguided.

The problem with the Good Place is that it is a hedonist reward in a non-hedonist universe created exclusively for people who have rejected a hedonist worldview. There is nothing wrong with pleasure. And the Good Place has a wide variety of pleasures: higher pleasures, like the pleasures of the intellect, are just as available as lower pleasures, like endless milkshakes. However, virtue requires temperance, being well-off with respect to pleasures, and the Good Place does not accommodate that virtue. It habituates its inhabitants to excess.[18] What makes the Good Place good, according to the architects who oversee it, is its pleasures. But what goodness is, according to the architects who created it, is not pleasure. The pursuit of morality is goodness, according to the laws of their universe, but the pursuit of pleasure is all that is permitted, according to the laws of the Good Place. That is why so many have to leave the Good Place to find meaning and happiness. A hedonistic reward might be nice for a while, but it cannot be all there is, and a hedonistic reward cannot be the Good Place, because it has no goodness in it.

The characters in the show realize this fact. In discussing what to do about Patty's conundrum, Eleanor announces, "The way to restore meaning to the people in the Good Place is to let them leave."[19] On both the happy interpretation and the tragic interpretation, this statement is correct. But its euphemistic explanation of death is actually a way out of the false dichotomy it creates between the Good Place and nonexistence. Tahani explains in her own revelation that she does not want to die: "Wait, I don't want to leave. . . . I also don't want to stay. I'm done here. But, I don't want to go there." "Those are kind of your only options," Chidi replies, stating what the characters of the show have, up until this point, believed to be true as an either/or fallacy. "No, they aren't," Tahani explains.[20] Of course, Tahani is right and Chidi is wrong. But the fact that there are more options does not lead the characters to think similarly for the other inhabitants of the Good Place or even for themselves. It places Tahani in a leadership role without being a trailblazer; nobody else takes her rejection of the false dichotomy between the door and staying.

In adding a door to the Good Place, the Soul Squad alters it, but does not improve it. In writing *Paradise Lost*, John Milton aims to "justify the ways of God to men."[21] In choosing to lose paradise, the characters of the Good Place must justify the ways of human beings to the divine. That is because the divine creation of the Good Place does not respond to human nature. Human beings do not want or need to have their every desire fulfilled nor their every pleasure achieved. What they want and need, as virtuous individuals, is to pursue the good. If the Good Place cannot allow them to do so, they must leave. But, the door does not solve the problem of the Good Place nor adequately respond to their natures, which are eternal. Only leaving to pursue good does that. Only Tahani's solution adequately responds to her virtuous and eternal nature by allowing her to pursue the good forever.

SUICIDAL IDEATION IN THE GOOD PLACE

With this framework in place, I resolve what I take to be the problematic treatment of suicidal ideation in the show. In the happy interpretation, the treatment of suicide in the show is, as I hope to have shown, morally problematic, philosophically incongruous, and literarily vacant. I now argue it is also medically negligent. If the happy interpretation is right, the show's use of themes related to suicide is wrongheaded and offensive. Instead, only the tragic interpretation of the finale I defend explains the finale in such a way that makes the show's treatment of suicide both responsible and moral.

To make this case, I first need to explain why I take walking through the door to be akin to death. The door is not the same as death in a literal sense; all the protagonists in the show have either already died, many of them several times (Eleanor, Chidi, Jason, and Tahani), or never lived (Michael and Janet). However, insofar as death is an ending to a psychological consciousness with a personal identity that exists over time containing memories and plans, the door does constitute a certain sort of death. Furthermore, since the show claims that our time on Earth is limited but our psychological souls are actually immortal, the death that the door provides is much more definitive than actual death. The door is a sort of "super-death" in which even those immortal souls cease their existence.

Under the DSM-5 diagnostic criteria of depression, loss of "interest in activities [individuals] once enjoyed" is a symptom that must be present for a diagnosis of depression and has come to be definitionally associated with a common understanding of depression.[22] The characters who chose the door could be construed as depressed under this definition.[23]

Each character is pursuing identifiable goals in the Good Place. Eleanor and Chidi pursue philosophy and their relationship; Tahani pursues familial relationships along with her skills; Jason pursues his relationship with Janet along with his video game playing; Michael oversees the Good Place and practices guitar. However, upon reaching these goals, the characters are not portrayed as happy, at least in the sense of a joyful attitude. Instead, they are described as losing interest in activities that they once enjoyed. . The achievement of a goal is often met with the character in question's face falling, and the cessation of the activity in question. "When you've already designed the ultimate one [neighborhood], it's kind of a letdown," Michael says, explaining that he fails to find pleasure in the activities that once brought him joy and why that led him to a door he couldn't take.[24] In addition, some characters also experience other symptoms associated with depression in conjunction with their decision to use the door. Chidi complains of fatigue; Michael uses alcohol and other drugs; all experience memory loss or the threat of it.[25]

One reason why there are guidelines on how to discuss suicide is that media representation of suicide and suicidal ideation can contribute to what is called suicide contagion or "copycat suicide."[26] Some empirical research supports this concern. For example, "more than 50 research studies worldwide have found that certain types of news coverage can increase the likelihood of suicide in vulnerable individuals," which frames this as a public health problem.[27] Thus, real-life dangers arise even from fictional accounts of activities associated with suicide. In the case of *The Good Place*, because going through the door bears similarities to suicide, its representation on media matters.

Media guidelines recommend against discussing suicide in sensationalist terms, normalizing language, and even recommend against discussing "suicide contagion" at all because it can create an influential and harmful norm. Guidelines also recommend against discussing the manner and location of the suicide. In addition, media guidelines recommend against talking about suicide as an acceptable response to hardship or other difficulties.[28] I argue that on the happy interpretation, the show violates each of these guidelines. Only when we view the finale as tragic does the problematic treatment of themes associated with suicide make sense as part of the show's larger purpose to criticize their choice. In fact, we can even view Eleanor and Chidi's deaths as examples of copycat suicide after Jason's, resulting from their experience of depression and the problematic representation of suicide they witness.

First, the characters speak of the door in normalizing tones. The title of the episode, for example, "Whenever You're Ready," is itself a normalizing approach to an act associated with suicide. It is taken from a moment in the episode where Janet is explaining the door to Jason and says, "You can sit on that bench as long as you want. Whenever you're ready, you just walk through." Here, she makes choosing death seem normal, and with the word "just," easy and encouraging. Similarly, when Eleanor and Michael are speaking of Chidi, they use similar language. "We've got a problem. I think Chidi's gonna leave," Eleanor says. "Really?" Michael asks. "Did he say he was ready?"[29]

The show also talks about death by suicide in sensationalist terms. The conversation between Eleanor and Chidi at the bar after their dinner with friends starts in normalizing terms. "Shakespeare went through the door," Chidi announces to Eleanor without emotion in his voice, presenting it as just another item of news or gossip. "Really?" Eleanor replies. "Yeah." Then he moves to sensationalist terms: "Everyone's talking about it."[30] This discussion is problematic because it sensationalizes Shakespeare's death, focuses on his death rather than his life, and places suicide in a prominent position in the show, each of which are violations of media guidelines. This problem of sensationalist descriptions is related to a concern of media representation of death by suicide that glamorizes or creates a spectacle. Jason's decision to have a big party before using the door could be seen as glamorizing or creating a spectacle in a similarly sensationalist way.

These conversations also include discussions of suicide as an epidemic in ways media guidelines oppose. For example, in a discussion later in the episode, Michael states, "I've loved being here, but Jason's gone. Chidi's gone. You know, even Doug Forcett (played by Michael McKean and Noah Garfinkel) went through the door."[31] This kind of expression—which talks about how everybody is doing it, and how even the best people are doing it—is problematic by itself. Evidence suggests talking about increasing numbers of suicide, epidemic proportions, or how so many people choose suicide specifically contributes to what is actually a public health problem that has solutions.[32]

Media recommendations on representations of suicide explicitly advocate for including resources for how to help people dealing with suicidal ideation, but characters in the show criticize this impetus to help.[33] In response to Eleanor's request to give Chidi new meaning or purpose in life, Janet says, "Forgive me, Eleanor, but if Chidi's ready to go, it's time for him to go."[34] This response to death that Janet displays can be helpful if death is inevitable, such as handling end-of-life scenarios in which death cannot be avoided. However, to use that kind of reasoning in a situation where death is chosen and avoidable upends this seemingly compassionate stance.

Third, the characters discuss the door as solutions to individual problems, another problematic treatment of suicide as described by media guidelines. For example, of Shakespeare's death, Eleanor states, "It's probably for the best. His last 4,000 plays were not nearly as good as the ones he wrote on Earth. I mean, did you see 'The Tempest 2: Here We Blow Again?' Woof. [BOTH LAUGH]."[35] Here, Chidi and Eleanor endorse Shakespeare's death as good because he was not creating high-quality art, an attitude that can directly harm struggling creatives. The statements have a predictable impact: Chidi, who is struggling with suicidal ideation, immediately responds by saying, "You mind if we go home? I'm tired." Here, he calls attention to a symptom of depression he is experiencing. Eleanor says of Doug going through the door, "That was probably for the best," just as she did about Shakespeare. Following up with a reason, she states, "That guy partied so hard when he was here."[36] This reason is a clear indictment of the Good Place, which only allows for hedonistic pursuits, while at the same time, problematically condemns someone's avoidable death as an overall good.

Fourth, the characters speak about the door using inappropriate language according to media guidelines, such as "failed" or "successful" attempts. For example, when Michael walks through the door and his "damn essence" does not return to "the damn fabric of the damn universe," he talks about going through the door in the "wrong way" and asks why going through the door is "not working."[37] Suicide prevention guidelines call such language inappropriate, because to deem surviving a suicide attempt a "failure" and dying by suicide "successful," is to describe death by suicide in value-laden, positive terms.

Last, the show depicts the manner and location of the suicides in great detail, which violates media guidelines. These depictions not only are problematic because of how they can contribute to viewers' mental health struggles, but are also glamorizing and sensationalizing, turning individual persons into sparks of glowing light and indicating the ways in which their memory will be especially preserved if they choose this sort of death.

According to the happy interpretation of the finale, there is no awareness or recognition of the way the door in the show bears resemblance to suicide in the real world, or if there is, the indication is that such glamorizing of suicide is acceptable or desirable. However, according to the tragic interpretation, we see a sensationalized depiction of suicide followed by a public health crisis in which a predictable series of copycat suicides and suicide attempts follows. These deaths are tragic side-effects of individuals who have lost their way, forgotten the meaning of life they once understood, and died because their cries for help and symptoms of depression were ignored or enabled.

In this section, I used guidelines for discussion of suicide in the media to argue that the treatment of the door in the happy interpretation is at best, problematic, and at worst, grossly negligent. Death by suicide is not good, is not a solution to life's problems, and does not give life meaning. When someone dies, even if their art was imperfect or they couldn't find meaning in endless parties, it is not "for the best." That's because, as Chidi states, "It turns out life isn't a puzzle that can be solved one time and it's done. You wake up every day, and you solve it again."[38] Completeness is not and cannot be our goal. Or as Scanlon writes, "Working out the terms of moral justification is an unending task."[39] "Boom!" Eleanor shouts in punctuation to reading these words from Scanlon aloud.[40]

THE GOOD PLACE AND THE ERA OF PEAK TV

So far, I have proposed a moral theory that fits with the point system of the show, explains some characters' actions and failures to flourish, and shows why their decisions to go through the door were unnecessary and perhaps even immoral. I argued that the tragic interpretation, and not the happy interpretation of the finale, is consistent and valuable from a literary, philosophical, moral, and medical perspective. I now argue that my interpretation of the finale fits with a larger interpretation of the era of Peak TV and the happy interpretation does not. In other words, the tragic interpretation makes the show consistent and valuable culturally, while the happy interpretation fails to fit with a relevant cultural narrative.

According to Steven A. Benko's view of Peak TV, as outlined in the introduction to this volume, "[This era of TV] emphasizes connection over self-actualization, community over individuality, and an uplifting vision of humanity, rejecting the nihilism of the previous era."[41] According to this definition of Prestige television, *The Good Place* as a TV show fits into a larger cultural milieu in which a life-affirming, optimistic approach to humanity is embraced by a significant portion of writers and directors creating content during the time period starting around 2011.[42]

The happy interpretation of the finale, in which individuals can find meaning in existence through mere mortality and not through an existence that includes what we owe to each other, relies on the Good Place as a place where self-actualization takes precedence over connection, where individuality takes precedence over community, and a literally nihilistic approach to the afterlife.[43] Connection, which is a process and ongoing, is sacrificed to an idea of self-actualization that allows individuals to reach a particular goal, after which life is not worth living. Similarly, individuality and self-interested desire take precedence over morality, what we owe to each other, and altruism on the happy view. The nihilism it endorses is one where non-existence is better than existence. Nothing really matters when faced with eternity on the happy interpretation.

The happy interpretation can be used retroactively among the audience viewing it as redefining Earthly existence to be meaningless and nihilistic. Why help others if we will all end up in the Good Place eventually? Why rack up points to get to the Good Place sooner if we will soon tire of it anyway? Why help others if our moral exemplars would choose not to when given the chance? Why practice an art on Earth if we will have eternal time to achieve perfection of skills in the Good Place? Why create relationships of caring connection if the creation of a perfectly open, loving, and reciprocal relationship will fail to bring joy or even begin to evoke boredom in eternity? The answers to these questions are only empty on the happy interpretation, which promotes an amoral universe over a moral one. According to the happy interpretation, achieving the virtues does not benefit the possessor, nor bring about the happiness we all seek, nor even truly help others. The purpose of acting virtuously is to make a cynical trade to achieve the life of pleasure we all really want deep down. Virtue can never be rewarding for its own sake, but can only ever lead to a hedonist reward given by a divine force.

On the tragic interpretation of the series finale, however, the Good Place is an eternal reward that ought not be eternal for those who deserve it. Billions of souls need help in the ethos of The Good Place, but individuals cannot help them from the Good Place. One must decline hedonism and leave the eternal reward in order to help others if one wants an afterlife-affirming existence in eternity. This result—the result that Tahani chooses—is the "joyful" ending that makes the audience feel "safe, loved, and inspired," in the words Dan Levy uses to describe the era of Prestige television.[44] Nothing matters in the Good Place; by definition, everything that happens there is inconsequential.

But everything matters outside of it. Only when we realize that Jason, Chidi, and Eleanor's deaths were the unnecessary and avoidable result of forgetting what virtue is do we realize the meaning of existence, in life and after it. Morality, and not mortality, provides that meaning.

BUDDHISM AND BEYOND

One objection to this interpretation is that the finale is not tragic, because the episode adheres to a Buddhist worldview in which the door represents Nirvana.[45] According to this view, Jason, Chidi, and Eleanor reach true enlightenment, while Michael and Tahani are left out of Nirvana. "Picture a wave in the ocean," says Chidi. "You can see it, measure it, its height, the way the sunlight refracts when it passes through, and it's there, and you can see it, you know what it is. It's a wave. And then it crashes on the shore, and it's gone. But the water is still there. The wave was just a different way for the water to be for a little while."[46] This story of a wave is a reference to a teaching by Thich Nhat Hanh writing in his book, *The Heart of the Buddha's Teaching*.[47]

Nirvana is sometimes described as a "blowing out," "extinguishing," or "quenching," which could fit with the episode. References to Buddhism begin in the very first episode, in which Jason is introduced as the Buddhist monk "Jianyu," who is adhering to a vow of silence. Additionally, the system that the Soul Squad introduces to the afterlife to create a path to the Good Place for all souls looks similar to the path of reincarnation (or rein-something, if not-carnate). Furthermore, the absence of an omniscient, omnipotent, and omnibenevolent deity adds to the Buddhist interpretation, though The Judge (played by Maya Rudolph) could fill this role.

Much more about the show, however, contradicts a Buddhist worldview. First, the show concretely endorses the existence of eternal souls endowed with a personal identity as well as memories existing over time.[48] All people in The Good Place universe are endowed with a permanent self and unchanging identity that the concept of the no-self (*anatta*) rejects.[49] In addition, plenty of opportunities to incorporate a concept of reincarnation into the show arose, from the Soul Squad's earthly returns to Michael's decision to go back to Earth in the finale. In each case, the show went in a different direction.[50] In fact, reincarnation as a taking on of a new body in another life on Earth is incompatible with the system as described in the show. Before Eleanor, Chidi, Tahani, Jason, and Michael, who returned to Earth in a decidedly non-reincarnation fashion, it is implied that no soul ever returned to earth in all of human and animal history, suggesting a rejection of tenets in certain versions of Buddhism.

Nirvana as a liberation from the path of rebirth does not make sense in a universe without an endless cycle of reincarnation, nor is it liberation from suffering (*dukkha*), as the Good Place already provides for that.[51] Applying Buddhist conceptions of death to the door is problematic in part because Buddhist teachings not to fear death are specifically tailored to a universe in which nothing is eternal, least of all a personal soul; death is inevitable; and good living on earth protects individuals in rebirth. Yet, the show rejects each of these conceptions.[52] Retaining the Buddhist teachings about death while rejecting the metaphysics that make those teachings possible would lead to an incongruous approach in the finale.

If the help we render others is accompanied by detachment and the rejection of emotional involvement, giving insight into a world of suffering characterized by the unreality of the self (*nekkhamma*), that teaching would not be very compatible with the Good Place, which is characterized by deep emotional involvement, the elimination of suffering through complete wish fulfillment, and a permanent and eternal unchanging self.[53] Although the characters may have created a universe where all things are impermanent at the end of season 4, by the conceit of the show, this view would have been false when the Buddha taught it.[54]

Mahayana Buddhism, in which compassion and help for others lead to the complete erasure of the self, is not something that would be easy to achieve after several eternities without providing any help for others, focusing exclusively on self-interested pleasures. Although it is possible that the protagonists all happened upon a Buddhist enlightenment independent of any Buddhist meditation and after explicitly rejecting Buddhist teachings, as well as avoiding Buddhist practices of shedding desires, this conclusion would be a happy accident and not the result of bringing the way of life to its fruition.[55]

In addition, Nirvana can be described as a "mental event," not a physical transformation or choice of non-existence as the door is depicted.[56] Nirvana, much more than a place or a transformation, is described as extinguishing desire and a negative state absent any suffering that attends negative emotions, something which could involve a psychological transformation but would not be the extinguishing of an eternal soul.[57] Meditation as a path to desirelessness and karma as a way to shed our unwelcome desires does not have much space for an afterlife in which complete desire fulfillment is a reward for a life without desires.[58] A better approximation of Nirvana would be the feeling the characters get before they go through the door, which, because of its desirelessness, should not bring the characters any discomfort to stay in. To seek nonbeing as soon as one experiences desirelessness, or to experience discomfort in continuing to exist after having achieved this state, would suggest a problematic consequence of Buddhist teachings. While accepting death and removing our fear of it might bring peace, seeking it out would be problematic.

Lastly, it is worth noting that if the door were Nirvana in the Buddhist interpretation of the finale, then Nirvana did not exist for thousands of years prior. According to this interpretation of the finale, the Buddha himself could not have attained Nirvana.

CONCLUSION

In this chapter, I defended a moral theory of the Good Place to justify an explanation of the series finale that offers a responsible resolution of the major themes of the show from a moral or philosophical, literary, psychological or medical, as well as cultural perspective. I oppose the happy interpretation, under which Jason, Chidi, and Eleanor's choice of the door is justified in favor of one that makes that choice tragic. However, I recognize that I could be wrong. Therefore, I will end this chapter with words from section 2 on p. 1,000 of Chidi Anagonye's 3,600-page book. "Of course, the exact opposite might be true."

NOTES

1. This essay includes major spoilers for all seasons of *The Good Place*. Thanks to the editor of this volume, Steven A. Benko, for his comments and input. Thanks to Lavender McKittrick-Sweitzer, Emily Crookston, Nora Hendren, Alison Reiheld, Christopher Pearson, Eric Brown, David Griesedieck, Waldemar Rohloff, Elijah Jauernig, and Jeff Armel for helpful conversations on the topic or comments on earlier drafts. Thanks also to Michael Tofte and the participants of UMSL Philosophy Department's Philosophy on the Reels.

2. Judy Berman, "'The Good Place' Finale Left Us With No Lessons, But Lots of Tears," *Time*, January 31, 2020. https://time.com/5775041/good-place-series-finale -recap-review/; Phil Harrison, "The Good Place: Was This the Most Devastating TV Finale Ever?" *The Guardian*, February 4, 2020. http://www.theguardian.com /tv-and-radio/2020/feb/04/the-good-place-was-this-the-most-devastating-tv-finale -ever; Linda Holmes, "A Goodbye To 'The Good Place,'" *NPR.org*, January 31, 2020, https://www.npr.org/2020/01/31/801540105/a-goodbye-to-the-good-place; Alan Sepinwall, "'Everybody Was Bawling': Kristen Bell on the End of 'The Good Place,'" *Rolling Stone* (blog), February 3, 2020, https://www.rollingstone.com/tv/tv -features/good-place-finale-kristen-bell-interview-947122/.

3. Ted Danson, "The Emotional Cast Talks Finale with Seth Meyers – The Good Place," interview by Seth Meyers, *Late Night with Seth Meyers*, January 31, 2020.

4. *The Good Place*, season 1, episode 1, "Everything is Fine," dir. Drew Goddard, aired September 19, 2016, originally released on NBC.

5. Derek Parfit, *Reasons and Persons* (Oxford: Oxford University Press, 1986), 25.

6. Furthermore, acting with a positive value is an especially low bar; the point system actually requires we maximize point values, creating a world in which, even if we rack up positive points, we might still have been able to act in such a way that produced more points, making our actual actions wrong. Eric Wiland, "Monkeys, Typewriters, and Objective Consequentialism," *Ratio* 18, no. 3 (2005): 352–60.

7. The next logical answer to the moral underpinning of the show is Scanlon's contractualism, since it is repeatedly discussed and upheld by the characters of the show. I endorse this understanding of the show to a large extent, but put aside this understanding here. While major elements of Scanlon's contractualism get worked into the final season, it is not an accurate representation of the point system, which is an aggregative measure. It also, by definition, does not pass the "reasonable rejection standard," which Scanlon describes by saying: "An act is wrong if its performance under the circumstances would be disallowed by any set of principles for the general regulation of behaviour that no one could reasonably reject as a basis for informed, unforced, general agreement" (Thomas M. Scanlon, *What We Owe to Each Other* (Cambridge, MA: Harvard University Press, 1998), 153). Since the Soul Squad do reject the original system, and do so from an impartial, well-informed, uncoerced stance, we can put aside contractualism for the time being. Instead, contractualism is a better explanation of the new system implemented by the characters of the show who form an impartial committee behind a veil of ignorance of sorts and unanimously agree on a new moral framework with full information, a rationally competent and autonomous freely given voluntary consent, and do so in a way that no reasonable person could (or does) reject. This new system is still based on virtue ethics, but virtue ethics is chosen not based on a teleological understanding of a human function, but rather as the result of a Scanlonian contractualist agreement.

Theories like care ethics fail to capture the impartiality of the point system, in which actions toward strangers have equal import to actions toward loved ones. Theories like moral particularism fail to capture the point system's universality and generality.

8. *The Good Place*, season 1, episode 1, "Everything is Fine," dir. Drew Goddard, aired September 19, 2016, originally released on NBC.

9. This failure of consequentialism and deontology to explain the system, and the incongruity of using a point system with a theory like virtue ethics, leads some to argue that the system does not adhere to any one moral theory but rather incorporates ideas from all. For example, James M. Russell argues, "So, in the end, there is a bit of everything at work in the ethical universe of *The Good Place*—and that is probably for the best" (James M. Russell, *The Forking Trolley: An Ethical Journey to The Good Place* (London: Palazzo Editions, 2019)). But Russell's rejection of virtue ethics might be too quick. He states, "If the world of *The Good Place* wasn't so explicitly based on a set of rules and points, this might lead us to conclude that the real aim here is for Eleanor to learn 'virtue.'" Rules are not an adequate characterization of

the point system, and in any case, some virtue ethicists do incorporate rules (Rosalind Hursthouse, *On Virtue Ethics* (Oxford University Press, USA, 2002)). In addition, Aristotle was not opposed to using a mathematical analysis of morality, and does so in several places in the Nicomachean Ethics (Aristotle, *Nicomachean Ethics* (Indianapolis, IN: Hackett Publishing Co., 1999), 1106a-b; 1106b25-30; 1131a10-1132b20). However, even if virtue ethics fails in the end to sufficiently capture the moral system of *The Good Place*, its close approximation to the show's view, and the failure of other theories to as closely approximate the theory of the show, can still be instructive.

10. Aristotle, 1098a7; 1109a20-25.

11. *The Good Place*, season 4, episode 11, "Mondays, Am I Right?," dir. Rebecca Asher, aired January 16, 2020, originally released on NBC.

12. They would have achieved a sort of McDowell-level silencing of their bad or vicious reasons that would have made unvirtuous actions inconceivable to them and virtuous actions the only salient and desirable possibility. McDowell, "The Role of Eudaimonia in Aristotle's Ethics," in *Essays on Aristotle's Ethics*, ed. Matina Souretis Horner Distinguished Professor Radcliffe College Professor of Philosophy Amelie Oksenberg Rorty (Berkeley, CA: University of California Press, 1980), 370. Or, if virtue does not completely silence competing reasons for actions, virtue always overrides them. Anne Margaret Baxley, "The Price of Virtue," *Pacific Philosophical Quarterly* 88, no. 4 (2007): 403–423.

13. Aristotle, 1099b25.

14. *The Good Place*, season 4, episode 13, "Whenever You're Ready," dir. Michael Shur, aired January 30, 2020, originally released on NBC.

15. *The Good Place*, season 2, episode 4, "Existential Crisis," dir. Beth McCarthy-Miller, aired October 12, 2017, originally released on NBC.

16. David Hume, *A Treatise of Human Nature* (Mineola, NY: Dover Publications, 2003), 347; John Rawls, *A Theory of Justice* (Cambridge, MA: Belknap Press of Harvard University Press, 1999), 110; 127.

17. *The Good Place*, season 4, episode 12, "Patty," dir. Morgan Sackett, aired January 23, 2020, originally released on NBC.

18. As Patty explains, "On paper, this is paradise. All your desires and needs are met. But it's infinite, and when perfection goes on forever, you become this glassy-eyed mush person." *The Good Place*, season 4, episode 12, "Patty," dir. Morgan Sackett, aired January 23, 2020, originally released on NBC.

19. Ibid.

20. *The Good Place*, season 4, episode 13, "Whenever You're Ready," dir. Michael Shur, aired January 30, 2020, originally released on NBC.

21. John Milton, *Paradise Lost: Penguin Classics*, ed. John Leonard (London: Penguin Books, 2003), 5.

22. Jessica Truschel, "Depression Definition and DSM-5 Diagnostic Criteria," *Psycom*, September 25, 2020, https://www.psycom.net/depression-definition-dsm-5-diagnostic-criteria/; American Psychiatric Association, "What Is Depression?" accessed February 10, 2020, https://www.psychiatry.org/patients-families/depression/what-is-depression.

23. Of course, one of the symptoms of depression is also "Recurrent thoughts of death, recurrent suicidal ideation without a specific plan, or a suicide attempt or a specific plan for committing suicide." Truschel. If the door is a proxy for death, then characters' discussion of the door meets this symptom, too. However, to rely on this symptom of depression would be circular for the purposes of my argument, since I am arguing a pre-existing depression is what helps explain why the talk of the door sounds like suicidal ideation in the first place. Still, it is relevant for my argument that all of the characters have recurrent experiences of the other symptoms of depression as well as the experience of suicidal ideation.

24. *The Good Place*, season 4, episode 13, "Whenever You're Ready," dir. Michael Shur, aired January 30, 2020, originally released on NBC.

25. Having argued that the door is akin to death, the characters' experiences are akin to symptoms of depression, and the characters' desire for the door is akin to suicidal ideation, it is relevant to point out that for the purposes of my argument, it is not necessary to classify the actions of the characters literally as suicide. It is because the actions bear some similarity to suicide that my argument holds, and not because what occurs in the show are literally cases of suicide.

26. Patrick W. O'Carroll, Lloyd B. Potter, Eugene Aronowitz, Diane Linksey, Elisa Bildner, Eve Moskicki, Jacqueline Buckingham, Jordon Richland, et al., "Suicide Contagion and the Reporting of Suicide: Recommendations from a National Workshop," *Centers for Disease Control and Prevention*, April 22, 1994, https://www.cdc.gov/Mmwr/preview/mmwrhtml/00031539.htm.

27. "Recommendations for Reporting on Suicide," *American Foundation for Suicide Prevention*, n.d., https://afsp.org/wp-content/uploads/2016/01/recommendations.pdf.

28. Reporting on Suicide, "Recommendations for Reporting on Suicide," accessed June 29, 2020, https://reportingonsuicide.org/recommendations/.

29. *The Good Place*, season 4, episode 13, "Whenever You're Ready," dir. Michael Shur, aired January 30, 2020, originally released on NBC.

30. Ibid.

31. Ibid.

32. Florian Arendt, Sebastian Scherr, Benedikt Till, Yvonne Prinzellner, Kevin Hines, and Thomas Niederkrotenthaler, "Suicide on TV: Minimising the Risk to Vulnerable Viewers," *BMJ 358*, August 22, 2017; Alia E. Dastagir, "Kate Spade's Death and the Unintentional Consequences of Suicide Coverage," *USA TODAY*, June 6, 2018, https://www.usatoday.com/story/news/2018/06/06/kate-spades-death-and-suicide-contagion-how-media-got-wrong-again/678314002/.

33. If you need help, resources are available. The number for the National Suicide Prevention Lifeline is (800) 273-8255 and the website is suicidepreventionlifeline.org.

34. *The Good Place*, season 4, episode 13, "Whenever You're Ready," dir. Michael Shur, aired January 30, 2020, originally released on NBC.

35. Ibid.

36. Ibid.

37. Ibid.

38. *The Good Place*, season 4, episode 9, "The Answer," dir. Valeria Migliassi Collins, aired November 21, 2019, originally released on NBC.

39. Scanlon, 362.

40. *The Good Place*, season 4, episode 13, "Whenever You're Ready," dir. Michael Shur, aired January 30, 2020, originally released on NBC.

41. Steven A. Benko, "TV: Better Living With Other People?" in Steven A. Benko, *Better Living Through TV* (Washington, DC: Rowman and Littlefield, 2022): 5.

42. Comedies in this time period, from *Broad City* on Comedy Central, to *Veep* on HBO, to *Schitt's Creek* and *The Unbreakable Kimmy Schmidt* on Netflix, as well as Michael Schur's television other shows such as *The Office, Parks and Recreation,* and *Brooklyn Nine-Nine*.

43. "Mortality offers meaning to the events of our lives, and morality helps navigate that meaning," Todd May states in the show, quoting his book. Todd May, *Death (The Art of Living)* (Milton Park, Abingdon-on-Thames, Oxfordshire, England: Routledge, 2014), 47.

44. Amber Dowling, "Emmys: How 'The Good Place,' 'Veep,' 'Russian Doll' Find Humor in Heightened Realities," *Variety* (blog), August 15, 2019, https://variety.com/2019/tv/awards/emmys-2019-heightened-comedies-veep-schitts-creek-good-place-marvelous-mrs-maisel-russian-doll-1203301330/.

45. I here aim to focus on "the neutral core" of Buddhism, acknowledging the vast diversity of thought within the tradition.

46. *The Good Place*, season 4, episode 13, "Whenever You're Ready," dir. Michael Shur, aired January 30, 2020, on NBC. Eleanor echoes the same sentiment later in the episode. She says, "The wave returns to the ocean. What the ocean does with the water after that is anyone's guess. But as a very wise not-robot once told me, true joy is in the mystery."

47. Thich Nhat Hanh, *The Heart of the Buddha's Teaching: Transforming Suffering into Peace, Joy, and Liberation* (New York: Harmony, 1999), 112, 124.

48. For a discussion of the role of memory in the show, see Alison Reiheld, "Some Memories You May Have Forgotten: Holding Space for Each Other When Memory Fails," in *The Good Place and Philosophy*, ed. Kimberly S. Engels and William Irwin, 1 Ed. (Hoboken, NJ: Wiley-Blackwell, 2020).

49. Owen Flanagan, "Buddhism," in *How to Live a Good Life: A Guide to Choosing Your Personal Philosophy*, ed. Massimo Pigliucci, Skye Cleary, and Daniel Kaufman (New York, NY: Knopf Doubleday Publishing Group, 2020), 15. Furthermore, beings like Janets, architects, demons, angels, committee members and other deity-like entities all have eternal natures rejected in the Buddhist notion of *anicca*. They also do not clearly fall into the category of bodhisattvas, and since they cannot walk through the door, as evidenced by Michael's attempt, their inability to attain Nirvana would be a problem if they were.

50. For example, Michael's return to Earth could have been a cut to a crying baby, or at least a version of himself that did not retain his full memories. Instead, the show decided to eschew reincarnation in its choices. Although there is a certain sort of reincarnation in the new system's tests and trials, it all occurs in the afterlife, a view opposed by a Buddhist approach to reincarnation and the afterlife in which whatever

happens in our temporary afterlives does not make a difference to our spiritual fates. The absence of reincarnation itself is not evidence of much, since Buddhism can be presented without it. Rather, I take the show coming so close to reincarnation while still eschewing it as evidence.

51. Paul Williams, *Buddhist Thought: Second Edition* (London; New York: Routledge, 2013), 31.

52. Hanh says of the wave, which does not die when it crashes into the shore because its true nature is water, "It would be sad if the wave did not know it is water. It would think, Some day, I will have to die. This period of time is my life span, and when I arrive at the shore, I will return to nonbeing. These notions will cause the wave fear and anguish. We have to help it remove the notions of self, person, living being, and life span if we want the wave to be free and happy." Hanh, 124. However, when the characters enter the afterlife, the true nature of the universe is revealed to them, and that nature includes notions of self, person, living being, and life span.

53. Reiheld.

54. Williams, 21.

55. For example, Eleanor says to Michael, "You know, it took me a while to figure it out, but earlier, when you were walking back and forth through the door it hit me. You will never be at peace until you get the one thing you truly want" (*The Good Place*, season 4, episode 13, "Whenever You're Ready," dir. Michael Shur, aired January 30, 2020, on NBC). Achieving peace by having every last desire you ever had sated is not an obviously Buddhist approach to contentment.

56. Williams, 69.

57. Ibid.

58. A desire for non-existence still falls under the category of such a desire. "Cravings include not just cravings for sensory pleasures, but also craving for continued existence—eternal life—and craving for complete cessation, non-existence, a complete 'end to it all.'" Williams, 32.

BIBLIOGRAPHY

American Psychiatric Association. "What Is Depression?" Accessed February 10, 2020. https://www.psychiatry.org/patients-families/depression/what-is-depression.

Arendt, Florian, Sebastian Scherr, Benedikt Till, Yvonne Prinzellner, Kevin Hines, and Thomas Niederkrotenthaler. "Suicide on TV: Minimising the Risk to Vulnerable Viewers." *BMJ* 358 (August 22, 2017).

Aristotle. *Nicomachean Ethics*. Translated by Terence Irwin, 2nd Ed. Indianapolis, IN: Hackett Publishing Co., 1999.

Baxley, Anne Margaret. "The Price of Virtue." *Pacific Philosophical Quarterly* 88, no. 4 (2007): 403–423.

Benko, Steven A. "TV: Better Living With Other People?" in *Better Living Through TV*, edited by Steven A. Benko. Washington, DC: Rowman and Littlefield, 2022.

Berman, Judy. "'The Good Place' Finale Left Us With No Lessons, But Lots of Tears." *Time*, January 31, 2020. https://time.com/5775041/good-place-series-finale-recap-review/.

Dastagir, Alia E. "Kate Spade's Death and the Unintentional Consequences of Suicide Coverage." USA TODAY, June 6, 2018. https://www.usatoday.com/story/news/2018/06/06/kate-spades-death-and-suicide-contagion-how-media-got-wrong-again/678314002/.

Dowling, Amber. "Emmys: How 'The Good Place,' 'Veep,' 'Russian Doll' Find Humor in Heightened Realities." *Variety* (blog), August 15, 2019. https://variety.com/2019/tv/awards/emmys-2019-heightened-comedies-veep-schitts-creek-good-place-marvelous-mrs-maisel-russian-doll-1203301330/.

Flanagan, Owen. "Buddhism." In *How to Live a Good Life: A Guide to Choosing Your Personal Philosophy*, edited by Massimo Pigliucci, Skye Cleary, and Daniel Kaufman. New York, NY: Knopf Doubleday Publishing Group, 2020.

Greenstein, Luna. "Why Suicide Reporting Guidelines Matter." NAMI: National Alliance on Mental Illness, June 15, 2018. https://www.nami.org/Blogs/NAMI-Blog/June-2018/Why-Suicide-Reporting-Guidelines-Matter.

Hanh, Thich Nhat. *The Heart of the Buddha's Teaching: Transforming Suffering into Peace, Joy, and Liberation*. 1st Broadway Books trade pbk. ed Ed.. New York, NY: Harmony, 1999.

Harrison, Phil. "The Good Place: Was This the Most Devastating TV Finale Ever?" *The Guardian*, February 4, 2020. http://www.theguardian.com/tv-and-radio/2020/feb/04/the-good-place-was-this-the-most-devastating-tv-finale-ever.

Holmes, Linda. "A Goodbye To 'The Good Place.'" NPR.org, January 31, 2020. https://www.npr.org/2020/01/31/801540105/a-goodbye-to-the-good-place.

Hume, David. *A Treatise of Human Nature*. New Ed. Mineola, NY: Dover Publications, 2003.

Hursthouse, Rosalind. *On Virtue Ethics*. Oxford University Press, USA, 2002.

May, Todd. *Death*. Milton Park, Abingdon-on-Thames, Oxfordshire, England: Routledge, 2014.

McDowell, John. "The Role of Eudaimonia in Aristotle's Ethics." In *Essays on Aristotle's Ethics*, edited by Matina Souretis Horner Distinguished Professor Radcliffe College Professor of Philosophy Amelie Oksenberg Rorty. Berkeley, CA: University of California Press, 1980.

Milton, John. *Paradise Lost: Penguin Classics*. Edited by John Leonard. Rev. Ed. London: Penguin Books, 2003.

O'Carroll, Patrick W., Potter, Lloyd B., Eugene Aronowitz, Diane Linksey Elisa Bildner, Eve Moskicki, Jacqueline Buckingham, Jordon Richland, et al. "Suicide Contagion and the Reporting of Suicide: Recommendations from a National Workshop." Centers for Disease Control and Prevention, April 22, 1994. https://www.cdc.gov/Mmwr/preview/mmwrhtml/00031539.htm.

Parfit, Derek. *Reasons and Persons*. Oxford: Oxford University Press, 1986.

Rawls, John. *A Theory of Justice*. Rev. Ed. Cambridge, MA: Belknap Press of Harvard University Press, 1999.

"Recommendations for Reporting on Suicide." American Foundation for Suicide Prevention, n.d. https://afsp.org/wp-content/uploads/2016/01/recommendations .pdf.

Reiheld, Alison. "Some Memories You May Have Forgotten: Holding Space for Each Other When Memory Fails." In *The Good Place and Philosophy*, edited by Kimberly S. Engels and William Irwin, 1 Ed. Hoboken, NJ: Wiley-Blackwell, 2020.

Reporting on Suicide. "Recommendations for Reporting on Suicide." Accessed June 29, 2020. https://reportingonsuicide.org/recommendations/.

Russell, James M. *The Forking Trolley: An Ethical Journey to The Good Place*. None Ed. London: Palazzo Editions, 2019.

Scanlon, Thomas M. *What We Owe to Each Other*. Cambridge, MA: Harvard University Press, 1998.

Sepinwall, Alan. "'Everybody Was Bawling': Kristen Bell on the End of 'The Good Place.'" *Rolling Stone* (blog), February 3, 2020. https://www.rollingstone.com/tv/ tv-features/good-place-finale-kristen-bell-interview-947122/.

The Good Place. Created by Michael Schur. Aired from September 19, 2016–January 30, 2020. Originally released on NBC.

Truschel, Jessica. "Depression Definition and DSM-5 Diagnostic Criteria." *Psycom. Net - Mental Health Treatment Resource Since 1986* (blog), November 25, 2019. https://www.psycom.net/depression-definition-dsm-5-diagnostic-criteria/.

Wiland, Eric. "Monkeys, Typewriters, and Objective Consequentialism." *Ratio* 18, no. 3 (2005): 352–360.

Williams, Paul. *Buddhist Thought: Second Edition*, 2 Ed. London; New York: Routledge, 2013.

Chapter 11

How Television Produces Invisible Communities in an Age of Loneliness

A Detailed Look at 13 Reasons Why

Denis Newiak

Narratives and aesthetics of loneliness become increasingly preferred in serial fictional television entertainment, especially with the rising popularity of streaming services.[1] In numerous successful television series of the recent past, discourses of loneliness dominate against the societal background of increasing individualization, urbanization, and medialization, as they decisively shape the late-modern way of life. According to Newiak, in the more and more risky, accelerated, and singularized societies of late-modernity, communities have a hard time, so that the feeling of social disintegration and distance becomes a trademark of post-industrial "highly developed" affluent societies.[2] According to Fukuyama, modernity threatens to become the age of a Nietzschean "last man" who tries to make himself as comfortable as possible in his eternal lonely boredom.[3] As Niethammer puts it, the modern subject "is running danger to become a degenerate, economically calculating, isolated and irresponsible individual."[4] For Bauman, as modernization progresses, society is increasingly transformed into a purely functional network of abstract relationships, into a "swarm" of anonymous individuals.[5] Following Giddens, traditional experiences of community such as family, local togetherness, and transcendence are increasingly disintegrating in late-modernity, leaving behind insecure individuals who hardly feel up to the demands of their life's reality.[6] These modern phenomena produce "an inner distance to other people and the associated longing for connectedness in satisfying, meaningful relationships" which can be understood as the most basic feeling of the late-modern subjects.[7] Loneliness becomes a general diagnosis of life in the highly modernized present-day societies, and thus a burden for the late-modern subject which longs for experiences of community and closeness in the midst of more and more isolating social circumstances. At the same time, late-modern humans understand that pre-modern expressions of Gemeinschaft—as Tönnies defined them for the rural, deeply religious, and stable living conditions—will gradually disappear in a more and more urbanized, secularized, and rapidly changing modern world. Aware of their growing sense of social isolation, modern people search for new concepts and methods to overcome (or at least stun) this feeling of distance between people.[8]

While modernity can be characterized as an age of ever-increasing existential loneliness, the search for ways out of this social crisis is becoming a driving force in many art forms, including television series, and for the hyper-modernized characters acting in them—generating a growing audience's demand for narratives and representations of those societal trends. Newiak suggests that one need only think of the successful sitcom formats of past two decades, such as *The Big Bang Theory* (USA 2007–2019), *Two and a Half Men* (2003–2015) and *How I Met Your Mother* (USA 2005–2014), which feed their cheerful narrative stock primarily from the countless (and only at the end successful) efforts of their characters to establish sustainable (couple) relationships as a way out of their tortures of loneliness.[9] This amusing obstacle-rich communalization dominates in sitcoms (and in comic formats in general) and requires loneliness as a dramaturgical premise which only dissolves in the finale. However, characters in the contemporary drama TV series "Quality TV" usually go through an agonizing loneliness, or "de-communalization," which becomes more and more oppressive episode by episode: In *Bates Motel* (USA 2013–2017), the world-famous up-and-coming motel manager is left in a tangled web of drugs, arms, and human trafficking with mother as his only lifeline in the midst of increasingly complex and confusing—seemingly uninfluenceable and thus impracticable— late-modern circumstances.[10] Similar forms of tragic spirals of late-modern social isolation (which often lead to catastrophic outcomes) are not only found in teen TV series such as *The End of the F***ing World* (GB 2017–), *The Rain* (DK 2018–), and *The Society* (USA 2019–) but also across genres and target groups in formats ranging from *Breaking Bad* (USA 2008–2013) to *Designated Survivor* (USA 2016–2019) and *Black Mirror* (GB 2011–). Here, in what Mácha identified as early as 1968 as the "inner characteristic of industrial civilization," loneliness becomes an omnipresent and inescapable "feeling of the individual that exists in the web of social relationships that are indifferent to him."[11]

This tendency of modernity to create ever denser and harder forms of loneliness is also the focus of four seasons *13 Reasons Why* (USA 2017–2020).[12] Hannah Baker (played by Katherine Langford), a Californian high school student, records her own sad history of decay on thirteen music cassettes, describing how she is exposed not only to age-typical and unavoidable misunderstandings and uncertainties but also to constant vulgarity, harassment, and ultimately severe physical and sexual violence. Her story talks primarily of a disoriented contemporary society, which is visibly overwhelmed by the specific challenges of modernization—with its tendency to constantly compete for wealth and relationships, the omnipresence of abstract communication technologies, the compulsion for spatial mobility and dynamically changing role expectations.[13] From this, the fatal courses of action first emerge: bit by bit, the last communities within the nuclear family, the clique, and the school collapse one after the other, not only for Hannah but also for her classmates, the teachers, and parents, until the resulting total abandonment in this narrative world leads to Hannah's suicide.

Against the background of a history of modernity as an age of a growing sense of social isolation, television series such as *13 Reasons Why* can be seen as expressions or "reflections" of the processes of late-modern desocialization. However, with the help of an interdisciplinary discourse analysis of theories from television studies, I would like to show that those depictions of loneliness cannot simply be hermeneutically interpreted in a sociological sense as a "representation" of "excerpts from social reality" in which "social fears, desires and interests are expressed."[14] Rather, TV serials themselves are actively participating in the modern processes of socialization. Whether in the form of collectively received, recited, and revered cult series, through their serialized ability to make visible social causation processes and the production of temporal orders, or through the behavioral offers they make for complex life situations in late-modern society: television series intervene directly in the real-world processes of communalization in front of the screen through the mechanisms of communalization inscribed in them.[15] TV audiences have always been attracted to serial programs as, television series can be understood as an apparatus of substitute communalization, providing modern viewers with a temporary community mediated by the televisual mass media system that enables them to find meaning, orientation, and support in the advancing lonely modern age, today, more than ever before. As the global TV audiences do not only recognize themselves through the lonely narratives and aesthetics of serial shows, but discover new ways to experience a sense of belonging to a greater whole, they understand themselves as a meaningful part of an influenceable and interconnected society—which only makes more rapid modernization possible, and in turn provokes only deeper experiences of loneliness.

In this contribution, we will show how television series contribute to the creation of strong experiences of community, which late-modern people depend on in order to survive the loneliness that dominates their lives. It is easier to live a modern life with television than without it, as it allows each single individual to navigate through tough decisions, challenging life situations, and moments of fatalism by providing the feeling that even modern society is influenceable through individual choices, organized by the universal categories of truth and causation, and commonly shapeable through a shared reality. Through watching its programs, telemedial seriality allows every single member of society to live through modernity as an age of loneliness by providing them a sense of belonging and importance, only to allow the late-modern subject to push its efforts to modernize. However, as such an active motor of accelerated modernization, the television series is thus creating its own prerequisites, because this modernization goes hand in hand with a further increase in loneliness. Television thus creates the necessity of ever stronger telemedial substitute communities—which must be subjected again to ever greater demands to compensate for this escalating loneliness.

From this point of view, the undeniable special status that television has had as a communication system within the highly industrialized societies for half a century is—as it will be argued in the following using the example of *13 Reasons Why*—primarily due to this unrivaled capacity for production of experiences of community and closeness in an age of isolation. In Hannah Baker's lonely tape narrative, a self-referential game with the communalizing logics of serial television fictions appears and its performance limits unfolds like hardly anywhere else. From this point of view, the series represents not only the processes of loneliness in late-modernity itself, but above all the modes of communalization of the television series, which are worked through in *13 Reasons Why* in an auto-reflexive manner—and at the same time are interconnecting the TV audience in front of the screens:

1. Seriality, causation relations, and rationalizations. Through the serially connected and systematically ordered cassette narration of their former classmate, the young people visualize that their own actions are parts of causal chains, just as television series illustrate the otherwise abstract and invisible social dependencies of late-modern social interactions and demonstrate the causal-logical order of actions in a social being.
2. Fatal decisions—subjunctive alternatives. The reconstruction of what happened and the revealing relationships of cause and effect from a contemporary perspective allow the reassessment of past individual decisions of the characters and a play with decision-making options, just as television series always demand of their audience to question their own real-world decisions within social life in relation to what can be observed within the fictional world.
3. Behavioral offers for late-modern life situations. Both the cassette series and the Netflix series offer themselves a stock of behavioral tools that characters and television viewers alike can use to perform appropriate and potentially community-building actions within complex late-modern

living conditions and situations, making both series important instances of socialization, and thus a progressive modernization of their audience.

4. Time foundations and collective memory. At the same time, Hannah's tapes act as a materialized cultural memory, as a store of collective recollections, whose course can no longer be influenced, but whose serial narrative places the past, present, and future in a logical relationship to one another, thereby generating—like a television series—a collective feeling for the orderly progress and structure of time, which only makes meaningful social interactions within a community possible.

5. Neo-religious cult communities. The concrete rules of use that Hannah envisages for her cassette series, which are intended to order communal use, as well as the emerging media appropriation practices (binge hearing, reproduction, fan fiction) that ritualize serial reception, can be read as neo-religious cult practices that give the tapes the character of a mythically charged relic, which are only reinforced by the media-nostalgic aura of the analog technology used, while fan cultures of collective "worship" are also forming around the television series itself.

6. Television as a producer of truth and order. Hannah's cassette narratives initiate an examination of "truth" and "fiction" as universal categories and produce their own concept of reality: just as television series can be understood as an important producer of social meaning, the tapes, too, create a collectively shared consensus on the nature of social reality. Despite all its shortcomings, the serial fictional narrative still seems more real than the fragmentary everyday individual perspectives of the potentially lying subject. Through the serial principle of repetition, they create a sense of social order and collectively shared meaning.

7. Television's power, hubris, and the Last Community. The positions developed by the tapes, the television series, and television theory provoke the question of influence and responsibility of individuals and media systems in a social structure. *13 Reasons Why*, after a public discussion about possible imitation suicides among young people, saw itself forced to take various intervention measures—which on the one hand strangely overestimate a possible negative social influence of television series and at the same time question the important community-building functions of serial fictional television in a problematic way.

Although Hannah's cassette narrative lacks the immediate visuality and vividness typical of television series, it turns into an insightful source of self-reflexive play with the serial practices of a TV series: there are astonishing parallels between the thirteen cassettes and television serials as a genre that allow for an enlightening (though not exhaustive) auto-reflexive examination of the communicative operating principles of television series through Hannah's serial narrative (cf. fig. 11.1). In the words of Kirchmann, one could say that *13 Reasons Why* "is the illustration of its own theory."[16] With the metaphorical tape series, TV contributes to a philosophy of its own, which at the same time only allows a scientific theory of television as it will be developed in this chapter: "[Media philosophy] has always taken place in the media and through the media. It can therefore only be encountered and exposed there, in and through the media themselves."[17]

SERIALITY, CAUSATION RELATIONS, AND RATIONALIZATION

Why did an outwardly cheerful young woman take her own life—and can this question even be answered afterward? The reasons for Hannah's decision become the series' main concern and remain at first opaque to the figures surrounding her: hardly anyone believes that their own individual behavior could be meaningful enough to provoke such fatal consequences. On the contrary, there is a chronic fatalistic pessimism among those young people that their own actions, all in all, are barely likely to have a significant influence on the course of events around them. This powerlessness appears to be an expression of a basic feeling typical of late-modernity, that in a world with a practically infinite number of possibilities and simultaneously active participants, "[t]he technical complexity and the degree of networking in the world have increased to such an extent that direct cause-and-effect relationships can only be established in exceptional cases."[18] In Rosa's words, "The social actors

Figure 11.1 *"I'm about to tell you the story of my life."* – Hannah's Serial Narrative Creates a Compulsion to Reflect Processes of Isolation and Communitization. *13 Reasons Why*, season 1, episode 1, minute 12, © Paramount Television Studios

experience their individual and political life as fleeting and directionless, i.e. as a state of frenzied standstill."[19]

In *13 Reasons Why*, the characters reach the limits of their ability to actively influence their environment. For instance, when they try to hold the rapist Bryce (played by Justin Prentice) accountable for his actions through legal means, he gets away with it unpunished. "Nothing does anything," Clay (played by Dylan Minnette) (as Hannah's most important companion) notes bitterly as he fails in the fight against the inertia and blindness of late-modern automatisms and institutions.[20] Only the privileged elite of the school are aware of their power and like to live it out, but most young people experience their social environment as a mostly indifferent and faceless mass, in which occasional, superficial, and inconsequential encounters take the place of stable and deep social relationships, and any attempt to make things positive must fail.

To still be able to experience community as influenceable and thus livable, it is necessary to regularly reassure oneself that society can still be shaped by individual actions. Hannah takes on this role in the form of her serial cassette story: every single negative episode in her life—the exposure after her first kiss, the spreading of compromising images on social media, the circulation of rumors, insinuating slurs, etc.—appears as a significant part of her suffering with an almost inevitable (if not entirely plausible) outcome. "Life is unpredictable, and control is just an illusion. . . . And sometimes all that unpredictability is overwhelming. . . . And it makes us feel small and powerless," Hannah dictates into her tape recorder, while she visualizes and tries to order the dense network of her social interactions in a diagram.[21] "And once I took a look back and I finally understood how everything happened"—piece by piece, Hannah acquires a logic of past events as a continuous narrative, which may not be complete, but is nevertheless self-contained.[22] While constantly occupying themselves with their compromising phones, the young, disorientated characters lack perhaps the most important instrument for visualizing late-modern life in all its complexity: the television series. In Engell's view, serial TV would be the only chance to develop an understanding of the principle of cause and effect:

> Only as a construction, causality is itself "causal" . . . For something to be made visible as the consequence of a cause and to become effective [. . .], it must be called the cause of a consequence, it must cause that consequence as the cause. In short: only in series can there be causes and consequences and thus causality. Causality and seriality are inextricably linked.[23]

But there are no TV sets present in the lonely world of *13 Reasons Why*, and the lost young people must help themselves. As in a crime thriller, Hannah takes the matter into her own hands, and she becomes a television detective in her own cause, thus creating—like the television series in which she lives—"a concept and practice of causation."[24] While Hannah forensically reassembles and painstakingly reconstructs the strands of causality, she makes the hardly comprehensible causal principles of the social actions in her environment sensually perceptible and clear again. In the style of a playwright, she thus rescues the "belief that the life of the individual really has a shape and a course, and the determining forces can be identified."[25] This feeling to be a vivid part of causation relations is necessary to live in a community in the first place: life in community must be perceived as something that can be shaped by individuals, so that they also feel bound by the collective mutual obligations and responsibilities. Maybe television only suggests that our lives, even under late-modern conditions of growing fragmentation and individualization, are still interconnected through relations of causation and a rationally logically ordered path of events, or as the characters put it over and over again, "Everything affects everything."[26] However, only this allows the audience to understand social reality as a susceptible system—a habitable place to live which can be shaped through individual decisions. "What happens to us, it may only have the sense that we make of it. But I do know that it's in telling the story that we learn who we are and maybe see who we might become," summarizes the psychotherapist in the last episode of the series.[27] Following Mittell, who uses the concept of "Complex TV" to describe the specific nature of contemporary "Quality TV," serial television is characterized by the fact that it combines the actions of the ensemble to a vivid and thus convincing "chain of events over time."[28] It is only in the face of television series that our otherwise fragmented and seemingly random social coexistence still appears as a coherent fabric of mutual conditions, obligations, and causes, in which actions entail consequences. A late-modern life with serial TV shows is better than a life without them, because they demonstrate that we still have a life that deserves the name as it can be lived together.

FATAL DECISIONS: SUBJUNCTIVE ALTERNATIVES

If, however, one's own actions actually have consequences, this leads to the agonizing question of whether one's own decisions are reasonable or wrong, communalizing or isolating. "One thing. If one thing had gone differently somewhere along the line, maybe none of this would have happened," analyses the successful football player, Zach (played by Ross Butler), but hardly any of the characters were able to fully appreciate the effects of their actions at the moment of their decisions.[29]

For Luhmann, it is a typical problem of large systems that the "long-term effects of decisions that can no longer be identified" are hardly transparent for the individual in view of the "over-complex and no longer tractable causal relationships," although "it is clear that without decisions damage could not have occurred."[30] The future must always remain "a horizon of uncertainty"; but, in a community, we want to be able to shape the future through our individual decisions.[31]

Television has the task of transforming this typically modern "uncertainty into security."[32] For these reasons, playing through certain key decisions and alternative courses of action becomes the leitmotif of both the cassette and the television series itself. The school psychologist regrets in court that he did not prevent a crying Hannah from leaving his office after the failed consultation meeting. While he imagines an alternative course of action, in which he speaks to Hannah with commitment, empathy, and insistence, gives her hope despite the hopeless situation, and finally rips the constantly ringing phone off the line and throws it aside, he confesses with tears: "I could have done more. . . . I was just trying to do the right thing. I was following protocol."[33] Interestingly, Porter (played by Derek Luke) was only able to make this admission because Hannah's cassette narrative allowed him to become fully aware of the consequences of his own wrong decision to let the person seeking help go without results. Even if the decisions can no longer be revised, the serial narrative gives justified cause for hope that future decisions could be made differently.

Clay also struggles with his decisions that could have been made with less isolating effects. The young man misses the chance to kiss Hannah at least four times, who is obviously interested in him, and to initiate a couple relationship. If the constantly changing role expectations, gender relations, and performance requirements under late-modern conditions create chronic uncertainties in decision-making, the cassette series at least allows an examination of alternative courses of action. This play with possibilities, initiated by Hannah's narrative, runs through the entire television series, in which decisions are repeatedly put to the test. This procedure appears to Kirchmann as a typical procedure for television series of a "reflexive thematization of alternative selection options in the narrative process itself, in the form of alternative and at the same time antinomic drafts of action within a narration."[34] As, in principle, every "narrative can be understood as a fundamental operation with options at every branching point, as a technique of event selection," Kirchmann observes, especially for late-modern television, "a massive increase in subjunctive narrative forms."[35]

The question of what is the right decision in a particular late-modern life situation, of what is considered appropriate and community-building, is increasingly becoming a challenge as modernization progresses, because the criteria and methods for systematic decision-making provided by modernity are not always functional, and the number of decision options is practically unlimited. Moral criteria, which emerged in relatively easily comprehensible living conditions of the pre-modern era, are (due to their rigid attribution criteria in view of the complexity and diversity of late-modern life situations) completely ruled out as a method of decision-making: they fail due to the multitude of morally ambiguous life situations. Earlier forms of traditional, institutionalized, and role-related dissemination of knowledge for problem solving thus reach their limits, and not all everyday decisions can be evaluated by modern special facilities like law and court.[36] In communities, all members must become aware of the effects of their decisions even beyond legal attributions and are also able to make appropriate decisions spontaneously and at the concrete moment.

Television series, in turn, take up decision-making in complex life situations that elude traditional problem-solving mediation by church, state, and family. Television shows such as *13 Reasons Why* help each single subject to understand its own responsibility and yet own capability to shape the path of life. "I should have kissed her," Clay reproaches himself again and again. Even if it must remain uncertain whether his intervention really could have redirected the tragic course of action, the "talking in the subjunctive" at least allows the soothing certainty "that everything could just as well have been or could have become completely different," and that decisions in a social context always have effects, even if they are not always immediately visible.[37] Due to the dramaturgical connotations, decisions can then be assessed on the basis of whether the following effects are desirable or undesirable, whether decisions have communizing or isolating consequences. While the characters in the fictional world have to try out their bad decisions in a dysfunctional universe, thus the television series allows the viewer to evaluate, on the basis of the recurring late-modern life situations and their variations of decisions, which of the courses of action shown are more suitable for community building than others and which would only intensify their loneliness.

BEHAVIORAL OFFERS FOR LATE-MODERN LIFE SITUATIONS

One of the main features of the late-modern way of life is the exponential increase in the number of opportunities to shape one's life generated by rapid social change. The number of morally or legally unambiguous life situations is constantly decreasing as the complexity of social interactions grows with modernization. Thus, in late-modernity, "individuals are forced to negotiate lifestyle choices among a diversity of options," and their life becomes a constant search for the "right" behavior in the "pluralization of contexts of action."[38] Inherently tenacious democratic processes of political decision-making, inflexible institutions such as schools, parties, and associations, and the nuclear communities of marriage, parenthood, and friendship, which are themselves struggling for survival, are not suitable anymore for making plausible and appropriate behavioral offers for the numerous new types of life situations.[39]

Serial fictional television increasingly enters this gap, becoming an almost unrestrictedly available, universally understandable, and permanently accessible institution of the enculturation process.[40] For Hickethier, one of the central functions of the television series is "to provide models and patterns of behavior, how one has to behave in the world."[41] To this end, television series allow their protagonists to "play through different types of behavior and opinions, which are juxtaposed and presented to the viewers on individual themes, and which must prove their appropriateness."[42] The constant changes taking place within modernity require each individual to adapt to these new conditions so that interactions between members of society remain possible and the community remains functional.

For this modernization process to succeed, the fictional life situations shown by television series must be sufficiently comparable with the real-world life experience of the television audience.[43] This is also the particular strength of contemporary television series. Although the young people in *13 Reasons Why* intellectually understand what their teacher tells them about Bandura's theory of social learning in the communication class, the reality of their lives speaks a different language: the girls, for example, feel pressured in a never-ending beauty contest and find themselves as fair game among disoriented young men, from whom social media, disproportionate wealth, and constantly available online eroticism have taken any sense of appropriate gender-related behavior.[44] Between alcohol abuse, sexually transmitted diseases, and the opioid epidemic, low-threshold access to anabolic steroids and weapons, a dysfunctional approach to rampant psychopathologies and experiences of sexual violence, our young heroes are mainly on their own. This is because even the adults, constantly preoccupied with themselves and their own problems, are haunted by the challenges of late-modern life.

But the teens are not completely alone. This becomes most obvious in the episode of dance. Such rituals of initiation offer the prospect of suspending the automatisms of loneliness, at least for the time being, which makes them (just like the party) particularly attractive to young people. But the ballroom remains alien to contemporary serial adolescents. On the one hand, because they are no longer used to participating in such a custom overloaded with physicality and subtle forms of non-verbal communication, on the other, because new rules of the game have long since been enforced here: flasks are pulled out of jackets, compromising images circulate on cell phones, and social belonging depends on the availability of an SUV smelling of new cars. While Lord Huron is gently singing of *The Night We Met*, Clay is visibly straining to find appropriate behavior for this unknown life situation. He therefore digs in his memory for fragments of behavior known from films: "I'm not really sure how this is done . . . I don't know if people actually ask people this like in the world, but I'm just saying: I wonder if you wanna dance."[45] After the hoped-for agreement, the slow song becomes a special challenge: while the other "gentlemen" have already put their hands suspiciously low on their partners, Clay considers these harsh approaches to be inappropriate. The social reality surrounding him is apparently not a good role model for him, and his parents and teachers did not teach him how to behave in such a situation. In this moment, he is forced to fall back on his extensive film knowledge, which he acquired as a temp at the local cinema, "Crestmont." He looks deeply into Hannah's eyes, puts his hands on her waist in a trusted and respectful manner, and remembers with Hannah the romantic "old dance movies we play sometimes at the Crestmont. Remember *Strictly Ballroom*?"[46] The constructed fictions of the cult film, even if, at times, they seem ridiculous, are sufficient at this point to navigate through the evening, creating, as Hickethier would say, a "present set of behaviors that offer the viewer a frame of reference within which he can move with some certainty."[47]

But *Strictly Ballroom* is not enough for the late-modern challenges that follow. Clay always reaches his limits when it comes to finding his way in unfamiliar situations. For example, as a young man, when a young woman, who has just given her unambiguous consent to shared intimacy, suddenly and unexpectedly rejects you and yells at you, should you, despite all caution, give in to this young woman's urgent request to leave the room or would it be appropriate, perhaps even necessary, to at least demand an explanation? (cf. fig. 11.2). Even if the fictional late-modern living conditions demand this of their characters, answers to these questions can hardly be demanded from anyone—not even from our television heroes, whose task cannot be to present ideal-typical and patent-like solutions for even the most improbable variations of everyday occurrences. It can also be confidently demanded of an advanced television viewer that they can assess that not every behavior shown is worthy of imitation in itself and that television characters are instructive role models precisely because of their misjudgments, naivety, and gaps in knowledge. Rather than simply providing copyable, "instant" behavioral patterns, television series design a process of "permanent behavioral modeling of the participants" for the purpose of a successful and sustainable "modernization of society."[48] The fictional young people in *13 Reasons Why* are then treated in exactly the same way as the television viewers. It is precisely because the characters lack television series in their world that the series narrative on the tapes, with its opportunities for behavioral modeling and offers for modernizing one's own behavior, is so important. In late modernity, serial television narratives thus stand between a multitude of still existing but dysfunctional socialization instances as perhaps the only effective mass medium, which probably plays the most promising role in the foundation of communities through modern behavioral offers, without substituting the multifaceted structure of socializing influences.[49]

Figure 11.2 "Why didn't you say this to me when I was alive?" – Clay Retrospectively Regrets His Decisions Which Intensified Isolating Effects. *13 Reasons Why*, season 1, episode 11, minute 44, © Paramount Television Studios.

TIME FOUNDATIONS AND COLLECTIVE MEMORY

Whereas a circular understanding of time dominated in pre-modernity, the transition to modernity for Anderson is characterized by the feeling of a "homogeneous, empty time" of simultaneity without direction.[50] In modernity, time became an important "medium for coordinating action," through which a community coordinates itself and thus becomes capable of acting.[51] Nevertheless, the culturally constructed time system must remain a foreign object as it opposes the natural perception of the time sequences of nature, body, and culturally and historically habituated rituals. In late-modernity, there is also "a mixing, individualization and pluralization of time patterns," and the uniformly running time as a collective experience threatens to break apart into a "polychronic time culture" of compressed individualized "subject times."[52]

Communities, however, need time, because all human communication, practices of consensus building and conflict resolution but also experiences of mental and physical closeness always have a temporal course. Thus, late-modern time culture stands in antagonistic contradiction to the principles and time needs of community building. But modernity, in order to defend its successes, is also dependent on a complex and dense time structure. Television, and in particular the television series, contribute their part to dealing with this contradiction in everyday life in a practical way, without being able to resolve it completely, by mediating between the two legitimate interests of time order: television series create a collective sense of time in which communities can be realized, and thus make possible the modernization processes within the accelerating social reality with its specific needs for temporal compression.

Under late-modern conditions, and not least due to the widespread popularity of non-linear distribution channels, television's time-founding functions through programming are subject to rapid change, which in *13 Reasons Why* are self-reflectively played out in a media-nostalgic way. But even if late-modern television lacks the programming process, the core principle of serialization, the organization of narrative and reception as interconnected parts, remains. Hannah Baker's tapes also signal their episodic-serial character through their physical form of presentation alone: they force an orderly listening to one cassette tape after the other and are divided into narratively meaningful units that are nevertheless dependent on and refer to each other. The possibility of the collective experience of time survives as the logical and future-oriented sequence of divided fragments of events that necessarily lie in the past. Community, albeit invisible, is thus no longer created here only by the immediate temporal simultaneity of reception but by the creation of a shared history that materializes in the serial narrative of Hannah's tapes as in *13 Reason Why* itself. The cassette series, which the listeners can access as a community, reassures them that they are all part of a shared past. The serial character of Hannah's narrative allows them to access and retrieve their mutual history collectively. History means sharing a common idea of the past and certain practices, reviving them so that they always remain part of the common present. While in late-modernism, the interest in shaping the future and in knowing the dynamic current events gains the upper hand, television series and their stories allow a return to one shared history. TV serials produce what Fabeck calls a "distance from the events, which represents their exclusive condition of experience . . . which makes [history] possible in the first place."[53] This allows us to pass on knowledge from one generation to the next, and even, due to rapid social change, to update it within a generation, that is to constantly modernize the society. Hannah's 13-part series season shows how the two decisive safeguarding functions necessary for the preservation of a collective memory are manifested in television, namely "'safeguarding forms of duration' through storage techniques," and "'safeguarding forms of repetition' through performative media such as rites as forms of renewal, participation, and appropriation."[54] One may watch television series alone, and yet one is taking possession of a common cultural treasure that television secures and makes available in duration and repetition. Just as every form of historiography simplifies, abridges, and idealizes the overwhelming complexity of the past into a representation that can be mastered by humans, Hannah's story, despite all efforts, is never able to grasp all the influential factors, let alone reproduce them. It is precisely this reduction of an endless stream of events to something mentally controllable that makes the experience of divided history possible in the first place.

This hope to experience a shared past of closeness is also the reason for the striking media nostalgia that drives the protagonists of *13 Reasons Why*: the old-fashioned tapes express a longing for past times that seem attractive because (according to the logic of modernization as an age of ever-increasing loneliness) communities must have once existed in them that were only lost with late modernity. Nostalgia is the memory of an idealized history of communities that can no longer be accomplished in the present. The physical materiality and haptics of the cassette tapes, the indexical inscription of Hannah's voice on the endless magnetic strip, the possibility of personal sharing and (temporary) appropriation of the common treasure of history—all these possibilities of direct access to history are the basis of a media nostalgia that has long since become an omnipresent stylistic device in many other television series such as *Stranger Things*, *Bates Motel*, and *Cobra Kai* as a promise of past communities. The rewinding of collective history makes it possible to recall moments of possible communalization to remember *The Night We Met*.

NEO-RELIGIOUS CULT COMMUNITIES

With her narrative as a suffering martyr who takes the burden of the modern "sins," Hannah creates a cult around her prophetic passion story and its incarnation of the 13 tapes. Hannah's cassette series produces phenomena that can be described for pre-modern scriptural monotheistic religions, such as Christian church morality. Just think about Hannah's rules about how to use her tapes as "sacred script" ("Rule number 1: you listen. Number two: you pass it on."[55]) and the "punishments" for those who resist following them, how the decoration of everyday objects with ornaments and iconographic symbols turns the industrial mass products (tapes, map, shoe box) into a unique "holy relic," the ritualized ceremonies of "worship," and interpretation to decipher the "deeper meaning" of the anecdotal story and its tragic dynamics, from which Hannah emerges as a lonely "martyr," uniting the world in a common "belief" that her pain should not have been in vain, how this story resounds through her disembodied and omnipresent voice like a melancholy "sermon," proclaiming a new "moral" order for late-modernity, how the collective repetition of the "Scripture" produces truthful "myths."

The cult phenomena that emerge in *13 Reasons Why* through Hannah's tapes refer to the diverse community-building functions of television series through the potential for meaning they offer, which arises from what Hills calls "neo-religiosity." Luckmann and Berger had described how societies are dependent on producing universally valid truths in order to be able to interact and communicate meaningfully with each other on the basis of this common understanding of the world. The fixed standardized stream of signs produced (for example) by religions creates a "symbolic universe" in whose order each individual is protected from the anomie of sensory loneliness can experience himself or herself as part of the greater whole and thus experience transcendence.[56] With modernization and secularization, the need for a worldview system that gives meaning is not lost.[57] On the contrary, according to the needs of an increasingly liberal, highly differentiated, and dynamically changing society the manifestations of religion have changed, as seen through the emergence of a market of religions, by moving the practice of religion into the non-public private sphere or by negotiating religious topics in popular culture.[58] For Hills, television is predestined to create such neo-religious experiences. Without allowing the fan cultures generated by television to be misunderstood as religion in the narrower traditional sense, television generates various practices of collective worship, canonization, and ritualization of its own, thus transferring the procedures of institutionalized church religion into forms that are applicable to modernity.[59] In modernity, television fulfills comparable functions of socialization like the pre-modern institutions of the church, but they are different systems which should not be mixed up.

The ritualization practices that are released from the serial have a communalizing effect—for the characters, but also for the audience in front of the TV. Modernization and secularization created a chronic lack of meaning, because ritual acts no longer play a primary role in them. Even the routines (e.g., commuting between home and work), habits (e.g., brand loyalty), and compulsive neurotic actions (e.g., checking whether the door is locked) that emerged with modernity may help to avoid losing oneself in the sheer infinity of possible actions, but they remain meaningless and do not come close to the transcending power of pre-modern cults.

In *13 Reasons Why*, too, the characters find their usual daily rituals increasingly pointless. The communal meals (when no one listens to each other and the ignorant father prefers to sink into the iPad), the over-staged narcissistic team sports tournaments, and even the daily showers are becoming an increasing burden: "I turned the water on just now, and I thought about it all, the whole thing, taking clothes off, dealing with hair, and I just . . . I couldn't do it. . . . We shower, like, every day, and it's just, a lot."[60] What everyday life has to offer here may create a certain degree of order, but hardly any communities, let alone transcendence. The ritual of listening to Hannah's tapes, on the other hand, is quite different. While young people ritualistically listen to Hannah's tapes and pass them on, in times of social fragmentation they experience themselves again as part of a larger whole. For the young people, this is not easy to cope with at first (not least because this experience is accompanied by feelings of guilt). Some even resist the possibility that their individualistic life, the idea of a completely independent and liberated subject, is just an ideology. The mythical reality of the cassette series becomes the basis for new and urgently needed joint communication, enlightenment, and reconciliation, which only become possible again through the ritualized listening that Hannah had prescribed and is then experienced as a commonly shared reality. This common reality allows young people to experience an unexpected community of meaning, just as television viewers of TV series such as *13 Reasons Why* become part of an invisible global community of "common sense." However, this reality is not a fixed entity. The heroes of the series in the fictional world, just like those watching the series on television, also produce their own text. "Seriality, textual density, and, perhaps especially the nonlinearity of multiple time frames and settings" of Quality TV shows "create the potentially infinitely large metatext," which fans expand into an independent universe of meanings through their own supplementary texts like their own characters, storylines, and pre-stories.[61] What is called "fan fiction" in reality also takes place in *13 Reasons Why*, when Clay records a 14th part on the rear side of Hannah's last tape. At the same time, new metatexts emerge in conversations, in court, and on the internet, through which Hannah's tale of woe becomes what Hills calls an "endlessly deferred narrative," and thus "cult."[62] Through their own speculations, interpretations, and fantasies, the young people, as well as the TV spectators, experience a complete, self-contained, and consistent world—a community of truth.

TELEVISION AS A PRODUCER OF TRUTH AND ORDER

Truth, as a binding consensus on the nature of shared social reality, is a necessary condition for people to be able to interact meaningfully with each other in a social context. But as the stability and reliability of the knowledge and value system within modern societies always remain fragile, this is associated with a chronic uncertainty as to the extent to which the other members of society still feel committed to a concept of interconnected, universally valid truth. Especially in an individualistic, liberal society, communities remain dependent on a consensus about what is generally accepted as true and what is rejected as untrue.

However, the young people in *13 Reasons Why* do not really know what they can believe in at first. Depending on their own interests, they all tell what they want; what is right and what is wrong gradually becomes indistinguishable. This mode of unrestrained spreading of rumors, defamation, and excuses is only met with bitter resistance with Hannah's cassette series. Even though almost all members of the school community are ultimately aware that Hannah's stories are essentially true, some stick to the mode they have practiced, which is to fob off her narrative (or at least parts of it) as freely invented. Because Justin (played by Brandon Flynn) was incapable of protecting his girlfriend from being raped by Bryce, he convinces himself and his girlfriend that the truth is not what Hannah had described on the tapes. Also, the rapist himself puts on a mask of sublime credibility for the court and tells an entirely fictional story, behind which he tries to hide his own deep loneliness, which appears to be implausible even to himself.[63]

Because each individual has no immediate interest in a concept of truth, from which responsibilities would arise, they fight against it. The fact that characters even consider it realistic to be able to artificially withhold the truth about their own misdemeanors appears as a strange underestimation of the ability of serial fictional narratives to appear vivid, logical, and plausible—and thus true. Of course, Hannah's subjective 13-part narrative cannot lay claim to complete accuracy of detail, and a certain appeal of the series is also that the television viewer as well as the characters can never be completely certain that the stories of the two series are "really" true at all times. But ultimately, the thirteen episodes of the cassettes generate their own power of an inescapable reality, which the young people—who lose themselves between dubious "photo-shopped" images, trivial pleasantries, and the pressure to constantly stage themselves and their success—have long since become unaccustomed to. As in the world of *13 Reasons Why*, there are no longer any TV series that could produce communities of meaning, so Hannah's cassette series creates an overwhelming sense of honesty that becomes a burden for the young people. But this honesty ultimately appears to be the last chance to overcome the late-modern loneliness, and is therefore ultimately no longer really questioned by anyone.

In that sense, the television viewers themselves can consider themselves lucky to live in a world in which television series exist. For Keppler, with reference to Gehlen, television becomes the central place for conveying meaning within late-modern societies: it conveys to viewers a feeling for "what the historical, social and cultural present beyond their own living environment is," it gives them "a more or less strongly shared understanding of what is possible and impossible here and now, tempting and repulsive, urgent or indifferent," and thus "makes a collective consciousness of the present possible."[64]

Television series are therefore not "mirrors of society," but they themselves participate in a complex interdependent process of founding social reality.[65] Despite (or perhaps because of) highly individualized, globalized, and networked living conditions, late modernity is also dependent on a more or less uniform canon of values and norms, which makes it possible to foresee the behavior of others to a sufficient degree, which is what makes social interaction within a complex society possible in the first place. Through the construction of universally valid self-evident facts, television series create the "minimum of mutual trust that must be presupposed for the existence of communities and thus for an entire society" which is at risk being lost in an individualized, heterogeneous, and solipsistic modern society.[66] Even if distribution channels, aesthetics, and usage practices are always changing, television series with their familiar characters, sets, and props create the certainty that what was true in the last episode will be true in the next episode: that truth is a stable, reliable matter.

Again and again, the young people in *13 Reasons Why* are plagued by the uncertainty that there are no longer things that can be taken for granted in their lives, that even the most basic categories which organize society—such as truth and falsehood, right and wrong, love and hate—could become ineffective and meaningless: "Everything's broken. And I don't think any of it can be fixed."[67] But through Hannah's series, they gradually regain the confidence that even within their late-modern social reality, there are generally valid concepts, binding criteria, and clear rules, which makes a sense of community possible again. In the cassette tapes, as in the television series itself, an inalienable, indisputable truth is thus inscribed: although television series are freely invented texts, an even stronger truth emerges from them, a meta-reality that seems more real than the intangible truths of science or the subjective everyday perception of reality. While life in late modernity here and then feels somehow surreal, like being part of an unreliable parallel world full of inconsistencies and lies, seriality produces—for our fictional TV heroes as well as for the "real-world" audience in front of the screens—a new concept of reality and common sense satisfying the high requirements of the late modernity to stabilize the confidence that collective life is possible even under the complex and isolating conditions of the contemporary society.

TELEVISION'S POWER, HUBRIS, AND THE LAST COMMUNITY

Just as *13 Reasons Why* is a media-reflexive exploration of the extent to which television series participate in processes of community building, the series provokes a very similar question as to how mass media can be held responsible for their real-world interventions. The television series led to an extremely controversial public discussion about the influence of television on the behavior of its young viewers. Parents, teachers, and psychologists have expressed concern that the series could have a bad influence on young people and even incite them to suicide; some professional associations have even demanded a ban.[68] Netflix felt compelled to create a variety of interventionist metatexts around the series: fade-ins, text panels, and introductory clips warn against "Language, Sex, Drugs, Sexual Violence" and the theming of "tough real-world issues."[69] In short videos, which precede the seasons, the actors hope for an open discourse on tabooed problems of young people and refer to the pastoral care on the phone and the offers on

13ReasonsWhy.info (cf. figure 11.3). The first three seasons are followed by a kind of "14th episode" entitled "Beyond The Reasons" with expert discussions between the actors, series creators, and experts, in which the central themes are dealt with and the decisions of the characters are also questioned and classified.[70]

The extent and variety of metatext arranged around a television series due to its possible negative effects seem unprecedented. "Enjoy the show. Enjoy the conversation. And take care of each other," is the actors' credo, and their characters also formulate well-meant but surprisingly explicit instructions for action within the fictional world; for example, when Clay leaves the office of the school psychologist and speaks to him, almost directly into the camera: "the way we treat each other, look out for each other, it has to get better somehow."[71]

In this variety of obviously strenuous intervention efforts, which are very atypical for television series, an astonishing mixture of boundless overestimation and at the same time astonishing underestimation of television and its audience is articulated. On the one hand, the series believes itself capable of making such an intense impression on young people that they would even harm themselves in individual cases. But, on the other hand, serial TV also does not want to rely on its own powerful communitization potentials. While in the series the "Suicide Prevention" posters in the high-school hallways

Figure 11.3 **"Once you start talking about it, it gets better." – The Nondiegetic Interventions in *13 Reasons Why* Partly Relativize the General Community-Building Functions of Serial Television.***13 Reasons Why*, season 3, episode 1, minute 1, © Paramount Television Studios.

are torn up by the angry characters, *13 Reasons Why* surrounds itself with an arsenal of self-protection methods.

In the series, the characters share a collective guilt among themselves: "You think you could have changed anything. What does that make you? God?"[72] This is the question that Tony (played by Christian Navarro) asks a terribly guilty-feeling Clay, who imagines that he has set in motion a chain of tragic misfortunes through a regrettable but trivial human misjudgment—but who only becomes aware of the dense interweaving of causes and effects, options and offers for action, history, and memory, beliefs and rituals, values, and norms in the social context through the cassette series. Contradictorily, the television series can, in Tony's words, be burdened with a godlike responsibility that rationalizes the complexity of social coexistence into individual factors, and thus at the same time totally over-simplifies societal interactions. A society that unilaterally ascribes systematic complicity in such tragic cases to its aesthetically demanding, narratively complex, and discursively progressive television series misjudges and endangers the important role of late-modern television series as perhaps the most important community-building institution that it still has left.

13 Reasons Why tells us—as it is typical for contemporary television series—about life in an age of increasing loneliness. Because the hostile living conditions of their late-modern reality have turned out to be unlivable for the young people, Clay sees in his nightmares a "post"-modern decayed world that has been destroyed by environmental destruction, robotization, and resource warfare. As in their own reality, the young people are completely on their own: "Fighting an inhospitable world that took away their childhood. Having to become adults before their time, trying to take their world back."[73]

Cynically, it is the death of Hannah Baker that becomes a turning point in the life of the lonely ones, as her cassette series gives hope for a new sense of community—behind and in front of the screen surface. In *13 Reasons Why*, people are initially trapped in a world in which nothing and no one can show them how it could be possible to lead a meaningful life and counteract late-modern isolation. But when fictional seriality finally enters their TV-free lonely world, their lives seem to be logically ordered again, positively changeable through appropriate behavior, connected by a shared history, common memories, a collective reality that makes communities possible. Hannah's painful truth seems at first to tear apart the already isolated figures; but in the end, it is precisely this series that slowly brings the solitary characters together again, and a sense of mutual responsibility, trust, and community is once again created. In the end, the completely exhausted and tormented characters can even bury the tapes, as Hannah's serial narrative has completed its task to build an invisible and immaterial, but tangible and durable community: "We had to love each other at the end of it all."[74]

Television series allow us to meet the challenges of modernity and to master its errors without questioning its obvious successes: a free, comfortable, progressive life. TV enables us to adapt to modernity by providing us with new experiences of community—and at the same time, by constantly modernizing us. At the same time, however, a tendency toward further modernization potentially only means new, even more overwhelming loneliness—and it is unclear whether the serial fictional television of the future will be able to counteract it.

NOTES

1. This chapter is based on my contribution to an edited book on *Fernsehwissenschaft und Serienforschung. Theorie, Geschichte und Gegenwart (post-)televisueller Serialität* ("Theory, Past, and Present of (Post-)Televisual Seriality") by Denis Newiak, Dominik Maeder, and Herbert Schwaab, published by Springer VS in 2021, cf. Newiak (2021).

2. See, Ulrich Beck, *Weltrisikogesellschaft: Auf der Suche nach der verlorenen Sicherheit* (Frankfurt a.M.: Suhrkamp, 2007); Hartmut Rosa, *Beschleunigung und Entfremdung: Entwurf einer kritischen Theorie spätmoderner Zeitlichkeit* (Berlin: Suhrkamp, [2013]2018); Andreas Reckwitz, *Die Gesellschaft der Singularitäten: Zum Strukturwandel der Moderne* (Berlin: Suhrkamp, 2017); Denis Newiak: Die Einsamkeiten der Moderne. Eine Theorie der Modernisierung als Zeitalter der Vereinsamung (Wiesbaden: Springer VS, 2022).

3. Francis Fukuyama, *The End of History and the Last Man* (New York, NY: The Free Press, 1992), 328.

4. Lutz Niethammer, *Kollektive Identität: Heimliche Quellen einer unheimlichen Konjunktur* (Reinbek: Rowohlt Taschenbuch, 2000), 513.

5. Zygmunt Bauman, *Liquid Love: On the Frailty of Human Bonds* (Cambridge; Malden: Polity Press, [2003] 2014), xi–xii.; Zygmunt Bauman, *Gemeinschaften: Auf der Suche nach Sicherheit in einer bedrohlichen Welt* (Frankfurt a.M.: Suhrkamp, [2009] 2017), 155–156.

6. Anthony Giddens, *Modernity and Self-Identity: Self and Society in the Late Modern Age* (Stanford, CA: Stanford University Press, 1991), 33–34.

7. Reinhold Schwab, *Einsamkeit: Grundlagen für die klinisch-psychologische Diagnostik und Intervention* (Bern/Seattle: Huber, 1997), 22; my translation.

8. Ferdinand Tönnies, *Gemeinschaft und Gesellschaft. Abhandlung des Communismus und des Socialismus als empirischer Culturformen* (Leipzig: Fues, 1887).

9. Denis Newiak, *Einsamkeit in Serie. Televisuelle Ausdrucksformen morderner Vereinsamung* (Wiesbaden: Springer VS, 2022).

10. Denis Newiak, "Nicht-Ort Bates Motel. Vorüberlegungen zu einer Ikonografie der Einsamkeit in der amerikanischen Moderne," *VZKF Schriften zur Kultur- und Mediensemiotik* 4, no. 5 (2018): 79–122.

11. Karel Mácha, "Der einsame Mensch in der Industriezivilisation," *Internationale Dialog-Zeitschrift* 1, no. 3 (1968): 291–297 (own translation).

12. Denis Newiak, "Telemediale Narrative und Ästhetiken spätmoderner Vereinsamung am Beispiel von 13 Reasons Why," in *Teen TV: Repräsentationen, Rezeptionen und Produktionen zeitgenössischer Jugendserien*, ed. Florian Krauß and Moritz Stock (Wiesbaden: Springer VS, 2020), 65–94.

13. Dieter Oberndörfer, *Von der Einsamkeit des Menschen in der modernen amerikanischen Gesellschaft* (Freiburg im Breisgau: Rombach, [1958] 1961).

14. Gregor Balke, *Episoden des Alltäglichen—Sitcoms und Gesellschaft: Eine Wissenssoziologische und Hermeneutische Lektüre* (Weilerswist: Velbrück Wissenschaft, 2015), 140; Lothar Mikos, "Fernsehen und Film—Sehsozialisation," in *Handbuch Mediensozialisation*, ed. Ralf Vollbrecht and Claudia Wegener (Wiesbaden: VS Verlag für Sozialwissenschaft, 2010), 247; my translation.

15. See Matt Hills, *Fan Cultures* (London: Routledge, 2010); Lorenz Engell, "Folgen und Ursachen: Über Serialität und Kausalität," in *Populäre Serialität: Narration—Evolution—Distinktion: Zum seriellen Erzählen seit dem 19. Jahrhundert*, ed. Frank Kelleter (Bielefeld: Transcript, 2012), 241–58; Irene Neverla, *Fernseh-Zeit: Zuschauer zwischen Zeitkalkül und Zeitvertreib. Eine Untersuchung zur Fernsehnutzung* (München: Ölschläger, 1992); Knut Hickethier, "Die Fernsehserie—Eine Kette von Verhaltenseinheiten. Problemstellungen für die Seriendiskussion," *Beiträge zur Film- und Fernsehwissenschaft* 33, no. 43 (1992): 11–18.

16. Kay Kirchmann, "Philosophie der Möglichkeiten: Das Fernsehen als konjunktivisches Erzählmedium," in *Philosophie des Fernsehens*, ed. Oliver Fahle and Lorenz Engell (München: Fink, 2006), 157; my translation.

17. Lorenz Engell, "Tasten, Wählen, Denken. Genese und Funktion einer philosophischen Apparatur," in *Medienphilosophie: Beiträge zur Klärung eines Begriffs*, ed. Stefan Münker, Alexander Roesler, and Mike Sandbothe (Frankfurt a.M.: Fischer-Taschenbuch-Verlag, 2003), 53; my translation.

18. Hans von Fabeck, *Jenseits der Geschichte: Zur Dialektik des Posthistoire* (München: Fink, 2007), 137; my translation.

19. Rosa, 64–65; my translation.

20. *Thirteen Reasons Why*, season 2, episode 11, "Bryce and Chloe," dir. Jessica Yu, aired May 18, 2018, digitally released on Netflix.

21. *Thirteen Reasons Why*, season 1, episode 12, "Tape 6, Side B," dir. Jessica Yu, aired March 31, 2017, digitally released on Netflix.

22. Ibid.

23. Engell, "Folgen und Ursachen," 249; my translation.

24. Ibid., 242–243.

25. Erving Goffman, *Rahmen-Analyse: Ein Versuch über die Organisation von Alltagserfahrungen* (Frankfurt a.M.: Suhrkamp, 2016), 598; my translation.

26. *Thirteen Reasons Why*, season 2, episode 13, "Bryce and Chloe," dir. Kyle Patrick Alvarez, aired May 18, 2018, digitally released on Netflix.

27. See *Thirteen Reasons Why*, season 4, episode 10, "Graduation," dir. Brian Yorkey, aired June 05, 2020, originally released on Netflix.

28. Jason Mittell, *Complex TV: The Poetics of Contemporary Television Storytelling* (New York, NY; London: New York University Press, 2015), 10.

29. *Thirteen Reasons Why*, season 1, episode 8, "Tape 4, Side B," dir. Gregg Araki, aired March 31, 2017, digitally released on Netflix.

30. Niklas Luhmann, *Soziologie des Risikos* (Berlin: de Gruyter, 1991), 35; my translation.

31. Niklas Luhmann, "Risiko und Gefahr," in *Soziologische Aufklärung* (Opladen: Westdeutscher Verlag, 1990), 130; my translation.

32. Ibid.

33. *Thirteen Reasons Why*, season 2, episode 9, "The Missing Page," dir. Kat Kandler, aired May 18, 2018, digitally released on Netflix.

34. Kirchmann, 163.

35. Ibid.

36. Alfred Schütz and Thomas Luckmann, *Strukturen der Lebenswelt* (Neuwied: Luchterhand, 1975), 292; Niethammer, 513.

37. Kirchmann, 171.

38. Giddens, 5.

39. Tim Dant, *Television and the Moral Imaginary: Society Through the Small Screen* (Basingstoke: Palgrave Macmillan, 2012), 119–120.

40. Larry Gross and Michael Morgan, "Television and Enculturation," in *Broadcasting Research Methods*, ed. Joseph R. Dominick and James E. Fletcher (Boston, MA: Allyn and Bacon, 1985), 223.

41. Knut Hickethier, "Fernsehen, Rituale und Subjektkonstitutionen: Ein Kapitel Fernsehtheorie," in *Medienrituale: Rituelle Performanz in Film, Fernsehen und Neuen Medien*, ed. Kathrin Fahlenbrach, Ingrid Brück, and Anne Bartsch (Wiesbaden: VS Verlag für Sozialwissenschaften, 2008), 53.

42. Knut Hickethier, "Die Fernsehserie und das Serielle des Programms," in *Endlose Geschichten: Serialität in den Medien*, ed. Günter Giesenfeld (Hildesheim: Olms, 1994), 67.

43. Hickethier, "Die Fernsehserie—Eine Kette von Verhaltenseinheiten. Problemstellungen für die Seriendiskussion," 15.

44. *Thirteen Reasons Why*, season 1, episode 3, "Tape 2, Side A," dir. Helen Shaver, aired March 31, 2017, digitally released on Netflix.

45. *Thirteen Reasons Why*, season 1, episode 5, "Tape 3, Side A," dir. Kyle Patrick Alvarez, aired March 31, 2017, digitally released on Netflix.

46. Ibid.

47. Hickethier, "Die Fernsehserie und das Serielle des Programms," 68; my translation.

48. Ibid., 71.

49. Dant, 144–145.

50. Benedict Anderson, *Imagined Communities: Reflections on the Origin and Spread of Nationalism* (London: Verso, 1983), 24.

51. Hermann Lübbe, *Im Zug der Zeit: Verkürzter Aufenthalt in der Gegenwart* (Berlin, Heidelberg: Springer, 2003), 315; my translation.

52. Irene Neverla, "Medien als soziale Zeitgeber im Alltag: Ein Beitrag zur kultursoziologischen Wirkungsforschung," in *Die Mediatisierung der Alltagswelt*, ed.

Maren Hartmann and Andreas Hepp (Wiesbaden: VS Verlag für Sozialwissenschaften, 2010), 184–185; my translation; Neverla, *Fernseh-Zeit*, 53; my translation.

53. von Fabeck, 161.

54. Aleida Assmann, *Der lange Schatten der Vergangenheit: Erinnerungskultur und Geschichtspolitik* (München: Beck, 2006), 58; my translation.

55. *Thirteen Reasons Why*, season 1, episode 1, "Tape 1, Side A," dir. Tom McCarthy, aired March 31, 2017, digitally released on Netflix

56. Peter L. Berger and Thomas Luckmann, *The Social Construction of Reality* (New York, NY: Anchor Books, 1967), 103.

57. Thomas Luckmann, *Das Problem der Religion in der modernen Gesellschaft: Institution, Person und Weltanschauung* (Freiburg: Rombach, 1963), 38.

58. Thomas Luckmann, *The Invisible Religion: The Problem of Religion in Modern Society* (New York, NY: Macmillan, 1967), 104.

59. Hills, *Fan Cultures*, 117. Matt Hills, "Media Fandom, Neoreligiosity and Cult(ural) Studies," in *The Cult Film Reader*, ed. Ernest Mathijs and Xavier Mendik (Maidenhead, Berkshire, England, New York, NY: Open University Press/McGraw-Hill Education, 2008), 117, 137–139.

60. *Thirteen Reasons Why*, season 1, episode 5, "Tape 3, Side A," dir. Kyle Patrick Alvarez, aired March 31, 2017, digitally released on Netflix.

61. Sara Gwenllian-Jones and Roberta E. Pearson, "Introduction," in *Cult Television*, ed. Roberta E. Pearson and Sara Gwenllian-Jones (Minneapolis, MN: University of Minnesota Press, 2004), ix–xx.; Robert Blanchet, "Quality TV. Eine kurze Einführung in die Geschichte und Ästhetik neuer amerikanischer Fernsehserien," in *Serielle Formen: Von den frühen Film-Serials zu aktuellen Quality-TV und Onlineserien*, ed. Robert Blanchet, Kristina Köhler, Tereza Smid, and Julia Zutavern (Zürcher Filmstudien 25. Marburg: Schüren, 2011), 40; my translation.

62. Hills, *Fan Cultures*, 143.

63. *Thirteen Reasons Why*, season 2, episode 11, "Bryce and Chloe," dir. Jessica Yu, aired May 18, 2018, digitally released on Netflix.

64. Angela Keppler, *Mediale Gegenwart: Eine Theorie des Fernsehens am Beispiel der Darstellung von Gewalt* (Frankfurt a.M.: Suhrkamp, 2006), 316–317.

65. Giddens, 27.

66. Peter L. Berger and Thomas Luckmann, *Modernität, Pluralismus und Sinnkrise: Die Orientierung des modernen Menschen* (Gütersloh: Verlag Bertelsmann-Stiftung, 1995), 68.

67. *Thirteen Reasons Why*, season 2, episode 9, "The Missing Page," dir. Kat Candler, aired May 18, 2018, digitally released on Netflix.

68. Anastasia Schnitzer, "Aufklärung über Suizidalität im Jugendalter in der Netflix-Serie 13 Reasons Why," in *Teen TV: Repräsentationen, Rezeptionen und Produktionen zeitgenössischer Jugendserien*, ed. Florian Krauß and Moritz Stock (Wiesbaden: Springer VS., 2020), 95–112.

69. *Thirteen Reasons Why*, season 1, episode 1, "Tape 1, Side A," dir. Tom McCarty, aired March 31, 2017, digitally released on Netflix.

70. Newiak, "Fernsehserien gegen spätmoderne Einsamkeiten," 148-151.

71. *Thirteen Reasons Why*, season 1, episode 13, "Tape 7, Side A," dir. Kyle Patrick Alvarez, aired March 31, 2017, digitally released on Netflix.
72. *Thirteen Reasons Why*, season 1, episode 11, "Tape 6, Side A," dir. Jessica Yu, aired March 31, 2017, digitally released on Netflix.
73. *Thirteen Reasons Why*, season 4, episode 8, "Acceptance/Rejection," dir. Sunu Gonera, aired June 5, 2020, digitally released on Netflix.
74. *Thirteen Reasons Why*, season 4, episode 10, "Graduation," dir. Brian Yorkey, aired June 5, 2020, digitally released on Netflix.

BIBLIOGRAPHY

Anderson, Benedict. *Imagined Communities: Reflections on the Origin and Spread of Nationalism.* London: Verso, 1983.

Asher, Jay. *Thirteen Reasons Why.* New York, NY: Random House, 2012.

Assmann, Aleida. *Der lange Schatten der Vergangenheit: Erinnerungskultur und Geschichtspolitik.* München: Beck, 2006.

Balke, Gregor. *Episoden des Alltäglichen—Sitcoms und Gesellschaft: Eine Wissenssoziologische und Hermeneutische Lektüre.* Weilerswist: Velbrück Wissenschaft.

Bauman, Zygmunt. *Liquid Love: On the Frailty of Human Bonds.* Cambridge; Malden: Polity Press, 2015.

———. *Gemeinschaften: Auf der Suche nach Sicherheit in einer bedrohlichen Welt.* Frankfurt a.M.: Suhrkamp, [2009] 2017.

Beck, Ulrich. *Weltrisikogesellschaft: Auf der Suche nach der verlorenen Sicherheit.* Frankfurt a.M.: Suhrkamp, 2007.

Berger, Peter L., and Thomas Luckmann. *The Social Construction of Reality.* New York, NY: Anchor Books, 1967.

———, and Thomas Luckmann. *Modernität, Pluralismus und Sinnkrise: Die Orientierung des modernen Menschen.* Gütersloh: Verlag Bertelsmann-Stiftung, 1995.

Blanchet, Robert. "Quality TV. Eine kurze Einführung in die Geschichte und Ästhetik neuer amerikanischer Fernsehserien." In *Serielle Formen: Von den frühen Film-Serials zu aktuellen Quality-TV- und Onlineserien,* edited by Robert Blanchet, Kristina Köhler, Tereza Smid, and Julia Zutavern, 37–70. Zürcher Filmstudien 25. Marburg: Schüren, 2011.

Dant, Tim. *Television and the Moral Imaginary: Society through the Small Screen.* Basingstoke: Palgrave Macmillan, 2012.

Engell, Lorenz. "Tasten, Wählen, Denken. Genese und Funktion einer philoso-phischen Apparatur." In *Medienphilosophie: Beiträge zur Klärung eines Begriffs,* edited by Stefan Münker, Alexander Roesler, and Mike Sandbothe. 53–76. Frankfurt a.M.: Fischer-Taschenbuch-Verlag, 2003.

———. "Folgen und Ursachen: Über Serialität und Kausalität." In *Populäre Serialität: Narration—Evolution—Distinktion: Zum seriellen Erzählen seit dem 19. Jahrhundert,* edited by Frank Kelleter, 241–58. Bielefeld: Transcript, 2012.

Fabeck, Hans von. *Jenseits der Geschichte: Zur Dialektik des Posthistoire.* München: Fink, 2007.

Fukuyama, Francis. *The End of History and the Last Man.* New York, NY: Free Press, 1992.

Giddens, Anthony. *Modernity and Self-Identity: Self and Society in the Late Modern Age.* Stanford, CA: Stanford University Press, 1991.

Goffman, Erving. *Rahmen-Analyse: Ein Versuch über die Organisation von Alltagserfahrungen.* Frankfurt a.M.: Suhrkamp, 2016.

Gross, Larry, and Michael Morgan. "Television and Enculturation." In *Broadcasting Research Methods*, edited by Joseph R. Dominick and James E. Fletcher, 221–34. Boston, MA: Allyn and Bacon, 1985.

Gwenllian-Jones, Sara, and Roberta E. Pearson. "Introduction." In *Cult Television*, edited by Roberta E. Pearson and Sara Gwenllian-Jones, ix–xx. Minneapolis, MN: University of Minnesota Press, 2004.

Hickethier, Knut. "Die Fernsehserie—Eine Kette von Verhaltenseinheiten. Problemstellungen für die Seriendiskussion." *Beiträge zur Film- und Fernsehwissenschaft* 33, no. 43 (1992): 11–18.

Hickethier, Knut. "Die Fernsehserie und das Serielle des Programms." In *Endlose Geschichten: Serialität in den Medien*, edited by Günter Giesenfeld, 55–71. Hildesheim: Olms, 1994.

Hickethier, Knut. "Fernsehen, Rituale und Subjektkonstitutionen: Ein Kapitel Fernsehtheorie." In *Medienrituale: Rituelle Performanz in Film, Fernsehen und Neuen Medien*, edited by Kathrin Fahlenbrach, Ingrid Brück, and Anne Bartsch, 47–58. Wiesbaden: VS Verlag für Sozialwissenschaften, 2008.

Hills, Matt. "Media Fandom, Neoreligiosity and Cult(ural) Studies." In *The Cult Film Reader*, edited by Ernest Mathijs and Xavier Mendik, 133–48. Maidenhead, Berkshire, England, New York, NY: Open University Press/McGraw-Hill Education, 2008.

———. *Fan Cultures.* London: Routledge, 2010.

Keppler, Angela. *Mediale Gegenwart: Eine Theorie des Fernsehens am Beispiel der Darstellung von Gewalt.* Frankfurt a.M.: Suhrkamp, 2006.

Kirchmann, Kay. "Philosophie der Möglichkeiten: Das Fernsehen als konjunktivisches Erzählmedium." In *Philosophie des Fernsehens*, edited by Oliver Fahle and Lorenz Engell, 157–72. München: Fink, 2006.

Lübbe, Hermann. *Im Zug der Zeit: Verkürzter Aufenthalt in der Gegenwart.* Berlin, Heidelberg: Springer, 2003.

Luckmann, Thomas. *Das Problem der Religion in der modernen Gesellschaft: Institution, Person und Weltanschauung.* Freiburg: Rombach, 1963.

Luckmann, Thomas. *The Invisible Religion: The Problem of Religion in Modern Society.* New York, NY: Macmillan, 1967.

Luhmann, Niklas. "Risiko und Gefahr." In *Soziologische Aufklärung*, 126–162. Opladen: Westdeutscher Verlag, 1990.

———. *Soziologie des Risikos.* Berlin: de Gruyter, 1991.

Mácha, Karel. "Der einsame Mensch in der Industriezivilisation." *Internationale Dialog-Zeitschrift* 1, no. 3 (1968): 291–297.

Mikos, Lothar. "Fernsehen und Film—Sehsozialisation." In *Handbuch Mediensozialisation*, edited by Ralf Vollbrecht and Claudia Wegener. Wiesbaden: VS Verlag für Sozialwissenschaft, 2010: 241–251.

Mittell, Jason. *Complex TV: The Poetics of Contemporary Television Storytelling.* New York, NY; London: New York University Press, 2015.

Neverla, Irene. *Fernseh-Zeit: Zuschauer zwischen Zeitkalkül und Zeitvertreib. Eine Untersuchung zur Fernsehnutzung.* München: Ölschläger, 1992.

———. "Medien als soziale Zeitgeber im Alltag: Ein Beitrag zur kultursoziologischen Wirkungsforschung." In *Die Mediatisierung der Alltagswelt*, edited by Maren Hartmann and Andreas Hepp, 183–194. Wiesbaden: VS Verlag für Sozialwissenschaften, 2010.

Newiak, Denis. "Nicht-Ort Bates Motel. Vorüberlegungen zu einer Ikonografie der Einsamkeit in der amerikanischen Moderne." *VZKF Schriften zur Kultur- und Mediensemiotik* 4, no. 5 (2018): 79–122.

———. "Telemediale Narrative und Ästhetiken spätmoderner Vereinsamung am Beispiel von 13 Reasons Why." In *Teen TV: Repräsentationen, Rezeptionen und Produktionen zeitgenössischer Jugendserien*, edited by Florian Krauß and Moritz Stock, 65–94. Wiesbaden: Springer VS, 2020.

———. "Fernsehserien gegen spätmoderne Einsamkeiten: Formen telemedialer Vergemeinschaftung am Beispiel von '13 Reasons Why.'" In *Fernsehwissenschaft und Serienforschung. Theorie, Geschichte und Gegenwart (post-)televisueller Serialität*, edited by Denis Newiak, Dominik Maeder, and Herbert Schwaab. Wiesbaden: Springer VS, 2021: 103–157.

———. *Die Einsamkeiten der Moderne. Eine Theorie der Modernisierung als Zeitalter der Vereinsamung.* Wiesbaden: Springer VS, 2022a.

———. *Einsamkeit in Serie. Televisuelle Ausdrucksformen moderner Vereinsamung.* Wiesbaden: Springer VS, 2022b.

Niethammer, Lutz. *Kollektive Identität: Heimliche Quellen einer unheimlichen Konjunktur.* Reinbek: Rowohlt Taschenbuch, 2000.

Oberndörfer, Dieter. *Von der Einsamkeit des Menschen in der modernen amerikanischen Gesellschaft.* Freiburg im Breisgau: Rombach, [1958] 1961.

Reckwitz, Andreas. *Die Gesellschaft der Singularitäten: Zum Strukturwandel der Moderne.* Berlin: Suhrkamp, 2017.

Rosa, Hartmut. *Beschleunigung und Entfremdung: Entwurf einer kritischen Theorie spätmoderner Zeitlichkeit.* Berlin: Suhrkamp, [2013] 2018.

Schnitzer, Anastasia. "Aufklärung über Suizidalität im Jugendalter in der Netflix-Serie 13 Reasons Why." In *Teen TV: Repräsentationen, Rezeptionen und Produktionen zeitgenössischer Jugendserien*, edited by Florian Krauß and Moritz Stock, 95–112. Wiesbaden: Springer VS, [2013] 2018.

Schütz, Alfred, and Thomas Luckmann. *Strukturen der Lebenswelt.* Neuwied: Luchterhand, 1975.

Schwab, Reinhold. *Einsamkeit: Grundlagen für die klinisch-psychologische Diagnostik und Intervention.* Bern/Seattle: Huber, 1997.

Tönnies, Ferdinand. *Gemeinschaft und Gesellschaft. Abhandlung des Communismus und des Socialismus als empirischer Culturformen.* Leipzig: Fues, 1887.

Chapter 12

Can Watching TV Make Me a Unicorn?

TV and the Ethics of Decency

Steven A. Benko and Eleanor Jones

Television shows record change while preserving the status quo. Locations and sets often remain the same: *Buffy the Vampire Slayer* had Springdale; *Community* had the study room in the library; Jerry Seinfeld never upgraded his apartment, maybe because it defied the laws of physics; *Friends* ended when the characters moved out of apartments they had lived in for ten television seasons. While places remain the same, television shows rely on changes—some big, some small—in order to create the conflict that drives the plot. Sitcoms may thrive on repetition, however characters or their circumstances need to evolve or the show becomes stale and boring. Shows will employ a story arc to create drama and conflict before a new status quo is established. Enough needs to remain familiar so that audience expectation is satisfied. Characters are a both/and: both static so that they remain familiar and predictable, and dynamic so that they do not become rote, boring, or stale. On *Schitt's Creek,* the Rose family had to struggle against and then make peace with their circumstances; characters on the CW's slate of super-hero shows (dubbed, "The Arrowverse") have to grow into their powers and the responsibilities that come with them; in *She-Ra*, Adora has to come to terms with her new identity while saving the planet from the Horde; the main characters on *Atypical* have to adjust their lives to their changing identities: Sam trying to live a "normal life" on the autism spectrum and Casey coming out as bisexual. The change-but-remain-the-same aspect of television reflects the experience of viewers: the audience remains in living rooms and houses that do not physically change but are the setting for physical, emotional, and psychological growth.

This chapter focuses on how characters, tethered to the show's premise, change over time by occupying different subject positions. These subject positions need to make sense to who the characters are but must also allow the

characters to act in new and meaningful ways. For example, on *Jane the Virgin*,
it was not just that Jane had to choose between Rafael or Michael, but she had
to be in a position to choose which meant that she had to be the person for
whom one choice and not another made sense from that particular subject position. The second concern of this chapter, then, is the moral dimensions of what
it means for the audience to see a character achieve, or fail to achieve, a certain
subject position. We argue that beyond watching television for entertainment
or aesthetic reasons, that TV, particularly in this era, is more intentional about
questions of moral character. The result is that the TV viewing can be an occasion for the audience testing out the possibilities of achieving that subject position and the moral meaning of what is possible from that position.

Premiering on CBS in the fall of 2019, *The Unicorn* was a traditional
sitcom about family, work, and friends. The plot of the show follows Wade
Felton (played by Walter Goggins) as he navigates being a widower, father
to two teenage daughters, and owner of his own landscaping company. The
show begins one year after the death of his wife with his friends encouraging
Wade to move on with his life and date again. Wade is reluctant because he
does not want to upset his daughters; his friends are insistent because they
feel Wade would take better care of himself and his daughters if he were hap-
pier and in a relationship. Upon signing him up for an online dating app and
seeing how many women respond to his profile, they dub him "the unicorn":

Michelle: You are a unicorn.
Wade: A what?
Michelle: A unicorn. You know that elusive creature that all single women are
    looking for? See, most of the men on these dating sites are having midlife
    crisis, they're getting divorced, buying Porsches. They're hooking up with
    25-year-olds.
Delia: You're a devoted father, you are a devoted husband, and not for nothing
    but you haven't had sex with anybody besides Jill in over 20 years. So, you're
    factory fresh, buddy.[1]

This setup establishes the tension that will move the plot of most episodes:
Wade has relative ease meeting women but is constantly worried about meeting his obligations as a father. He will only schedule plans if they do not
conflict with his parenting responsibilities and will cancel any plans should
his daughters need him. Each step in any relationship is thought through with
how it will impact his daughters.

The Unicorn was not a major show on CBS. It had low ratings and only
lasted for thirty-three episodes before being cancelled (season 2 was cut short
due to COVID). What makes *The Unicorn* noteworthy is that it is obvious
in its efforts to show how the characters think about themselves from very

specific subject positions. Those positions shape or influence what matters to the characters. Wade Felton's daughters matter the most to him; the influence of his memories of his deceased wife also matter, however, that fades over time as he opens himself up to new relationships. Wade's friends matter to him and Wade and his daughters matter to Wade's friends; they are often shown as acting as surrogate parents or authority figures when Wade cannot be there or realizes that he cannot meet his daughters' needs. The Feltons, the other adults and their children, all function as one large, extended family. Because of the ways they matter to one another and the intensity of those investments they becomes more or less obligated to behave certain ways around each other. The three families socialize together, frequently eating meals with one another, and coordinate child care when one of them has a work or personal obligation. While the men (Forrest, played by Rob Corddry and Ben, played by Omar Benson Miller) are friends in their own right, they met through Jill's friendship with their wives (Delia, played by Michaela Watkins and Michelle, played by Maya Lynn Robinson).[2]

The Unicorn shows Wade, as well as the other characters, anchored by what matters to them while actively thinking about and attempting new ways of being as they approach midlife transitions through kids growing up and becoming more independent, as well as professional successes and failures. Because of this premise, it provides useful examples of the ways that television shows can model different subject positions for the audience based on what matters to the characters and what then matters to the audience. Wade's successes become possible ways of being a father; Wade's struggles and failures can be read as warnings of moving too far away from what should matter, or how the different things that matter ought to be prioritized, if one is going to successfully occupy a specific subject position.

What *The Unicorn* demonstrates, and many shows of this particular era of television demonstrate as well, is how what matters to a character maps how they interact with other characters, what they invest in emotionally and materially, and how other things come to matter relative to what matters to someone in a particular subject position. Because mattering differentiates people and groups from one another and is about resource allocation, mattering is both political and moral: mattering involves questions of who or what ought to matter, who or what deserves to matter, and to what extent can someone or something that matters make a claim to emotional and material resources, especially since someone or something matters to them, too.[3] The moral question of mattering has to do with the effort to satisfy one's moral obligations and demands while at the same time preserving the individuation that mattering creates. Television is uniquely poised to show this tension because it is the conflict between desire and obligation that fuels conflict, moves the plot, and makes characters interesting and dynamic. Negotiating this tension between what matters to an individual or community and ethical and moral obligations that would call for less self-interested, more altruistic, behavior is what Todd May calls "decency" in his book *A Decent Life: Morality for the Rest of Us*. May gives form to what is usually a vague term meant to convey a sense of goodness and amiability. The audience of *The Unicorn* watches Wade Felton become a decent father in the sense that he is justified in giving attention to what matters to him but, recognizing that something matters to others, specifically his daughters, him getting his way is not at their expense. Wade Felton is not a unicorn because of his attractiveness to women; his consistent decency is what makes him a unicorn.

TELEVISION AND MAP MAKING

The Unicorn does not fit some of the most common definitions of "prestige TV." It was never nominated for any awards, it did not redefine the sitcom genre, and the low ratings make it difficult to think that it was "appointment viewing." What it does reflect, though, is what Martin Shuster identifies in *New Television*: that the current era of television reflects an awareness of normative breakdown or normative emptiness and that, absent any objective moral truths to guide or make sense of behavior, TV shows are navigating how to live in a morally empty universe.[4] *The Unicorn* is not as heavy as other shows that have navigated this terrain (e.g., *The Sopranos, Breaking Bad*, or *The Wire*). However, the occasion of the mother's death and the need for Wade to step out of his defined role and be both father and mother, as well the need for Delia and Michelle to fulfill the role of family friends, quasi-aunts, and mother figures, reflects a breakdown in the traditional roles that each character inhabits. The show slowly peels away the layers of saying goodbye to Jill as each of the characters finds out who they are in this new space. The uniqueness of their situation has them mapping out new ways of relating to each other, though the ways they work and do not work shows what is possible and impossible from the different subject positions each character inhabits.[5] In S2E7, "Swerve and Volley" Wade is struggling to teach Grace (played by Ruby Jay) how to drive. Ben offers to help but his extreme caution stresses Grace; Ben is Grace's soccer coach but they cannot relate to each other this way. His wife Michelle steps in to help, but her enthusiasm for the freedom that driving brings also stresses Grace out. Michelle tells Grace that having a driver's license is the next step to adulthood and lists all the new opportunities coming her way. Grace is upset because the death of her mother forced her to grow up too fast, and she feels overwhelmed by the thought of more adult responsibilities. Here, Ben and Michelle are stepping in for both Wade and Jill, but ultimately it is not their place, and Wade has to set everything right. Grace has to negotiate her own experiences as a teen on the cusp of adulthood and comes to a new understanding of herself as both young and responsible.

The Unicorn can depict Wade getting parenting right—and sometimes getting parenting wrong—not just because it is a standard sitcom trope that father knows best (though that is part of it) but because the way that Wade parents both is, and can be, a possibility for the viewer. For Shuster, though television screens a possible reality for the viewer, there has to be a conflict to move the plot.[6] The source of that conflict is dissatisfaction with the way things are; the resolution provides a new way that things are that is either an endorsement (this is the way they ought to be) or lament (this is how it is going to be). Television may be fictional, but the demand that the plots make sense to the viewer makes television real. Television becomes how the viewer understands what it means to occupy a specific subject position from which the world is made sense of. Shuster puts it thusly,

> How can we acknowledge the fictional nature of television series even as, on the other hand, we acknowledge the role these works of art play in our world—that they are constitutive of how we make sense of our world, of each other, of ourselves? Put most simply, what does it mean to view such works of art as relevant to understanding how we go on with each other? Or do not?[7]

Television maps the possible by creating and reflecting the reality that the audience inhabits. In order for that reality to create and reflect a familiar world for the viewer, there has to be a practical engagement with meaningful people and objects.[8] The viewer watches characters engage with things or people that matter to them. How well that does or does not go, or how meaningful those interactions are, becomes a script for how the viewer engages what matters to them. Sitcoms like *The Unicorn* must present everyday life in realistic and familiar ways. Beyond that, the show ought to depict, so that the viewer can see, how the character engages with something that matters to them. That engagement has to be in a way that makes sense to the viewer, something along the lines of "if this matters, then one ought to behave thusly" and vice versa.[9] In Shuster's words, TV allows viewers to "go visiting"—to see how people occupying a certain subject position interact with others and pursue what matters to them (and whether they do so successfully or unsuccessfully): "it allows those listening to visit other perspectives, perspectives that open up temporalities and spaces they are otherwise unable to occupy."[10]

As much as television shows allow viewers to see the consequences of other perspectives and behaviors played out, television both suggests what it would look like to occupy a certain subject position and engage with people and things from that perspective, and the need to move from one position to another when being in that subject position prevents access to what matters. No episode of *The Unicorn* does this better than S2E3, "It's the Thought That Counts." Forrest gifts Ben's son Noah (played by Devin Bright) a water gun. Ben takes it away because he knows it is dangerous for his son to be seen holding something shaped like a pistol, even if it is blue; he tells Forrest, "It's not the color of the gun. It's the color of my son."[11] This episode problematizes the White habitus that Delia and Forrest live in.[12] It is from inside this White habitus that Forrest believes Ben and Michelle to be free from the harms of racism. Because Forrest is blind to their color, he believes that the world treats Ben and Michelle in a colorblind way as well. This instance causes a disruption of Forrest's and Delia's White habitus that leads them to rethink their interactions with Ben and Michelle. They wonder if behaviors that made sense to them are actually forms of micro and macro-aggressions.

The episode features conversations between the different characters articulating their perspectives on race and what they think about themselves and what they aspire to be. Each character is a possibility for differently positioned audience members: the White friend (Delia) who has been too familiar with her Black friend and now wonders if she has said something wrong; the Black woman (Michelle) who is frustrated and tired of educating everyone around her about how oblivious they are to the experience of Black Americans:

Michelle: Well, any time you take a toy away from a child, it's a big deal. But if you're serious about rededicating yourself, it's gonna take a whole lot more than . . . You know what? I'm gonna stay out of this one. 'Cause I just had this talk last week with my study group, and after Zoe's gymnastics, and I'm only halfway through Delia's mile-long "how can I help you?" e-mail. I am exhausted. My Black hurts.[13]

Forrest claims that he wants to undertand and be an ally to Ben and Michelle. Ben then tells Forrest that to be the ally he thought he was and wants to be that he needs to listen and believe Black people when they tell them about the racist discrimination that they face:

Forrest: I want to do better.
Ben: But this, what you're doing now, this isn't better. Come on, man, you're putting all your guilt on me, because you want me to make you feel better about the things I have to deal with.
Forrest: I-I don't know if I'd put it exactly like that, but. . .
Ben: Forrest, I love you, and I know you mean well, but I cannot do your work for you.
Forrest: I know it's hard out there for Black people, but I didn't think it was like that for you.
Ben: Why not?
Forrest: Because I know you.

Ben: Oh, so you think the struggle with racial injustice only applies to the Black people you don't know.

Forrest: Apparently I did, yeah.

Michelle: Okay, I couldn't help but overhear . . . Screw it, I was eavesdropping. Now, this type of thing might be new to you, but this is all we've ever known. It's our life every single day. Do you know how often I-I am followed around a store, or somebody touches my hair without my permission?! Ooh, don't get me started. I was about to get started. Ben: Don't get started, babe.

Forrest: [whispers] I'm glad she didn't get started.

Ben: You really want to know what you can do?

Forrest: Yes.

Ben: Listen.

Forrest: Listen. Yeah. Great. Ah, good, good, good. Listen. Mm. Listen . . . to . . .

Ben: Me!

Forrest: Right.

Ben: Black people.

Forrest: Black people.

Ben: And believe us. Because we get told that we're imagining things when we talk about our own experiences. Yeah. Or that when we protest, we shouldn't. Or that we're doing it wrong. Even though that is the only way anything has ever changed for us.

Forrest: [exhales sharply] I believe you.

Ben: Thank you.[14]

Typical of *The Unicorn*, the conversation is light but candid. Because the characters have been shown to care about each other, be in each other's homes, and have honest conversations with one another, the viewer is not challenged to imagine this sort of conversation taking place. It is the sort of conversation these characters can have. Furthermore, the dialogue guides the viewer through these difficult conversations by pointing out the error of thinking that racial reconciliation is work for Black Americans but goes no further than saying that listening is the work that White people need to do.[15] To be sure, it is a safe perspective for the viewer to adopt, but it might represent a shift in their perspective on race, or at the very least, a disruption of the White habitus they live in. This, though, is what practical engagement with someone who matters, about something that matters, looks like open-ness, patience, dialogue, perspective sharing. If this is not where the viewer is on the issue of race, this scripted conversation can become their script for moving to an emotional or intellectual space where they are. This supports Shuster's conclusion that television shows "suggest a possibility—no mat-ter how small—beyond or outside of the normative emptiness that they also display" of a world that the audience member desires to live in (or, alternatively, avoid at all costs) because of their own moral sensibilities.[16]

Moral perspective taking occurs through the imaginative linking of what viewers see on the screen and what they experience in their own lives. Their experience of relationships, things, emotions, or events (Shuster's example is pain) provides the criteria they use to evaluate and make judgments about what they see on the screen. However, perspective taking is not an uncritical adoption of another point of view; it is the evaluation and ranking of other criteria relative to what matters to the viewer. Shuster writes that

> to the extent that film and television series screen a world, they offer us likely the most *worldly* way of exploring criteria, whether our own or entirely distinct from ours, past or present, and they do all of this without resorting to experiments in the human world. . . . Worlds on a screen offer a means of examining the boundaries and implications, if not outright rejections and avoidances, of our criteria—when, how, if, why, to what extent, and in which ways they apply. Or do not.[17]

The viewer starts from their own subject position and can move toward or away from another place or point of view. The shift is always relative. Moving from one position to another shifts the perception or attitude toward other things or people that matter. On *The Unicorn*, Wade prioritizes his daughters and will speak openly about seeing things from their point of view. However, when he feels more comfortable wanting something or someone for himself—when his desire for that other thing, person, or relationship intensifies—his perspective shifts, and there is an emotional realignment of his priorities. By suggesting what is valuable, what is practical, what matters, and also the opposite, viewers watch characters map and remap their world. Then they evaluate those maps from their own subject position in a way that fortifies their own map, or is the occasion for the viewer shifting their own map so that they gain access to what new thing matters to them.[18] Television shows clarify what matters (what can matter, should or should not matter) in a way that establishes a meaningful and moral universe for the characters and the viewers.

TELEVISION AND MATTERING

Investment in a television show, a storyline, or characters occurs when what matters on the show intersects with what matters to the viewer. The viewer sees the character inhabit a world that allows for meaningful engagement with practical matters and concerns defined by what matters to those characters. *The Office* is a show for people who have to endure clueless bosses with boundary issues. *Arrested Development* is for people negotiating dysfunctional families. *The Unicorn* is a show for people who are invested in relationship dynamics and midlife, mid-career parenting. What makes *The Unicorn* interesting is how transparent it is about how what matters to those characters is what is supposed to matter to them given their respective subject positions. This is validating to the audience because the overlap between what matters to them and what they see on the screen shines a positive light on what is meaningful to them (the opposite is also true). Because it feels good to matter, and because it is validating when what matters also matters to others, then it makes more sense to say that the primary driver of what matters is not economic utility, but confirmation and validation that what one thinks matters actually does matter in meaningful ways.[19] To build on what Shuster argued in *New Television*: television shows viewers what is possible and lets them try out different perspectives; television shows that it is possible to realize and experience what matters as well as different avenues and arenas for realizing it.

Mattering is when a person feels like they matter and that the things they invest in emotionally and materially also matter. Philosopher Rebecca Newberger Goldstein laid the foundation for what is called "mattering theory" and defines it as a way to understand what motivates and differentiates individuals from one another. She treats mattering as foundational for human existence and connects mattering, which she defines as living a life where one pursues goals, relationships, or projects that matter, to identity and agency.[20] Newberger Goldstein claims that the mattering instinct is universal: every person has a desire to matter and have something matter to them. Every person has something that they want to achieve, the characteristics that they want to display and be recognized for, and the things that they value about themselves and others. Each of the characters on *The Unicorn* wants to be seen as a good parent. Next, they want to be understood as caring for their friends and about those friendships. The push and pull of one of these elements affects the others such that if the children are not OK, the group's attention is pulled to that. If Wade is not happy, then the group focuses on him. When Forrest loses his job, his wife Delia is most affected, but the other adults lend moral and logistical support as well.

Mattering is not just about what matters. Beyond establishing group identity and affiliation, mattering also individuates. Because mattering is how a life becomes distinct from other lives, each character on the show needs something unique that matters only to them. For example, in S1E11, "If It Doesn't Spark Joy" Michelle organizes a yard sale and encourages

the others to donate. Forrest goes through all of his belongings and realizes he has nothing to donate because he does not have "a thing" that is
his; he realizes that he is lost and adrift because nothing matters to him
(his daughter matters to him, but she also matters to his wife, Delia).
Forrest is lost until Ben gives him some vinyl LPs and that becomes his
thing. Cultural theorist Lawrence Grossberg pinpoints why Forrest feels
lost: mattering is essential to our sense of self for how it differentiates
us from others. Grossberg says "we redefine our own identity out of the
relations among our differences; we reorder their importance, we invest
ourselves more in some than in others," and it is those differences that
individuate us even though we are drawn toward contexts, events, or ways
of being that we have been told matter more than others.[21] Forrest's sense
of aimlessness culminates in him trying to revamp his job but he ends up
getting fired (S1E14: "The Wade Beneath My Wings"). He tries to find
meaning in not working but he becomes a burden to his wife. When he
has the insight that he thrives in the structure provided by employment
and getting out of the house, he commits to finding a new job and does
(S1E18: "No Matter What the Future Brings").

Forrest's struggle to find meaning in work reflects the push and pull
between what he has been told should matter to him—his job—and what
comes to matter to him. Though what matters is individuating and is a
way to distinguish oneself from another, what comes to matter is never
totally up to the individual. Society encourages and discourages certain
things from mattering more or less to individuals. Wade's decision that
his daughters matter most was not really his decision. To occupy the
subject position of "good father" his daughters had to matter the most.
How he acted from that position and what could or could not matter to
him (more or less intensely) is largely defined for him. He had room to
maneuver, but only so much. If Wade wanted to think of himself a certain way, and be seen by others a certain way, then he had to show that
his daughters mattered most to him, or rather, the greatest intensity of
mattering on his own mattering map was his daughters. He had room to
maneuver and create a space for himself in a role that was largely defined
for him. Mattering, then, is the give and take between the individual and
the social: individual preference has been shaped by repeated experiences
of social norms and expectations of what should matter and how much it
should matter. Wade's most serious relationship in season 1 is with Anna,
a doctor who works with Delia. Wade goes on multiple dates with her and
as a result ends up giving less time to his daughters. In S1E10 "Anna and
the Unicorn" Wade allows his daughters to have friends over while he is
out with Anna; this is to make them OK with him being out and for him
to feel less guilt about not being there for his daughters. He returns home

to a house filled with teenagers and realizes that he has been neglecting his responsibilities at home. He tells Anna that while he still wants to see her, he needs to spend time with his daughters:

Wade: I was. . . I was trying to tell myself that I could do this every night and I could still be a good dad, but I . . . I can't. And it's breaking my heart because I really like you. So I hope that when I say that. . . that I can't see you tomorrow, that you'll still want to see me the day after tomorrow, because I really believe that there's something here.[22]

Though Anna understands that his daughters matter to him, the relationship ends when she realizes the degree to which the memory of his late wife still matters to Wade. Before that, though, she rewards his confession with a passionate kiss and his daughters express their approval of the relationship. What Wade is doing is what Loewenstein and Moene call "self-signaling behavior," which are behaviors or activities arising from uncertainty or insecurity about what matters. People perform self-signaling behaviors to show "that they are the type of person who would engage in those activities."[23] Wade is not just letting Anna know that they matter most; in a moment of crisis, he is reminding himself that he is the person puts his daughters first. Wade's self-signaling behavior becomes a script for the audience because they see him rewarded and validated for realigning his priorities with what should matter most to him. Validation is always experienced as pleasure, and it is pleasurable to be validated. What matters is pursued because of the overlapping of pleasure and validation.[24] This is how television, among other forms of mass culture, interpellates individuals into hegemonic norms and behaviors. Merely being told that something should matter, and how it should matter, does not make it matter. But seeing how a character feels pleasure and validation at experiencing what matters to them creates a desire in the viewer to experience that pleasure and validation for themselves, and this could intensify their own mattering maps or shift the location of things and people on them.[25]

   Thinking of mattering as a map that places objects closer or further away from what matters most to the individual explains both the relational nature of what matters to an individual and also how an individual will position and move (as well as be positioned and be moved) on that map. Newberger Goldstein coined the phrase "mattering map" to explain the relativized way things that matter come to matter more or less. If something matters then something else will also matter because of its relationship to that first thing. Maps shift as new things come to matter. In season 1, Wade feels he has to sacrifice time with Anna because he worries that his daughters need him. In season 2, he begins to chafe at having to make the same sacrifices.

In S2E06, "Overnight Sensation" Shannon (played by Natalie Zea) spends the night at Wade's house. Shannon is embarrassed when Wade's younger daughter sees her coming down from the bedroom in Wade's shirt to get coffee.[26] Wade's response is an example of how different things that matter create tensions until they are rearranged on the map relative to other things that matter. Everyone's comfort matters to Wade, so he becomes upset because Shannon is upset. He makes her feel better by suggesting that she make breakfast (Shannon is a professional chef) for the family. In this way, Wade satisfies what matters to him: he is able to maintain his relationship with Shannon; she is able to feel comfortable by doing something that she is good at; and Wade's daughters are included in his life, which now includes Shannon. Where before, the women that Wade dated were further away from what mattered to him the most—his daughters—his map has been redrawn so that his daughters and his girlfriend are in closer proximity to one another.

Having something matter is not in itself satisfying, but being able to identify, access, and experience what matters is satisfying and gives a feeling of agency and control. If what mattered was not possible to access and experience, then one of two things would happen: life would be frustrating and unfulfilling, or something accessible would come to matter so that life would become meaningful and fulfilling. Loewenstein and Moene claim that people are able to change what matters to them and adjust their mattering map accordingly. They write that "when different things matter in different social settings then, rather than attempting to maximize according to what matters in their own immediate social environment, people can shift toward social settings in which their existing capabilities are valued."[27] Mattering maps get redrawn so that life has passion, and events and relationships can be experienced as pleasurable. The experience of something that matters being affirmed is validating because of the transfer between the thing that matters and the person that it matters to. Beyond it being validating, it is also empowering because it gives the person the space to act, to reiterate their investment, and to invest further in things that matter or divest from things that do not. Grossberg writes that empowerment "refers to the reciprocal nature of affective investment: that is, because something matters (as it does when one invests energy in it), other investments are made possible. Empowerment refers to the generation of energy and passion, to the construction of possibility."[28] Most importantly, empowerment provides the energy necessary to go on in a particular way, and, as long as that way is affirming and validating, then one will keep going in that way.

This is because being validated by what matters is validating to the point of being empowering. Being empowered then creates the possibility of performing meaningful actions from a particular subject position. Where Shuster talks about television opening up the viewer to the possible, mattering maps take that a step further: the possible, or what can be the case, is what the character and viewer want to be the case because it matters to them that it would come to pass. The intensity with which the character and the viewer invest in what they want to be the case becomes a moral ought: the possible ought to be the case.

Understanding mattering as a map explains behavior not as binary choices but as investments on a spectrum based on the intensity of what matters most at that moment. That intensity transfers over to other objects on the map, with objects in close proximity mattering more and objects further away mattering less. What accounts for an object mattering more or less is investment and return. If what matters does not provide an adequate return on the investment in time and emotion, then the map will be redrawn and something else will have to matter more. This is because "maps tell us where and how we can be absorbed—not into the self but into the world—as potential locations for our self-identification, and with what intensities."[29] Beyond that is the idea that being able to invest in what matters is empowering. The fun that Wade's daughters have with Shannon, demonstrated by their enthusiasm for her cooking, transfers back to Wade in that their investment in Shannon makes his investment in her more intense and meaningful. Wade is validated because something that matters to him matters to people that also matter. This is difficult to navigate on a sitcom like *The Unicorn* because if investment in what matters is what tells a person where they can be absorbed, Wade over-investing in what mattered to him at the expense of his daughters would come across as self-absorbed. In order for Wade to remain familiar to himself and for the show to remain familiar to the audience, the writers and actors have to keep Wade grounded in his concern for his daughters without that becoming tedious, inappropriate, or boring. It is not that Wade's daughters matter less to him, it is that what he wants comes to matter more. It is fair to say that his daughters come to matter differently to him, maybe less intensely, than they did in the immediate aftermath of their mother's death. What Wade has internalized is the idea that his happiness, in the form of what matters to him, makes his daughters happy. This is expressed in season 1, episode two when his daughter Grace says, "Dad, if you're unhappy, that means that Natalie and I are unhappy."[30] What the viewer sees is the ebb and flow of what matters and what is safe, possible, and beneficial to invest in (the opposite is also true) if one wants to remain familiar to oneself and live a meaningful life.

A DECENT UNICORN

What does the viewer gain from watching *The Unicorn*? Watching Wade and the other parents negotiate midlife parenting and relationships provides suggestions for how to negotiate similar situations. The premise of *The Unicorn*, different from shows like *The Sopranos* or *Breaking Bad*, is that it is possible to experience what matters but not at the expense of other people. *The Unicorn* is part of a cluster of shows—of which *The Good Place* is the best—that explore the social dimensions of being a better or decent person. Prior to *The Unicorn*, CBS tried and failed with shows that were in a similar vein to *The Good Place* (*Living Biblically* and *God Friended Me*, to name two). One difference between *The Good Place* and *The Unicorn* is that the characters on *The Good Place* start at a deficit and have to become good people; the characters on *The Unicorn*, particularly Wade, are already good, and his challenge is to remain so as he navigates new situations and relationships. Wade organizes his behavior by prioritizing what matters most to him: his daughters. Though there are television shows where the main character is defined by their willingness to sacrifice for others (*Highway to Heaven* or *Touched By an Angel*), and viewers can aspire to be like these characters, it would be impossible to sustain their level of altruism. What is usually the case is that a show starts with characters at some kind of moral deficit that they overcome through the maturation that occurs over time, through new relationships, or through major life changes (except on *Seinfeld*). *The Unicorn* is premised on the main character being uniquely good and changing to become good in other ways.

To keep Wade good and interesting, the writers had to justify his self-interest. Because his daughters were grieving the loss of their mother, his investment in them made sense. It had to make sense for him to come to care about himself more than he did when the audience first met him, but over time, the challenge was to avoid making him look selfish. What mattered to Wade had to shift and his new self-interest had to make emotional sense to the characters and the viewer. It made sense to the other characters because they wanted him to be happy; by extension, the audience wanted him to be happy, too. The balance that the show had to strike was that Wade could be happy but not at the expense of others. Where the show starts out showing Wade putting the needs of others before his own, the moral vision of the show, and what truly makes Wade a unicorn is his ongoing concern that he not take advantage of others in order to get what he wants. Wade's girlfriend in season 2, Shannon, who is also divorced, calls him out for not telling her that he was a widower and suggests that he could exploit his situation for selfish gain:

Shannon: We can't all have these easy, clean divorces the way you obviously have.
Wade: Right.
Shannon: What?
Wade: I-I didn't mention this?
Shannon: What?
Wade: Uh, I'm not divorced. My wife Jill, she-she died.
Shannon: Oh. But I'm the one keeping secrets. I mean, don't. . . I'm sorry. Sorry, don't get me. . . I feel, I feel terrible. You poor thing.
Wade: Uh, thank you, but. . .
Shannon: But how could you not tell me that?
Wade: I-I should have.
Shannon: [LAUGHS]: Yeah. Yeah. You bet your ass you should have.
Wade: Okay. I'm sorry.
Shannon: Wow. You're a widower. And a father, you own your own business. You must get laid a ton.
Wade: Uh, uh, no. No. Uh, I'm not that kind of guy.
Shannon: Uh-huh.
Wade: I mean, I could be. But I am not. I'm not.[31]

This short exchange reveals the essence of Wade's character: he knows who he is and how he is positioned in society. If he were to take advantage of the sympathy generated by his status as a widower, he would be taking advantage of other people. Wade knows that he can, but ought not to do that, if he is going to be true to what matters to him.

The ethics of mattering is an ethics of decency or being decent. Mattering can be intoxicating and pull people away from personal or social values: if mattering is individuating, it sets people apart from one another and creates in-and-out group dynamics based on what does and does not matter to a group of people; if having access to and experiencing what matters is validating, then there is an incentive to experience it and be validated even at the expense of others. Mattering may involve an element of self-interest, but that interest need not be expressed as selfish behavior at the expense of others. Television is an appropriate place to watch people try to negotiate what matters to them relative to what matters to other characters because this creates the conflict that drives the narrative forward and is the occasion for character growth and change. Television is an opportunity to watch people negotiate trying to be decent (or altruistic or selfish) because at the end of the day their behavior has to be justified and the audience has to be OK with the character's desires being satisfied or frustrated. What *The Unicorn* shows is that there is a link between what matters and how one treats what matters. If what matters is another person, then there is an obligation to treat them with respect. A benefit of taking this approach to what matters is that it creates stronger, more intense, bonds between individuals and what matters to them thus allowing them more opportunities to experience what matters to them relationally.

Television screens the possible and shows viewers examples of what practical engagement with people and things that matter looks like. This opens up opportunities for changes in perspectives that would allow viewers to consider feelings or points of view different from their own. Seeing what matters to other people allows the audience to see what matters to others, why it matters, and how people go about accessing and experiencing what matters to them. It is this last part—how people experience what matters to them—that marks *The Unicorn* as unique in this era of television. *The Unicorn* shows how to approach what matters decently by showing how Wade lives a fuller, more complete life by being decent toward those who matter to him.

Todd May fleshes out what it means to be decent in *A Decent Life: Morality for the Rest of Us*. May is no stranger to ethics on television: he was one of the philosophy consultants on *The Good Place*. In *A Decent Life,* he makes an argument for dialing back the requirements and expectations of normative ethical theories like Kantianism, Virtue Ethics, and Utilitarianism. He argues that they encourage a kind of altruism that is unattainable thus creating a situation where the perfect becomes the enemy of the good enough. None of us are perfect, and a life spent sacrificing what mattered would not be meaningful. May characterizes a meaningful human life, one that matters, as one where people are able "to engage in projects and relationships that unfold over time; to be aware of one's death in a way that affects how one sees the arc of one's life; to have biological needs like food, shelter, and sleep; to have basic psychological needs like care and a sense of attachment to one's surroundings."[32] The type of constant sacrifice that altruism demands would discourage people from investing in what matters to them and would make it impossible to live a meaningful life. May writes that "our lives involve projects and commitments whose importance to us may conflict at points with moral requirements. And at times we simply are not up to the task. We want to be moral beings, but for a variety of reasons, and for better or worse, our lives get in the way."[33] The things that get in the way are the obstacles to what matters. Those obstacles can take a variety of forms, from the emotional to the practical, but when those obstacles seem illegitimate or undeserved, moral shortcuts that would allow one to realize what matters become more attractive.

Decency is necessarily social. To be decent is to recognize that other people have lives to live too, and they share a time and space with us; to be decent is to not frustrate another person's access to what matters to them: "it is a matter of recognizing others as having lives to live and seeking to incorporate that recognition into our lives in ways that are reasonably workable, or, to put it in a more positive light, to navigate through the world with a certain moral gracefulness."[34] On *The Unicorn,* there is a consensus that the children are what matter most but as they become more independent a space opens up for other things to matter to the adults. When Michelle and Ben's youngest child starts kindergarten she decides that she needs to complete her education and enrolls in college. This requires a reshuffling of responsibilities in the home, but they make it work. Rarely on *The Unicorn* are someone's interests or goals diminished or played for laughs. Each person has something that matters to them and other people act in ways that show that it matters to them too. Each of the characters on *The Unicorn* respects each other; there are very few instances where they undermine each other, even if it is just for laughs. This is how the audience knows that they are decent people.

Decency on *The Unicorn* is portrayed as a reasonable sacrifice that is not altruistic. When one of the characters acts selfishly, the correction is not toward altruism but toward a more morally appropriate way of accessing or experiencing what matters to them. In S2E12, "Out With the Old," Ben is nervous about a colonoscopy and sabotages his procedure three different times; this is selfish because it upsets his wife, Delia. Wade and Forrest offer to get colonoscopies at the same time to lend moral support and because the preventative procedure would provide a benefit for the children. Wade and Forrest are able to reframe the procedure to make it less about Ben and more about care for others. Altruism would have been doing it for Ben. Decency is supporting Ben while recognizing that there is something in it for them too. Indecent behavior is not just selfish; it is also doing something that violates the norms of the subject position that one inhabits. In season 1, episode 16, "The Client," Wade is hired by a recent divorcee, Denny (played by Donal Logue), who promises Wade a large contract if he also shares tips with him about picking up women; Wade tries to play along because he needs the money. When their time together pulls Wade away from home and Denny equates his single status with Wade's, the latter is offended. Wade's signal that he is not acting like himself is that another person misidentifies what is important to Wade. Wade tells Denny that that he would rather lose the contract and money than be away from his daughters. However, he does not abandon Denny: Wade helps Denny, who is drunk, get home safely and defends

Denny as a person who is going through a difficult time and just needs a friend. He turns down Denny's request for help making a dentist appointment (he chipped his tooth biting into a frozen burrito he did not heat up enough) but Wade says he will help him and gives him a stray dog to take care of. Wade sets Denny on a path to self-sufficiency and being able to take care of another living thing. Reflecting on what just happened he tells his accountant that he can "be a good businessman and a good person."[35] For Wade, this means being a decent father, where being a decent father is putting his daughters first. This is another instance of Wade's self-signaling behavior and the viewer sees that being decent, in this case non-judgmental and supportive of another person in need, gets Wade what he needs and what he wants. In the world of *The Unicorn*, decent people get rewarded for being decent and this is why the show can function as a script for the viewer in their own life.

A criticism of *The Unicorn* is that decency only occurs at the local level. There are no episodes where there is concern about what it would mean to be decent to people who live far away or are yet to be born, two aspects of decency discussed by May in light of the current environmental crisis; *The Unicorn* keeps its ethics local and interpersonal. Decency on *The Unicorn* is in our homes, with our neighbors, families, and at work. It is a lesson in how to be decent to those who are in our immediate surroundings. On *The Unicorn,* an ethics of television viewing is about finding meaningful subject positions in situations similar to what is shown on the screen. A different television program could inspire more geographically widening concerns and reorient the viewer's mattering map on a global scale. However, for this to occur, viewers need to move beyond the idea that television consumption is passive or for entertainment purposes. The audience must see viewing as a part of a moral conversation. The reason that TV is an excellent source for mattering maps, both reiterating them and being the occasion for redrawing them, is that TV shows how complicated people are. People are complicated because of the relational nature of their mattering maps and how the changing intensity of one area of the map impacts other areas. These mattering maps with shifting intensities are illustrated in the current eras of TV. Prestige and Peak TV are defined by complex characters that cannot be reduced to one defining trait, motivation, quirk, or behavior. Complicated characters show that we are all more than just one thing and that helps to avoid reductive thinking. Part of the pleasure, then, of watching television, becomes the validation that comes from enjoying the validation of others in their particular subject positions and understanding how that desire for validation transfers back to the viewer as a strategy or tactic for negotiating what matters to them. Understood as a moral moment where what matters is emphasized or redrawn on the viewer's mattering map, television viewing is biographical. Television shows are a way that people can communicate what matters to them.

NOTES

1. *The Unicorn*, season 1, episode 1, "Pilot," dir. John Hamburg, aired September 26, 2019, originally released on CBS.

2. Writing for the *A.V. Club*, Danette Chavez says that part of the appeal of the show was its refusal to be boxed into one subgenre of sitcom: "*The Unicorn* is as much a hangout comedy as it is the story of an unconventional family. Wade's relationships with his daughters, Grace (Ruby Jay) and Natalie (Makenzie Moss), are just as developed as his friendships with married couples Delia (Michaela Watkins) and Forrest (Rob Corddry), and Michelle (Maya Lynne Robinson) and Ben (Omar Miller.) And Delia et Al. are involved in Grace and Natalie's lives, too, making this one big, happy, extended family." Danette Chavez, "The Search for Love—and Natalie Zea—Begins Anew in *The Unicorn* Season 2 Premiere," *The A.V. Club*, November 12, 2020, accessed May 15, 2021, https://www.avclub.com/the-search-for -love-and-natalie-zea-begins-anew-in-the-1845660717

3. Loewenstein and Moene make this point in "On Mattering Maps" though they are talking about it in slightly different context: mattering does indeed differentiate, however, their concern is the threat to self-esteem when someone feels as if they do not matter or that what matters to them does not matter to others. Those who threaten self-esteem by denying the value of what matters are relegated to out-group status so that self-esteem might be preserved. See George Lowenstein and Karl Moene, "On Mattering Maps," in *Understanding Choice, Explaining Behaviour: Essays in Honour of Ole-Jørgen Skog*, ed. Jon Elster (Oslo: Oslo Academic Press, 2006), 159–160.

4. Shuster draws from Arendt's take on modernity as a disconnect from the past: "the thread of tradition has become severed, implying that our access to the past is beset by uncertainty and our potential conviction in it undermined." Drawing from Benjamin, Arendt uses the image of the pearl diver who retrieves bits and pieces of a decayed, crystallized past that can be used to explain how and why things are. Storytelling reckons with these moments and helps the viewer understand what is currently the case and what might be possible in the future. On *The Unicorn* it is memories of Wade's wife, Jill, that are often brought to the surface in order to make sense of their experiences. See Martin Shuster, *New Television: The Aesthetics and Politics of a Genre* (Chicago, IL: The University of Chicago Press, 2017), 6, 60–61.

5. After an era dominated by male protagonists where misogyny was a defining character trait, there seemed to be a turn toward character who cared more about their moral character. For shows like *The Sopranos, Breaking Bad*, or *Mad Men,* the absence of a defined moral universe dislodged men, specifically white men, from their privileged status; these shows map ways for men to reassert themselves in this empty landscape. Shows like *The Good Place, The Unicorn, Living Biblically*, and *God Friended Me* still seem impacted by the disappearance of a normative morality but stress cooperation and collaboration instead of self-realization at the expense of others.

6. See Shuster, 18: "What's essential is that films produce a world, that is, they screen or project *reality*" (emphasis in original).

7. Shuster, 69.

8. See Shuster, 21.

9. The change from one subject position to another is a change in the possible. As much as a subject position is determined by social factors, it is also a perspective or attitude toward what is possible and impossible from that subject position. Certain actions and behaviors blocked in one subject position become possible in another. The subject, denied access to what matters to them, or denied access to it in a way that matters to them, shifts subject positions (or is shifted) and gains access to what matters to them or reorganizes their investments so that they have access to what (now) matters.

10. Shuster, 72.

11. *The Unicorn*, season 2, episode 3, "It's the Thought That Counts," dir. Matthew A. Cherry, aired December 3, 2020, originally released on CBS.

12. "White Habitus" is defined by Bonilla-Silva as "a racialized, uninterrupted socialization process that *conditions* and *creates* whites' racial taste, perceptions, feelings, and emotions and their views on racial matters" in Eduardo Bonilla-Silva, *Racism without Racists Color-Blind Racism and the Persistence of Racial Inequality in America* (Lanham, MD: Rowman & Littlefield, 2018), 121 (emphasis in original). Burke continues, "They argue that the white habitus prevents whites from understanding their isolation and segregation as the result of racial dynamics, using instead a colorblind lens of preference or naturalization." In Megan Burke, *Colorblind Racism* (Cambridge: Polity Press, 2019), 74.

13. *The Unicorn*, season 2, episode 3, "It's the Thought That Counts," dir. Matthew A. Cherry, aired December 3, 2020, originally released on CBS.

14. Ibid.

15. One criticism of this episode is that it is filmed from a White perspective and that the show has not completely purged itself of microaggressions and tropes that reinforce anti-Black stereotypes. It is true that the episode centers Forrest and his desire to do better, but it also lets him sit in his unease and discomfort when he realizes that he does not know what to do. More importantly, Ben and Michelle are given plenty of space to express their concerns and grievances but do not give Forrest, or the audience, a script to follow that would make the solution seem pat and quick. Ben tells Forrest that "I cannot do your work for you" and that anti-racist behavior begins with listening, but must go beyond that. See Danette Chavez, "The Unicorn Gets Topical with Some Help from Matthew A. Cherry," *The A.V. Club*, December 4, 2020, https://www.avclub.com/the-unicorn-gets-topical-with-some-help-from-director-m-1845804952.

16. Shuster, 201.

17. Shuster, 80.

18. This might feel like giving too much credit and importance to television. Shuster suggests that film and television "form a node in our very being in the world, determining lines of salience and creating possibilities, all while potentially delineating and highlighting formal elements of our agency" (Shuster, 81). This is in keeping with the idea that while television is an opportunity for perspective taking, beyond the adoption of a point of view is the opportunity for the viewer to think how a particular

action or behavior would play out for them in their life. For example, catch phrases like "that's what she said" or "how you doin?" or "you know nothing Jon Snow!" come with predictable and, in most cases, safe responses from others.

19. Loewenstein and Moene make the point that mattering disrupts standard rational choice theory but that is because what matters does not have to be something that can be bought and sold. They write that mattering is complicated by how changing social settings and roles can shift what matters to a person. Ultimately, though, they conclude that "whether it is beneficial to maximize within a particular social environment, or to shift social environments, will depend on a variety of factors. Most obviously, it will depend on which of these options provides greater opportunities for enhancement of utility" (163). What Loewenstein and Moene do not discuss is that what matters might create harm. Mattering does not operate in the neat, economical way that Loewenstein and Moene argue; the realization of what matters can bring pleasure and be validating at the same time that its realization is not advantageous to the individual or the group. See Loewenstein and Moene, 163–164.

20. Newberger says of mattering that it is necessary to believe that one matters and that one can access those things that matter, saying that "we can't pursue our lives without thinking that our lives matter" and "to be a fully functioning, non-depressed person is to live and to act, to take it for granted that you can act on your own behalf, pursue your goals and projects. And that we have a right to be treated in accord with our own commitment to our lives mattering." In Rebecca Newberger Goldstein, "The Mattering Instinct," Edge.org, March 16, 2016, https://www.edge.org/conversation/rebecca_newberger_goldstein-the-mattering-instinct.

21. Lawrence Grossberg, "Is There a Fan in the House?: The Affective Sensibility of Fandom," in *The Adoring Audience: Fan Culture and Popular Media*, cd. Lisa A. Lewis (London: Routledge; Taylor & Francis Group, 2003), 58. Mattering is about feeling familiar to oneself and feeling safe and comfortable in one's surroundings. He writes that mattering maps create "sites at which we can, at least temporarily, find ourselves 'at home' with what we care about" (60).

22. *The Unicorn*, season 1, episode 10, "Anna and the Unicorn," dir. Jay Karas, aired December 12, 2019, originally released on CBS.

23. Loewenstein and Moene, 159.

24. Grossberg writes that pleasure can take a variety of forms: satisfaction of doing what others want, enjoyment from doing what one wants to do, the fun of breaking rules, the fulfillment of desires (even if only temporary), the feeling of catharsis, the comfort that comes from escaping negative situations, reinforcement of identifying with a character, and the thrill of sharing one's emotional life. Television produces these pleasures in a variety of ways, predominantly through identification with a character and then seeing them feel pleasure and validation from a certain subject position. Grossberg's point is that a viewer is a consumer, actively engaged in the construction of meaning. They will draw meaning maps that create opportunities to feel pleasure and validation. See Grossberg, 54–55.

25. What comes to matter only does so in relation to what already matters and the intensity of what matters (or what newly matters) depends upon the possibility of realizing or actualizing those concerns. Frustration is the feeling of not getting to

experience what matters; enough frustration might lead someone to shift what matters to them (unless it matters so intensely that they continue to invest in it) so that they can experience the validation and confirmation that comes from experiencing what matters.

26. In addition to being embarrassed by the situation, Shannon's overreaction is an example of what Newberger says happens when what matters to one person is not validated by another: over-investment in what matters as a way of signaling its importance. The insecurity that comes from feeling that what matters is insignificant to others can intensify investment in those objects.

27. Loewenstein and Moene, 163.

28. Grossberg, 64.

29. Grossberg, 57.

30. *The Unicorn*, season 1, episode 2, "Breaking Up Is Hard to Do," dir. John Hamburg, aired on October 3, 2019, originally released on CBS.

31. *The Unicorn*, season 2, episode 2, "It's Complicated," dir. John Hamburg, aired on November 19, 2020, originally released on CBS.

32. Todd May, *A Decent Life: Morality for the Rest of Us* (Chicago, IL: University of Chicago Press, 2019), 156. May continues: "To treat people with dignity requires that we not shut people off from developing important life projects and significant relationships or bar them from meeting their basic biological needs. In order to thrive people must, in addition to fulfilling needs like food, sleep, and shelter, be able to engage in projects of various sorts that unfold over time, often with other people who matter to them. These projects can be of various kinds: friendships, meaningful work, love relationships, even hobbies. To prevent people from doing these things is to fail to acknowledge their dignity, that is their intrinsic value as human beings" (May, 157).

33. May, 27.

34. May, 49.

35. *The Unicorn*, season 1, episode 16, "The Client," dir. Rebecca Asher, aired on February 20, 2020, originally released on CBS.

BIBLIOGRAPHY

Bonilla-Silva, Eduardo. *Racism without Racists Color-Blind Racism and the Persistence of Racial Inequality in America*. Lanham, MD: Rowman & Littlefield, 2018.

Burke, Megan. *Colorblind Racism*. Cambridge: Polity Press, 2019.

Chavez, Danette. "The Search for Love—and Natalie Zea—Begins Anew in *The Unicorn* Season 2 Premiere." *The A.V. Club*, November 12, 2020. https://www.avclub.com/the-search-for-love-and-natalie-zea-begins-anew-in-the-1845660717.

Chavez, Danette. "The Unicorn Gets Topical with Some Help from Matthew A. Cherry." *The A.V. Club*, December 4, 2020. https://www.avclub.com/the-unicorn-gets-topical-with-some-help-from-director-m-1845804952.

Grossberg, Lawrence. "Is There a Fan in the House?: The Affective Sensibility of Fandom." In *The Adoring Audience: Fan Culture and Popular Media*, edited by Lisa A. Lewis. London: Routledge, Taylor & Francis Group, 2003.

Lowenstein, George, and Karl Moene. "On Mattering Maps." In *Understanding Choice, Explaining Behaviour: Essays in Honour of Ole-Jørgen Skog*, edited by Jon Elster. Oslo: Oslo Academic Press, 2006.

May, Todd. *A Decent Life: Morality for the Rest of Us*. Chicago: University of Chicago Press, 2019.

Newberger Goldstein, Rebecca. "The Mattering Instinct." Edge.org, March 16, 2016. https://www.edge.org/conversation/rebecca_newberger_goldstein-the-mattering -instinct.

Pribram, E. Deidre, and Jennifer Harding. "Losing our cool? Following Williams and Grossberg on Emotions." *Faculty Works: Communications* 9 (2007): 1–24.

Shuster, Martin. *New Television: The Aesthetics and Politics of a Genre*. Chicago, IL: The University of Chicago Press, 2017.

The Unicorn. Created by Grady Cooper. Aired from September 26, 2019–March 18, 2021. Originally released on CBS.*Steven A. Benko and Eleanor Jones*

Chapter 13

The Baby Yoda Effect
A Kantian Analysis of Mandalorian Ethics
James Rocha

At first glance, *Star Wars* appears to present a simplistic moral vision: Jedi good/Sith bad. This Jedi/Sith dichotomy presents an especially problematic moral viewpoint since the Jedi's alleged moral superiority clearly derives from cutting off their feelings, while the Sith's evil is connected to their embrace of so-called negative feelings (you are more powerful if you accept your fear, anger, and hatred). In actuality, it is normal and morally neutral to have feelings, but we judge someone for whether and how they act on those feelings. Of course, morality is much more complicated: it involves attachment, being in touch with all of one's feelings, and regularly experiencing at least some moral uncertainty.

To be fair, any deep dive within the *Star Wars* universe reveals that this surface depiction is misleading and the truth is much more complicated. After all, the Jedi take force-sensitive children away from their homes and pressure them into Jedi training without meaningful consent (which these children cannot give), often engage in warfare despite claiming to be pacifists (and sometimes without thoroughly examining whether they are even on the just side, as they fought for Palpatine during the Clone Wars), and betrayed Ahsoka Tano by refusing to believe her when she was being framed by another member of the Jedi order.[1] For this and other reasons, the Jedi have no reasonable claim to moral superiority, which is an idea that is explored in the sequels to the original trilogy.

Furthermore, the Jedi/Sith moral framework does not represent all of *Star Wars*. Things are much more morally complex in the various worlds that exist outside of this binary. This chapter focuses on the ethics of the Mandalorians, who can be both pacifists (under the rule of Satine Kryze) and proud warriors. They are resistant to joining either the Empire of the Sith or the Republic of the Jedi. They often take up the morally complicated trade of bounty hunting,

279

while also sticking ardently to their Creed (although there is some complexity here). The Mandalorians are depicted like many others in the *Star Wars* universe: navigating a complex array of competing values that are sometimes good and sometimes bad, but that always make demands on time and actions.

By examining the life of Din Djarin (from here on, Mando, played by Pedro Pascal) in the first season of Disney+'s *The Mandalorian* the inherent complexity of life outside of the Jedi/Sith binary is made clear. Mando readily presents himself as fully committed to two value systems: the bounty hunter code and the Mandalorian Creed. While the Creed is not specifically linked to any known religion inside or outside the *Star Wars* universe, it is not dissimilar from many religious doctrines that the audience would be familiar with. If the references to the Creed or the Way do not call to mind a specific doctrine, the audience would at least be familiar with the way that the characters on the show respond to them when they are mentioned: with a spiritual reverence that the audience would reserve for the most sacred doctrines and creeds. Furthermore, bounty hunting is Mando's job, but it is also clearly something well beyond that: to be a bounty hunter is to be committed to hunting bounties in a very specific way. The bounty hunter code, as articulated by the guild that legitimate bounty hunters work for, forms a central part of the bounty hunter identity at the same time that it allows for them to find meaningful employment and a chance to earn a living.

Given Mando's resolute commitments to both of these codes, it would appear that Mando would be immoral according to Kantian ethics: Kant requires that agents place the moral law as their ultimate authority—above any such code of conduct. To have a good will, the agent must set the moral law as the ultimate authority for all of their action choices. Yet, Mando clearly allows his Mandalorian Creed and his occupational duties to serve as his highest practical priorities, thus supplanting the top role that Kant demands be given to the moral law. Mando is not only occasionally immoral for Kant, but, in this picture, he would be evil: he knowingly places something other than the moral law as his highest priority.

But, and perhaps unfortunately for Kantian ethics, many agents exhibit similar priorities in their lives: they prioritize their religious codes (just as Mandalorians do with their Creed). Not many people who watch *The Mandalorian* are bounty hunters, but for the audience, jobs partially define who they are as persons, and they often find a variety of other values that they consistently highlight as codes they try to follow without wavering. Perhaps another reason (besides Baby Yoda/Grogu) that *The Mandalorian* is so popular is because the tension between professional and personal creed is something that resonated with the audience. It may be that *The Mandalorian* reveals that Kantian ethics is too demanding for people to follow all of the time, similar to how some of the Jedi chafed at the strict moral binary it imposed upon its members.[2] Or, perhaps, there are other moral lessons to be gleaned from season 1 of *The Mandalorian*, specifically, by looking at the relationship between Mando and Baby Yoda in the first eight episodes.

The Child (from here on, Baby Yoda) provides the spark that ignites Mando's recognition that his moral duty does ultimately take precedence over religious or occupational creed.[3] In this fashion, *The Mandalorian* exhibits how Kantian ethics can place the high demand on agents that they always prioritize the moral law while also recognizing that they also prioritize so many other things. The bounty hunter code would require that Mando hand over the bounty to the Client (played by Werner Herzog), the person who placed the bounty on Baby Yoda's head. Per the bounty hunter code that Mando follows, his job requires that he hand over the bounty without asking any questions. While it is less clear what the Mandalorian Creed requires (though at the time, Baby Yoda is his enemy), it is true that a plethora of Mandalorians will end up dying due to Mando's choice. It is precisely because Mando has elevated the bounty hunter code to the status of moral law, meaning that satisfying the code is his duty and highest moral priority, which creates the internal conflict in Mando. Ultimately, he abandons the bounty hunter code and saves Baby Yoda's life.

Thus while it might seem at first that season 1 of *The Mandalorian* presents a sci-fi version of the conflict between independent moral vision, or conscience, with occupational responsibilities and religious doctrines, in fact the opposite is true: *The Mandalorian*, through Baby Yoda, exhibits how Kantian ethics is much more plausible than it may at first appear, especially in the pre-COVID American society when the first season was initially released.[4] Most viewers came to *The Mandalorian* with busy lives that dictated a stream of conflicting values that seemed to simultaneously and inconsistently demand complete attention: in order to survive, jobs must be prioritized; in order to be happy, family must be a priority, too; religion, friends, and individual pursuits and hobbies are also included in the list of things that matter and must be given attention. Yet, Kantian ethics demands that the agent should prioritize morality and not allow any of these other responsibilities or preferences supersede the place of morality in deciding what one ought to do. If the audience thought that they were watching *The Mandalorian* because it satisfied their need for original programming, or that it deftly explored a part of the *Star Wars* universe not yet developed in film, cartoons, or comic books, the truth is that they may have showed up to follow the adventures of Baby Yoda and his faceless Space Dad, but they stayed for an exploration of our current social and moral moment: the negotiation of our multiple responsibilities and social roles. The moral message of *The Mandalorian* is that people can embrace Kantian ethics in an overly complex contemporary world because when morality truly shows itself to us, the agent can—and must—drop the other priorities and satisfy their duty by meeting the demands of the moral law. Mando's commitment to Baby Yoda, best explained in season 1 as him meeting what the moral law requires of him in terms of keeping his word and respect for others, can serve as a reminder to the audience that there are times—and maybe the COVID-19 pandemic was/is one of them—when moral responsibilities are clear: there is a duty to protect others who are vulnerable. For this reason, Kant is correct in his argument that morality ought to come before any other consideration or preference. Maybe *Star Wars* has it right: maybe morality is simpler than is commonly thought, even if it is not the simple binary the Jedi/Sith distinction implies.

KANTIAN ETHICS: RESPECT IN
THE DIVERSE UNIVERSE

Immanuel Kant (1724–1804) based his moral system on the idea that the way humans (and any other rational beings) act is through our rational wills, and so morality involves willing correctly, or, really, willing rationally.[5] Though there are many complications, the idea is rather simple. For Kant, the will is the faculty that moves humans to action (a free will implies you are able to freely act).[6] And the way humans get themselves to act is by forming a rule to act on (for Kant, the will forms rules of action, which he refers to as "maxims").[7] It can be something like: "I will secure the Darksaber (means) to unite the Mandalorians (end), as long as I don't run into Darth Maul (a limit to my planned action)."

Since humans act from wills whose job consists in forming rules, then the measure of whether wills are good is rationality (generally speaking, rules are well made when they are rational).[8] In other words, you act well when your will forms a rational rule of action, or maxim. If your maxim is irrational, such as if it is inconsistent and self-defeating, then it is not well formed.[9] For instance, if I will to secure the Darksaber (means) to make sure that I never get challenged for having the Darksaber (end), then I have willed poorly. I have willed a means that does not help with my end and I am being irrational. To have a good will, you must form rational maxims.

It turns out, as Kant argues, that to will rationally, you must be consistent in treating all humans (or any other rational beings) well; willing rationally means the agent must act from moral maxims.[10] Although there are many complications that need not be discussed here, the idea again is simple: moral agents act through the will by forming maxims. Agents act well when they form rational maxims. Part of being rational is being consistent. One area for consistency is treating all rational beings (whether human, Togruta, or Gungan) in the same, respectful ways. Any maxim that fails to treat all people as equals is an irrational maxim. Thus, any immoral maxim is an irrational maxim.

Although it is possible to do a deep dive into imperatives, formulae, and much more, the Kantian view of ethics can be summarized in a way that is simplified, but also hopefully fair and plausible. The way humans (or Lasats or any other rational beings) act is by forming maxims through their wills. They act well by forming rational maxims. Significantly, a maxim can only be rational if it is moral, and so we only act well if we act from moral maxims.

Before moving on, it is important to note that Kant also believes the moral law should outrank all other values.[11] In a way, this view is not surprising. Every maxim must be moral to be rational. Yet, the agent can relinquish any other requirements if doing so is necessary to ensure that the agent's maxim is rational. For instance, suppose Mando had lived a life-long quest to obtain the Darksaber.[12] Similarly, his career of being a bounty hunter is essential to how Mando understands himself. Yet, Mando would be required to give up his quest for the Darksaber or his career as a bounty hunter if he could find no rational path to satisfy his rationally chosen goals and ends. If it turned out that the Darksaber was lost or that it came with responsibilities that Mando did not want to accept, he would have to abandon his quest. If it turned out that Mando could not make a living as a bounty hunter, it would be rational to leave that line of work so that one can satisfy one's duties of self-care and self-preservation. No matter how important a goal is, if it cannot be rationally pursued or maintained, it is morally permissible to give it up.

The only exception is morality because it is always rational to be moral. So, for Kant, the agent must seek to be moral in every situation, regardless of various other goals the agent might want to pursue (no matter how important they are). Perhaps Kant's requirement, though, is too much of a burden. All moral agents have a variety of life goals that are important to them such that it is unthinkable to consider giving them up (for example, Bo Katan's quest for the Darksaber in season 2). While some may think that Kant goes too far and is too demanding, it is possible that he provides a kind of moral clarity that helps individuals see through the haze created by competing logistical and emotional demands.

BOUNTY HUNTING: A COMPLICATED CODE

Mando's imperial client acknowledges that "bounty hunting is a complicated profession."[13] Morally speaking, this point is clearly true. A bounty hunter captures people with bounties on their head, turns them in, and then collects the money. Bounty hunters have always been part of the *Star Wars* universe, but very little is known about them or how they work. Part of the allure of

The Mandalorian is that it fills in some of these gaps. Bounty hunters work for profit and typically do not know the back-story of the person they are capturing. While bounty hunters will chase people who are wanted by official agencies (courts, police, etc.), there are often exceptions. Bounty hunters are rarely shown deciding whether a bounty has merit or is warranted. So, it is the nature of bounty hunters to capture people without knowing whether those individuals are innocent or suspect, if the reasons are official, legitimate, or specious; they are then required to turn the fruits of their labor over to the clients who may or may not be intending to treat them fairly.

Due to the moral complications that are inherent in the practice, bounty hunters, surely in fiction and quite likely in real life as well, have codes that they live by. To some extent, these codes are meant to ease moral concerns, though they are also largely intended to alleviate inefficiencies and risks that are inherent to the job. For instance, when programmed as a bounty hunter, IG-11 (voiced by Taika Waititi) both goes by this code without fail, and, surprisingly, seems to expect others to do the same. He is not programmed to anticipate or prepare for subterfuge or betrayal from other bounty hunters.[14] In the first episode, IG-11 expects the people who possess (or are guarding) the bounty to surrender and comply as the Bondsman Guild Protocol Waiver requires. Notice, though, that the bounty hunter code in this instance is meant to make things more efficient and painless: if everyone follows the code, then the first bounty hunter on the scene can make the capture without any bloodshed. If bounty hunters were constantly fighting with their targets and each other, then it would be a much more dangerous job. Without their code, bounty hunters may become violent with each other, harm innocent bystanders, and appear to be completely without moral qualms in their pursuit of their targets. Part of the bounty hunter code is practical as it is meant to ensure safety and efficiency, even if the means to achieve those ends is often violent, random, and causes pain, property destruction, and sometimes death (via disintegration). Thus, their code is both practical and honor seeking: without it, bounty hunting would be impossible logistically; with it, they are respected and feared, thus making their profession something others aspire to. However, even if bounty hunters operate according to a code, that does not mean it is a moral one.

Mando breaks the bounty hunter code in two significant ways, one of which is practical, and the other of which is moral. The practical requirement is that bounty hunters ought to ask no questions about the job or the person they are hunting. The second requirement, the moral requirement, is to not betray the client. Yet, because of Baby Yoda, Mando very much has questions and he asks them: he does not wish to see Baby Yoda harmed and the Client clearly has malicious intentions. The Client even remarks on how Mando is breaking the code: "Is it not the Code of the Guild that these events are now forgotten?"[15] Of course, Mando eventually saves Baby Yoda from the Client, an act which most definitely betrays the Client who had already paid Mando.

The rightness of Mando's actions in saving Baby Yoda from the Client and fledgling First Order is clear. To establish why, it is important to focus on the different types of requirements that bounty hunters face. As we can see in Mando's situation, the practical requirement not to ask questions is not a moral requirement. If bounty hunters never ask questions, then they would return their targets both in cases where it is morally permissible to do so and where it is not. The failure to ask about the target ensures a system where the bounty hunter could just as easily be acting morally or immorally. The bounty hunter neglects their moral responsibility by refusing to find out the back-story. Of course, practically, this practice ensures more money for bounty hunters since they can take morally problematic cases and simply refuse to learn the details at hand. The benefit of the practice derives entirely from profit, not moral concern.

On the other hand, some parts of the bounty hunter code are morally driven, at least in theory, such as the idea that they ought not to betray their clients. The bounty hunter and the client enter into an agreement when the bounty hunter accepts the job. The bounty hunter consents to deliver the target, while the client consents to pay for the delivery. Notice that the practice of bounty hunting requires the respecting of the consensual agreement. If you refuse to pay your mechanic after your car is fixed, then the mechanic has the leverage of holding onto your car. If the client refuses to pay the agreed-upon amount, the bounty hunter may have a human body that they can't otherwise make money off of. Furthermore, we regularly see in fiction the idea that the target can attempt to outbid the client ("If you don't turn me in, I'll pay you double what your client is paying you"). If bounty hunters often agreed to take the target's money, then there would be no point for clients to hire bounty hunters. Thus, there are clearly practical considerations to ensure that bounty hunters stick to their consent, which will often involve an unwavering and unquestioning commitment to their clients—something that Kant would surely question.

At the same time, bounty hunters are also morally committed to respecting their own consent. While it is true that, practically speaking, it would undermine bounty hunting if bounty hunters regularly broke their consent, it would not undermine the practice if some bounty hunters just sometimes performed this kind of betrayal. But it is always immoral to commit betrayal for the sake of making more money. While the bounty hunter could occasionally profit nicely from a betrayal, it is clearly immoral to not live up to their consent simply because it would make them more money.

The moral commitments of the bounty hunter code can become undone by the practical commitments, as is the case in season 1 of *The Mandalorian*. If the bounty hunter refuses to determine whether their overall activity is morally permissible, then even keeping their prior agreement could turn out to be immoral. Trivially, it would be immoral to keep an agreement if the agent agreed to do something immoral. If Mando does not know who the target is and does not know why the client is interested in capturing the target, then there is a good chance that Mando is depriving someone of their freedom without justification. Being committed to keeping his word and delivering the target is no longer morally praiseworthy if he agreed to deprive someone of their freedom without justification.

So, is the bounty hunting code a moral code? No, and no one should expect it to be. After all, no rational agent would expect a moral code to allow someone to say things like, "I can bring you in warm or I can bring you in cold."[16] The bounty hunter code is a professional code whose primary purpose is to ensure the survival of the profession. And, to a certain extent, moral duties may be subsumed under the code, but only insofar as they maintain the profession, such as by maintaining its respectability. Furthermore, those moral duties may give way in other ways because they are not primary within the code. Bounty hunters may treasure and respect consent, honesty, and not violently harming each other, but they may only treasure these things insofar as they instrumentally support their profession. While some bounty hunters may personally feel committed to moral codes, including consent, honesty, etc., those personal commitments are separate from and not essential parts of the moral code. Ultimately, the bounty hunter code is about doing what is best for bounty hunting as a profession, and this is not always a moral matter.

Bounty hunting is indeed a complicated profession. The bounty hunter code is a professional code with moral components. Importantly, it is also a professional code that matters deeply to its proponents in part because there is so much room for trouble. And this is common with similar professional codes. For instance, doctors, lawyers, and engineers all have very stringent and complicated professional codes because they very easily can have things turn out poorly and the public very much needs to trust that they are doing their jobs well. Bounty hunters work in a field that is potentially violent, that involves depriving people of their freedom, and that requires the public to trust that they are doing their jobs well. So, it is of the utmost importance that bounty hunters stick to that code as it ensures their payment and lifestyles. And so, it is clear that Mando, at least at the start, appears to be very committed to the bounty hunter code, but not as much as he is committed to the Way.

THE MANDALORIAN CREED: THE NATURE OF THE WAY

All the Mandalorians say it with the same inflection and reverence: "This is the Way."[17] Yet, it is not entirely clear what type of thing the Mandalorian Creed is. Mandalorians treat it with a level of reverence that is usually reserved for religious creeds and dogmas. Not even "May the force be with you" is uttered with the same solemnity as "This is the Way." What the Way is, or what sort of religion it might be, is not entirely clear. At one point Mando says, "I'm a Mandalorian: weapons are part of my religion."[18] However, none of the other Mandalorians depicted in *The Clone Wars*, *Rebels*, or the expanded universe/legends have ever spoken about a Mandalorian religion or "Way." Instead, it appears that the Mandalorians, after having been nearly wiped out by the Empire, either adopted the Creed anew, became much more hardened adherents to it, or at least developed new customs and rituals. Although the audience cannot be certain at this point whether the Creed is part of a religious doctrine, it likely has that kind of feel because the Mandalorians needed to become ardent and even fanatical to survive after the attack by the Empire. I will argue that the Creed is somewhere between a military-style band of brothers and sisters and a religion, and I will explain why Mando is entirely and unquestionably committed to the Creed.

One of the main things the audience knows about the Creed is the fact that Mando cannot be seen by others without his helmet on. As Mando tells IG-11, "No living thing has seen me without my helmet since I swore the Creed."[19] The audience is left to guess why this ritual developed. Yet, as previously indicated, Mandalorians have been shown without their helmets in other *Star Wars* shows. Even the members of Death Watch, the extremely militant band of Mandalorians from *The Clone Wars*, take off their helmets. Sabine Wren, of *Rebels*, appears to have no issue doing so. As far back as *Attack of the Clones*, Jango Fett is shown acting as a bounty hunter with his helmet on but interacting with others, including Boba and Obi Wan Kenobi, with his helmet off.[20]

Viewers do not know much about the ancient ritual of always keeping on one's helmet, but they can make an educated guess that it is a matter of projecting immense pride that can also protect the honor of their Creed. If Mandalorians never remove their helmets, they are advertising to everyone around them that they not only are Mandalorians but also heavily proud of being Mandalorians. None of them would be allowed to hide their identity as Mandalorians, no matter how convenient doing so may be, which further enforces this public display of pride. And, of course, as Mando moves around the universe, many people who engage with him both immediately see him as a Mandalorian and are impressed to have met one. Of course, there could be a number of other reasons for the helmet.

It is essential to stress the problematic implications of requiring that others not be able to see them without their helmets on. As we see in "The Sanctuary," Mando will struggle to find love even if he meets someone he may bond with, as he is unable to show them his face. To be explicit, not only would sex be strained, but he cannot even share a meal with a potential partner. Mando clearly will have no dating life, which also suggests that the Mandalorians will struggle to improve their dwindling numbers through reproduction.

At the same time, it can be inferred that reproduction is not necessarily the plan. The Mandalorians perhaps are not so worried about sexual reproduction because they are not a race, but a Creed, an idea explored in episode eight of season 1, "Redemption." It is not the *race* that they are trying to replicate, but the *Creed*. So, they need not spread their genes—they must instead spread their *ideas*. So their Creed is not merely something they adhere to, but it is also something to which they intend to convert others.

This Creed appears to be spread not so much through proselytizing, but more through militant action. For instance, we learn that Mando becomes a Mandalorian after Mandalorians save him from a battle in which his parents are killed. Like Baby Yoda, Mando is an orphan or foundling. Mando's commitment to the Creed is not ideological, but derives from the fact that he owes the Mandalorians his life. Furthermore, we see that Baby Yoda is becoming a member of the Mandalorians because he is bonded to Mando through a series of battles and the saving of each other's lives. Violence and blood debt spread the Creed. As far as the audience can tell, the Creed may not be a set of doctrines, stories, or commandments. If it has any of these standard religious aspects, the audience has not fully seen them yet. Instead, the Creed connects Mandalorians through their commitments and duties to each other, as born from militant encounters. The Creed, in this sense, is closer to a militant band of brothers and sisters who are bonded together to ensure mutual survival on the battlefield. The Creed lies somewhere between the commitment found among soldiers in war and a true religion.

Seeing the Mandalorian Creed as related to militant bonding does not entail that it is always practically sound. Mando's protection of Baby Yoda does not follow from the Creed initially since Baby Yoda, as Mando explains to the Armorer, is an enemy. Yet, when the other Mandalorians risk (and some eventually lose) their lives to support Mando, they are of course following the Creed, and even explain that "This is the Way."[21] Of course, military bonding can induce this kind of impractical self-sacrifice. It is a common militant creed to "not leave a brother [or presumably sister] behind." Such a creed is meant to at least imply a commitment to risk everyone's life (including the person left behind) to try to save one person. Following this creed too far would of course leave any military unit vulnerable to being wiped out: there are almost always fellow soldiers endangered in war, and the attempt to save all of them would result in saving no one. Yet, such a militant creed offers peace of mind (soldiers can believe they will be rescued in spite of horrible odds), which in turn can motivate greater dedication to the cause (soldiers can take greater risks with the belief that they would be rescued if caught). And so it makes sense that all the other Mandalorians are willing to risk their lives for Mando because it is the Way.

The Mandalorian Creed then is similar to other methods of military bonding. Yet, it is also clearly much stronger than that as it has a religious feel, as if "the Way" was a spiritual entity that motivated even greater adherence. The Creed may require rituals that do not necessarily make sense to the audience, such as always wearing the helmet, but these rituals add to the religious-like quality that helps motivate the Mandalorians to do whatever is necessary simply because it is the Way. Of course, as stated, Baby Yoda is an enemy, and so Mando does not save him because of the Creed. Ultimately, Kantian ethics better explains Mando's most important decision more than either the bounty hunter code or the Mandalorian Creed.

OVERRIDING PRINCIPLES: MORAL BESKAR

Mando does not wish to be shot. He obviously does whatever he can to avoid being shot and has many moves and skills that he has likely worked on to avoid getting shot. But if he does get shot, he wears that outer layer of beskar that clearly protects him from most of the weapons of his time period, which was a long time ago.

In Kant's picture, we can understand morality as metaphorical beskar. Kant believes humans act from rational rules, which he called "maxims," and the highest requirement for forming a maxim is that it be moral since an immoral maxim is always irrational.[22] An immoral maxim is irrational because it treats some persons like things in an inconsistent fashion (I can't steal your ice cream cone because that would treat your value as a human inconsistently with mine, as if I were better than you—but we are both human, and neither of us is worth more or less than any other human).[23] So, for Kant, the highest rule for forming rational maxims is that you must form moral maxims.

That means that we can set all kinds of core values, but the outer layer of our values must be the value of morality for Kant. Individuals can have values that are very localized and immediate: where to eat breakfast, lunch, and dinner, for example. The agent can have values that are much more long term (maybe writing a book about the philosophical aspects of *Star Wars*).

And the agent can have overriding values that are always or almost always in play. Examples of overriding values might include a career (Mando upgrades his armor and weapons in order to be a better bounty hunter), family, religion, and so on. Overriding values are ones that the agent may just check against no matter what else they are doing. Before one eats lunch, they check that doing so right then does not violate their job requirements, their religious beliefs, their adherence to the law, and does not hurt their family. Obviously, in most cases, this check is perfunctory and the agent may not think about it at all. But in other cases, they have to do more work because things are more complicated. For instance, suppose someone on a Star Tours trip to Dathomir finds a pyramid-shaped holocron and considers taking it home. Taking the holocron home could start an intergalactic incident or it could offend residents of Dathomir, who could take out their anger on a later, unsuspecting Star Tours tourist group. So, if they are just having lunch, overriding values need not even take a second of their time, but when they are potentially stealing a holocron that may belong to Nightsisters or Zabrak warriors, a more careful check is in order.

Kantian morality operates, at least metaphorically, like beskar: the agent has to allow morality to act as their greatest shield that protects them from their own inclinations to perform immoral actions. Just as beskar is the Mandalorians' final defense from attack, for Kant, morality is the agent's final defense to make sure their maxim is rational. The only difference is that beskar protects the agent from attack from outside, while morality protects the agent from immoral inclinations to act irrationally and immorally, from within. For example, if Mando is preparing to fight for the Darksaber, his immediate values are to win the fight and to obtain the Darksaber. Before starting, he may check on a few different overriding values, such as his strong overriding value of survival (what are the chances he will lose?), his job (did he check to see if he had any outstanding bounties to collect or is he free to battle?), his family (is this the Way and is Baby Yoda protected in his floating infant carrier?), etc. But, for Kant, the ultimate and final check is morality: is it morally permissible for Mando to fight for the Darksaber? For Kant, if morality checks out, then the agent can act. If the action fails to be rational, then it is immoral and the agent can be held as morally blameworthy if they do act.

Morality should be the ultimate check of every maxim to ensure that the agent is acting well, which means acting rationally.[24] Like with other overriding values, checking morality may often come easy, and the agent can pursue any number of day-to-day actions without any moral issues coming up. Yet, other times, it seems clearly necessary to make sure that before the agent acts that they are not being guided by a maxim that is immoral (either violates the principle of universality or treats another person as a means only, and not as an end). Consider the Dathomir holocron: there, the ultimate check would be whether it was morally permissible to take the holocron to display on a mantle. Even if the tourist could legally and practically take the holocron, they should not morally do so. So, for Kant, the last thing to do is check whether an action is morally permissible. Sometimes this is easy and the agent barely even notices they are doing it; sometimes it is much harder and the behavior requires more thoughtful deliberation.[25]

It is also possible that different overriding values might come in tension. For Kant, that agent is always supposed to choose morality and morality will always give one right answer as to what to do because moral duties cannot conflict. Mando shows the viewer why Kant may be correct that behavior can be reduced to one primary motivation or concern. Mando's immediate values are capturing the target (Baby Yoda) and earning beskar from the Client. Mando's first overriding value is his thorough commitment to the bounty hunter code—a commitment that has earned him a positive reputation with people like Greef Karga (played by Carl Weathers). Furthermore, Mando's higher overriding value is clearly the Mandalorian Creed. And it seems that all of these mentioned values are aligned when he turns over Baby Yoda, collects the beskar, and adorns a new, shiny set of Mandalorian armor.

Yet, Mando goes back. Mando rescues Baby Yoda even though doing so neither fulfilled his immediate values nor his two major overriding values. He broke the bounty hunter code by betraying his client. While the audience does not know too many details of the Mandalorian Creed, they know it is a militaristic creed and it is likely that keeping your word is considered to be a strong positive. He also of course risked the lives of his fellow Mandalorians, almost all of whom would end up dying because of Mando's actions. Furthermore, Mando had clearly identified Baby Yoda as an enemy, and it certainly does not seem to be the Way to risk the lives of almost all of the surviving Mandalorians to save an enemy.

Yet, Mando does indeed go back. It was just too morally wrong to leave Baby Yoda with the Imperial Client. Mando's rescue of Baby Yoda represents the triumph of morality over all other values. I am not claiming that Mando is a morally perfect person. He should not have returned Baby Yoda to the Client in the first place. He also should not be in a line of work that places him in this kind of situation. By not asking questions, he risks committing grave moral wrongs. Mando is clearly a morally flawed person; we have to acknowledge that fact. He should not be in this position in the first place.

And so the point is that morality, like beskar, is the protection from going awry from the path of moral behavior. When morality's call became too loud, Mando could no longer look the other way. Mando has surely too often lived according to the bounty hunter code and the Mandalorian Creed without always checking whether the moral law might override both. Yet, part of being human—even (maybe especially) a morally flawed human—are the moments it becomes clear that morality's demands are too significant to ignore. Some may try to listen to morality's demands almost all of the time. Some may have psychological difficulties that make it challenging to account for some or all of morality's demands. Most people, though, can be grouped in with Mando: they might ignore morality when the requirements are low or they think they have good rationalizations ("it is my job after all"), but they will definitely listen when the gravity of the situation becomes too severe. Who wouldn't go back for Baby Yoda?

DO THE MAGIC MORAL THING

Ultimately, the audience learns the moral message from *The Mandalorian* that Kantian ethics is neither as mysterious nor stringent as it may seem. It is often thought that Kant asks too much since he thinks morality must always win. What he means by that is simply that before every action, the moral will ought to be consulted and considered. Usually this check is quick and trivial: not all actions are moral actions so, of course, teeth can be brushed in the morning without a deep consideration of whether that behavior ought to be universalized (it should) or if brushing one's teeth denies other people their freedom or dignity (it does not). That is because brushing one's teeth has never in the past led to anything immoral and is pretty much not likely to do so now. Of course, turning a baby over to an Imperial thug is the kind of action that should prompt deep moral reflection before proceeding with what one thinks one ought to do.

Every person has a variety of overriding values and concerns that matter to them, and all Kant asks is that the agent check that morality be the final test to ensure that any action is ultimately rational. Maybe *The Mandalorian* resonates with so many people because careers tend to override other values, or, there are too many examples of people betraying what they claim are their clear moral values and concerns for the sake of their careers. They do this because they value their jobs or what their jobs provide them; at the very least, people value their jobs because the jobs (hopefully) keep the lights on and put food on the table. Thus, the audience can identify with how Mando's commitment to the bounty hunter code creates internal conflict for him when something else, in this case, the way that Baby Yoda intersects with the Mandalorian Creed and the Way.

The audience can likewise identify with Mando's stronger commitment to the Mandalorian Creed, which is depicted as being a part of a larger group, a band of brothers/sisters, or a religious community. Many in the audience belong to at least one of those groups and would understand the heightened sense of belonging and dedication that either can inspire. Yet, television, films, literature, history, etc. have shown that these kinds of powerful bonds, whether in the military or in religions, can become dangerous. Clearly, throughout history, both armies and/or religions have led violent and unjustifiable attacks on innocent communities. Given tons of historical evidence, the audience knows not to assume that strong commitments to exclusive groups or ideologies will guarantee moral behavior.

Kant's ethic is neither mysterious nor burdensome. It just says that the agent must always check morality, even when they have other overriding values. The agent still ought to do what is morally correct, and Mando eventually comes around to that point of view. He does not see it all the time—neither do any of us. He does not see it easily—everyone struggles from time to time. But the audience can learn through watching Mando's realization that, ultimately, morality must win out.

The reason the audience can learn so much better by watching Mando is that it is so striking when Baby Yoda's life is at stake. Baby Yoda is vulnerable, and is as cute as he is dangerous. Though season 1 of *The Mandalorian* aired just before schools in America were closed, some began working from home, and many braved dangerous working conditions because they were deemed "essential workers," the show reflects many of the moral questions raised by the COVID-19 pandemic. Audiences can turn to *The Mandalorian* to answer questions about keeping others safe, what individuals owe others who are near and far from them, and how to prioritize our own wishes, desires, and preferences over the needs of others when it comes to protecting them from a deadly airborne disease. Maybe more people need to adopt Mando's commitment to covering their face. And this moral difficulty—the difficulty in suddenly prioritizing morality above all of your other concerns—is highlighted in season 1 of *The Mandalorian*. Thus, through the pandemic, we all clearly saw that we can learn more about ethics from a TV show like this one. By watching *The Mandalorian* and seeing the more overt Baby Yoda effect on Mando, the audience learns something from Kantian ethics that is relevant to their lives. It is fair to note that the show simplifies complex matters, but sometimes simplifying moral dilemmas is necessary to avoid all of the rationalizations and excuses, or to put it another way, to avoid paralysis by analysis. Yes, there are often times many ways, but there are moments where Mando and Kant demonstrate the strength, purpose, and clarity that come from asserting that "this is the Way."

I have spoken.

NOTES

1. See *Clone Wars*, season 5, episodes 17–20.

2. For example, Anakin Skywalker.

3. The audience did not learn his name until season 2, episode 5, "The Jedi." Because this chapter reflects on the moral dimensions of season 1, many of which are challenged or undone in season two, I will be referring to The Child by his season 1 name, "Baby Yoda."

4. Season 1 of *The Mandalorian* began airing on November 12, 2019; the season 1 finale aired on December 27, 2019. While the dates for COVID arriving in America are not entirely clear, Americans became more aware of its presence in early March of 2020.

5. To learn more about Kant's views, the first primary sources I would recommend are: Immanuel Kant, "Groundwork for the Metaphysics of Morals," in *Practical Philosophy*, ed. and trans. Mary J. Gregor (Cambridge: Cambridge University Press, 1996) and Immanuel Kant, "Metaphysics of Morals," in *Practical Philosophy*, ed. and trans. Mary J. Gregor (Cambridge: Cambridge University Press, 1996). For secondary sources, I would recommend: Barbara Herman, *The Practice of Moral Judgment* (Cambridge, MA: Harvard University Press, 1993); Christine Korsgaard, *Creating the Kingdom of Ends* (New York, NY: Cambridge University Press, 1996); Christine Korsgaard, *The Sources of Normativity* (Cambridge: Cambridge University Press, 1996); Onora O'Neill, *Constructions of Reason* (New York, NY: Cambridge University Press, 1989); and John Rawls, *Lectures in the History of Moral Philosophy* (Cambridge, MA: Harvard University Press, 2000).

6. The following notes will all be from Kant's "Groundwork for the Metaphysics of Morals." Since there are many different versions of this text, it will be useful to use the standard (Academy edition) pagination on the side. For instance, for this current note, I will use the following citation to reference the places (as noted by the standard pagination) where Kant explains the will, free will, and the good will: *Groundwork* 4:393–401, 412–413, 446–447. Kant, "Groundwork for the Metaphysics of Morals."

7. Ibid., 399–401.

8. Ibid., 412–413.

9. Ibid., 399–417.

10. Ibid., 402–403.

11. Ibid., 399–403.

12. It is clear that this is not the case. See season 2, episode 16, "The Rescue."

13. *The Mandalorian*, season 1, episode 1, "Chapter 1: The Mandalorian," dir. Dave Filoni, aired on November 12, 2019, digitally released on Disney+.

14. This works against him in S1E01 when he anticipates that Mando will live up to the bounty hunter code but instead, Mando betrays him and shoots IG-11 in the head. *The Mandalorian*, season 1, episode 1, "Chapter 1: The Mandalorian," dir. Dave Filoni, aired on November 12, 2019, digitally released on Disney+.

15. *The Mandalorian*, season 1, episode 3, "Chapter 3: The Sin," dir. Deborah Chow, aired on November 22, 2019, digitally released on Disney+.

16. *The Mandalorian*, season 1, episode 1, "Chapter 1: The Mandalorian," dir. Dave Filoni, aired on November 12, 2019, digitally released on Disney+.

17. As noted previously, this chapter concentrates on season 1. In season 2, we learn that the surviving Mandalorians are diverse and Din Djarin is likely part of a more extreme faction of Mandalorians.

18. *The Mandalorian*, season 1, episode 2, "Chapter 1: The Child," dir. Rick Famuyiwa, aired on November 15, 2019, digitally released on Disney+.

19. *The Mandalorian*, season 1, episode 8, "Chapter 8: Redemption," dir. Taika Waititi, aired on December 27, 2019, digitally released on Disney+.

20. Of course, this work has been analyzing the show through a concentration on season 1, but in the season 2 episode, "The Heiress," Bo-Katan Kryze explains that Mando and his group of "zealots" derive their creed from the ancient ways, which Mandalorians no longer follow.

21. *The Mandalorian*, season 1 episode 3, "Chapter 3: The Sin," dir. Deborah Chow, aired on November 22, 2019, digitally released on Disney+.

22. Kant, "Groundwork for the Metaphysics of Morals," 399–403.

23. Ibid., 428–431.

24. Ibid., 395.

25. Ibid., 406–407.

BIBLIOGRAPHY

Herman, Barbara. *The Practice of Moral Judgment.* Cambridge, MA: Harvard University Press, 1993.

Kant, Immanuel. "Groundwork for the Metaphysics of Morals." In *Practical Philosophy*, edited and translated by Mary J. Gregor, 37–108. Cambridge: Cambridge University Press, 1996.

Kant, Immanuel. "Metaphysics of Morals." In *Practical Philosophy*, edited and translated by Mary J. Gregor, 353–604. Cambridge: Cambridge University Press, 1996.

Korsgaard, Christine. *Creating the Kingdom of Ends.* New York, NY: Cambridge University Press, 1996.

———. *The Sources of Normativity.* Cambridge: Cambridge University Press, 1996.

O'Neill, Onora. *Constructions of Reason.* New York, NY: Cambridge University Press, 1989.

Rawls, John. *Lectures in the History of Moral Philosophy.* Cambridge, MA: Harvard University Press, 2000.

The Mandalorian. Created by Jon Favreau. Aired from November 12, 2019–Present. Digitally Released on Disney+.

Chapter 14

A Black Captain America

Race in The Falcon and the Winter Soldier

Alisa Johnson and Steven A. Benko

The Marvel Cinematic Universe (hereafter MCU) has been criticized for its lack of diversity. A *Forbes* magazine article analyzed the twenty films that comprise Phases 1–3 in the MCU and found that with the release of *Avengers: Endgame*, a majority 61 percent of actors in the MCU are White, 20 percent are African American, 8 percent are multiracial, 4 percent are Spanish/Hispanic/Latino, 5 percent are East Asian, 1 percent are South Asian, and 1 percent are Middle Eastern/Arab. There are no characters of Native Hawaiian/Pacific Islander or Native American/Alaskan Native descent.[1] These numbers become worse if one excludes *Black Panther* from the totals.[2] After years of criticism that the MCU avoided politics for the sake of entertainment and profit, *The Falcon and the Winter Soldier* (hereafter *TFATWS*) directly addressed both the previous effects of American's institutionalized racism and its contemporary manifestations. Series lead Mackie commented on the failure of previous MCU projects to depict complex notions of race and racism characterizing the omission of actors and characters of color as a blind spot that had to be rectified:

> I don't think what's happening is a racism problem. I think it's an unawareness problem. With Marvel, I really think with most companies, they feel like they're doing what they should be doing. In no way, shape, or form, is it enough. My big thing is, put your money where your mouth is. You can't cast a Black dude as one of your main superheroes and not expect him to have that conversation. It's just in my DNA to have that conversation. It's a huge opportunity for me to be part of the Marvel universe so it's my job to make sure the Marvel universe is as good as it can be. Anyone who's big in our industry, if they have a party at their house, their party is 98 percent white. If you go to their office and their office is 98 percent white, that reflects their reality.[3]

Mackie's words show that the conversations about race in America that need to happen can only happen if people and actors with different life experiences and viewpoints come together to actually have those conversations. While the diversity in the MCU is increasing, whether its audience hears and appreciates Mackie's (or the Falcon's) words may be dependent on the racial and ethnic identity of that audience.

The Whiteness of the MCU makes the overt references in *TFATWS* to America's racist past and present compelling television. Those references are even more significant when one considers when it was filmed and released (during what is termed the second Civil Rights movement) and that it was distributed by Disney, a company that eschews controversy as it tries to reach the largest possible audience by projecting a conventionally moral, historically White, family-friendly image. In an era where television is raising questions about race, and more importantly, avoiding pat answers so as to not alienate viewers and advertisers, *TFATWS* asks the audience to consider multiple questions about race and racism in America and consider different perspectives and alternative points of view. This brief exchange from the second episode between Sam Wilson, the Falcon (played by Anthony Mackie) and a young boy playing in the street demonstrates how *TFATWS* draws the viewer into conversations about race that might call them out from their own perspective on race and identity toward something more complex and nuanced:

Young boy: Hey, it's Black Falcon. What's up?
Wilson: It's just Falcon, kid.
Young boy: No, no. My daddy told me it's Black Falcon.
Wilson: Is it because I'm Black and I'm the Falcon?
Young boy: Well, technically, I mean, yes.
Wilson: So are you, like, Black kid? (Chuckles) I got him, right?
Young boy: Whatever, man. (Chuckles) Whatever.[4]

Wilson's brief exchange with the youth offers a wealth of racial discourse for the audience to reflect upon and is a microcosm of the larger questions about race and identity posed in the series. Relative to this brief exchange, a Black audience could interpret it as a gentle commentary on the role of color, rooted in good-natured teasing between a youth and an adult, both in society and the MCU. Some White audience members may interpret Wilson's statements as a denial that race is part of his identity, a powerful confirmation of the post-racist belief that America has moved beyond racism, and therefore no longer requires a systemic response. For our purposes, the question is to what extent *TFATWS* challenges the complacency of White viewers by asking them to re-examine their assumptions about race while at the same time allowing Black viewers to be seen in ways that Marvel does not often allow them to be seen. If the audience pauses over even this brief exchange and considers the multiple meanings contained within it, then the show has done something that would be considered moral improvement: empathetic identification with points of view different from one's own. Therefore, it is possible for a television show to offer a complex and nuanced discussion of race that can both educate and influence its audience; the question is whether the audience is too entrenched in their perspectives on race and racism to be altered by that discussion.[5] When the audience projects their own views onto the different characters so that their own attitudes about race and racism are reinforced, no alteration or progress is possible. *TFATWS* attempts to avoid being the occasion for the reiteration of the racial status quo by shifting point of view characters and making racial awareness or healing part of each character's personal journey.

The success of the MCU is testimony to their ability to make the heroic journey an entertaining spectacle. Most of the heroic journeys depicted in the MCU focus on the superhero overcoming personal flaws or demons that stand in the way of their ability to serve the greater good. *TFATWS* is different because it asks the audience to consider the history, social problems, and entrenched attitudes toward race that might prevent the hero from wanting to help others, thereby interrupting or stalling that heroic journey. The hero's journey in *Iron Man*, or *Thor*, or *Black Widow* can entertain without indicting the audience for any bias or attitude they might hold. *TFATWS* does not take that approach as it combines a difficult but much-needed conversation on race within a standard, formulaic, MCU superhero plot: villains being villainous, heroes being heroic, fighting and joking as they save the day. This makes it difficult to claim that a mass-market television show can successfully challenge its audience to think more critically about America's racial legacy. The critiques of mass art by Adorno and the Frankfurt School still haunt efforts to see pop culture as much more than mindless entertainment meant to pacify the audience and distract them from the economic and political realities that perpetuate their alienation. The scope and enormity of the MCU, coupled with the corporate desire to keep generating more revenue streams, makes these products uniquely susceptible to these critiques. Yet art, even mass art, can be both edifying and transformative such that because of the large amount of pop culture space that the MCU occupies, it is no longer safe or interesting to be safe. In the era of Peak TV, there is more of an expectation that questions of representation, race, gender, sexuality, and class will be included in even the broadest pieces of pop culture, but whether these questions can be handled with the depth and nuance they deserve remains to be seen. The approach taken in *TFATWS* was to include three distinct presentations on the relationship between race and identity, though, as has been the case with the majority of MCU properties, the focus is on the male hero and his journey.

Typically, the hero's journey can only be completed when the hero learns something new about themselves or reconciles themselves to some larger truth, thus allowing them to overcome whatever obstacle is in their way. In *TFATWS*, the thing that the heroes have to learn about themselves is how to better relate to the ongoing legacy of racism in America. The characters need to situate themselves in a larger conversation about race because the show makes the point that one cannot be a hero in contemporary America without having an understanding of the relationship between race and power.

CAPTAIN AMERICA AFTER STEVE ROGERS

TFATWS is one of the latest offerings in the MCU, a short series (just six episodes long), that continues the story of Sam Wilson/Falcon and James "Bucky" Barnes/the Winter Soldier (played by Sebastian Stan) in a post-Blip world after half the life in the universe had been restored. The audience has seen a good deal of Wilson, but has been shown very little about Wilson's personal life. Introduced in *Captain America: The Winter Soldier* (2014) and included in *Captain America: Civil War* (2016), he is a victim of the Blip in *Avengers: Infinity War* (2018), but returns triumphantly with the dusted heroes in the climactic battle of *Avengers: Endgame* (2019). In these films, Wilson is defined by his loyalty to Steve Rogers, which he offers because of his belief in Rogers's bravery, fairness, loyalty, and willingness to sacrifice himself for the greater good. At the conclusion of *Endgame*, Rogers passes the mantle of Captain America to Wilson, but the act leaves Wilson conflicted. As he indicates in this scene from *TFATWS*, Wilson respects Rogers but sees him as a symbol of a different era, a bygone time:

Wilson: Steve represented the best in all of us. Courageous, righteous, hopeful. And he mastered posing stoically. (All chuckle) The world has been forever changed. A few months ago, billions of people reappeared after five years away, sending the world into turmoil. We need new heroes. Ones suited for the times we're in. Symbols . . . are nothing without the women and men that give them meaning. And this thing . . . I don't know if there's ever been a greater symbol. But it's more about the man who propped it up, and he's gone. So, today we honor Steve's legacy. But also, we look to the future.[6]

Early in the series, he will tell James Rhodes/War Machine (played by Don Cheadle) that he is reluctant to carry the shield because "It's a new day, brother."[7] Wilson sees Rogers as the best representation of his era, but clearly believes that era has passed, but how does a White audience read Wilson's reluctance to take up the shield? Is it physical, because Wilson is not enhanced like Rogers? Is it moral, because Wilson does not believe he is as noble or selfless as Rogers? How likely is it that a White audience would see Wilson's unwillingness to be Captain America as a political statement about race relations in America? A Black audience would be more attuned to the problematic symbolism of a Black American becoming Captain America. Later in the series, Isaiah Bradley (played by Carl Lumbly) elaborates on these concerns and gives them historical depth by connecting his experiences to Wilson's situation. Him doing so educates the White audience about the long history of racism in America and reassures the Black audience that the show will not efface or avoid the question of race. Different audiences are going to interpret Wilson's journey differently; the success of the moral vision of the show hinges on whether those who are likely to see his journey as a struggle to overcome personal limitations can be moved to a place where they see his journey as an effort to find their place in a larger conversation about race in America.

From Wilson's initial reluctance to take on the mantle of Captain America and implicit identification of race as the reason for that reluctance, *TFATWS* raises three questions about race and identity: first, while Sam Wilson is aware of the many ways systemic racism has impacted African Americans, including his own family, he is uncertain of what it would mean to invest more of himself in—and become the public face of—a program and social role steeped in racism. His journey includes his learning more about the racist legacy of the Super Soldier/Captain America program of which he is a part. In uncovering the history of Isiah Bradley, an African American man victimized by the Super Soldier program, both Wilson and the audience are reminded of the ugly race-based violence that is a part of America's medical history. As this tragic history is being presented, *TFATWS* challenges the audience to examine where they place their sympathies: do they elide that racist past and identify with Walker (played by Wyatt Russell), a White character who is also used and abused by the Super Soldier program, or with Bradley, a Black character whose suffering was made worse by the era's racism?

Second, in addition to *TFATWS*'s focus on historical, specifically medical, racism, the series uses Bucky Barnes to raise important issues about morality and redemption as part of an exploration of identity. Barnes wrestles with a racist legacy that he is both aware and unaware of. Different from Wilson he is aware of the racism embedded in the Super Soldier program but unaware (or not as sensitive as he should be) to societal racism. As a result of his journey to find himself, Barnes is able to reevaluate his understanding of race, including the way his previous silence about Isaiah Bradley helped perpetuate the violence Bradley suffered. Barnes initially believes that his silence was a way to protect Bradley—and perhaps, on some level, to protect Steve Rogers from having to confront the racist legacy of the Super Soldier program—but it also allowed Barnes to escape Rogers's criticism. As a character whose point of view is important, Barnes's journey provides an opportunity for the White audience to reflect on the ways their silence about issues of race is self-serving and perpetuates cycles of violence against persons of color.

The third question about race and identity presented in *TFATWS* has to do with the legacy of racist violence and what, if anything, can be done to name and identify that violence in a meaningful way. Isiah Bradley's anger and bitterness about his suffering, torture at the hands of the Super Soldier program, and the bitter payment for his heroism, offers another important perspective in the show's discourse on race. His experience is a poignant reminder of the way Black Americans historically have been treated by the government, but also a reminder of the way Black heroes in comics have also been treated, primarily relegated to the service of White heroes. However, while Bradley is able to move beyond the pain of his past because of the significant changes in society, it remains to be seen if the audience connects his inclusion in the Captain America story to the possible reforms made in the institutions that used and abused him. The series ends on a high note: Bradley's inclusion in the museum exhibit implies that society has changed enough that Bradley can be a public figure without risk of harm to himself and his family and the new Captain America is Black. However, the focus on the individual and their heroic journey might obscure for the audience the need to reform real institutions.

THE FALCON AND SYSTEMIC RACISM

In the series, the journey that Sam Wilson takes in order to move from the Falcon to Captain America is both powerful and instructive. It involves his growing awareness of the racist legacy of the Super Soldier program and ends with his choice to integrate that knowledge into the work that Captain America is obligated to do. Sam's journey invites the audience to question their own perspectives on America and to determine whether they believe in the legacy of Captain America and his shield at all. Along with Wilson, the audience could deliberate on "the idea of a black man confronting the stars and stripes and whether it's even appropriate to carry that shield."[8] Over the course of the series, the audience is able to observe his deepening understanding of what it means to be a hero. In fact, Wilson's growth into Captain America can be linked to his growing comfort with using his position to speak out for, if not demand, inclusion and fairness. Instead of simply focusing on the physical welfare of others, Wilson acknowledges that he is responsible for drawing attention to systemic injustices that affect their emotional and psychological welfare. Selflessness was the defining characteristic of Steve Rogers, the original Captain America, who went so far as to jump on what he thought was a live grenade to save members of his troop. (In the series, Bucky Barnes asks John Walker if he ever attempted the same selfless act in order to determine if he is worthy of the shield and the Captain America name.)[9] While the willingness to sacrifice oneself for the good of others was a hallmark of the previous Captain America, the racial situations that the series illustrates indicate self-sacrifice is not enough. Wilson's journey is less about what he learns about himself than it is about how he comes to see himself, his role, and his responsibilities if he is going to become the new Captain America.

Wilson's growing awareness of his responsibility to both act and advocate for others begins when he is forced to confront a personal problem: unlike Tony Stark, who is fabulously rich, he has no clear source of income. (Other MCU heroes such as Natasha Romanov, the Black Widow, and Clint Barton, Hawkeye, have the same issue. Bucky Barnes appears to have access to funds in the series, but the source is unknown. Wilson, a former Air Force pilot, seems to be working freelance as Falcon at the start of the series, but what, if any, salary he receives for the missions he undertakes is unclear.)[10] Wilson's money woes are not presented as a personal foible or something that he can overcome through discipline or hard work. His and his family's financial situation is the result of systemic injustices that have harmed Black Americans for generations.

The social cause of Sam Wilson's financial situation becomes painfully relevant when his family is faced with losing their business and home. The fishing boat that the family owns is in disrepair, and his sister Sarah (played by Adepero Oduye) has no collateral with which to secure a loan. At first, Wilson believes that he can secure the loan because of the goodwill he has earned as an Avenger; he has helped many others, so therefore help should be available to him. At one level, the services Wilson has performed for his country should be all of the collateral that he needs to secure the loan. At another level, because superheroes help individuals, Wilson feels that if he approaches the loan application at a personal level, his good work and sacrifice will be recognized. Unfortunately, as the series makes clear, Wilson's stature does not protect him from discrimination. When he and Sarah go to the bank to apply for a loan, he and the banker have an ironic exchange:

Banker: Is there some kind of fund for heroes? Or did Stark pay you when he was around? My condolences, by the way.

Wilson: Thank you, but no, it doesn't really work like that. There's a tremendous amount of goodwill and because of that, people are inclined to help, which applies to the business.

Banker: Yeah, right. But were you living off of goodwill this whole time?

Sarah Wilson: I don't get what you're going for here. Are you trying to help us, or indict us?

Banker: You have no income over the last five years. How can you have income if you don't exist?

Sam: Sarah. Uh . . . (Stutters) I've been gone like several billion other people. But if you look at our plan, I have government contracts, so, that's proof of earnings. And I know for a fact that we qualify for a SBA loan.

Banker: Under the old terms, sure. But these days, what, with everyone just showing up, well, things tightened up.

Sarah Wilson: Funny how things always tighten around us.

Banker: Whoa. Easy there. Look, I'm on your side. After all, he's a hero. Is there any chance, and of course you could say "no," that I could get a selfie with your arms out?[11]

Wilson has done nothing wrong yet he will not be helped. The failure is not his own; instead he is told that the system works by failing him and his family. For many White viewers, Wilson's treatment at the bank and the denial of his loan may be their first encounter with discriminatory lending practices, but many Black viewers would be all too familiar with the racial dynamics at play. They would be more likely to know that as Delgado and Stefancic specify in *Critical Race Theory* that while low-income White families, with the help of social and economic systems, are often able to change their socioeconomic status within a generation or two, Black families are unable to do so for decades.[12] Therefore, Black audience members would perceive more quickly than Whites how devastating the rejection of the bank loan is to Wilson and his family. The scene at the bank stirs up difficult feelings for Wilson, forcing him to question who he should be helping: his country or his family, and where he can make a meaningful difference.

Wilson's experiences at the bank are one way that *TFATWS* shows how systemic racism impacts individuals. As he is pulled away from his family—but not his financial concerns—in order to chase down Karli Morgenthau (played by Erin Kellyman) and the Flag Smashers, his inner conflict grows. When challenged by Morgenthau that "the people I'm fightin' are trying to take your home, Sam. Why are you here instead of stopping them?" he sees her logic and returns home to help his family.[13] Morgenthau gets Wilson to realize that his problems are a microcosm of the problems that many others face; others who are similarly situated suffer the same impersonal discrimination and racial/ethnic violence. This part of Wilson's journey is juxtaposed to his sister's continued alienation—an alienation rooted in feelings of racist exploitation and abandonment—from the American dream. In a private conversation between Morgenthau and Sam's sister Sarah over his continued pursuit of her and the Flag Smashers, and his continued involvement with the new Captain America, John Walker, Sarah says to Morgenthau, "My world doesn't matter to America, so why should I care about its mascot?"[14] Sarah's response speaks to the impact of racism on Black Americans, an impact that Wilson has also experienced. This realization stirs in Wilson a desire to not just help others, but be an agent of change for those who cannot make that change alone. Here, Wilson recognizes that up until this point his heroism has supported a system that has not supported him and his family. If he is going to be the hero that he thinks America needs now then he is going to have to find a way to be a hero that challenges and changes the system that has oppressed so many for so long. Caught between his reality as a Black American and his work as a superhero, Sam Wilson wants to support his family and his community while showing people around the world what Black men are capable of. However, Morgenthau's question causes him to refocus his priorities. After their encounter, he realizes that he could and should put the needs of his family and his community on par with saving the world and that he has every right to leverage whatever authority or power that he has for that purpose.

Wilson has two realizations that alter his attitude toward the altruistic nature of being a superhero. First, as the scene in the bank demonstrates, helping others does not generate any real credit for Wilson or his family; second, while villains like Baron Zemo (played by Daniel Bruhl) are a threat to the social order, systemic racism and violence do just as much to diminish the well-being and lives of ordinary citizens. These realizations make Wilson less self-sacrificing and more unwilling to work alone. He realizes that the fight against the system requires changing the system. For that, he is going to have to enlist the help of those who have seen how systemic racism is just as harmful even if the harms and machinations are not as obvious as they are with a villain like Zemo. The first indication of this change is in a scene with Shannon Carter (played by Emily VanCamp). Wilson says that he will help her secure a pardon if she helps him find Morgenthau:

Wilson: We need your help, Sharon. I can get your name cleared.
Sharon: You haggling with my life? Not like that. I don't buy that. You pretending like you can clear my name.
Wilson: Okay, maybe it is hypocrisy. Maybe you're right. What happened to you. But I'm willing to try if you are. They cleared the bionic staring machine, and he killed almost everybody he's met.
Barnes: I heard that.[15]

Wilson's decision to offer his influence in exchange for Sharon's help is an indication of the growing shift in his perception. The line "I'm willing to try if you are" signifies a switch in his approach to being a hero from serving others for the greater good to serving with others so that they see themselves as a necessary part of the change in the institutions that are victimizing them too. While it is clear that Wilson has no illusions that he will receive Sharon's help simply by asking for it—an awareness he may not have had as clearly before the incident in the bank—he is also much more aware of his personal power and is willing to use it in the service of his cause.

Wilson's journey to becoming the superhero that he believes America needs would not have been possible without his interactions with Isaiah Bradley. Bradley's experiences both deepen Wilson's understanding of America's racist past and directly implicate him when he is called out for not seeing how the past is still present. When, after meeting Bradley, Wilson expresses his frustration to him over the fact that he, as the first Black Super Soldier, did not assume a leadership role, Isaiah counters that such action would not have been possible. Despite his powers, Bradley would have been killed for drawing attention to himself. And, given his treatment, he had no wish to advocate for a government that could abuse him in such a manner. Angry at Wilson for not realizing that, he tells him: "Man, that's why you're here? You think things are different? You think times are different? You think I wouldn't be dead in a day if you brought me out?"[16] Bradley's anger, rooted in his physical and emotional abuse, is justifiable, and while Wilson does not share it, he understands it. Bradley's accusations remind Wilson once again that for a Black man, being a superhero is no protection from racism and discrimination, just as being a superhero was no protection from a legacy of racist lending practices that harmed his family's ability to become financially secure. The series indicates that part of Wilson's journey is learning to first, claim his personal power, and the power of Captain America, in the light of America's racial past, and second, to leverage that power to persuade people to extend themselves for the greater good. Sam Wilson's ability to navigate America's racial past is complicated because he, like the rest of his family, sincerely wants to help others. In the penultimate episode of the series, Wilson sees his sister prepare extra lunches for children whose father cannot wake up early enough to prepare lunch for them. Watching his sister, Wilson is reminded that his family has been helping people in their community for years while asking nothing in return. However, in the light of his growing awareness, he realizes that he can ask the community for favors and, unlike the bank or Sharon, he can count on their help. When he calls on his neighborhood for help, people show up in droves—including Barnes with a special gift from Wakanda—to help Wilson and his family repair their boat and business. Although Wilson is both a member of a beloved and respected family and a celebrity, he does not need to leverage either to receive the help he needs. The warmth and unity of the scene, in which people of different ages, races, and sexes come together in work and celebration is markedly different from the bank scene. Sam Wilson's community values him and his family, and therefore offers their help without reservation; whereas the banker who rejected Wilson's loan did not, and refused to help. Both realities are part of the world that Wilson must navigate, and this awareness aids in his movement toward reclaiming the shield.

What Bradley teaches Wilson is that a costume and a shield cannot protect someone from the harsh realities of racism. For that reason Wilson cannot simply reclaim the shield that he and Barnes took back from Walker after a fight in a warehouse/refinery. To have done so would have been a denial of his personal past as Falcon, the past he embodies as a Black American and the future he wants to create as Captain America, albeit a different Captain America. His mission to draw from the past in order to create a different future is symbolized by his retaining his Falcon wings and merging them with the Captain American iconography and shield. After the climactic battle scene in which Wilson and Barnes defeat the terrorists, two men in the crowd surrounding Wilson respond differently when they see him as Captain America. One identifies him as Captain America, and the other identifies him as Black Captain America. The two responses dramatically reflect the journey Sam Wilson has taken to become Captain American and indicate the challenges he will continue to face. As a Black Captain America, the implication is that his race will be recognized before anything else. Wilson recognizes this and in a call back to the scene from the second episode with the young boy playing outside, he is not coy, playful, or ambiguous about his identity and who he is. Wilson uses his platform as savior and hero as an opportunity to define himself and the type of Captain America he is going to be. When accused by a senator of failing to understand the seriousness of the refugee situation, Wilson, who fought against other Avengers in Berlin and twice fought against Thanos's armies for the fate of the universe, respectfully but firmly disagrees. His response indicates that he knows exactly how serious both the refugee situation and his assumption of the mantle of Captain America are, and he sees both as interconnected.

Wilson: You know what? You're right. And that's a good thing. We finally have a common struggle now. Think about that. For once, all the people who've been begging, and I mean, literally begging for you to feel how hard any given day is . . . Now you know. How did it feel to be helpless? Now if you could remember what it was like to be helpless and face a force so powerful it could erase half the planet, you would know that you're about to have the exact same impact. This isn't about easy decisions, Senator.

Senator: You just don't understand.

Wilson: (Scoffs) I'm a Black man carrying the stars and stripes. What don't I understand? Every time I pick this thing up, I know there are millions of people out there who are gonna hate me for it. Even now, here . . . I feel it. The stares, the judgment. And there's nothin' I can do to change it. Yet, I'm still here. No super serum, no blond hair, or blue eyes. The only power I have is that I believe we can do better. We can't demand that people step up if we don't meet them halfway. Look, you control the banks. Shit, you can move borders! You can knock down a forest with an email, you can feed a million people with a phone call. But the question is, who's in the room with you when you're making those decisions? Hmm? Is it the people you're gonna impact? . . . Look, you people have just as much power as an insane god or a misguided teenager. The question you have to ask yourself is, "How are you going to use it?"[17]

Both Wilson and *TFATWS* indicated that, going forward, Captain America is going to mean different things to different people. Some people are going to focus on race, while others will not. However, Wilson's question in the previous scene about who is in the room when decisions get made echoes the actual statements actor Anthony Mackie made about the lack of diversity in the MCU. The position espoused by the show at its conclusion is that there are perspectives that have been excluded from conversations where important matters need to be decided, and that has to change. Wilson's response to the senator in the final scene emphasizes the importance of recognizing the importance of multiple perspectives, particularly in the light of America's legacy of racism and discrimination. Wilson as Captain America charges everyone with the responsibility to consider other, previously excluded perspectives, so that they can come to see differently and make a difference: those who have been in a position to do so but have not, as well as those who have been excluded from the opportunity to contribute to America's long-overdue reckoning with its racist past. This is why Wilson can have this exchange with Bradley:

Eli Bradley: What you want, Black Falcon?
Wilson: Hey, you need to learn some manners.
Bradley: He ain't a Falcon anymore, but he's still Black. I saw what you did out there. And it seems, so did everyone else. I heard the GRC was standing down on those plans of theirs, so you must have done somethin' right. I ain't gonna lie. You're special.
Wilson: Thank you.
Bradley: I mean, you ain't no Malcolm, Martin, Mandela, but . . .
Wilson: No argument there. But I know what I've gotta do.
Bradley: So, a Black Captain America, huh?
Wilson: Damn right.
Bradley: (CHUCKLES) The fight you taking on ain't gonna be easy, Sam.
Wilson: Yeah, I might fail. Shit, I might die. But . . . We built this country. Bled for it. I'm not gonna let anybody tell me I can't fight for it. Not after what everybody before me went through. Including you.
Bradley: (VOICE SHAKING) Shit. I almost bought that.

Wilson: Man, do you ever lighten up?
Bradley: Nope.[18]

As part of his final transformation, the new Captain America asserts that he will model for people the behaviors necessary for addressing America's racist past.

As the new Captain America, Sam Wilson offers a firm anti-racist perspective when he challenges those in power to change their attitudes and their plans and include those who have not had a voice in decisions that impact them.[19] For the audience, both Black and White, Sam's speech in the final scene is a call to action—if they choose to hear it. In the MCU, it is expected that heroes who fight villains will also fight injustice; those viewers willing to incorporate the message from the series into their real lives are also called to fight injustice in the most effective ways—that is, demonstrations, voting, and community service. Complacency in the face of suffering is unacceptable, for Wilson's Captain America and his fans. As Wilson reminds the audience, "What would be the point of all the pain and sacrifice if I wasn't willing to stand up and keep fighting?"[20]

On the other hand, the limitations of the superhero genre might undermine the point that Wilson is trying to make. The Peter Parker principle, "with great power comes great responsibility" (a gloss on John F. Kennedy's "for to those to whom much is given much is required" and Luke 12:48, "From everyone who has been given much, much will be demanded; and from the one who has been entrusted with much, much more will be asked") means that those who are super-human, either because of ability, technology, or both, are responsible for being superheroes. Conversely, not much is required to those to whom very little or nothing has been given. Wilson's Captain America points out that much has been given to some only they have not—or choose not—realize it. Wilson's call for change is not problematic: it requires that they (specifically, the Senator he is speaking to, the audience the message is being broadcast to, and the audience watching the show at home) recognize how their privilege has benefited them and what it has provided them. The question is whether the narrative undermines the point that Wilson is trying to make. Throughout the series Wilson and Morgenthau engage in lengthy conversations about power and representation and what types of actions are necessary in order to enact meaningful, systemic change. Given that the only character who articulates any critique of the system or calls for systemic change is Karli Morgenthau, the terrorist, it is debatable as to whether the series expects the audience to believe real systematic change will take place. On multiple occasions throughout the series, Wilson expresses sympathy and support for Morgenthau's politics, even though he rejects her tactics. However, the connection between Wilson's support of Morgenthau's position and his call for greater inclusion of diverse voices, experiences, and points of view (which would lead to systemic change) might not be apparent to an audience unused to hearing calls for systemic change. Black members of the audience may be more sympathetic to Wilson's support for Morgenthau's position, since it echoes the same critiques and calls for systemic change that have been part of the first and second Civil Rights Movements.

THE WINTER SOLDIER AND THE WHITE HABITUS

Like other MCU characters such as Iron Man, Black Widow, Thor, and to a certain extent, Rocket Raccoon, Bucky Barnes is searching for an identity, as well as a path to forgiveness for past wrongs. At the beginning of the series, much of Barnes's identity is derived from his relationship with Steve Rogers. Rogers was the moral conscience of the MCU: he opposed the Sokovia Accords, was proven right for believing in Barnes, and offered counseling to people who lost loved ones after the Snap. Rogers's belief in Barnes was personally validating, because if Captain America invested in him, it meant that he was worth investing in. Rogers's faith in Barnes was the only thing that made Barnes feel good about himself and provided him with a lens through which Barnes could see himself as something more than the Winter Soldier. Barnes's frustration with Wilson's decision to give up the shield is rooted in his need to believe that Steve Rogers never made a mistake in assessing a person's character. Barnes says as much to Wilson in an impromptu therapy session:

Barnes: Why did you give up that shield?
Wilson: Why are you making such a big deal out of something that has nothing to do with you?
Barnes: Steve believed in you. He trusted you. He gave you that shield for a reason. That shield, that is . . . that is everything he stood for. That is his legacy. He gave you that shield, and you threw it away like it was nothing.
Wilson: Shut up.
Barnes: So maybe he was wrong about you. And if he was wrong about you, then he was wrong about me.
Wilson: You finished?
Barnes: Yeah.[21]

At the beginning of Barnes's journey, he attempts to take responsibility by making a list of the people he has wronged in order to make amends, but the task proves difficult because he is not emotionally or psychologically ready to admit his guilt. As the series progresses, Barnes moves away from his desire for revenge against those he put in power as the Winter Soldier and is even willing to spare Zemo and turn him over to Dora Milaje and the Wakandans. However, Barnes's unwillingness to confess his sins to those he harmed, particularly Yori Nakajima (played by Ken Takemoto), or to articulate his pain, are major obstacles to his emotional recovery and a new sense of self. Barnes can only move forward when he is able to relinquish his self-imposed silence, which includes his silence about Isaiah Bradley's treatment at the hands of the Super Soldier program, and speak up for the things that matter to him.

Just as Wilson had to come to a deeper understanding of the racist past of the Super Soldier program, Barnes must also explore and accept how he contributed to those racist goals by not telling Steve Rogers about Isaiah Bradley. Wilson's story indicates that the hero's journey is neither race-free or race-neutral, and that racism and discrimination are part of the battles a hero must fight. Like Sam Wilson, Barnes must grow into a new identity, one which involves speaking out for those in need, and speaking up for fairness and justice. *TFATWS* uses Barnes's acceptance of his prosthetic Vibranium arm as a visual marker of his coming to terms with his past: his sense of wholeness, completeness, and unity is both emotional and physical. The fact is particularly important for Barnes, since many of the actions he took as a tool for Hydra helped preserve the racist status quo in many countries. There are several moments in the show where he is forced to question whether his actions served the common good, or whether his loyalty to the Super Soldier program and his silence harmed marginalized people.

The superhero costume marks the hero as different from the general population. While the costume is often functional (for example, Batman's utility belt) it is also a visual representation of their identity (again, Batman's is dark, mysterious, and ominous). As the Winter Soldier Barnes had a costume and mask that hid his identity, but his real power came from being augmented by the Super Soldier serum and his prosthetic Vibranium arm. Different from other superhero costumes, both were imposed upon Barnes against his will. For that reason, his journey toward reconciling himself to his past as the Winter Soldier includes reconciling himself toward his prosthetic arm. His relationship with his arm is ambivalent: it makes him more lethal, but it also makes him less human. Bucky Barnes's body is organic, but the Vibranium arm represents that part of him that will always be the Winter Soldier. Barnes's attitude toward his Vibranium arm changes over the course of the series, and he comes to see his Vibranium arm as something other than a weapon of death. When Barnes comes to Louisiana to help Wilson repair the family boat, he closes a leaky gas valve with a wrench instead of his prosthetic hand. When Wilson asks why he did not use his Vibranium hand he replies, "Well . . . I don't always think of it immediately. I'm right-handed."[22] In the ensuing montage, where Barnes bonds with Wilson, his family, and his community, he is shown switching between hands, though eventually leading with his prosthetic, in a sign he has incorporated the arm more fully into his psyche. In one part of the montage, Barnes is shown letting children hang from his outstretched arm. In the final episode, Barnes demonstrates his successful incorporation of his prosthetic arm into his body, and his past into his psyche, when he chooses to pull open the van door rather than punch through it in order to save the people inside.

Barnes coming to accept his prosthetic arm and the powers that it grants him is a familiar superhero trope, even if it is an inversion of how that journey is normally played out. Superheroes who get a new piece of technology that makes them more powerful are usually overwhelmed by it at first, make several awkward attempts to use it successfully, and then are eventually able to harness and control its power (for example, Tony Stark's early attempts at the Iron Man suit). Because the trope of coming to terms with or mastering superhero technology is so familiar, an audience watching Barnes's transformation might be less likely to see the prominence race plays in his journey to self-forgiveness and wholeness. While it is impossible to guarantee that a particular narrative or story arc will produce a specific perspective in the audience, it is possible to identify obstacles that might obscure or prevent certain insights. In the case of *TFATWS*, it would be a type of audience identification with Barnes that obscures the racial nature of his actions. An audience situated in what Bonilla-Silva calls a "White habitus" would be more likely to accept Barnes's explanation for why he never told Rogers about Bradley (to protect him and because Barnes felt that Bradley had suffered enough) instead of seeing Barnes's actions as an example of White silence that perpetuated the privileged status that Steve Rogers enjoyed as "the first Avenger."

A White habitus is defined by Bonilla-Silva as "a racialized, uninterrupted socialization process that *conditions* and *creates* Whites' racial taste, perceptions, feelings, and emotions and their views on racial matters."[23] A White habitus consists of (supposed) commonsense attitudes about other races that advantage White people. This advantage can take a variety of forms: first, claims of cultural, historical, political, social, and religious superiority of traditions and institutions created by White people; second, is the reiteration of these claims through education, law, and culture at the expense of other histories, traditions, religions, philosophies, or ways of knowing. A White habitus is perpetuated by segregation in housing, education, and in social experiences. The result of segregation means that White people do not engage with people of color at all, or often enough, to understand their experience of racism. From within a White habitus, White people come to view themselves and people of color in White terms. A White habitus allows White people to occupy a privileged position where their perspective becomes the norm and other perspectives are marginalized as abnormal. And as Bonilla-Silva points out, "the more distant the group in question is from the White 'norm,' other things being equal, the more negative Whites will view the group."[24]

An audience situated in a White habitus would be more likely to not be bothered by examples of White privilege. For example, they are likely to understand why Walker was chosen to be Captain America:

> On paper, Walker is qualified for the position: a special ops combat vet who graduated from West Point, testing off the charts in speed, endurance and intelligence. But to be frank, the subtext is that when the government resurrected Captain America, they chose Walker because they felt that America's symbol needed to be white. The blue-eyed and blonde-haired Walker even gets a Black sidekick, Lemar Hoskins/Battlestar (Clé Bennett), like the original Cap.[25]

Additionally, they are not likely to be bothered when Walker does not hesitate to use the power and privilege that comes with being Captain America excusing these actions as necessary in the moment or as standard superhero behavior: he arranges Barnes's release from prison (for missing a court-ordered therapy session) in order to force Barnes to work for him and makes sure that Barnes knows about the power and authority he possesses as Captain America. Walker is indifferent to the fact that he violated normal protocol and ignored other concerns and priorities in order to get his way; an audience situated inside a White habitus would be indifferent to those violations of protocol too.[26] Yet despite Walker's swagger, *TFATWS* indicates that he is uneasy and uncomfortable with the role because he is aware that he might not have earned it. Walker's sense of entitlement and his insecurity about his ability to do the job of Captain America lead him to ignore advice and rush in when standing down would have been a better option.[27]

Unlike Walker, Barnes is aware of the responsibility that comes with power because he has mostly used his power to harm others. For that reason, unlike Walker, Barnes has a healthy respect for his power. But like Walker, Barnes has supported institutions that abused and mistreated people of color, if not by active participation then by deliberate silence. Barnes chose not to speak up for or about Isaiah Bradley, allowing the Super Soldier program to keep its abuses hidden from the world. *TFATWS* implies that silence, in combination with privilege, is a manifestation of White supremacy, which allows those in power to maintain their societal advantages without being seen as directly involved in racism and oppression. While Walker displays his privilege by flouting rules and conventions, Barnes performs his privilege through his silence. Specifically, his silence allows a great evil to remain hidden and saves others the difficult task of confronting the truth about themselves and the institutions they support. By avoiding that confrontation himself, and enabling others to do likewise, Barnes participates in the ongoing erasure of people of color from history, an action that, as Isaiah Bradley tells Wilson, has been going on for 500 years.[28]

How could an audience situated in a White habitus read Barnes's decision to keep silent about Bradley and the racist elements of the Super Soldier program? If White silence is "a defending of the status quo of white supremacy—a manifestation of holding on to one's White privilege through inaction," then Barnes is a direct example of this inaction.[29] Evaluating that decision through the perspective of a White habitus means accepting Barnes's explanation that he intended no harm. It might mean working to find similarities between Barnes and Bradley, for example, that they were both given the Super Soldier serum against their will, or they were both experimented on, and they were both treated as disposable by governments and agencies, and using those similarities to see them as similarly situated. However, doing so elides the very real differences in their experiences due to race. To see Barnes's actions outside of a White habitus is to deny Barnes the opportunity to center his feelings and perspective on the situation and judge him for protecting Steve Rogers from knowing the larger truth about the Super Soldier program, and more than that, protecting himself from having to face the possibility that Rogers might not have responded to Bradley or his experiences in a noble and socially responsible way. Had that happened, the light that Barnes needs Rogers to shine on him might have been a bit dimmer. When Barnes introduces Bradley to Wilson and admits that he knew about what had been done to Bradley, he begins to accept his role in preserving the status quo and hiding an injustice that deserved to be revealed.

Just as Barnes is awakened to his own complicity in perpetuating the injustices perpetrated by the Super Soldier program, he is also awakened to a more complex understanding of the power of his own voice. In the latter part of the series, he apologizes to Wilson for not doing more to educate Rogers about Bradley. Barnes tells Wilson, "When Steve told me what he was planning, I don't think we understood what it felt like for a Black man to be handed the shield. How could we? I owe you an apology. I'm sorry."[30] The brevity of Barnes's apology is significant: he does not attempt to highlight his own intentions, nor does he use the apology to showcase his own transformation; different from how he treated Bradley, he is not centering himself. He confesses his limitations as he understands them, and then he stops talking. This silence, however, is profoundly different from his silence about Bradley. In remaining silent after he apologizes to Wilson, Barnes both acknowledges the potential hurt he may have caused and opens up a space for Wilson to respond to his actions. Barnes's apology is tangible proof of his desire to accept responsibility for his actions and deepen his connection to Sam Wilson, whom he now sees clearly as a friend.

In its exploration of race, *TFATWS* highlights the fact that the mutual respect necessary for reconciliation to occur requires that people recognize the limitations of their own experience and become willing to cede the stage to others so that they can speak their truth. An audience that is sensitive to the racial dimension of Barnes's journey will understand that he is demonstrating this new sensitivity to this fact in the final episode: when Wilson is giving his speech to the Senator and the world, the camera quickly cuts to Barnes standing off to the side, silent and respectfully listening to the new Captain America explain his vision for racial healing. Barnes claims the power of his voice, which is, in many ways, as powerful as his Vibranium arm, by demonstrating to the audience when to use it and when to remain silent. He also indicates his awareness that others should have the same choice and the same power and shows his willingness to ensure that they have both. His journey from problematic silence to a silence that is appropriate is a template that the audience can follow.

In *TFATWS*, both Sam Wilson and Bucky Barnes grow into their ability to be of service to one another and to other people. Barnes and Wilson began the series linked primarily through their individual relationships to Steve Rogers; fighting with him brought them together, and losing him (when he makes his decision to remain in the past) pushed them apart. However, by working together to stop the terrorist threat, they overcome their differences, grieve their shared loss, and learn to support each other physically and emotionally. The two men become friends, and form the basis for a meaningful and effective alliance. Barnes can be of service to Wilson and be his ally (in many ways) by both listening and lending support, and Wilson can be of service to Barnes and be his ally by sharing his experience and claiming his personal power. While both could and did accomplish a great deal separately, the series indicates that it is only by working together that they can bring about significant social change. Change begins, as Wilson indicates to Barnes, with an acknowledgment of past harms and the desire to make amends:

Wilson: You up for a little tough love? You want to climb out of the hell you're in, do the work. Do it.
Barnes: I've been making amends.
Wilson: Nah. You weren't amending, you were avenging. You were stopping all the wrongdoers you enabled as the Winter Soldier, because you thought it would bring you closure. You go to these people and say "sorry," because you think it'll make you feel better, right? But you gotta make them feel better. You gotta go to them and be of service. I'm sure there's at least one person in that book who needs closure about something, and you're the only one who can give it to 'em.

Barnes: Probably a dozen.
Wilson: That's cool. Start with one.[31]

ISAIAH BRADLEY AND THE LEGACY OF (CAPTAIN) AMERICA'S RACIST PAST

Like Wilson and Barnes, Isaiah Bradley's journey in the series is one of personal growth, though it is much less developed. After a number of scenes that
explored Bradley's anger at and distrust of the government, the series ends
Bradley's story on a very positive note. Sam Wilson takes Bradley and his
grandson to the museum shown in the season's first episode. They briefly tour
the Steve Rogers/Captain America exhibit, and then Wilson shows Bradley
a new addition: a statue of him and a small plaque (which, unfortunately, the
viewing audience is unable to read). The statue indicates that Bradley's story,
or at least part of it, is finally being told. Bradley's emotional response to the
museum exhibit marks a distinct change in the attitude he showed toward
his past earlier in the series. He is clearly moved by the statue, and grateful
to Sam Wilson for clearly making it possible. Bradley's and its place in the
exhibit is proof that Wilson was right: some things have changed. Bradley
is no longer erased, and his existence and experiences are part of the public
record and the Captain America legacy. In ensuring Bradley's rightful place
in the Captain America saga, the series validates Wilson's belief in the ability
of the society to change and, to a certain extent, right its wrongs as well as his
belief that good and necessary things happen when the right people are in the
room having conversations and making decisions.

Although Bradley is poised to receive the acclaim that he deserves, nothing
can make up for his suffering at the hands of his own government. As his story
is revealed, Bradley's long-standing distrust of the government that betrayed
him is shown to be justified and his disdain for Black people loyal to that government understandable. Wilson tells Bradley that they need to share his story
so that other people can know about him. Bradley's response is not positive:

Bradley: No. Leave me dead. My name is buried.
Wilson: But the world's different now. I know people.
Bradley: Man, that's why you're here? You think things are different? You think
times are different? You think I wouldn't be dead in a day if you brought me
out? You wanna believe jail was my fault because you got that white man's
shield. They were worried my story might get out. So, they erased me. My
history. But they've been doing that for 500 years. (CHUCKLES) Pledge allegiance to that, my brother. They will never let a Black man be Captain America.
And even if they did, no self-respecting Black man would ever wanna be.[32]

Despite Wilson's claims that the world was different, Bradley did not share his optimism at the time. However, Bradley's inclusion in the exhibit validates Wilson's position and indicates that, at least to a certain extent, the world has changed. Bradley achieves the status of a hero, and his story can be added to stories of other American heroes, though none of the admiration he will receive can undo the pain that he has suffered. Although many troubling questions about Bradley's ordeal and its aftermath remain, the ending of his story is positive on a personal level, as it reflects a progress that he did not think was possible. The society that abused him has grown enough to accept not only a Black man in the Super Soldier program, but a Black man as Captain America. Bradley's story provides the foundation for the series' assertion that racial healing in society is possible. The change in the relationship between Bradley and Wilson also indicates that intergenerational conflicts can be reconciled, and each generation can learn from the other.

However, while the positive conclusion to Bradley's story may be emotionally satisfying to audiences, it indicates the limitations of the series' racial explorations. While Wilson, Barnes, and Bradley have grown and changed in positive ways, separately and together, the institutions that allowed Bradley to be tortured, Wilson to be overlooked as the successor to Captain America, and Barnes to be weaponized and manipulated are still in place. There is no indication that the bank that denied Wilson and his family a loan has changed its lending policies, though through Bradley the audience learns that the Global Repatriation Council has postponed their plans to deport refugees. Typical of the superhero genre, the focus is on the individual and their redemption, not larger systemic changes. Audiences can expect Bradley's frustration and anger to dissipate over time, but there is no reason for those feelings to go away completely. His healing, to the extent that it is possible, has begun, but the extent of that healing is unknown. The addition of Bradley's statue is an important and necessary gesture, but it is a gesture nonetheless. No gesture, no matter how well-meaning or well-deserved, could restore to Bradley what has been taken from him. To the extent that the audience feels that the statue in the museum means that all's well that ends well supports criticism that, as a medium, television is unable to address systemic social issues in a meaningful way. The show's efforts to open up conversations and new perspectives on race are undermined by standard superhero tropes that focus on interpersonal dynamics as the occasion for personal growth: after making his speech to the senator, Wilson flies off to help catch more terrorists and Shannon Carter has her name cleared. In its positive conclusion, *TFATWS* asserts that personal growth helps to make racial progress possible, but it cannot deny the fact that there are wounds, both personal and cultural, that may be too deep to ever fully heal and that systemic change is difficult to dramatize.

CONCLUSION

The ending of *TFATWS* is not very different from the ending of other MCU properties: it teases future movies or television shows that will continue what started in 2008 with *Iron Man*. Sam Wilson is now Captain America; Bucky Barnes might lean into his White Wolf persona now that he has closed the book on the Winter Soldier; John Walker is no longer Captain America, he is U.S. Agent; most surprisingly, Sharon Carter has been revealed as the Power Broker and will now use her position in the U.S. government to sell weapons and secrets to the highest bidder. Her line about having access to something for everyone could be the mantra of the MCU which aspires to appeal to a global audience. While "something for everyone" might have been the approach prior to *TFATWS*, the emphasis on race and race relations in America was certain to divide audiences and critics. Responses to *TFATWS* and the ending were mixed, especially compared to the critical acclaim that *WandaVision* received. To be fair, due to its episodic nature, *WandaVision* provided the audience with an air of mystery and intriguing misdirection, while *TFATWS* was structured much like a six-hour movie. While both series dealt with serious issues, *TFATWS* direct confrontations with race and fairness may have made it less appealing to some than *WandaVision*. Despite lower internet traffic, *TFATWS* gained viewers every week, and the season finale "finished with 855 million minutes viewed per Nielsen" (the most common measuring system for a show's success on streaming or cable).[33]

While it could be argued that the *TFATWS* presents a multilayered and complex response to race and racism, critics were divided on the show's engagement with the topic. One reviewer was impressed that such a clear and damning depiction of race relations in America even made it to television, let alone in a property as culturally relevant as the MCU.[34] Critic Aurich Lawson applauded the show for its depiction of the Black superhero experience, saying that the same plot in a film "would have been too superficial; the show was able to do moments that would have been cut to make runtime otherwise."[35] This opinion is countered by critic Jennifer Oullette, who claimed that "[*TFATWS*] tries to do too many things at once, and thus doesn't do them as well as it could."[36] Writing in *Colorlines*, critic Joshua Adams faulted the show for not having more conversations between Wilson and other White characters on the topic of race.[37] Critic Scott Woods wrote, "The idea bubbling underneath Isaiah's story is that America may not deserve and certainly hasn't earned what a Black Captain America represents. The idea underneath Sam's actions is that working harder and through adversity defeats racism, which is patently false."[38] Some of these reviews oversimplify what the show was trying to do while others indict the show for failures that are native to television; they are blaming the show for not transcending its medium. Different from many shows, and certainly different from other superhero shows, *TFATWS* allows the audience access to different points of view about race and gives them the opportunity to learn from the characters' experience. Sam Wilson, a powerful Avenger, learns to claim his power and his voice. Bucky Barnes learns to take responsibility for his silence and his speech. Isaiah Bradley, the first Black Super Soldier, confronts America's racist past through his pain. Each character has a valuable perspective, and each must be understood within the universe of the show. While it is unclear what audiences will take from the show, it is clear that the series attempts to provide them with insight into America's racial problems.

TFATWS is what television in the era of Peak TV should be doing. Wilson's vision for a Captain America that believes that people—all people and not just superheroes—ought to learn, grow, and contribute to solving the world's problems is an inversion of the most recent Golden Age approach that saw other characters as occasions for (really, fodder for) the main character's (usually a White male) journey to self-understanding. This is a necessary moral improvement that shows the audience the value of community and sincerity to, and for, others. Though TFATWS comes to television from the world of comics and film and inserts itself in the tropes and features of this era of television, it earned its place among other Peak TV programs by addressing complex social issues with a sophistication that would not have been possible in other eras. The strength and weakness of *TFATWS* are that it presents a complex and nuanced discussion of race and racism but does not provide many, or easy, answers. The series appears as a brief moment in a long, much-needed conversation, one that suggests a way forward, but does not explain how to arrive at the destination. The series insists that the system can be reformed, but also illustrates the real and immediate needs of those waiting on that reform. The characters grow in their understanding of themselves, America's racial past, and the need to work for positive change, but audiences do not get the chance to see how they will act on their new knowledge.

If anything, *TFATWS* presents the audience with a lively and engaging storyline that gives them the opportunity, if they wish, to have conversations about race. The blurring of in-universe and out-universe examples and experiences provides the audience several touchstones with which to grapple with about how race is lived in America and how it is depicted in pop culture—but only if they are willing to dig deeply and think critically about a cinematic universe that used to be merely for entertainment.

NOTES

1. Anhar Karim, "The Marvel Cinematic Universe Is 61% White, but Does That Matter?," Forbes (*Forbes Magazine*, October 20, 2018), https://www.forbes.com

/sites/anharkarim/2018/10/10/the-marvel-cinematic-universe-is-61-white-but-does
-that-matter/?sh=43566f934482.

2. Phase 4 is a vast improvement over phases 1-3. Movies like *Shang-Chi and the Legends of the 10 Rings* (2021) and *The Eternals* (2021) showcase characters and actors that are of Asian descent.

3. Donna Freydkin, "Anthony Mackie Is Black Captain America," Fatherly, July 29, 2020, https://www.fatherly.com/play/anthony-mackie-interview-marvel-captain -america-black-lives-matter-falcon/.

4. *The Falcon and the Winter Soldier*, season 1, episode 2, "The Star-Spangled Man," dir. by Kari Skogland, aired March 26, 2021, digitally released on Disney+.

5. For the purposes of this essay we will focus on Black and White responses to *TFATWS* as it is outside the scope of the essay to consider how other populations might respond to the show.

6. *The Falcon and the Winter Soldier*, season 1, episode 1, "New World Order," dir. Kari Skogland, aired March 19, 2021, digitally released on Disney+.

7. Ibid.

8. Adam B. Vary, "Why 'the Falcon and the Winter Soldier' Is so Pointed about Race, Nationalism and the World Today," Variety (Variety, March 21, 2021), https://variety.com/2021/tv/news/falcon-and-winter-soldier-race-nationalism-mal-colm-spellman-1234935019/.

9. *The Falcon and the Winter Soldier*, season 1, episode 2, "The Star Spangled Man," dir. Kari Skogland, aired March 26, 2021, digitally released on Disney+.

10. In an interview with Variety, series creator Malcolm Spellman says that he was surprised by the amount of interest and debate this question generated. He said, "Every single person I'm sitting with went crazy over that scene. It satisfied some-thing very deep for people. What's a trip is when we got to that moment, and that question came about naturally, the entire Marvel structure chimed in. That was a really, really fun moment, where what was supposed to be a scene that mostly dealt with the issues of, you know, a Black family from a certain background dealing with a bank loan, and the fact that him being a celebrity does not transcend him being Black, turned into way more fun of, Wait, how do superheroes make their money? I can't tell you the volumes of documents that came out in building what is this much dialogue [holds fingers inches apart] in the episode." In Vary.

11. *The Falcon and the Winter Soldier*, season 1, episode 1, "New World Order," dir. Kari Skogland, aired March 19, 2021, digitally released on Disney+.

12. Richard Delgado and Jean Stefancic, *Critical Race Theory: An Introduction* (New York, NY: New York University Press, 2017), 119.

13. *The Falcon and the Winter Soldier*, season 1, episode 4, "The Whole World Is Watching," dir. Kari Skogland, aired April 9, 2021, digitally released on Disney+.

14. Ibid.

15. *The Falcon and the Winter Soldier*, season 1, episode 3, "Power Broker," dir. Kari Skogland, aired April 2, 2021, digitally released on Disney+.

16. *The Falcon and the Winter Soldier*, season 1, episode 5, "Truth," dir. Kari Skogland, aired April 16, 2021, digitally released on Disney+.

17. *The Falcon and the Winter Soldier*, season 1, episode 6, "One World, One People," dir. Kari Skogland, aired April 23, 2021, digitally released on Disney+, our emphasis.

18. Ibid.

19. Anna North, "What It Means to Be Anti-Racist," Vox (Vox, June 3, 2020), https://www.vox.com/2020/6/3/21278245/antiracist-racism-race-books-resources-antiracism.

20. *The Falcon and the Winter Soldier*, season 1, episode 5, "Truth," dir. Kari Skogland, aired April 16, 2021, digitally released on Disney+.

21. *The Falcon and the Winter Soldier*, season 1, episode 2, "The Star Spangled Man," dir. Kari Skogland, aired March 26, 2021, digitally released on Disney+.

22. *The Falcon and the Winter Soldier*, season 1, episode 5, "Truth," dir. Kari Skogland, aired April 16, 2021, digitally released on Disney+.

23. Eduardo Bonilla-Silva, *Racism without Racists Color-Blind Racism and the Persistence of Racial Inequality in America* (Lanham, MD: Rowman & Littlefield, 2018), 121 (emphasis in original).

24. Ibid., 140.

25. Joshua Adams, "The Falcon and the Winter Soldier Is Weird about Race ...," *Colorlines*, May 26, 2021, https://www.colorlines.com/articles/falcon-and-winter-soldier-weird-about-race.

26. *The Falcon and the Winter Soldier*, season 1, episode 2, "The Star Spangled Man," dir. Kari Skogland, aired March 26, 2021, digitally released on Disney+.

27. Adams writes, "Over the course of the show, Walker's humility, for example, his nervousness before being presented to the world as the new Cap, transforms into a sense of entitlement. Walker begins to feel like Wilson, Barnes and others around him should submit to his authority simply because of who he is. Walker ignores Wilson's suggestions on how to handle the Flag-Smasher's leader Karli Morgenthau (Erin Kellyman), and this same arrogance eventually leads Walker to get whooped by the Dora Milaje, the all-female royal guard of the kingdom of Wakanda." In Adams.

28. *The Falcon and the Winter Soldier*, season 1, episode 5, "Truth," dir. Kari Skogland, aired April 16, 2021, digitally released on Disney+.

29. Layla F. Saad and Robin DiAngelo, *Me and White Supremacy: Combat Racism, Change the World, and Become a Good Ancestor* (Waterville, ME: Thorndike Press, a part of Gale, a Cengage Company, 2020), 54.

30. *The Falcon and the Winter Soldier*, season 1, episode 5, "Truth," dir. Kari Skogland, aired April 16, 2021, digitally released on Disney+.

31. Ibid.

32. Ibid.

33. Patrick Hipes, "'The Falcon and the Winter Soldier' Tops Nielsen Streaming Charts for First Time." Deadline (Deadline, May 13, 2021), https://deadline.com/2021/05/the-falcon-and-the-winter-soldier-nielsen-streaming-charts-april-12-18-1234755790/.

34. David Zurawik writes, ""The Falcon and The Winter Soldier" has already done its culture work. It is outstanding popular culture because of the way it connects to some of the deepest and most powerful currents of American life today with its core

narrative of Wilson's journey. It feeds off and amplifies for entertainment audiences the kind of discussion the nation is having in connection with events like the trial of former Minneapolis police officer Derek Chauvin who was convicted Wednesday of murder and manslaughter in the death of George Floyd. It challenges viewers to reflect and re-evaluate what they think they know about race and history in the United States. The series also speaks directly to what feels like a yearning for new heroes and leadership at this moment in American life." See David Zurawik, "Disney's Falcon and Winter Soldier: A Journey of Racial Reckoning Made for Today's America: Commentary," baltimoresun.com, April 23, 2021, https://www.baltimoresun.com/ opinion/columnists/zurawik/bs-ed-zontv-0425-falcon-soldier-disney-20210423-kph i7urduvfmjdvvmls6rxkxhq-story.html.

35. Quoted in Jennifer Oullette, "Review: The Falcon and the Winter Soldier Aims High but Falls a Bit Short," Ars Technica, April 25, 2021, https://arstechnica.com/ gaming/2021/04/review-the-falcon-and-the-winter-soldier-aims-high-but-falls-a-bit -short.

36. Ibid.

37. Adams, "The Falcon and the Winter Soldier Is Weird about Race ..."

38. Scott Woods, "'The Falcon and the Winter Soldier' Sends the Wrong Message about Being Black in America," Medium (LEVEL, April 29, 2021), https://level .medium.com/the-falcon-and-the-winter-soldier-sends-the-wrong-message-about -being-black-in-america-c35bed1b3a73.

BIBLIOGRAPHY

Adams, Joshua. "The Falcon and the Winter Soldier Is Weird about Race ..." Colorlines, May 26, 2021. https://www.colorlines.com/articles/falcon-and-winter -soldier-weird-about-race.

Bonilla-Silva, Eduardo. *Racism without Racists Color-Blind Racism and the Persistence of Racial Inequality in America*. Lanham, MD: Rowman & Littlefield, 2018.

Delgado, Richard, and Jean Stefanic. *Critical Race Theory: An Introduction*. New York, NY: New York University Press, 2017.

Freydkin, Donna. "Anthony Mackie Is Black Captain America." Fatherly, July 29, 2020. https://www.fatherly.com/play/anthony-mackie-interview-marvel-captain -america-black-lives-matter-falcon/.

Hipes, Patrick. "'The Falcon and the Winter Soldier' Tops Nielsen Streaming Charts for First Time." Deadline. Deadline, May 13, 2021. https://deadline.com /2021/05/the-falcon-and-the-winter-soldier-nielsen-streaming-charts-april-12-18 -1234755790/.

Karim, Anhar. "The Marvel Cinematic Universe Is 61% White, but Does That Matter?" Forbes. *Forbes Magazine*, October 20, 2018. https://www.forbes.com/ sites/anharkarim/2018/10/10/the-marvel-cinematic-universe-is-61-white-but-does -that-matter/?sh=43566f934482.

North, Anna. "What It Means to Be Anti-Racist." Vox. Vox, June 3, 2020. https://www
.vox.com/2020/6/3/21278245/antiracist-racism-race-books-resources-antiracism.

Oullette, Jennifer. "Review: The Falcon and the Winter Soldier Aims High but Falls a
Bit Short." Ars Technica, April 25, 2021. https://arstechnica.com/gaming/2021/04/
review-the-falcon-and-the-winter-soldier-aims-high-but-falls-a-bit-short.

Saad, Layla F., and Robin DiAngelo. *Me and White Supremacy: Combat Racism,
Change the World, and Become a Good Ancestor.* Waterville, ME: Thorndike
Press, 2020.

The Falcon and the Winter Soldier. Created by Malcom Spellman. Aired from March
19, 2021–April 23, 2021. Originally released on Disney+.

Vary, Adam B. "Why 'the Falcon and the Winter Soldier' Is so Pointed about Race,
Nationalism and the World Today." Variety. Variety, March 21, 2021. https://vari-
ety.com/2021/tv/news/falcon-and-winter-soldier-race-nationalism-malcolm-spell-
man-1234935019/.

Woods, Scott. "'The Falcon and the Winter Soldier' Sends the Wrong Message
about Being Black in America." Medium. LEVEL, April 29, 2021. https://level
.medium.com/the-falcon-and-the-winter-soldier-sends-the-wrong-message-about
-being-black-in-america-c35bed1b3a73.

Zurawik, David. "Disney's 'Falcon and Winter Soldier': A Journey of Racial
Reckoning made for Today's America: Commentary." *Baltimore Sun.com.* April
23, 2021. https://www.baltimoresun.com/opinion/columnists/zurawik/bs-ed-zontv
-0425-falcon-soldier-disney-20210423-kphi7urduvfmjdvvmls6rxkxhq-story.html.

Subject Index

Character Index

Episode Index

About the Contributors

Steven A. Benko is a professor of religious and ethical studies at Meredith College in Raleigh, North Carolina. He is the co-editor (with Andrew Pavelich) of *The Good Place and Philosophy* and *Ethics in Comedy: Essays on Crossing the Line*. He received his B.A. from Loyola University, New Orleans, and his M.A. and Ph.D. from Syracuse University. His interests lie in ethical subjectivity, pop culture studies, comedy studies, and ethics. Additionally, he has presented and published on critical thinking pedagogy, *Monty Python's Life of Brian*, how affect theory contributes to laughter and comedy theory, the comedy of and Aziz Ansari, the links between an ethics of otherness and comedy of incongruity, the comedy of Dave Chappelle, and posthumanism. His current research is on how stand-up comedy shapes ideas of masculinity.

Jill B. Delston is associate teaching professor of philosophy at the University of Missouri–Saint Louis. She is the author of *Medical Sexism: Contraception Access, Reproductive Medicine, and Health Care* (2019) and co-editor of *Applied Ethics: A Multicultural Approach* (editions 5 and 6). She received her B.A. in liberal arts from St. John's College in Annapolis, Maryland, and her M.A. and Ph.D. in philosophy from Washington University in St. Louis.

John Hillman is a researcher, writer, educator, and image-maker engaged in the interdisciplinary areas of photography, image, and visual culture. He is associate professor and director of research into an expanded view of photography at Birmingham City University. His interests lie in philosophical approaches to contemporary culture and understanding how images and media technologies shape our experience. His research is interdisciplinary in form and covers the social, political, and philosophical dimensions of contemporary experience. What unifies his interests is the exploration of how theory can enrich and offer new insights into creative practice and lived experience. His approach is distinctive in its foregrounding of theoretical ideas and in how it attempts, not to explain phenomena through theory, but to elucidate theory as it appears within contemporary culture.

Douglas L. Howard is academic chair of the English Department on the Ammerman Campus at Suffolk County Community College. He has published widely on television, film, and literature. He is also the editor of *Dexter: Investigating Cutting Edge Television* and the co-editor of *Television Finales: From Howdy Doody to Girls, The Essential Sopranos Reader,* and *The Gothic Other: Racial and Social Constructions in the Literary Imagination.*

Matt Hummel (M.A.L.S. in ethics and values & Grad. Certificate in humane education, Valparaiso University) of Evansville, Indiana, works as a paralegal in the Public Defender's Office. He has taught legal studies and legal ethics at Ivy Tech Community College and has started teaching introduction to sociology at the University of Evansville, his alma mater, from fall 2021. He has been published three times for both Wiley and Open Court's series on pop culture and philosophy, including topics in *Dungeons and Dragons, Star Wars*, and *Rick and Morty.* He is also a seasoned actor in community theater and a motivated environmentalist.

Alisa Johnson is assistant dean in the School of Arts and the Humanities and associate professor in English at Meredith College, where she teaches American and African American literature and introduction to film. She received her B.A. in English at Guilford College, and her M.A. and Ph.D. at the University of North Carolina at Chapel Hill. Her areas of research include African American literature, film studies, Chinese Wuxia films, and pop culture. She is currently the coordinator of the Meredith College Documentary Film Festival and juror for local film festivals.

Eleanor Jones is pursuing an M.A. in environmental philosophy, completing a graduate certificate in women's, gender, and sexuality studies, and is a teaching assistant in the Philosophy Department at the University of Montana in Missoula. She received a B.A. from Meredith College in Religious and Ethical studies. She has published work on comedy of incongruity and affectively charged feminism in the book *Ethics in Comedy: Essays on Crossing the Line.* Her areas of research include feminism, environmental ethics, culture, and comedy, and she is currently working on integrating ecofeminism and environmental justice frameworks and research into community programming.

Dutton Kearney is an associate professor of English at Hillsdale College where he teaches eighteenth-century literature as well as theology and literature. He is the editor of the Ignatius Press edition of *Gulliver's Travels* and has published several essays on Jonathan Swift. He is also the director of the Visiting Writers Program at Hillsdale.

Leigh Kellmann Kolb is an assistant professor of English and journalism at East Central College in Missouri. She's contributed to *Sons of Anarchy and Philosophy, Philosophy and Breaking Bad, Twin Peaks and Philosophy, Amy Schumer and Philosophy, The Handmaid's Tale and Philosophy*, as well as *The Women of David Lynch: A Collection of Essays*. She's also written for *Vulture* and *Bitch Magazine* and serves as a screener and juror for multiple Missouri film festivals.

Matilde Accurso Liotta is an independent researcher. After a bachelor's degree in Italian literature at the University of Milan, she has earned two master's degrees in comparative literature at University of Pisa (2017) and University of Turin (2020), respectively. During her studies, she has delved into gender and media studies, leading into a summer school in women studies at Sapienza University of Rome in 2020.

Denis Newiak studied media studies at the University of Potsdam, Germany, and film studies at the Freie Universität of Berlin. He also studied abroad at the University of Copenhagen and conducted research at the Library of Congress in Washington, D.C. His research focuses on the following areas: aesthetics and narratives of loneliness in television series, social functions of serial television entertainment, and disruptive events in science fiction movies. His current publications include "Fernsehserien gegen spätmoderne Einsamkeiten: Formen telemedialer Vergemeinschaftung am Beispiel von '13 Reasons Why'" in *Fernsehwissenschaft und Serienforschung: Theorie, Geschichte und Gegenwart (post-)televisueller Serialität*, edited by Denis Newiak, Dominik Maeder, and Herbert Schwaab (2021), and *It's All Been There Before. What We Can Learn about the Coronavirus from Pandemic Movies* (2021).

Douglas Rasmussen graduated with a Master of Arts in English from the University of Saskatchewan where he wrote on the television series *Breaking Bad*. His research interests are film studies, genre studies, and popular culture. Currently, he is writing a number of book chapters on subjects ranging from *Star Trek,* horror films, women in action films, and cult Japanese cinema.

James Rocha is associate professor of philosophy at California State University, Fresno. James is the author of many works of popular culture and philosophy, with chapters in *Twin Peaks and Philosophy, Westworld and Philosophy*, and *Psych and Philosophy,* among others. Additionally, James is the author of *The Ethics of Hooking Up* (2020) and co-author of *Joss Whedon, Anarchist?* (2019).

James Shelton is an independent scholar whose research focuses on narrative mechanics, with specific reference to the way in which retribution acts as a driver of narrative changes.

H. Peter Steeves is professor of philosophy and director of the Humanities Center at DePaul University where he works in phenomenology, ethics, aesthetics, and philosophy of science. Steeves is the author of nine books, including, most recently, *Being and Showtime* (2020; www.beingandshowtime.com). His current research focuses primarily on cosmology and astrobiology—on the origin events of both the universe and life. He lives in Chicago with his wife and his *agita*.

Martina Vanzo is an independent scholar in religious studies. She completed her master's degree in cultural anthropology at the University of Turin, Italy (2019). Her main research interests concern new spiritualities, including neopaganism, exploiting an interdisciplinary perspective that also requires the study of the media and their impact on society.

www.ingramcontent.com/pod-product-compliance
Lightning Source LLC
Chambersburg PA
CBHW022300280326
41932CB00010B/928